THE

DISTRICT OF BAKARGANJ

THE

DISTRICT OF BAKARGANJ

ITS HISTORY AND STATISTICS

BY

H. BEVERIDGE, B. C. S.

GYAN

Published by

Gyan Publishing House
5, Ansari Road
Daryaganj, New Delhi-110002
Phone: 011-47034999, 9811692060
E-mail: books@gyanbooks.com

Distribution Network
gyanbooks.com
India, USA, Canada, UK, Australia

ISBN: 978-81-212-7069-4 (PB)
First Published, 1876

2nd Impression 2024

Printed at: Gyan Press, Delhi.

THE DISTRICT OF BAKARGANJ
Author: H. BEVERIDGE

THE

DISTRICT OF BÁKARGANJ.

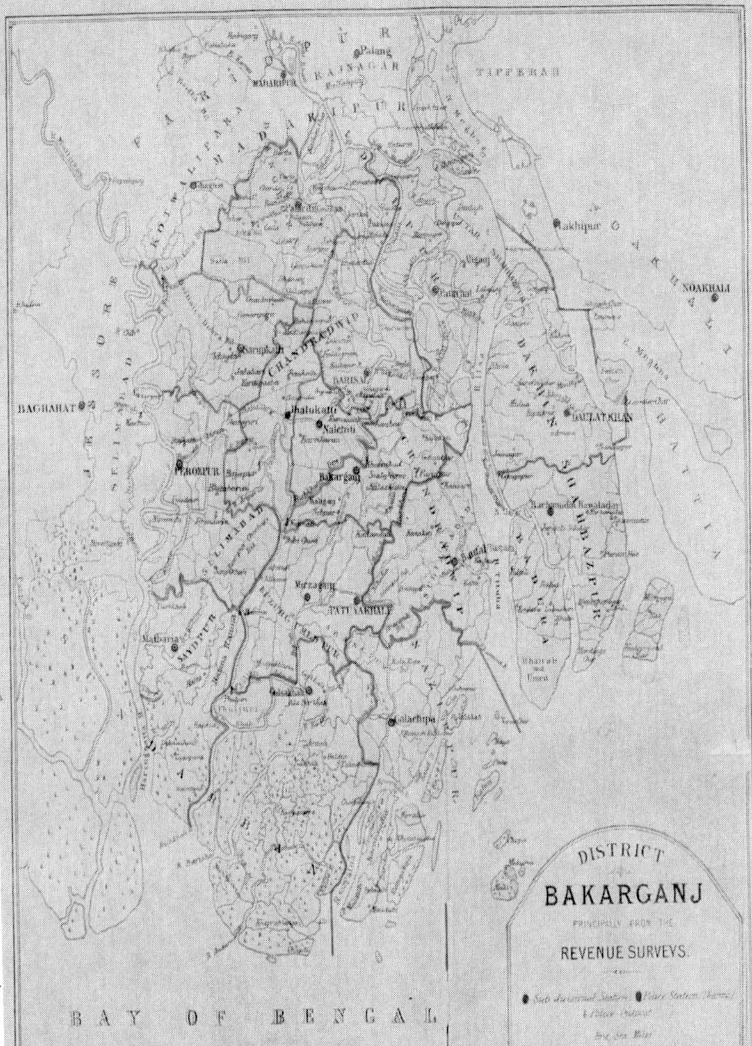
DISTRICT
BAKARGANJ
PRINCIPALLY FROM THE
REVENUE SURVEYS.
BAY OF BENGAL
TIPPERAH
NOAKHALI
BAGHAHAT
MADARIPUR
RAJNAGAR
CHANDRADWIP
Bakarganj
Jhalukati
Nalchiti
Mirzaganj
PATUAKHALI
Galachipa
DAULATKHAN
PIROJPUR
SELIMABAD
SAYDPUR
Matbaria

THE

DISTRICT OF BÁKARGANJ

ITS HISTORY AND STATISTICS

BY

H. BEVERIDGE, B.C.S.

MAGISTRATE AND COLLECTOR OF BÁKARGANJ

LONDON

TRÜBNER & CO., LUDGATE HILL

1876

I DEDICATE

This Book

TO

THE INHABITANTS OF THE DISTRICT

WHICH IT ATTEMPTS

TO DESCRIBE.

PREFACE.

THIS work is the result of nearly five years' experience in Bákarganj, and of subsequent researches in the India Office and the Library of the British Museum. My primary object has been to write a book which would be useful and interesting to the officers of Government and the inhabitants of the district, and therefore there is much in it which can have no attraction for the general reader. It is pleasing to think that so many district-histories are now in print, and that we are beginning to have for Bengal some such statistical account as the industry and patriotism of Sir John Sinclair caused to be prepared for Scotland.

Among older works we have the accounts of Rangpúr, Dinagepúr, and Purneah, by Francis Buchanan; that of Cuttack, by Mr Stirling; and the excellent description of Dacca, by Dr Taylor.[1] Among the more recent we

[1] This work was published by Government in 1839, and is now out of print. It is much to be desired that Government would correct and reprint it.

have the reports on the districts of the Dacca Division, Mr Brown's report on Tipperah, Colonel Gastrell's reports on Jessore, Farídpúr, and Bákarganj; Mr Hunter's description of Birbhum in his "Rural Annals," and the same author and Mr Toynbee's books on Orissa, Mr Glazier's account of Rangpúr, and, above all, Mr Westland's admirable report on Jessore. The reports on the Dacca districts owe their origin, I believe, to the forethought and public spirit of Mr Buckland, but more than three-fourths of the work was executed by competition-civilians; and I am proud to think that four of the other books I have mentioned have been written by members of the same class. In other parts of India this new class of civilians has not been idle, and I have been told on good authority that one of the best district-histories is the account of Ghazipúr, by Mr Oldham, B.C.S.

It will perhaps be thought that I have written too much about such an obscure district as Bákarganj, but my own consciousness is that I ought to have written a great deal more, and that I have often been very meagre in my treatment of important subjects. The truth is, no one man can write an exhaustive district-history, and still less can a foreigner adequately depict a district of Bengal. What I have chiefly laboured have been the descriptions of the parganas and the official history of the district. I did this not because they were the most important, but because they were less likely to be done by others. My idea always has been that the proper person to write the history of a district is one who is a native of it, who has lived all his life in it, and who has abundance of leisure to collect information. It is only a Bengali who can treat satisfactorily of the productions of his country, or of its social condition—its castes, leading families, peculiarities of language, customs, &c. I have not attempted to go minutely into these matters, but my hope is that I have done enough to stimulate discussion, and that I may serve to ring the fuller writer in. I have said very little about the mode of cultivating rice or other agricultural methods, both because I do not think that there are any which are peculiar to the district, and the ordinary practices have been repeatedly described already, and because I have observed that such parts of a book are always the first to become out of date.

In the chapter entitled "General Remarks" I have indulged in the luxury of making some observations of wider scope than were admissible in the earlier part of the book. Perhaps some may think that these observations are out of place in a district-history, but I hope they have some connection with it, since they presented themselves to me while writing this book. I do not think that there is anything singular or novel in the observations. Indeed, I should be the first to allow that they had no value whatever if I thought that they expressed nobody's opinions but my own. The only value, or at least the only practical value of opinions about India, or perhaps about any subject, is that they are shared by numbers of people, and are such as naturally suggest themselves to fair and reasonable persons who are conversant with the subject-matter. With regard to the question of the gradual abandonment of India, which is mooted by me in a note to the General Remarks, I am glad to be able to fortify myself with the following remarks by my late father at the conclusion of his "History of India:"—

"To the attempts made to christianise India, it has been objected that the inevitable result of their success would be to destroy the British rule. The inhabitants made aware of their natural rights, and become capable of self-government, would throw off our yoke and declare their independence. Unquestionably they would. But what then? Is it meant that, for the purpose of perpetuating our empire in the East, we must endeavour to keep our subjects there in a state of semi-barbarism, and discountenance all endeavours to raise them to our level in respect of intelligence, religion, and general civilisation? The time has been when such selfish and heartless policy would have been looked upon with favour, but a better spirit now prevails; and the determination, as announced in the Queen's proclamation, and cordially acquiesced in by all classes of society, is to do justice to India, and more than compensate her for all the wealth she has bestowed upon us by furnishing her with the means of rising above her present degraded state, and attaining to the highest form of European civilisation. Should the effect be to enable her to dispense with our tutelage, we shall have the satisfaction of feeling that we ourselves have been the willing instruments of her emancipation, while she, even in severing the political ties by which she is now bound to us, will not forget how much she shall then owe to us for the enlightened and generous policy which gradually prepared her for freedom. Should the day ever come that India, in consequence of the development of her resources by British capital, and the enlightenment of her people by British philanthropy, shall again take rank among the nations as an independent state, then it will not be too much to say that the extinction of our Indian Empire by such peaceful means sheds more lustre on the British name than all the other events recorded in its history."

In the above passage my father speaks of christianising India.[1] I should have preferred the word "civilise," unless, indeed, the term christianise be used in a different sense than it is at present. I have not the slightest expectation that the inhabitants of India will ever become Christians in the ordinary sense of that

[1] Much of my father's history was written against time and in failing health, but the vigour of his mind becomes apparent whenever a suitable subject for discussion presents itself. Few pieces of writing, for example, can be more vigorous than his reflections on the administration and trial of Warren Hastings. See also his remarks on the Permanent Settlement and the annexation of Oude.

word, nor do I suppose that any well-informed person believes that missionary efforts are making progress in India.

The plan of my book is first to give an account of the land. Thus I begin with the physical features, and then go on to a description of the parganas, the Sundarbans, and the Government estates. After that I notice the various kinds of tenures, and I have endeavoured to give some information about the numerous under-tenures of the district.

The chapter on antiquities and early history has been placed third in the book, in order to lead up to the constitution of the parganas and the financial history of the district.

In Part II. I have described the people and the natural productions, &c.; and in Part III. I have given a history of the administration, and chapters on detached points, such as the town of Barisál, the jail, &c.

The question of the correct spelling of the proper names is one I have taken some trouble with, but I am aware that I have omitted the accents in many places, and that also the spelling is often wrong. It is not in every case easy to know the etymology of a proper name, and in the absence of this knowledge we are very apt to make mistakes in spelling.

A considerable part of the book is taken up with the Appendices, and I trust that whatever judgment be passed on the rest of the work, it will be found that the Appendices contain something of value. I regret that I have been obliged to print the letters of Messrs Douglas and Massie from the imperfect copies in the Barisál office, and that there are therefore some passages in them which are probably incorrect. The reports of the Collectors at the time of making the Permanent Settlement are the most important documents in the history of each of the districts of Bengal, but it appears that very few of them have yet been printed. They are fast mouldering away in our record-rooms, and I hope that before it is too late Government will publish a volume containing all the correspondence about the Permanent Settlement of each district.

Since writing the note about early travellers in Bengal (Appendix, p. 444) I have seen the first volume of Ramusio's "Collection of Travels" (Venice, 1550), and I am almost convinced that the lost city of Bengala is neither more nor less than the famous city of Gour, in the Maldaha district. One of the most valuable accounts of early India appears to be the narrative of Edward Barbessa or Barbosa, who was a native of Lisbon, and finished his book in 1516. He afterwards sailed with Magellan on his voyage round the world, and was killed at the island of Zebu in 1521 (Biographie Universelle). Barbessa gives a description of the city of Bengala (p. 330), and it appears from it that it was a Mahomedan town—at least the king of it was a Mahomedan, and he appears to have resided in it. The narratives of Varthema, and of the anonymous author of the "Summary of the People of the East," &c., appended to Barbessa's account, also describe the king as being a Mahomedan, and this fact appears to me to render it almost certain that Bengala is Gour, as the latter was the only great Mahomedan city in Bengal. If Bengala had been a Hindu city, and governed by a Hindu king, we could understand its disappearance; but if there had been any large Mahomedan city in Bengal except Gour, it would certainly have been mentioned by the Mahomedan historians. The anonymous author above referred to says that the king of Tripura was tributary to the king of Bengala, and that Bengala was a port two days' journey from the mouth of the Ganges. This was written in the beginning of the sixteenth century, when Gour must have been much nearer the sea than it now is. What the origin of the name Gour is I do not know, but I believe that, like Bengala, it was a name given to the country as well as to the town. We find it in other places than in Maldaha; for example, some years ago there was a village called Gournadi—*i.e.*, the river of Gour—in the northern part of Bákarganj.[1]

[1] Dr Wise has referred me to a passage in Ortelius which says that Appian considered Bengala to be the emporium of Barakoura mentioned by Ptolemy, and that Gastaldi thought Barakoura was Bacala. (See the "Thesaurus Geographicus," under "Baracura.") Perhaps this name Barakoura is the origin of Le Blanc's remark about Batacouta. Appian is properly Apianus, and this again is the Latin appellation of Peter Bienewitz (both *apis* and *biene* signifying a bee), who was professor of mathematics at Ingolstadt in 1520, and published a cosmography. If Gour be thought too far

There is an interesting remark made by Barbessa which bears on the question of the conversion of the Hindus of Eastern Bengal to Mahomedanism discussed by me at p. 247. He says that the king of Bengala being a Mahomedan, many of his Hindu subjects are every day becoming Mahomedans in order to get favour with the king and his governors. The anonymous author of the summary tells us that the kings of Bengala had been Mahomedans for three hundred years, and this statement nearly corresponds with the date of Bakhtyar Khilji's conquest of Bengal (1203). The statement in my Appendix that Varthema was the first traveller in Bengal is incorrect, as Nicolo de Conti preceded him by nearly a hundred years. Conti was a Venetian, and his travels are printed in the first volume of Ramusio.

In conclusion, I wish to say that the Indian Government is in no way responsible for any of the opinions expressed in my book, and that these must not be regarded as having any official value whatever. I trust, however, that I have not said anything rashly, or which is other than a fair expression of opinion, and I do not think that I have said anything which could give just cause of offence to any one.

inland for Bengala, then Hugli, which was early a Mahomedan town, may be the place meant. (See the dictionary of Bruzen de La Martinière (1730), under the word "Bengale.") This writer says, "Dans le grand nombre de voyages de l'Indoustan que j'ai lus je n'en ai jamais trouvé où il soit parlé de Bengale comme d'une ville dont on ait dit quelques particularités capables d'en certifier la position ni même l'existence.

I have to express my obligations to the report on Bákarganj by Mr Sutherland, to Mr Westland's Jessore, to Colonel Gastrell's report, and to the disquisition of Professor Blochmann on the geography and history of Bengal. I have also been assisted by the Bengali account of Bákarganj by Naba Kanth Chattanji, which is a very good little manual, though I am sorry that the author has not acknowledged how much he has borrowed from Mr Sutherland. Finally, I have to declare how much assistance I have derived from the native officials of Bákarganj, and especially from the Collectorate Peshkar, Babu Koilas Chandra Ganguli.

The map prefixed to the work is a reduction from the Revenue Survey map, and I have made some alterations in it in order to bring it more into accordance with the existing state of the country, and also to exhibit the names mentioned in the book. I am indebted to the Indian Government for permission to make use of the Revenue Survey map.

H. BEVERIDGE.

LONDON, 23*d March* 1876.

CONTENTS.

PART I.

CHAPTER I.

CHAPTER II.

CHAPTER III.

CHAPTER IV.

CHAPTER V.

CHAPTER VI.

CHAPTER VII.

PART II.

CHAPTER VIII.

CHAPTER IX.

CHAPTER X.

PART III.

CHAPTER XI.

CHAPTER XII.

CHAPTER XIII.

CHAPTER XIV.

CHAPTER XV.

CHAPTER XVI.

CHAPTER XVII.

CHAPTER XVIII.

CHAPTER XIX.

APPENDIX A.

APPENDIX B.

APPENDIX C.

APPENDIX D.

APPENDIX E.

APPENDIX F.

THE

DISTRICT OF BÁKARGANJ.

PART I.

CHAPTER I.

INTRODUCTION.

THE district of Bákarganj is situated in Eastern Bengal, and is one of the four collectorates which compose the Division or Commissionership of Dacca. It lies in the lower portion of the delta which has been formed by deposits from the united waters of the Ganges or Padma, the Bráhmaputra, and the Meghna, and falls within latitudes 21° to 23° N., and longitudes 89° to 91° E. The boundaries of the district of Bákarganj are given in detail in the "Calcutta Gazette" of 16th September 1874. Briefly it may be described as bounded on the north by Farídpúr, on the west by Farídpúr and the Baleshwar river (which separates it from Jessore), on the south by the Bay of Bengal, and on the east by the Meghna and its estuary. Its length from north to south is about 85 miles, and its breadth, including the island of Dakhin Shahbázpúr, is about 60 miles. Its area is about 4300 square miles. It is thus more than half the size of Wales, the area of which is 7397 square miles, and it is slightly larger than the two counties of Somerset and Devon, the united area of which amounts to 4225 square miles (1636+2589). The area of Yorkshire, to which also it may be compared, is 5983 square miles.[1] It must, however, be confessed that the area of Bákarganj is not quite accurately known. The figures which I have given are derived from the Topographical Survey, but that survey was made in the years 1860 to 1863, and considerable changes must have taken place since then in an alluviating district such as Bákarganj. Also, I do not know the precise alteration of area which has been made by the transfer of the greater part of the Mádaripúr subdivision to Farídpúr.

The population of Bákarganj, according to the census of 1872, and after exclusion of the transferred portion of the Mádaripúr subdivision, is 1,878,144, of whom about two-thirds (1,254,429) are Mahomedans. The remaining third is composed of Hindus, with the exception of a few thousand Buddhists and Christians.

Bákarganj was made a *zila* or district for magisterial purposes in 1797 by Regulation 7 of that year, but it did not become a Collectorate till 1817. Barisál is the chief town, and the seat of the courts. It is about 180 miles east of Calcutta. The number of villages or townships in the district appears to be 3312. The land revenue is about thirteen lacs and seventy thousand rupees (£137,000), and the total revenue from all sources may be stated as sixteen lacs.[2] The cost of the local administration is under three lacs.

[1] The area of 4935 square miles which is assigned to Bákarganj in the Bengal Administration Report for 1872–73, includes the subdivision of Mádaripúr, which is now part of Farídpúr.

[2] In the Bengal Administration Report for 1873–74, p. ix. of the Statistical Returns, the land revenue of Bákarganj is given at Rs.1,511,278, and the gross revenue at Rs.1,905,464, but this includes Mádaripúr.

CHAPTER II.

PHYSICAL FEATURES.

I. GENERAL DESCRIPTION.

THE whole district of Bákarganj is an alluvial formation, and the most general observation which can be made concerning it is that the ground is everywhere flat. There is not a hill in any part of it. The general slope is from north to south, but it is very slight. From the Ganges to the Bay of Bengal (this description includes Farídpúr) the difference in level is only about 22 feet over the whole distance of 150 miles, or an average slope of 1·8 inch per mile. There is also a general depression towards the centre of the district (*vide* Colonel Gastrell's Report). The western part of the district and the central and southern portions down to the Sundarbans might almost be described as forming one vast rice-field, sprinkled with trees and villages, and intersected by numerous watercourses. The northern and eastern portions are higher, and produce large quantities of cocoa and betel nuts, sugar-cane, *pán*, and some jute and cotton.

The district consists partly of mainland, and partly of islands in the estuary of the Meghna. The islands are quite flat, but are for the most part well raised above the level of the sea; and as there are no rivers in them, they are generally less swampy than Bákarganj Proper. Commonly they present the appearance of a low table-land, of a rich soil, and yield many kinds of crops. Two or three are, however, uninhabited and uncultivated, and are for the most part covered with tree jungle. The largest island is Dakhin Shahbázpúr, which is the seat of a subdivision, and has an area of about 800 square miles, and a population of about 220,000 persons. The other principal islands are Kali, also called Panchkháli, Kázal, Bara Baisdia, Chota Baisdia, and its adjuncts Koralia and Rangabali, Kalmi, Chopa, Kúkri Múkri, and Manpúra. The last of these has a population of about 4500.

The proper Bengali word for an island is *upadwip*, and in legal phraseology the Persian word *jazira* is employed, but the word in common use is *char*. This name is applied indifferently to large islands, and to mere shoals and sandbanks, even though the latter fringe the mainland. Many chars are submerged at every tide; hence the aspect of the rivers varies much during each day. At flood, the estuary of the Meghna presents the appearance of a vast expanse of water, tempting one to think that it might be a highway for all the ships of the world. But the ebb shows the deceptiveness of this waste of waters, for then long lines of sand gradually emerge even in mid-channel. The navigation is so uncertain that the native boatmen, sailing in flat-bottomed country boats which draw only one or two feet of water, do not like to set out much after slack-water, lest they should ground as the ebb advances, and so expose themselves to being caught by the bore; if they have a fair wind, a man called the *goliya* or bow-man is continually thrusting a bamboo into the water ahead of the boat to ascertain the depth. English-built ships have, I believe, never ascended the Meghna, but sloops from Chittagong sail up it in the cold weather to

Naraingan, and also cross over to Dakhin Shahbázpúr, laden with earth-oil, and bringing away in exchange cocoa and betel nuts.

I have said that the district is an alluvial formation. In fact, it may be looked upon as a conquest won by the Ganges and the Meghna from the Bay of Bengal. With its central depression, and its deeply-indented southern boundary, it has somewhat the appearance of the outstretched palm of the hand. Thus a fanciful eye might regard it as a glove flung down by the Ganges to the ocean, in gage of battle, and as an augury of future victories.

As might be expected from its flatness, the scenery of Bákarganj is somewhat monotonous and uninteresting. As most of the district is of comparatively recent origin, it has not many fine trees, nor are there any ancient buildings to give picturesqueness to the landscape. In fact, there is something peculiarly unromantic and prosaic about the first impressions of Bákarganj. It strikes one as being a sort of agricultural Manchester, producing bread-stuffs instead of cotton cloth, but without the art culture for which Manchester is so justly famous. There is no ancient history of Bákarganj: no battles have been fought in it, or at least no traces of them now remain; there are hardly any resident aristocracy; and there are no art products of any kind. Other districts have their workers in ivory and silver, their shawlmakers, &c., but Bákarganj has none of these. Committees for International Exhibitions can get nothing from it to show in Europe as trophies of Indian skill or taste. It must be confessed, too, that there is something depressing in the air of Bákarganj, and in the continual prospect of swamps and muddy rivers. One longs for a dry tract of country, dotted with mango topes and tamarind-trees, across which one could ride or walk without being brought to a stand every three or four hundred yards by the slimy bank of a *khál.* Boats are all very well, and one acknowledges that there is no other mode of conveyance which is so economical, or so effectual for the transport of heavy or fragile goods, but one wishes that it could be dispensed with occasionally. It is fatiguing to find that you cannot reach a place only ten miles off on the map in less than eight or nine hours, and that if wind and tide be against you, you may not reach it in less than a day and a half.

Yet, in spite of all these disadvantages, the district is not without its interest and its beauty. A writer in the "Calcutta Review" endeavours to conjure up a feeling of admiration for a Bákarganj river, by suggesting that its muddy waters have come down from the magnificent valleys of the Himalayas; but I am afraid that this is an idea which will not readily come home to men's bosoms, at least except of that small minority which has seen Gangotri, &c. I would rest the claims of Bákarganj to the possession of some beauty and interest on more tangible and more human grounds, and would especially insist on the greenness and freshness which characterise its scenery. There is at least nothing arid or barren about the Bákarganj landscape; and one who has seen the weary plains of Cawnpore or Delhi must, I think, turn with delight and refreshment to the waving palm-trees, the wide sheets of green rice spreading without let or hindrance of hedge or wall almost as far as the horizon, and the full and flowing rivers, which meet the eye in Eastern Bengal. The Mahomedans called Bengal the Paradise of countries; the Englishman, panting in the heat, and longing for a sight of something more inspiriting than a uniform plain, is inclined to question the justice of the epithet. But there is a sense in which it is justifiable, and that too one which is perhaps higher than any mere sentimental feeling for fine scenery can be. As Macaulay teaches us, the love of rocks and mountains is a product of civilisation; so that we may utter the paradox, that the love of nature is an artificial taste. But no apprenticeship, and no study of poets and painters, are required for the admiration of a field of standing corn, or of a wide plain of rice. Such things appeal to our sympathies as men, and are lovely, as the face of a friend may be dear to us, not because of its mere beauty, but because of its associations. If we look at the homesteads of the Bákarganj peasantry, standing like "moated granges" embowered in bamboos, *ják* fruit and plantain trees, tamarinds and palms, and surrounded by luxuriant rice-fields, we cannot help feeling that the inhabitants enjoy a considerable amount of physical wellbeing, and that they are just objects of envy to the residents of other countries. The general character of Bákarganj scenery is that of open plains, called *kholas* (opens), of various sizes, separated from each other by ribands of fruit-trees, and traversed by numerous watercourses. The ribands represent the villages, the houses being always scattered and shrouded in trees. There are hardly any towns in Bákarganj, and every house in it has the appearance of a detached villa, and is, with its orchard, a sort of *rus in urbe.* The houses are literally "moated granges," for every ryot's house in Bákarganj is surrounded by a trench, the earth from which is used for raising the foundation of the homestead and the garden-ground. With the same object, it is common to dig a tank whenever a homestead is made. The lines of villages are like living walls, the bricks and lime being replaced by tree-stems and green leaves; and when the sunlight falls on them, or they are seen in the calm moonlight, the effect is very beautiful.

Rivers are always objects of interest in a landscape, and though those of Bákarganj are wanting in the picturesqueness of mountain streams, yet some of them are noble bodies of water, and their banks are often well-wooded and pleasant to the eye. There is, perhaps, not a more graceful sight in nature than a group of areca palms standing on the bank of a river. The spreading banyan, the sacred fig with its wealth of acuminated leaves, the *gáb*, conspicuous by its somewhat dome-shaped habit, and its massive, dark-green foliage, and the clumps of feathery bamboos, have all their attraction; but perhaps the most beautiful tree is the tamarind, which often attains a large size, and has a peculiarly elegant appearance, from its pinnated leaves and its air of ease and freedom. The branches are long and drooping, and fall about the stem with the luxuriant and unstudied grace of a woman's hair escaped from a fillet. The banks of some of the smaller rivers are exceedingly pretty. For example, the khál at Rahamatpúr, commonly called the Rajah's Moat (from a tradition that it was dug as an entrenchment for the palace at Madhabpásha), is very picturesque, both banks being richly clothed with fruit-trees, flowering creepers, &c.

The rivers frequently present an animated appearance from the number of boats which traverse them, and there is something cheering and inspiriting in the sight of a fleet of white-sailed boats trooping through a long reach of one of the larger rivers. Such a sight is often seen to great advantage in the cold weather at Barisál, when boats of many shapes and districts come sailing down under the north wind, and sweep past the town on their way to Bákarganj and other rice-marts. The traffic on the rivers is no doubt very large, but their tidal nature may sometimes make it appear greater than it really is. Boatmen are very gregarious in their habits, and like to keep near other boats as much as possible. This is partly from a desire for companionship, and partly is a reminiscence of the times when it was not safe to travel alone in Bákarganj on account of the dacoits; but independently of this, it is easy to see that if rivers are tidal, and boatmen have to trust chiefly to their oars and towing-ropes, the boats must keep a good deal together. Cargo-boats never row against the tide, and though they will tow against it, the river-banks are not always, or even generally, provided with towing-paths; so that unless there is a particular reason for hurry, they come to a halt with the turn of the tide. It is not always the same tide which is required throughout a single journey. Boat-travelling is very circuitous, and the tides run up and down the rivers and kháls in a very perplexing manner. Thus the journey from Barisál to Calcutta is far from being an ebb journey throughout. It is ebb as far as Jhalukátti, then flood, then ebb again; and there are one or two changes before the Baleshwar is reached and ascended with the flood. A boat arriving at a place where a change of tide is required, before the tide which has brought it has run out, moors or casts anchor, and thus gives time to other boats to come up. Hence the sight so frequently seen of a crowd of boats anchored at some turn of the stream. As soon as the required tide commences they set off together, and the river appears to be covered with boats; but if we were to return to the place in another hour, we might perhaps not see a single boat. The river now appears deserted, and will remain so till a turn of the tide bring a fleet of boats from the opposite direction.

II. CLIMATE.

The climate of Barisál, the headquarters of Bákarganj, and of most of the cultivated tracts, may be said to be good. The temperature is decidedly lower than that of most places in Bengal. In a report for 1871, the Civil Surgeon (Dr Bensley) writes as follows: "The climate of Barisál, though cool, is very relaxing, and recovery from any severe disease is extremely tedious, often necessitating a change. The past year (1871) has been remarkably cool; the average temperature during the three seasons was 67·835° in the cold season, 75·932° in the hot season, and 78·895° in the rainy season. The rainfall, as measured by the standard gauge, was 89·41, being 15·41 in excess of the previous year. The prevailing winds are south-west and north-west—the former about eight months of the year; it is generally cool and refreshing.[1] Barisál, being about fifty miles from the bay, and having a large river, the wind is thereby further cooled and purified before reaching the town. Our north-west is not similarly protected, and during the prevailing winds from that quarter, the town suffers considerably from malarious diseases." The months of March, April, and May, which are usually so hot in Calcutta and in Western Bengal, are comparatively cool in this district. The rains commonly set in about the middle of June, and continue

[1] It is observable that the breeze generally comes in with the tide, and dies away with the ebb.

into October. The worst time of the year, and also the hottest, is the period between the rains and the setting in of the cold weather. The sun is exceedingly powerful in the month of October, and even up to the middle of November. Perhaps the most disagreeable period of the whole year is that from the 15th of October to the 15th of November. This is the time of sudden changes of temperature—*sardi garmi* (cold and hot), as the natives call it—and the result is a large amount of fever. The dampness and steaminess of the climate also make themselves felt most at this time. An officer (Mr Wintle) describing to Government, in 1801, the climate of the station of Bákarganj, writes, "The atmosphere depresses the spirits in such a manner as to cause a sensation as if a person was only half alive." The cold weather is pleasant, but it is not so bracing as that of the more northern districts, and does not last more than four months. It is said that the proximity of Bákarganj to the sea prevents its climate from ever being very cold. The general complaint against it is of its dampness. This depresses vitality, and is also most injurious to furniture, books, &c. It is impossible to keep a house dry unless it is built on arches. Many of the native government officials and professional men, and even many of the traders, belong to other districts, especially to Dacca. They complain of the salt air (*lona howa*) of Bákarganj, and say that it gives them fever and indigestion. The healthiest place in the district used to be Mádaripúr, and police constables and others used to be transferred there when in bad health. Mádaripúr is now in Farídpúr, and probably the most healthy parts of the present district are the portions of Gournadi thana which face the Arial Khan, and the islands in the estuary of the Meghna. Dakhin Shahbázpúr and its chief town, Daulat Khan, seem to be healthy, except when, as happened in May 1869, a cyclone passes over the island and destroys the tanks. Cholera is endemic in the district, usually occurring in the beginning of November, and again in April and May; for several years, however, it has not been very severe. Fever and dysentery appear to be the most deadly diseases. Dyspepsia, spleen, and rheumatism are common. As a remedy for rheumatism many of the inhabitants are in the habit of keeping an open issue (seton) in the arm or leg. Dyspepsia often assumes the form called *pítshul.* Dysentery and diarrhœa prevail throughout the year, the mortality being greatest at the termination of the rains, and during the cold season. During September and October a slight scorbutic tendency is often observed, owing to the absence of sufficient fresh vegetables, the country being at the time more or less under water (*vide* Bensley's Report for 1871). Cutaneous diseases—ringworm, itch, &c.—are very common. The first is seen especially among boatmen and others who work in water, the soles of their feet being often drilled with holes like a sponge.

In 1860 there was a great mortality from fever in the islands of Kali, Kázal, &c., and in 1869 there was a similar but more widely-spread epidemic of fever in Dakhin Shahbázpúr. It is noteworthy that the Barisál jail has always been unhealthy. The same was true of the old jail at Bákarganj, and Mr Wintle writes (7th September 1801) that 242 prisoners had died within the past twelve months.

The only meteorological observations made in the district are those of the rainfall. There are four rain-gauges—viz., one at Barisál, and one at each of the three subdivisional stations. The following table shows the rainfall for three years :—

Jan. 1 to Dec. 31.	Barisál.	Peroz-púr.	Daulat Khan.	Patuyakháli.
	Inches.	Inches.	Inches.	Inches.
1871	93·04	92·45	113·26	No observation.
1872	82·14	62·53	81·49	90·73[1]
1873	61·71	57·18	101·08	91·73

In connection with the subject of climate it is necessary to notice the curious phenomenon called the Barisál guns. This is a sound, resembling the discharge of cannon, which is heard in Bákarganj and part of Dacca, Farídpúr, and Jessore at the beginning of the rains—that is, in May and June. At Barisál the sound comes from the south and south-west, and is generally heard in a south wind and before rain. It is sometimes heard only for a minute or two; sometimes it continues for one or two hours, at intervals of two or three minutes between each discharge. It seems to be heard usually in the evening and at night, but perhaps this is only because the attention is more drawn to it when there are fewer other noises. It has been supposed by some that the sounds are merely those of guns fired at marriages; by others, that they are caused by the falling in of the river-banks. But they are heard away to the south, among the Sundarbans, where there are no marriages, and where there are no high river-banks to fall in. They are heard down at Kúkri Múkri, the most southerly island in the district, and the Mugs there assured me that they are distinct from the noise of the breakers or of the tide coming in. The natives

[1] From the 13th of May 1872.

poetically account for the sound by saying that it is caused by the opening and shutting of Ravan's gates in the island of Lanka (Ceylon). This fiction is valuable, in so far as it shows that the sound generally comes from the south. The Mahomedans say that it is caused by the firing of cannon to announce the approach of their Imam. It is not altogether impossible that it originates in that curious submarine depression in front of Jessore and Bákarganj, which is known by the name of the Swatch of No Ground.[1]

III. CYCLONES.

The most destructive hurricane which has ever occurred in the district of Bákarganj was that which began on the 6th of June 1822, and lasted till the 9th idem. (For an account of its ravages see Chapter XIII.) On the 1st of November 1867 there was a cyclone which injured the crops in the eastern part of the district, especially in the island of Dakhin Shahbázpúr, then under Noakháli. The next cyclone occurred on the 16th of May 1869. It did much damage to the roads and villages generally, and carried away the station road on the east side of Barisál. Many cattle were drowned, and the *owsh* crop was injured. The cyclone was followed on the 8th, 9th, and 10th of the next month by an inundation, which did great damage in Dakhin Shahbázpúr, as it destroyed most of the fresh-water tanks. In consequence, probably, of the scarcity of

[1] Vol. liii. of the Philosophical Transactions for 1763 contains two interesting accounts of the Chittagong earthquake of 2d April 1762. In that given by Mr Gulston is mentioned the curious circumstance that "at the time of the first shake great explosions were heard like the noise of cannons, of which Mr Plaisted and others counted fifteen."

good drinking water, an epidemic of fever broke out in the island, which is said to have decimated the population.

IV. TIDES.

The subject of the tides in the Meghna is very interesting, but I am not competent to discuss it, and can only state a few facts concerning it. There are two tides in its estuary, which are known by the names of the Chittagong and the Daula tides. The Chittagong tide passes up between Sandwip and the Chittagong coast, turns west, round the north of Sandwip, and then flows south along the east coast of Dakhin Shahbázpúr. It meets the Daula tide about half-way down the latter island, overpowers it, and drives it back. The Daula tide flows up between Dakhin Shahbázpúr and Hattia, coming in about three-quarters of an hour before the Chittagong tide. Its waters are comparatively fresh, so that inundations by it are much less dreaded by the peasantry than those of the Chittagong tide. The bore occurs at new and full moon. It is only felt in shallow water, where it rushes up in a white wall, said to be twenty or thirty feet in height. Boatmen do not like to put out on the days of the bore, and especially object to setting out with the ebb, lest they should ground on a char, and there be overtaken by it. It is called the *bán*, also the *shar*, both words, in Bengali, signifying arrow.

V. RIVERS.

The rivers of Bákarganj are very numerous, but all draw their waters, directly or indirectly, from the Ganges or the Meghna. Three great rivers flow through or past the district in a southerly direction—viz., the Meghna, the Arial Khan, and the Baleshwar.

1. The Meghna flows down the east side of Bákarganj, and opens out into an estuary at the head of the island of Dakhin Shahbázpúr. At the north-east boundary of the district, the Meghna many years ago broke through to the westward by an opening called the Naya Bhangni or New Opening. Tradition says that the new channel was formed in a single night. It is not known in what year this took place, but it must have been less than a century ago, for the passage is not marked in Rennel's map. In a report by Babu Dinu Bandhu Maulik, a Deputy-Collector, it is stated that the channel was formed in B.S. 1200 (A.D. 1793). It is also called the Harinathpúr river, and is the channel south of Haturia.[1] In successive parts of its course the Meghna is called the Satbaria, the Ilsa (*i.e.*, Hilsa), and the Títulia.[2]

2. The Arial Khan is a branch of the Ganges or Padma. It enters the district east of Palardi (the site of the Gournadi police station), and pursues a south-easterly course till it joins the estuary of the Meghna, by the Máskátta and Kalinga channels. In the lower part of its course it is called the Dakaitia and the Jahapúr river. An offshoot from the Arial Khan flows past Barisál, and is therefore called the Barisál river.

1 The name Naya Bhangni is not given to the Muladi river, although it is marked as such in the survey map.

2 Wilford, Asiatic Researches, vol. xiv., says that the Meghna is the Magone of Megasthenes as cited by Arrian, and mentioned as one of the rivers which fell into the Ganges. It is the Meghanád or Meghabahana of Sanskrit writers, and derives its name from *megha*, a cloud, in allusion to the obscurity of its origin. This is in contradistinction to the Bráhmaputra, whose existence of course is accounted for by his being the son of Bráhma.

3. The Baleshwar is formed by the junction of the Madhamati and the Saldaha. It flows past the west side of Bákarganj, is joined, at some distance below Perozpúr, by the Kacha, and enters the sea under the name of the Haringháttá.

There is considerable difficulty in enumerating the Bákarganj rivers, on account of their frequent change of name. At every ten miles of its course, or at an even less interval, the name of a river is generally changed. The names, too, are commonly insignificant, and are merely those of the principal bazárs or villages on the bank. Thus we have the Barisál river, the Nalchiti river, and the Bákarganj river. This frequent change of name is common enough throughout East Bengal, but it is especially marked in Bákarganj, probably because there are more rivers in it than in any other district, and because its rivers have less appearance of continuity—are, in short, less like rivers than those of districts farther from the sea. In many places the so-called rivers are rather marine creeks or arms of the sea. All of them are tidal, and it is only in the height of the rains that their waters do not turn with the tide. In March and April the waters of most of the rivers south of Barisál are salt, or at least brackish.

After the three already mentioned, the following are the principal rivers of Bákarganj :—

4. The Barisál river flows west by Nalchiti and Jhalukátti. Part of its waters then go down by the Dhánsiddhi into the Kaukháli and Kacha rivers. Another part flows into the Bishkháli. About three miles below Barisál a branch of the Barisál river flows southward by Ranihát and Bákarganj, under the name of the Khairábád river.

5. The Pándab, in the east of Bákarganj thana.

6. The Kárkhána, in Bákarganj and Baufal.
7. The Dhulia, in the north of Baufal thana.
8. The Khairábád. (See No. 4.)
9. The Nohalia, in Bákarganj and the Patuyakháli subdivision. In the lower part of its course it is commonly called the Galachipa, on account of its flowing past the Galachipa bazár and thana.
10. The Bishkháli is a very large river, flowing past Niamati and Kala Megha, east of and parallel to the Baleshwar and Haringháttá.
11. The Bighai is in Mirzaganj and Gúlsakháli, and is probably the widest river in the district.
12. The Andarmanick, a large and wide river in the Gúlsakháli thana.
13. The Barishar, which may be considered a continuation of the Bighai.
14. The Kacha is formed partly by the Kaukháli river and partly by the Káliganga, which issues from the swamps of the Kotwalipara and Sarupkátti thanas. It is a very deep river, and joins the Baleshwar below Perozpúr.
15. The Sápleza (snake's tail), in Matbária thana, the Agunmúkha, the Kázal, between the island of Kázal and the mainland, the Dárchíra (destroyer of oars), between Big and Little Baisdia, and several others, are rather arms of the sea than rivers.

Nearly all the above-named rivers have a southerly course. The cross-rivers which connect them, and which generally flow in an easterly or westerly direction, are commonly called *dōnes.* The word *dōn* is applied rather loosely, but it generally means a channel which is larger than a khál, but not sufficiently wide or long to deserve the name of river. It is also distinguished from a khál or river by the fact of its having no source, properly so called. It generally has two mouths, one at each end of its course, and both may be equally large. Perhaps this characteristic may be the origin of the name dōn, which seems to have its root in the Bengali word for *two*.

The following are the principal dōnes :—

a. The Bishkháli, which connects the Bishkháli river (at Niamati) and the Khairábád river (near Kótarhát).

b. The Amua dōn, in Matbária thana, connects the Bishkháli and the Baleshwar rivers.

c. The Muradia dōn begins at Kadamtolli Hát, in the Bákarganj thana, and joins the Nohalia, north-east of Patuyakháli. It is the chord to a loop of the Nohalia.

d. The Damuda connects the Kacha and the Baleshwar, and is on the steamer route from Calcutta to Barisál.

e. The Patuyakháli, between the Nohalia and the Bighai.

f. The Aila, and its continuation, the Khák dōn, are deep and wide, and connect the Bighai and the Bishkháli rivers.

g. The Bagi, between the Andarmanick and the Aila rivers.

h. The Gajalia, between the Bishkháli and the Kaukháli. It is the usual steamer route, being preferred now to the Dhánsiddhi.

i. The Kalijiri is sometimes called a river. In the upper part of its course it is called the Sugandha, or the Fragrant, in allusion to the tradition that when the goddess Kali was cut in pieces her nose fell into it.

It would be an endless task to enumerate all the kháls of Bákarganj. Many of them exist only during the rains, when every village has its khál, and often two or three. The following are the most important, not on account of their size or length, but for their usefulness :—

(1.) The Jóbkháli khál, on the Barisál river.

(2.) The Jhalukátti khál, on the same river. These two kháls are important on account of their shortening the distance to Calcutta. The Jhalukátti was widened and deepened by the Public Works Department some years ago, at a cost of 11,000 or 12,000 rupees.

(3.) The Lakutia khál flows through the town of Barisál, where it is generally called the Jail khál. It is about six miles long, and shortens the journey to Dacca and the north of the district. It was originally made in a great measure by the liberality of the Lakutia zamindar, Babu Raj Chandra Rai. The Road Committee has since spent several thousand rupees in deepening it.

(4.) The Agarpúr khál.
(5.) The Shikarpúr khál.
(6.) The Turki khál.
} These three are in the north of the district.

(7.) The Srimantapúr khál, also called the Sibpúr khál, flows past Bákarganj and Sibpúr.

(8.) The Rajar Ber, at Rahamatpúr, so called because of a tradition that the Rajah of Chandradwip had it cut as a moat to his palace at Madhabpásha.

(9.) The Bhola khál, in Dakhin Shahbázpúr, extends across the island, and has been widened and deepened at a considerable expense.

Many of the kháls and dōnes have a double tide—that is, the tide flows in from each end and meets in the centre. This makes them apt to silt up. All the rivers and kháls wear away their banks, and often do much damage to the adjacent lands; but the most destructive in this respect are the Arial Khan and the Meghna. They often change their course, and carry away great tracts of country. It is true that they restore the land farther down; but this seldom compensates the proprietor, especially as the new formations remain for many years as barren sandbanks. At the present time the Ilsa—*i.e.*, the Meghna—is cutting away its west bank very rapidly in thana Mendiganj, and the estuary of the Meghna is doing the same with the east side of Dakhin Shahbázpúr. The Arial Khan has for many years been diluviating its east bank, and throwing up large chars at Kalkini and Gournadi. The old village of Gournadi, which was the seat of a police station, has been altogether washed away, and the station is now at Palardi. New chars have, however, now formed on part of the old site of Gournadi village and east of Palardi. Close to the Palardi police station there is a curious mark of the changes which have taken place. This is the abutment of an old bridge, which must have been made at a time when there was much country to the east of the police station. The river came and swept away the country to the eastward and the bridge which at that time spanned a narrow khâl. Palardi char has now formed opposite to the remains of the bridge, and the passage has become a khâl once more. Three or four years ago the Arial Khan cut across the long neck of land at Kewaria, east of Palardi, and the appearance of the country is now in consequence very different from that represented in the survey map. There is something very desolate in the appearance of the country near these large rivers, when the force of the stream begins to be directed against any particular tract. The peasants make haste to remove their houses, and to cut down their groves of betel and cocoa nut trees; as the diluviation advances, nothing is to be seen near the bank but stumps of trees, the earthen foundations of houses, and the broken walls of tanks. The irruption of the Meghna into the tanks is perhaps the most melancholy of such sights; for Dakhin Shahbázpúr and Hattia have many large tanks, which must have been constructed at much expense and labour. They are surrounded by high walls of earth in order to keep out the salt water, and when a breach is made in them they become useless, and whole villages suffer in consequence. When the peasants are thus driven away by the rivers, they sometimes merely move farther inland; but when they cannot get fresh land there, they are obliged to go to new chars, or to distant parts of the country. They are sometimes expressively called *nadi-bhanga lôk—i.e.,* river-broken people.

Generally it may be remarked of Bákarganj rivers, that they are deep on one side and shallow on the other. It also seldom occurs that they have high banks on both sides. The most common case is that one bank is high and wooded, and the opposite bank low and sandy. The high bank is always the one which the river is cutting away, but it does not always remain on the same side of the river. On the contrary, the general appearance is a high bank on, say, the right side, and a char on the left; then in the reach lower down a high bank on the left side, and a char on the right. The high bank of a river is commonly higher than the country farther inland, hence these river-banks are often useful as roads and towing-paths. They are also frequently the sites of villages, and are used for the cultivation of crops which require high land, such as sugar-cane, pán, betel-nut, &c. The volume of water brought down by the Ganges and Meghna must be very great; perhaps nothing can give a clearer idea of this than the fact that in October, and even, I believe, up to December, the water surrounding Kúkri Múkri is perfectly fresh. A reference to the map will show that this island is almost in the Bay of Bengal.[1]

VI. LAKES AND SWAMPS.

During the rains most of the country is a swamp, and the rice-fields do not dry up till January or February. There are also extensive depressions, in which the water remains all the year round, and which are generally known by the name of *bíls*. Of these, the principal are the Jhanjhania bíl, in Gournadi and Sarupkátti; Rampúr Chechari bíl, in Matbária; and Dharandi, Adampúr, and Kala Rajah bíls, in thana Baufal. The Kotwalipara bíls have for the most part been transferred to Farídpúr. The large bíls yield fish in considerable quantity, and there is some export trade in this article from the Sarupkátti and Kotwalipara bíls to Calcutta. They are also valuable for the large quantities of reeds they produce, which are extensively used in making mats, and are also exported. The Kala Rajah bíl is supposed to derive its name from one of the Chandradwip Rajahs.

Small bíls are common all over the district, there being one in almost every large village. They are valu-

[1] In speaking of the amount of soil brought down by the Ganges, Lyell remarks that "it is scarcely possible to present any picture to the mind which will convey an adequate conception of the mighty scale of this operation, so tranquilly and almost insensibly carried on by the Ganges. It may, however, be stated that if a fleet of about 2000 ships, each freighted with 1400 tons of mud, were to sail down the river every hour of every day and night for four months continuously, they would only transport to the sea a mass of solid matter equal to that borne down by the Ganges in the four months of the flood season."—*Principles of Geology*, p. 282.

able from their yielding reeds and cattle-grass, and also because they afford convenient ground for the herding of buffaloes. Shells abound in the bíls, and in many places are collected and converted into lime.

The name Sundarbunds, or more correctly, Sundarban, is said to derive its origin from the sundari-tree (*Heritiera minor*), and this again is said to be called *sundari*, or the beautiful, on account of the red colour of its wood. Probably this etymology of the word "Sundarban" is correct; but it is a singular fact that the sundari-tree is by no means common in many parts of the Bákarganj Sundarbans. Thus, in the island of Kúkri Múkri, which is covered with tree-jungle, there is apparently not a single tree of sundari; and in the neighbouring island of Chopa I was able to find two or three trees only, and these very young.[1] The prevailing tree in these and other chars is that called the *kerua*. In the neighbourhood of Chapli, also, the sundari is not so common as the *goma* and other trees. The Mugs, however, who live there, account for its comparative scarcity by the greater demand for it in the market. The area now covered by the Sundarbans is much less than it was in former years, and cultivation is still advancing. Many tracts—such as Ramna-Bamna, Aila, and Tushkháli—have been reclaimed, and now bear luxuriant crops of rice. Even now, however, there are extensive forests along the southern face of the Bákarganj mainland. The aspect of these forest-tracts is by no means cheerful. The woods are dark and silent; the trees are seldom tall

[1] The name may possibly be connected with Sundarkúl, which was the old name of a tract of country in Bákarganj. It may thus mean "the forest of the river Sunda;" or the word may, after all, be Sundarbund, and mean "the embankment of the Sunda."

enough to be handsome; and the rivers and creeks are sullen and muddy, and suggestive of fevers and alligators.[1]

[1] An interesting article on the physical characteristics of Bákarganj was published by Mr Pellew in the "Calcutta Review," and I have taken the liberty of transferring a long extract from it to my Appendix. This extract refers to the drainage system of Bákarganj. I do not feel competent to discuss the subject, but I am sure that whether Mr Pellew's views are correct or not, his remarks are worth reading.

CHAPTER III.

ANTIQUITIES AND EARLY HISTORY.

THERE is not much to be said about the antiquities or the early history of Bákarganj. It has always lain remote from the stream of Indian history, and has been happy in having no annals.

According to one tradition, much of the present district was formerly the bed of a large river, called the Sugandha or Fragrant. This river threw up chars or alluvial formations on either side, the lands on the east receiving the names of Bákla and Bákla-Chandradwip, and those on the west the name of Selímábád. The name Sugandha is still preserved under the shortened form of Sunda, in the name Sundarkúl—*i.e.*, bank of the Sunda—which is applied to a village in the neighbourhood of Nalchiti.

It is certain that the general name for much of the present district was Bákla, and that the territory was ruled over by a Hindu family. This family was one of the twelve *bhuyas* or rulers of Bengal, who were also poetically known as the twelve suns of Bengal. Its members are generally known by the name of Rajahs of Chandradwip, and their history has been given by me under that *pargana*.

Bákla is mentioned by the traveller Ralph Fitch, who visited it in 1586. He says, "From Chatigam, in Bengala, I came to Bacola, the king whereof is a Gentile [*i.e.*, Hindu], a man very well disposed, and delighteth much to shoot in a gun. His country is very great and fruitful, and hath store of rice, much cotton cloth, and cloth of silk. The houses be very fair and high builded, the streets large, the people naked except a little cloth about their waist. The women wear great store of silver hoops about their necks and arms, and their legs are ringed about with silver and copper, and rings made of elephants' teeth."—*Quoted by Blochmann.*

This Bacola has entirely disappeared, and it is only a conjecture which identifies it with Kachua, the ancient seat of the Chandradwip Rajahs. Fitch does not mention how he came to it from Chatigam—*i.e.*, Chittagong—nor is there any local tradition of there ever having been a town called Bacola or Bákla. If a town so large and flourishing as that described by Fitch ever existed in Bákarganj, it must have been washed away by the Meghna very many years ago. Bákla was famous amongst the Hindus as the seat of a school of pandits, who it is said ranked higher than those of Nuddea. Mr Taylor, in his history of Dacca, speaks of an astrological almanac which used to be drawn up by the Bákla pandits. There are still several pandits at Nalchira, in Gournadi.

In the "Ain i Akbari" (Gladwin's translation) there is the following notice of Bákla: "Sarkár Bákla is upon the banks of the sea; the fort is situated among trees. On the first day of the moon the water begins to rise, and continues increasing till the 14th, from which time to the end of the month it decreases gradually every day. In the twenty-ninth year of the present reign, one afternoon at three o'clock, there was a terrible inundation which deluged the whole *sarkár*. The Rajah was at an entertainment, from which he embarked in a boat; his son, Pannanand Roy, with many people climbed to the top of a Hindoo temple, and the merchants betook themselves to the highlands. It blew a hurricane, with thunder and lightning, for five hours, during which time the sea was greatly agitated. The houses and boats were swallowed up, nothing remaining but the Hindoo temple on the height. Near 200,000 living creatures perished in this calamity."

This inundation appears to have taken place in 1583 or 1584, and it is a very extraordinary circumstance, that Fitch, who visited the place two or three years afterwards, says nothing about it.[1]

We should have expected that such a catastrophe would have left, for many years, conspicuous marks of its occurrence, and that the country would not after so short an interval have worn an aspect of richness and prosperity.

The next reference to Bákla occurs in the letters of Nicholas Pimenta, who was a Jesuit priest stationed at Goa, at the close of the nineteenth century. These letters are referred to in "Purchas's Pilgrimage" (London, 1625), book v. p. 513, and the name Bacola occurs there; but for fuller information it is necessary to consult the original work. Pimenta's letters were written from Goa in the year 1600, to Claude Aquaviva, who was then general of the Jesuit Order. There is, properly speaking, only one letter, but it is a comprehensive one, describing the success of the mission, and containing

[1] Professor Blochmann (Asiatic Society's Journal for December 1868) gives a somewhat different translation of this passage. He says the merchants got upon a *tálar* (not highlands), and explains that a tálar is a wooden house built on four pillars, and used by musicians as an orchestra —a *naub at-khana,* in fact. He gives 1585 as the date of the inundation—*i.e.,* only one year before Fitch's visit. I have recurred to this subject in the chapter on the Sundarbans.

extracts from the letters of the missionaries. In fact, it is a missionary report. The letter was originally published in Italian at Venice, and was reprinted at Constance in 1603. It was then translated into Latin, and published at Mayence. The title of this edition is as follows: "De felici statu et progressu rei Christianæ in India Orientali Epistola R. P. Nicolai Pimentæ Societatis Jesu ibidem visitatoris ad admodum R. P. Claudium Aquavivam ejusdem Societatis Jesu Præpositum Generalem, Calendis Decembri anno MDC. data."

Pimenta commences by giving a short sketch of the history of Bengal, and states that the government of it was at that time in the hands of twelve princes who had formed a secret league among themselves, and had got the better of the Moghals. He adds that the most powerful of the twelve were the lords of Sripúr and Chandecan, but above all the Maafaddin or Masanddin (?). Perhaps this is Ísá Khan Masnad i Ali of Khizrpúr, described by Dr Wise as the most celebrated of the twelve bhuyas. Nine of the twelve, says Pimenta, are Mahomedans, and this circumstance very much retards the work of conversion.[1] He then goes on to describe the success attained by the missionaries who were sent into Bengal in 1598 and 1599.

These missionaries were Francis Fernandez, Dominic da Sosa, Melchior da Fonseca, and Andrew Bowes. The first two left Cochin for Bengal on 3d May 1598, and the other two in the following year. Fernandez appears to have been the chief of the four, and he wrote to Pimenta from Sripúr on the 22d December 1599,[2] giving an account of the proceedings of himself and his comrades. They appear to have sailed first from Cochin to

[1] According to Du Jarric, the three Hindu princes were those of Sripúr, Chandecan, and Bacalu.

[2] There is also a letter from him, dated Sripúr, 16th February 1599.

Chittagong, or Porto Grande, as the Portuguese called it, and then to have gone on to Dianga. Fernandez writes as follows: "Shortly after our arrival at Dianga, Melchior de Fonseca departed for Ciandeca, in accordance with the instructions of your Reverence, and while he was travelling through Bacola, the Portuguese who lived there, and also the other Christians, being inflamed with a desire to obtain a priest from whom they might receive the sacrament (for whole years pass away without ever one priest coming), took care that he should be brought before the King. The latter received the father gladly, and honourably entreated him, and even gave him a letter of authority (*literæ patentes*), which I here subjoin.

"'Ego Rex Bacolæ potestatem facio Societatis Jesu patribus hactenus in regna Bengalæ admissis et aliis quotquot veniant ecclesias erigendi in ditione mea universa et annunciandi veri Dei legem omnesque ad Christum quotquot potuerint trahendi citra fortunarum, officiorum, vel dignitatum quas gerunt detrimentum. Immo omnem honorem, favorem, et benevolentiam deferem illis tanquam subditis, mandaboque omnibus Præfectis et Dominis ut cum omnibus novellis Christianis idem faciant; et si quando ex patribus cognovero quempiam huic meo mandato non obsecundasse severe sciat se mulctandum.'"

On 20th January 1600, Melchior Fonseca wrote himself from Ciandeca, and gave an account of his success. He says that he left Chittagong in the month of October, and that he passed through the kingdom of Bacola at the request of the Commander (Il Capitano) and the other Portuguese, who for two years had been without any administration of the holy sacraments: "And it appeared to be by the disposition of our Lord that when I was about to go to Arracan in the place of Fernandez, who was ill with fever, I too should fall ill, and should be transferred to Ciandeca; so that in this journey the Company gained a residency in the kingdom of Bacola. I had scarcely arrived there, when the King (who is not more than eight years old, but whose discretion surpasses his age) sent for me, and wished the Portuguese to come with me. On entering the hall, where he was waiting for me, all the nobles and captains rose up, and I, a poor priest, was made by the King to sit down in a rich seat opposite to him. After compliments, he asked me where I was going, and I replied that I was going to the King of Ciandeca, who is 'the future father-in-law of your Highness;' but that as it had pleased the Lord that I should pass through his kingdom, it had appeared right to me to come and visit him and offer him the services of the fathers of the Company, trusting that his Highness would give permission to the erection of churches and the making of Christians. The King said, 'I desire this myself, because I have heard so much of your good qualities,' and so he gave me a letter of authority, and also assigned a maintenance sufficient for two of us."

Fonseca then told the Portuguese that Fernandez would soon come to receive their confessions, and that in the month of May fathers would be sent to commence a residence. Fonseca goes on to give a description of the route from Bacola to Ciandeca, which I give in the original Italian: "Il viaggio di Bacolà sin a Ciandecan è il più fresco, delitioso ch' io mai vedessi, per i varii fiumi con alberi alle rive ch' irrigano il paese, e per vedersi da una parte correre numerose schiave di cervi, per l' altra pascere moltitudine di vacchi; lascio le campagni spatiose di riso, e li molti canneti de canne mele, gli sciami d' api per gli alberi, e li simi andar saltando da uno albero al' altro e altri particolarita di grande ricreationi a viandanti. Non mancono però tigri e crocodili che si pascono di carne humana per transcuragine e peri peccati d' alcuni. Sono ancora per quelle silve rinoceroti ma io non ne hò visto verruno."

This description of Bákarganj and the Sundarbans is interesting, both on account of its liveliness and because it makes it not so improbable after all that the word "Sundarban" may really mean beautiful wood, and may have been applied in this sense to the forests by the Bráhmans. For if a poor Roman Catholic priest could see the beauty of these woods in spite of the tigers and crocodiles, why might not a Bráhman priest do so also?

Fonseca arrived at Ciandeca on the 20th November 1599, and was there received by Father Sosa and others. Sosa's being there is explained by Fernandez, who says that after he returned to Sripúr (from a visit which he seems to have paid to Ciandeca) he found that the regulus in Ciandeca, called Rajah, was displeased because they did not return to him, and so to pacify him it was necessary to send Dominic Sosa to him. A passage descriptive of Fernandez' proceedings at Sripúr may be here quoted: "I held discourses with the people every Sunday, and also on festival days, after the manner of the Goa College, and this thing being new in Bengal, wonderfully attracted everybody. Little, however, was done towards conversion, from the fault of the people, and also from my ignorance of the language."

Fernandez, in describing Fonseca's success at Bacola, adds that he had wished to visit Bacola before the departure of the Indian fleet, and to obtain more accurate and personal information which he might send to Pimenta. He had, however, been prevented by his having had to wait for a reply from the King of Arracan. He then says that he had now heard of Fonseca's arrival at Ciandeca, and that he had been received with much honour and kindness by the King and people, and that he had a church in which mass could be celebrated. This was the first church of the Company in Bengal, and was on that account called by the holy name of Jesus. "It now remains that the necessary workmen be obtained, and that so noble a vineyard may be fervently commended to the Lord."

From the work of Pierre du Jarric,[1] who was also a Jesuit, and who wrote a book entitled "Histoire des Choses plus memorables advenues tant aux Indes Orientales que autres Pays de la Decouverte des Portugais" (Bordeaux, 1608), we learn that Ciandeca was the first church in Bengal, Chittagong the second, and Bandel the third. He adds that the latter was built by Diego Mugnes de Villalobos, and that it was finer than that of Chittagong.

The favourable hopes entertained by Fernandez and his companions were doomed to be speedily disappointed, and the mission came to a melancholy end. War broke out, as Du Jarric tells us, between the Portuguese and the King of Arracan about the possession of Sandwip; and a tumult arose at Chittagong, where Fernandez then was. The immediate cause of this outbreak was a dispute about port dues. The Arracanese apparently took advantage of this tumult to try and carry off into slavery some children whom Fernandez

[1] Pierre du Jarric was born at Toulouse in 1565, and was for fifteen years professor of theology in that town. He died in 1616. His information was partly derived from a Spanish work written by one Felix da Guzman, and published at Alcala in 1601. Du Jarric's book, however, is the more valuable of the two, and contains nearly everything that is to be found in Pimenta, &c. It has been translated into Latin.

had under his instruction. Fernandez interfered on behalf of the children, and was severely beaten and blinded in one eye. He was then put in prison, and on the 14th November 1602 the poor old priest, says Du Jarric, "changed the miserable prison of this earth for a celestial mansion." Andrew Bowes buried him in the church, which was now in ruins. Bowes was in prison too, with chains on his legs and neck; and though his jailers took the chains off his legs, they retained that on his neck when they allowed him to bury Fernandez. What grieved Bowes most of all was to see the holy chalice in the possession of the Arracanese chief, and used by him as a spittoon. After Fernandez' death, the priests left Chittagong and took refuge in Sandwip; but they soon afterwards left that island, and with the other Christians dispersed themselves over Sripúr, Bacola, and Ciandeca. At Ciandeca, Carvalho, the commander of the Portuguese, was treacherously murdered by the Rajah, who hoped thereby to make his peace with the King of Arracan. This was the end of the Bengal Mission; for of the four fathers who remained, two were ordered off by their Superior to Pegu, and two returned to Cochin.

Du Jarric also tells us the fate of the boy-king of Bacola who had entertained Fonseca, and gives what is probably the true account of the downfall of the Chandradwip family. His words are: "The King of Arracan was proud of having taken the island of Sandwip from the Portuguese; and desiring now to pursue his design of conquering all the kingdoms of Bengal, he suddenly threw himself upon that of Bacola, of which he possessed himself without difficulty, as the King of it was absent and still young." I may add here, that, according to Wilford, "the King of Arracan assumed the title of lord of the twelve *bhuniyas, bhatties,* or principalities of Bengal. The kings of Arracan and of Commillah," he says, "were constantly striving for the mastery, and the former even conquered the greatest part of Bengal. Hence to this day they assume the title of lord of the twelve bhuniyas, bhatties, or principalities of Bengal."— *Wilford, Ancient Geography of India,* vol. xiv. *of Asiatic Researches.*

Although the island of Sandwip does not belong to Bákarganj, yet its history is in some measure mixed up with that of Bákla, and I shall therefore state some facts about it which I have collected from Du Jarric and others. Sandwip is evidently a very old island, and seems to have been of more importance three hundred years ago than it is now, because it was one of the chief sources from which Bengal was supplied with salt. The first notice of it apparently is that given by Cæsar Frederick, a Venetian merchant, who stayed in it for more than a month. He commenced his travels in 1563, and after travelling in many parts of the East, left Pegu on his homeward journey in 1569. He went from Pegu to Chittagong, as small ships sailed thence for Cochin. On the way to Chittagong, in August 1569, his ship was caught in a typhoon. After having been tossed about for some days, an island was discovered at no great distance, on which they landed to see what land it was. "We found it a place inhabited, and, to my judgment, the fertilest island in all the world; the which is divided into two parts by a channel which passeth between it. With great trouble we brought our ship into the same channel, which parteth the island at flowing water." I have quoted this sentence on account of its giving some description of the configuration of the island. Cæsar Frederick's description of the fertility of the island, &c., may be seen in Blochmann, p. 22. Du Jarric devotes a chapter (cap. 32 of book vi.) to a description of Sandwip. He tells us that it is opposite Sripúr, and that it supplies all Bengal with salt. The island belonged of right to Kedar Rai of Sripúr, but for several years he had not had possession of it, because the Mogores (Moghals) had taken it from him. However, in 1602, Carvalho, a Portuguese, and a native of Montargil, who was in the service of Kedar Rai, took possession of it. As, however, he was not strong enough to keep it, Emmanuel de Mattos came from Chittagong to help him, and then he and Carvalho divided the island between them. Afterwards Philippe de Brito built a fort on it. The King of Arracan was offended at these proceedings, consequently the Portuguese either left it, or were driven out by him.

Afterwards, however, Sebastian Gonzales, a Portuguese adventurer, landed on the island in 1018 H., or A.D. 1609, and took possession of it.

"This Sebastian Gonzales," says Stewart in his "History of Bengal," "became absolute sovereign of the island of Sandwip, and was obeyed by the natives and Portuguese as an independent prince. In the course of a short time his forces consisted of 1000 Portuguese, 2000 Indian soldiers, 200 cavalry, and 80 sail of vessels of various sizes, and well mounted with cannon; and as his government was conducted with equity, many merchants resorted to the island, and by their commerce contributed much to increase his revenue. The neighbouring chiefs, astonished at the prodigious success of Gonzales, sought his friendship, and deprecated his wrath; but as he was of a violent and covetous disposition, he listened not to their friendly overtures; and although he was under great obligations to the Rajah of Batecala [a mistake for Bákla], who had first given refuge to the Portuguese in their distress, he ungratefully seized upon the lands of Shahbázpúr and Patelbanga [?], which belonged to that chief, by which means his territories became as extensive as those of some independent prince, and consisting entirely of islands, was secure from the attacks of any enemies so long as the Portuguese were masters of the sea."

Stewart derived his information chiefly from the work of Manuel de Faria y Sousa, called "Asia Portuguesa," and published at Lisbon in 1666. An English translation of this work was published in 1695 by Captain John Stevens, and appropriately dedicated to the Dowager Queen of England, Catharine of Braganza. I have gathered the following additional particulars from Faria y Sousa's work. "Sebastian Gonzales Tibao was," he says, "a man of obscure extraction, as born in the village of St Antony del Torzal, near Lisbon, a place which never yet produced any worth note either for parentage or worthy action. In the year 1605 he embarked for India, went on to Bengal, enlisted himself as a soldier, and then fell to dealing in salt, which is a great merchandise in these parts. Thus by this trade he soon got as much as purchased a *jalia*—that is, a sort of small vessel. In this vessel he went to Dianga, a great port of the kingdom of Arracan. . . . Tibao stipulated with the King of Bacola that he would give him half the revenue of the island of Sandwip if he assisted him to conquer it. The King sent some ships and 200 horse. Afterwards, however, instead of giving the King of Bacola half the revenue of the island, he made war upon him."

Faria y Sousa adds that Emmanuel de Mattos, commander of Bandel, had been lord of Sandwip, and that

Fatteh Khan had held it for him, but that on Mattos's death Fatteh Khan had kept the island for himself.

In the end Gonzales was ruined, for after the unfortunate issue of a battle in 1615, "the King of Arracan fell on him in his island, took it, and reduced him to his former miserable condition. So his sovereignty passed like a shadow, his pride was humbled and his vileness punished." Such are the unsympathising remarks of the Portuguese historian about a man who at least possessed vigour and ability, and who owed his fall in great measure to the impetuosity of the Portuguese officer who was sent from Goa to assist him, but who was too proud or too rash to co-operate fully with him. The Viceroy was also to blame, for he directed his officer not to wait for Gonzales. We cannot but think that if Gonzales had been an Englishman, and his historian of the same nationality, we would have heard a great deal about Anglo-Saxon energy, the Berserker-spirit, and the Vikings.

Sandwip was finally taken by the Mahomedans from the Arracanese in 1666. I may here note that according to some the proper name of the island is Soma-dwipa—*i.e.*, island of the moon. Much information about the history of Sandwip will be found in the article on the Feringhies of Chittagong, "Calcutta Review," vol. liii. for 1871. See also article "Mofussil Records," in vol. liv. for 1872, of same Review, p. 216, for reference to an important petition by zamindars of Sandwip dated 1789.

In the Asiatic Society's Proceedings for January 1838 an account is given of a copperplate inscription found in the pargana of Idilpúr. The inscription records that three villages were given to a Bráhman in the third year of Keshab Sein—*i.e.*, 1136 A.D. These three villages cannot now be identified, and though it is possible enough that they have been long ago washed away by the Meghna, which flows past Idilpúr pargana, it may also be that they never belonged to the district of Bákarganj. The fact of the inscription having been found in a Bákarganj pargana does not necessarily imply that the villages belonged to that neighbourhood, and there does not appear to be anything in the inscription to connect it with Idilpúr. Another copperplate inscription (*sásanam*) was found about three years ago near Mádaripúr, and has been presented to the Asiatic Society, but it has not at present been deciphered.

The only clear memorial of the ancient times of Bákarganj is a mosque in the Sundarbans, which bore an inscribed slab (now removed to the Asiatic Society's Museum) purporting that the building had been erected in 1465. This mosque is built of brick, and is situated in a place called Masjidbari, near a tributary of the Bighai, and a few miles west-north-west of Gúlsakháli police station. It thus lies in the Patuyakháli subdivision, and in the southern part of the district. It was discovered at the time of the Sundarban Resumptions, and was, when found, surrounded by jungle. Mr Reilly, who was the Commissioner of the Sundarbans, wrote[1] an account of the mosque, and a translation of the inscription was furnished by Colonel Lees. The translation is: "The Prophet of God (on whom be peace, &c.) said, 'Whoso buildeth a mosque, God shall build for him seventy palaces.' This mosque was built in the reign of the Sultan, the mighty pillar of the Church and State, Aboo-al-Mozaffar Barbek Shah, son of the Sultan Mahmood Shah, by Khan Moazzam Ozyal Khan, year of Hijira 870" (= A.D. 1465).

I visited this mosque in 1874, and found it in good preservation. It is, however, quite devoid of architec-

[1] A. S. J., vol. iv. of 1860, p. 406.

tural interest or beauty. The woods which once surrounded it have been cleared away, and it now lies in the midst of rice-fields. A faqir has assumed the charge of it, and is supported by the gifts of occasional visitors.

There is another old mosque in Sialghuni village, thana Bákarganj, which is said to have been built by one Nasrat Ghazi. It appears to have been at one time richly ornamented, and still has some carved flowers and arabesques. The inhabitants told me that there had once been an inscription, but that it had fallen down and disappeared. Near it there is a village called the Fílkhana or elephant stables, which would seem to indicate that elephants had once been kept in it. There is, however, no tradition to this effect. There are, as far as I am aware, only two other old mosques in the district, one is in the village of Bíbí Chini, near the Niamati outpost, and is said to have been built by a lady named Bíbí Chini, sister to the Niamat who founded the village of Niamati. The other is in the village of Ramsiddhi, thana Gournadi, and is said to have been built by Sabhi Khan. It is a much handsomer building than that in Bíbí Chini, and has four stone pillars. Two of the pillars are slender, and are said to have been worn away by devotees clasping them, in the hope of thereby obtaining fulfilment of their wishes.

SUJÁBÁD.—About five miles south-west of Barisál, and on the north bank of the Nalchiti river, there is a small village called Sujábád, which derives its name from Shah Suja, the ill-fated brother of Arangzeb. In it there are the remains of a fort, which appears to have been erected by Shah Suja when he was Viceroy of Bengal, and had to defend the country against the incursions of the Mugs or Burmese. The fort was rectangular and surrounded by an earthen wall, with a mound at each corner. Inside were four small tanks separated by roads, and in the centre of the inner space, where the four roads met, was the prince's dwelling-house. A great part of the wall has fallen into the river, the tanks inside are nearly choked up and most of the space is covered with jungle. The whole village contains only 77 acres, and there is an interesting document in the Collectorate record-room showing that it was given rent free by Shah Suja to the families of some Afghans who had fallen in battle against the Mugs. It is further said that the fight lasted two days, and that Shah Suja's force was victorious. It is said that four forts were built, and this probably refers to the fortifications at each corner of the rectangular space. In 1845 it was proposed to resume the grant, and an *amín* went out to make a map of the locality, from which it appears that there was then more of the earthen wall standing than is now visible. The land was then in possession of the descendants of the Afghans, who succeeded in obtaining its release though they had lost the original grant or *sanad*, which they stated had been destroyed in the great inundation of 1822. None of them now reside on it, and their rights have passed by purchase into other hands. There is a tragical story told of Asman Singh, one of the last Afghan residents in Sujábád, which has been made the subject of a popular ballad. He had a wife who was unfaithful to him. News was brought to him, while away at Nalchiti, that his wife's paramour (a Mahomedan) was in his house. He armed himself with a sword, and rushed home to avenge himself. On pretext of illness his wife delayed to open the door, and thereby gave her lover time to escape. At last Asman Singh burst open the door and aimed a blow at his wife, but she had her child in her arms, on whom the stroke fell, and who was killed. Asman Singh was tried for the murder, and having been found guilty, was hanged in chains on the river-bank, near the scene of his crime. The ballad adds that his brother in Calcutta succeeded in obtaining a pardon for him, and hurried with it to Barisál, but that he arrived just too late to stay the execution.

There are the remains of two forts in the Jhalukátti thana—viz., one at Rupashia, near Jhalukátti, and another at Indrapásha, near Rajapúr outpost. Nothing appears to be known of their history.

In Major Rennel's map,[1] made from surveys in 1764 and 1772, two mud forts are shown in the southern part of the district. They had been built to repel the Mugs. No trace of them now exists, but there is a village called Sónárkót, near Adampúr, in the Baufal thana, which stands near the site of one of them, and seems by its name to indicate that it was once a fort (the word *kót* often meaning a fort). There is also a place near it which still goes by the name of the Killaghátta, or landing-place of the fort.

The map above referred to, which has been reproduced by Colonel Gastrell in his statistical report, is an interesting record of the former state of the district.[2]

1 Though the map generally bears the name of Rennel, it appears from Markham (Indian Surveys) that the credit of the Sundarban and sea-coast portion is chiefly due to Captain Ritchie, who was hydrographical surveyor from about 1770 to 1785. Ritchie's work is still in MS. in the India Office. The glory of making the first correct map of India seems due to the French, whose great geographer D'Anville preceded Rennel.

2 Professor Blochmann has given a reduced copy of De Blaev's map.

An inspection of it shows that Barisál, the present headquarters, was already a place of note, and that a great part of the Sundarbans had been depopulated by the Mugs. At that time Bákarganj was the headquarters of the district, and a road led from it to Kótarhát and thence to Sitaluri, which is near the modern Jhalukátti. From Sitaluri it proceeded to Madhabpásha, and thence by Idrakpúr, in Gournadi, across the swamps to Maxadpúr. The tract of country called Sundarkúl is represented in this map.

The history of the Chandradwip Rajahs, and notices of the old buildings at Kachua and at Raikátti, will be given in the accounts of the Chandradwip and Selímábád parganas.

AGA BÁKAR.[1]—The district of Bákarganj derives its name from one Aga Bákar, who was a servant of the Nawab of Murshidábád, and was proprietor of pargana Buzurgumedpúr, and of 11½ anas of Selímábád. He apparently founded the mart of Bákarganj, which was situated in his zamindari of Buzurgumedpúr, and was formerly the headquarters of the district. He is said to have taken possession by force of the 11½ anas of Selímábád, and to have retained them until his death in 1160 B.S., when he was executed for rebellion (Thomp-

There is a very interesting old map by Van den Broucke in the fifth volume of François Valentyn's work (ed. 1724–26) which ought to be reprinted. Bacola is marked on it, but only as an island. There is a place marked as the "Hoek" or Cape of Sancraan, and from its position I think this must be Sangrám, which was an old Moghal fort in the Mendiganj thana (see Wintle's account in Appendix). Van den Broucke marks the whole of the Sundarban coast as unknown, and states that the "Ter Schelling" was wrecked in this neighbourhood. Sangrám Fort is referred to in the Alamgirnáma, quoted in article on the Feringhies of Chittagong, "Calcutta Review," vol. liii. p. 73. It was fortified in 1665.

[1] Bákar is an Arabic word, and the correct transliteration of it is Baquir; hence some write Báqirganj.

son to Board, 28th December 1793). (See account of Selímábád.)

Dr Taylor, in his "Topography of Dacca" (p. 83), has the following notice of Aga Bákar and his son: "Shamat Jung Nowazish Mahomed Khan, the nephew and son-in-law of Aliverdi Khan, was next invested with the government in succession to Sarferaz Khan. Like his predecessor, he resided at Murshidábád, and acted in the twofold capacity of Imperial Dewan and Deputy Nazim, appointments which he held for many years prior to the British conquest of the country. He employed as his deputy at Dacca, Hosein Addeen Khan, the nephew of Hosein Kuli Khan, his minister at Murshidábád. When Aliverdi Khan declared in favour of his adopted son Seraja Daulah as his successor to the Masnad, feuds arose between the heir-apparent and Shamat Jung, which ended in the assassination of Hosein Addeen Khan at Dacca, and that of his uncle at Murshidábád. Aga Sadoc, the son of a wealthy zamindar in the Bákarganj district, was employed by Seraja Daulah to carry his plans into effect at this place. This person, who had proceeded to Murshidábád to appeal against a decision of Hosein Addeen, instead of obtaining the redress he expected, was detained a prisoner there by Hosein Kuli Khan. He was soon induced, therefore, to listen to the proposals of Seraja Daulah. Effecting his escape from Murshidábád, he returned to Dacca, where his father Mahomed Bákar was now residing, and prevailing on him to join in the conspiracy on the promise of being made Nawab, the party contrived to get admission into the palace at dead of night, and murdered Hosein Addeen. When the assassination became known the following morning, the inhabitants of the town rose in a body and attacked

Mahomed Bákar and his son. The former, on being required to produce the sanad for his appointment to the Neabat, pointed to his sword, and was immediately killed, but Aga Sadoc, though severely wounded, contrived to escape."

The accounts of this affair in Mr Scrafton's "Reflections," and in the "Siyar al Mutakhereen," may also be inserted, as they contain one or two additional particulars. It will be seen that, according to Mr Scrafton, Aga Bákar held the office of governor of Chittagong: "The conduct of this affair was left to Surajah Doulah, who chose for his instrument one Aga Sadoc, whose father was governor of Chittagong, but resided at Dacca. The son, an extravagant, debauched youth, was then under confinement at Nowazis Mahomed Khan's palace, being left there as hostage till he paid a large sum due for the revenues of his government. Surajah Doulah assisted him to escape. He landed at Dacca the 1st of December 1755, and engaged his father in the enterprise, deluded probably by the promise of Surajah Doulah to make him governor of Dacca. The father and son, with twelve of their dependants, surprised the governor in the dead of night, and after some little resistance, in which the father was wounded, they cut off his head and proclaimed it to be done by the order of Surajah Doulah. But the next day an order arriving from Nowazis Mahomed Khan to seize Aga Sadoc, the great men of the city immediately assembled their forces and attacked him. The son, with some of his desperate followers, cut their way through their opponents and made their escape, but the father and the rest of their party were killed. This news reaching the capital, the different parties were immediately in arms; but the old Soubah assuring his nephew that Aga Sadoc had made this attempt entirely in revenge for his confinement, the weak, timid Nowazis was appeased, and the consequence was that Surajah Doulah, a few days afterwards, murdered Hosein Kuli Khan in the street of Muxadabad."—*Scrafton's Reflections on the Government of Hindustan,* p. 49, London, 1763; reprinted 1770.

See also "Siyar al Mutakhereen," vol. ii. p. 646, Calcutta, 4th edition, 1789: "To ensure success to his [Surajah Daulah's] design he made use of some art to gain the heart of a young man, who, having had disputes with the officers of Hosein Kuli Khan, deputy-governor of the province of Dacca, had found means to lay his case before Nowazis Mohamed Khan, who concerned himself on his behalf. His name was Aga Sadoc, and his title Sadakut Mohamed Khan, son of Aga Bákar, a considerable zamindar of these parts. Surajah Daulah engaged him to return to Dacca in order to kill Hosein Addeen Khan, the nephew of Hosein Kuli Khan, and the latter's deputy at Dacca, a young man who for some reasons had fallen into a melancholy that had disordered his senses. The man did exactly as he was bid. Such a murder committed so openly struck terror and consternation into the minds of all the inhabitants of that great city, who concluded that an action of that high nature would never have been perpetrated had not some person of the first rank afforded it countenance, so that every one remained silent and thoughtful until it became known that the perpetrator had no order and no evidence in his hand. He was therefore set upon by the inhabitants and by the friends of Hosein Kuli Khan, who missed the murderer, but by mistake killed his father, Aga Bákar. The son having escaped so great a danger, fled to Murshidábád, and by such a step [the assassination ?] threw away both his peace of mind and safety of his person."

There is a curious reference to an Aga Bákir in Paton's "Arracan," vol. xvi. of "Asiatic Researches." He says that in 1113 of the Mug era (1751 or thereby), Aga Bákir, the Dacca Nawab, having been worsted in a contest near Dacca by a chief named Umed, applied to the King of Arracan for assistance. He sent a Sardar named Laya Murari with one thousand war-boats to the assistance of the Nawab, and enabled him to gain the victory.

I do not know if this be our Aga Bákar or not, but if he is, there is some mistake in describing him as Nawab of Dacca. Our Aga Bákar was Governor of Chittagong, which of course renders his connection with the King of Arracan probable enough.

Besides Bákarganj bazár there is a small village, called Bákarkátti or the clearing of Bákar, near Kótarhát, which probably also owes its name to Aga Bákar.

It will be observed that most of the parganas bear Mahomedan names, showing that the country was not portioned out till the Mahomedan dynasty. The names are probably derived from the first grantees. Thus we have Sultanábád, Shaistábád, Selímábád, Shahbázpúr, &c. The Selímábád pargana is the largest and most important of these, and extends over a great portion of the Perozpúr subdivision, and also westwards into Baghahát in Jessore.

Probably Bákarganj and its neighbourhood were the first places where the Mahomedans settled, for it is hereabouts that we find most traces of them. Thus there is a large tank near Bákarganj called Boran Khan's Tank, and Niamati and Bíbí Chini are not far off. In the latter there is the old mosque already noticed, which is chiefly remarkable for the height of the mound on which it is built.

There is also a mosque at Mendiganj, near Bákarganj, which bears an inscription purporting that it was built by one Mahomed Shuffee in 1161 B.S. (A.D. 1753.)

In the northern part of the district the most conspicuous name is Sabhi Khan, who has immortalised himself by the roads and bridges which he constructed. According to one account, he was a Kótwal, and Kotwalipara is said to derive its name from him. The following story is told to account for his beneficence. He was, it is said, the son of a wealthy merchant, but was stolen from his home during his infancy, and brought up in the forests. In course of time he grew up to man's estate and became a hunter. Meanwhile his father's house was attacked by enemies, who killed his father and drove his mother out into the jungles. There Sabhi Khan found her one day while he was hunting, and, in ignorance of their relationship, he took her as his wife. They lived together for awhile, but one morning the mother observed a spot on the sole of Sabhi Khan's foot, and knew thereby that he was her son. She told him the miserable discovery she had made, so Sabhi Khan went to a holy man, and asked him how he should expiate the terrible sin he had involuntarily committed. The answer was, that he should atone for it by doing works for the public good, and hence he set about making roads and building mosques. His roads traverse parts of the Gournadi and Kotwalipara thanas, and are still in use. They are known by the name of Sabhi Khan's *jangáls.* They have been obliterated in many places, but where they exist they are broad and remarkably well raised. There is also a village called Sabhi Khan's Pár,[1] which owes its name to him. The word *pár* refers to the village being situated on the side of an old tank which is said to have been excavated by Sabhi Khan.

[1] It is commonly spelt Chobikapár.

CHAPTER IV.

FINANCIAL HISTORY AND DESCRIPTION OF THE PARGANAS.

I. HISTORICAL SKETCH OF THE LAND SETTLEMENTS.

THE materials for the early financial history of Bákarganj are very scanty. The following facts have been gleaned from Mr Grant's "Analysis of the Finances of Bengal," printed in Appendix No. 4 to the Fifth Report of the Committee of the House of Commons, 1812, and from Professor Blochmann's monograph. As has been already stated, the name Bákarganj is of comparatively recent origin, and it does not occur in Mr Grant's work. At the time of Rajah Todar Mal's Settlement in 1582, the greater part of the present district appears to have been included in the ancient zamindari or pargana of Chandradwip, which belonged to sarkár Bákla, also called Ismáilpúr. Bákla was one of the nineteen sarkárs into which the Khalsa or Exchequer lands of Bengal Proper were divided by Todar Mal, who was Finance Minister to the Emperor Akbar. Sarkár Bákla contained only four *mahals* or parganas, the names of which are given by Professor Blochmann as Ismáilpúr or Bákla, Srírámpúr, Shahzádpúr, and Adilpúr. The three last still exist, and I suppose that Bákla was identical with Chandradwip. This pargana is still occasionally called Bákla-Chandradwip. The following account of Bákla is taken from Mr Grant's work: "Bákla or Ismáilpúr, eastward of Khalífatábád, chiefly on the western bank of the Padma or great Ganges, and extending to its mouth near the island of Rabnábád, which forms the south-east angle of the Bengal delta, as also the further extremity of the lowlands of Bhatty, commencing on the west from Hidjili. Two years subsequent to the date of this account (1582), fixed for convenience at the commencement of Todar Mal's financial operations, though not completed before his death in 1589, the whole sarkár now described was overwhelmed and laid waste by an inundation, and from the succeeding ravages of the Mugs continues to this day in great part depopulated."

The revenue of the four parganas in it was Rs.178,266 (sicca).

The eastern portions of the district, including North and South Shahbázpúr, belonged to sarkár Fathábád. Selímábád, in the west of the district, part of which now belongs to Jessore, was also included in this sarkár. Buzurgumedpúr, another large pargana in Bákarganj, was probably formed at a later period. It was included in sarkár Bazuha.

In 1658 another Settlement of Bengal was made by Sultan Suja, one of the sons of Shah Jehan. In this Settlement the Sundarbans were included under the name of Muradkhana or Jeradkhana. Perhaps the village and river of Muradia, in the northern part of the Patuyakháli subdivision, are parts of this Muradkhana.

In 1722, or 1128 B.S., a third Settlement was made by Nawab Jaffar Khan in the reign of Mahomed Shah. On this occasion the old sarkárs were included in *chaklas*, and sarkár Bákla, and portions of sarkárs Fathábád and Bazuha were included in chakla Jehangirnagar—*i.e.*, Dacca. A few years before this—namely, in 1717—the seat of Government had been removed from Dacca to Murshidábád.

Jaffar Khan's Settlement was improved and confirmed by his successor Suja Khan in 1728, or 1135 B.S. He divided the *suba* or province of Bengal into *ihtimams* or zamindaries, and the greater part of Dacca, Farídpúr, and Bákarganj appears to have been included in the ihtimam of Jalálpúr.

A fourth Settlement was made by Mir Kasim in 1763.[1]

The next Settlement of which we need take account is the Decennial or Permanent Settlement of A.D. 1790, or 1197 B.S. With regard to this Settlement the Fifth Report observes that "a medium of the actual produce to Government in former years, drawn from the scanty information which the collectors had the means of procuring, was the basis on which the assessment on each estate, whether large or small, was ultimately fixed."

The Permanent Settlement of the Bákarganj district was made during the collectorship of Mr William Douglas, who was then Collector of Dacca. At that time the Dacca Collectorate was called Dacca Jalálpúr.[2]

[1] From Warren Hastings' letter of 23d November 1773, about Provincial Councils, &c., printed in Judicial Papers, 1774, India Office Library, we find that Dacca, which then included Bákarganj and Farídpúr, was put into the Fifth Division. This was composed of Dacca, Sylhet, Attia, Kagmari, and Barbazu. The first members of the Council were Barwell, Purling, Thackeray, Shakespeare, and Holland. Barwell was Chief, and drew Rs.3000 a month, but, on the other hand, he was not allowed to trade, while the other members were allowed this privilege.

[2] There were formerly two jurisdictions—viz., Dacca Jalálpúr and the city of Dacca. These were amalgamated by Reg. 5 of 1833. Jalálpúr is the name of a large pargana in Farídpúr and Dacca, and Dacca Jalálpúr district included Farídpúr. There was a *Diwani Adâlat* for Dacca Jalálpúr and another for the city of Dacca. The jurisdiction of the latter extended over the city and the places adjacent (Reg. 3 of 1793, section 4). It appears, however (section 3 of Reg. 7 of 1797), that the Court of Dacca Jalálpúr was situated in the city of Dacca. It was removed to Farídpúr apparently in 1812 (Bengal Administration Report for 1872–73, p. 45).

The districts of Farídpúr and Noakháli were not then in existence, nor was Bákarganj, which was included, along with Farídpúr and Dacca, in Dacca Jalálpúr. The arrangements with the zamindars were made at the Revenue Court of Dacca, and not in this district.

The first reference to the Decennial Settlement which I have been able to find is contained in a letter, dated 6th April 1790, from Mr Douglas to the Board of Revenue. He mentions in it that he has received the Board's letter of the 18th March, and its enclosed copy of the resolutions of his Lordship in Council. I have thought it advisable to print this letter in the Appendix. It appears from it that the proposals for the Settlement were supplied by Mr Douglas's predecessor, Mr Day, in accordance with a circular which had been issued on 10th August 1787. It appears from a letter of Mr Day's, printed in an appendix to the Governor-General's Minute of 3d February 1790 (Fifth Report), that he was Chief of Dacca in 1786, and that he had resided for fifteen years in various parts of the district. It might therefore have been expected that Mr Day would have been well qualified to assess the revenue on the zamindars. It appears, however, from Mr Douglas's reports, and also from subsequent occurrences, that many of Mr Day's assessments were extravagantly high. I may add here that the early correspondence appears to show that Mr Douglas was a man of good sense and humanity, and possessed of a breadth of view which has never been very common among officials. Take, for example, his remark in a letter of 29th March 1790, about the administration of justice by the zamindars: "The zamindars also had the privilege of administering justice in their respective jurisdictions, acting something like justices of the peace in our own country, settling trifling disputes, and rendering easy and speedy redress to the injured party, which would have been rendered very difficult indeed if a poor man had to travel to the *Hazoor* and prefer his complaint through a regiment of corrupt *matsadies* [clerks], every one of whom must have been bribed before he could obtain what a respectable zamindar could have granted him on the spot in a day's attendance."

The making of the Settlement occupied a year or two, and it was not until 31st July 1792 that Mr Douglas sent up the papers "of the proposed Novennial Settlement, commencing with the Bengal year 1198 (A.D. 1791) and ending with 1206." The Settlement was called Novennial because, in consequence of the delay in making it, it commenced one year later than the Decennial Settlement. From a letter of Mr Massie, dated 31st March 1801, it appears that the Board's instructions on the subject of the Settlement were issued on the 30th December 1790, and that the formal tender of the Settlement to the landholders commenced on 20th May 1791. In the same report Mr Massie points out that sufficient regard was not paid at the conclusion of the Settlement to the ascertainment and record of the names of the real owners of the land, and he goes on to observe that a practice has prevailed in the district (Dacca Jalálpúr) from time immemorial, of conducting all the affairs of an estate from generation to generation in the name of the original proprietor, or of some fictitious name formed by him. As the letter gives several specimens of the manner in which the Settlement was made, I have printed it in the Appendix.

In another report, dated 7th March 1801, Mr Massie refers to certain abuses which were committed at the time of the Permanent Settlement: "The first is the frauds committed by zamindars at the time of the separation of the independent *taluqdars,* in causing *taluqs* that had never existed, or had been before consolidated, to be separated at a certain *jama* from their estates. The second is the frauds committed by zamindars subsequently to the separation of the independent taluqdars, in causing the lands of separated taluqs, of which they were the proprietors, to be clandestinely annexed to their zamindaries, leaving only small parcels of waste or jungle lands as the separated taluqs. The third is the frauds committed by the independent taluqdars, after their separation from the zamindars, in causing fictitious or unproductive taluqs to be separated from their taluqs, and inserted gradually in the accounts of the ziladars. This last species of fraud, your Board will observe, must have been committed with the connivance of the ziladars, and though I fear it has been carried to a great extent, it appears hitherto to have escaped detection, owing to the immense number of separated taluqs in this district, and the impossibility of the Collector himself entering so minutely into the details of the accounts of them." From the same letter it appears that the district of Dacca Jalálpúr was divided into ten zilas or collecting circles, and that Mr Massie proposed to increase their number to thirteen. These ziladars were liable to imprisonment, and on 11th January 1800, Mr Massie reports that he had put seven of them into jail for not giving up their papers. He adds that three of them immediately resigned.

The great number of separated taluqs is a peculiarity in the land settlement of Bákarganj and Dacca. In fact, the larger portion of the land revenue of this district is paid by taluqdars. There are 3232 estates—*i.e.*, lands—subject to the payment of revenue, for which separate engagements to Government have been executed (No. 8 of 1800, section 13), and no less than 2700 of these are independent or separated taluqs. The total revenue paid by zamindars is under four and a half lacs (444,107), whilst that paid by the taluqdars is over five lacs (507,714). *N.B.*—This does not represent the whole of the revenue of the district, there being also farms and also estates held under direct or *khas* management.

The difference between a zamindar and an independent taluqdar is nowadays merely nominal. The revenue paid by both is equally fixed, and their other rights and privileges are the same, and the difference of title is only important as a matter of social consideration. The nominal distinction even is not always observed, for sometimes the same landholder is called indifferently a taluqdar and a zamindar. The distinction, however, as generally made is as follows. If a landholder owns a pargana, or an aliquot portion thereof, he is called a zamindar, and also generally receives by courtesy the title of *chaudhari;* but if his estate bears no relation to a pargana or its divisions, he is merely a taluqdar. The districts of the British administration are a modern arrangement. The old divisions appear to have been into sarkárs and parganas for revenue purposes, and into thanas for purposes of police. The word *zila* is now taken as equivalent to district, but the zilas at or about the time of the Permanent Settlement were not districts in the modern sense, and were, as we have seen, merely collecting circles. Among the common people the word *zila* is at the present day very frequently employed to signify the headquarters of a district. Parganas are divided in the first instance into sixteen parts, corresponding to the divisions of a rupee, and if a landholder holds one-half or one-quarter of a pargana, he is described as the holder of eight anas, or four anas, as the case may be. But the subdivision does not stop here, for each ana, or even fraction of an ana, may be assumed as the unit and again divided into sixteen parts, and so on. Thus it is common to describe a person as the holder of eight anas, or one-half of a one-ana share of a pargana considered as a sixteen-ana property, and such a person is, I believe, always entitled to be called a zamindar. A taluqdar's estate generally consists of one or more *mozahs* or villages, or of portions of them. These portions are also divided into sixteen parts, and it may be mentioned here that this mode of dividing property is universal in Bengal. A man is never described as the holder of so many *bighas* or acres, but as the holder of two anas, or one pie, or five gandas, or two cowries, and so on, of such a taluq or *howala*, or other tenure. The taluqdars of the Permanent Settlement are of two sorts, first, the independent or *hazuri* taluqdars, who had already paid direct to Government; and secondly, those who were then separated for the first time from the zamindars. The separation of the taluqs was not a part of the original scheme of the Permanent Settlement, but it was a favourite idea with Lord Cornwallis, and was eventually carried out. In his minute of 3d February 1790 his Lordship remarks, "The proprietors of the smaller zamindaries and taluqs in general conduct their own business, and I make no doubt would improve their lands were they exempted from the authority of the zamindars, and allowed to pay their revenue immediately to the public treasuries of the collectors." In another place he says, "When the demand of Government upon the zamindars is fixed they can have no plea for levying an increase upon the taluqdars, for I conceive the taluqdars in general to have the same property in the soil as the zamindars, and that the former are to be considered as proprietors of lesser portions of land, paying their revenues to Government through the medium of a larger proprietor, instead of remitting them directly to the public treasury. The pernicious consequences which must result from affording to one individual an opportunity of raising the public revenues assessed upon the lands of another at his own discretion, and for his own advantage, are evident; and on this account I was desirous that all proprietors of land, whether zamindars, taluqdars, or chaudharies, should pay their rents immediately to the European Collector of the district or other officer of Government, and be subject to the same general laws. The number of names upon the rent-roll will add little to the business of the Collector, provided that the sum to be paid by each proprietor of land is fixed. In support of this opinion I have annexed some extracts from the proceedings of the Committee of Circuit, the members of which must have been well acquainted with the customs and practices of the Mogul Government."

"These extracts afford convincing proofs of the proprietary rights of the inferior zamindars and taluqdars, and that their being made to pay their rent through the superior zamindar of the district was solely for the convenience of the Government, which found it less difficult to collect the rents from one principal zamindar than from a number of petty proprietors."

The following remarks from the same minute may be quoted as showing the materials with which the Permanent Settlement was made, and the Governor-General's views of their sufficiency: "Twenty years have been employed in collecting information. In 1769 supervisors were appointed; in 1770 provincial councils were established; in 1772 a Committee of Circuit was deputed to make the Settlement, armed with all the powers of the Presidency; in 1776 amíns were appointed to make a *hastabud* of the country; in 1781 the provincial councils of revenue were abolished, and collectors were sent into the several districts, and the general control and management of the revenues was lodged in a Committee of Revenue at Calcutta under the immediate inspection of Government. Like our predecessors, we set out with seeking for new information; and we have now been three years in collecting it. Voluminous reports have been transmitted by the several collectors on every point which was deemed of importance."

His Lordship goes on to say, "I must declare that I am clearly of opinion that this Government will never be better qualified, at any given period whatever, to make an equitable settlement of the land revenue of these provinces, and that if the want of further information was to be admitted now, or at any other future period, as a ground for delaying the declaration of the permanency of the assessment, the commencement of the happiness of the people and of the prosperity of the country would be delayed for ever."

The data on which the assessments at the Permanent Settlement were fixed are clearly stated in the Bengal Special Orders, published at section 68 of Regulation 8 of 1793. "The jama—*i.e.*, revenue—of the preceding year, compared with the account and information supplied by the collectors, and the recommendations of the Board of Revenue founded thereon, is to be the standard." Certain qualifying sections follow, and it is expressly ordered (section 70) that no abatement from the revenue of the preceding year is to be allowed without the special sanction of the Governor-General in Council. Section 75 of the same Regulation observes that the statement above referred to is inapplicable to the separated taluqs, or to any instances where the actual produce may have been ascertained. In such cases the assessment is to be regulated so as to leave the proprietors a provision for themselves and families equal to about ten per cent. on the amounts of their contributions to Government. But taluqdars who had paid at a fixed rent for the last twelve years were allowed to settle at this revenue.

It has been often said that the Permanent Settlement ruined those who accepted it. This statement is probably true of the larger zamindars, but it is not applicable to the taluqdars, many of whom got their lands on easy terms, and have handed them down to their descendants to the present day. No doubt the rule, that if they had paid a fixed rent for twelve years it was not to be enhanced, proved the safety of many of them. The smallness of their estates, and the great number of them, must also have enabled them to escape, for the collectors could not know, or even guess at the real value of their properties, and were obliged to take what they offered, or what they had been paying hitherto. It may generally be said that the owners of the backward and less known zamindaries fared better than those of which the resources had been developed, and were supposed, at least, to be accurately known. Thus, Rajnagar and Chandradwip were probably over-assessed, and the owners were ruined, whereas Arangpúr and Selímábád were somewhat lightly assessed, and are to this day in the hands of descendants of the original proprietors. This remark applies to more districts than Bákarganj, and perhaps accounts for the light assessment and great prosperity of the zamindars in such remote districts as Mymensing and Eastern Bengal generally. It was not merely, or even chiefly, that the collectors knew less about the eastern districts than they did about Burdwan or Nuddea, but because cultivation was much more backward in the former districts. Hence the burden on the zamindars in these districts got lighter every year as cultivation advanced and more ryots came in, whereas in Burdwan or Nuddea the zamindars had not the same margin for making profits.

On the other hand, the zamindars in Eastern Bengal were much more exposed to loss from diluviation, owing to the great rivers which flow through or skirt their estates, and many flourishing parganas have in this way almost disappeared. For example, pargana Srírámpúr in this district, which was one of the four original parganas of sarkár Bákla, has been nearly all washed away by the Meghna, and the zamindars of it have long since disappeared. Pargana Dakhin Shahbázpúr has also suffered much from the same cause. I do not know whether it is to this cause, or to the abuse of the practice of subdivision, that the zamindars of Kotwalipara owe their poverty, but the fact is certain that the Kotwalipara zamindars (they now belong to the Farídpúr district) are among the poorest and pettiest, if not the very poorest zamindars in Bengal. As the rivers wash away estates, so also do they form new ones, and it might have been thought that the new formations would compensate the zamindars for their losses, but this has been far from the case. Not only do the new formations remain unproductive for many years, so that the zamindar may be ruined by the loss of his old lands and sold up before he can get any benefit from the substitutes for them, but also the chars, or new formations, are, or at least were, in general resumed by Government and assessed anew. The above is somewhat of a digression, but I have been led to enter upon it in order to counteract a common impression that all zamindars are wealthy men. In fact, there are more poor zamindars than there are rich ones—*i.e.*, comparing them with other classes, such as traders, and even professional men—and there are many taluqdars, both independent and dependent (*kharija*, or *hazuri*, and *shikami*), who are richer than their zamindar.

Mr Westland remarks that the zamindars, in accepting the Settlements, set the seal to their own ruin. This is true, but the fact is that they had not much option in the matter. If they did not accept the Settlements, they were ousted, their lands were managed by officers called *Kurak amíns*, or *Kurak sazawals*, or were let in farm, and though they were supposed to be allowed ten per cent. on the net collections, it was practically very difficult for them to get the allowance. A letter from the Collector, dated 20th February 1794, shows that no proprietors of estates held khas—*i.e.*, under direct management—had got the *mashahara*, or allowance sanctioned by the Regulations, except the proprietors of the three divisions of Selímábád. In short, it may be said that by not accepting the Settlements the zamindars were ruined at once, and by accepting them they were ruined after some interval. In some cases the acceptance of the Settlement appears to have been even less voluntary than the reluctant acquiescence in a hard bargain. One zamindar—he was a descendant of the great Rajah Raj Ballab—complained in 1797 that the Collector (Mr Thompson) demanded agreements from him and his partners, and that when he refused to give them he was confined under a guard of sepoys, and prevented from bathing, praying, or eating, and thereby driven to sign an application for settlement. The technical word for the zamindar's agreements is *tahút.* Many of them are preserved in the Collectorate, and are small, insignificant pieces of brown country paper, containing little except the obligor's name, the amount of the annual revenue, and the instalments in which it is to be paid. The agreements are in Persian, and are surmounted by the Collector's signature or initial.

The troubles of the collectors did not end with the general completion of the Permanent Settlement. The arrangements about the separated taluqs took time, and on 12th August 1793 the Collector reported that there were nearly 4000 taluqs (this is in all Dacca Jalálpúr) which had been separated but of which no settlement had been made. Some zamindars, as we have seen, would not come to terms, and the collectors had to manage their estates directly, or to grant temporary leases of them; and in other cases, although the zamindars accepted the Settlement, they fell into arrears, and their estates had to be sold, or the revenue of them to be collected by special officers.

SAYER DUTIES.—Besides the revenue from land, the Mogul Government was in the habit of levying taxes upon professions, and each tax was called a *mahal*, and let out in farm, just as if it had been a landed property. Thus there was a tax on washermen, which was called the *Gázar-mahal*, and yielded about Rs.60 a year. There were also the *Dhúmdari-mahal*, which was collected from bird-catchers, snake-charmers, &c., and yielded about Rs.1450; the *Bajantri-mahal*, collected from musicians, and yielding about Rs.310; the *Mahai-mahal*, collected from the dealers in dried fish; *Char-mokundia*, levied on sellers of vegetables; *Chappa-jam-danny*, levied on weavers, &c. I do not find that there was any tax on the sale of spirits in the Dacca division, and probably there was none, on account of the aversion of the Mogul Government to derive any profit from this source.

Mr Douglas, in his report of the 5th May 1790, objected to the abolition of the above taxes on the broad ground that professional men should contribute their quota to the general income of the country. He writes: "As far as I have been able to learn, they [the taxes] are in general of the same nature as taxes on the same articles in other countries, and I am inclined to think they are not considered as oppressive even by the natives themselves. . . . I shall not, therefore, take on me to recommend their discontinuance, whereby the Honourable Company must sustain considerable loss, while at the same time the benefit arising to individuals would scarcely be a compensation for giving up so much revenue, which is necessarily appropriated to the general defence of the State, and in the benefits of which every individual participates. I therefore see no reason why professional men, tradesmen, and artificers of every kind should not contribute their quota to such a useful and necessary purpose as well as the ryot or husbandman, more especially in times of pressing exigencies." It is perhaps to be regretted that these views did not prevail, and that a tax to which the people had got accustomed should have been allowed to fall into desuetude. However, the Government of the day took another view, and abolished these miscellaneous taxes. They also abolished the taxes levied at bazárs and markets from shopkeepers and market-vendors, and gave the zamindars compensation for the loss of them in the shape of a deduction from the land revenue. In fact, however, the zamindars did not cease to levy such taxes, and probably it never was intended that zamindars should be prevented from establishing such bazárs and markets and deriving revenue therefrom. Nearly all the markets, and probably most of the bazárs in Bengal, have been established since the Permanent Settlement, and on zamindars' land, and it seems legitimate that the zamindars should get at least ground-rent from those who make use of them. I have printed Mr Douglas's letter about the bazárs and markets in the Appendix.

II. TERRITORIAL DIVISIONS OF THE DISTRICT AND THEIR HISTORY.

The subordinate divisions under a sarkár or chakla are variously called *parganas, tappas, tarafs, girds,* and *joárs.* The pargana is the largest and most common of them, and it is generally understood that the word *tappa* prefixed to the name of a tract of country implies that it has been formed out of part of a pargana. Thus, tappa Nazirpúr and tappa Sultanábád are supposed to imply that they were formed out of pargana Chandradwip. The unit in the division of tracts of land is generally the mozah or village, though this is sometimes divided into *kismats* or *paras*—*i.e.*, hamlets. A pargana consists of a number of mozahs, but their number and size are quite uncertain, and hence parganas vary greatly in size and importance.

The number of parganas, &c., in Bákarganj is reckoned at forty-seven. They are of very different ages and importance, and in some cases the divisions appear to have no better foundation than the notions of the *Taujihnavis* — *i.e.*, the officer of the Revenue Roll Department. They are also far from being compact, and it has been found quite impossible to make them the basis of administrative divisions. Still they are well known to the natives, every ryot being able to tell to which pargana his village belongs, and there is little likelihood of the names of the chief parganas becoming obsolete. Pargana rates of rent no longer exist, nor do even the same weights and land-measures always prevail over a whole pargana; but still the word *pargana* is used by the public as a rough means of classification, and the rate of rent commonly, though not invariably, prevailing in a pargana is often appealed to as the standard. I have, therefore, resolved to take up the parganas one by one, and give a short history of each, more especially as this gives a convenient opportunity for noticing the principal native families, as their history is for the most part connected with that of their parganas.

In the following list I have arranged the parganas chiefly according to their geographical position, though I have deviated somewhat from this arrangement in order that I might begin with the four great parganas of Chandradwip, Buzurgumedpúr, Selímábád, and Idilpúr. Some of the parganas also are so scattered—*e.g.*, Baikanthpúr—that it is difficult to find a place for them.

The number of parganas (forty-seven) on the list appears large, but many of them really belong to other districts, and are only represented in Bákarganj by a few outlying taluqs. Thus Rajnagar and Kasimpúr Selapati substantially belong to Farídpúr, and Bikrampúr and Jalálpúr to Dacca; and by far the greater portion of their revenues is paid in those districts. But at the time of the Revenue Survey, and on other occasions, it was found that some taluqs which had been separated from the zamindaries were geographically situated within this district, and therefore their revenues were made payable at the Bákarganj treasury. I have not thought it necessary to give any account of these extraneous parganas, and have relegated them to the end of the list. The first thirty-seven names on the list comprise all the parganas which are territorially important, and even many of these are very small and insignificant. Speaking generally, it may be said that the north of the district belongs to Bangrora, Birmohan, Idrakpúr, and Chandradwip; the eastern portion to North and South Shahbázpúr, Idilpúr, Sultanábád, Nazirpúr, and Ratandi Kalikapúr; the central portion to Chandradwip, Selímábád, Buzurgumedpúr, and Arangpúr; and the western portion to Selímábád and Syedpúr. The south of the district belongs for the most part to the Sundarbans, and is not included in any pargana. If we study the subject, we find that the positions of the parganas are by no means so arbitrary as they appear at first sight, and we can recognise the fact that most of them were originally tolerably compact. Indeed it is reasonable to suppose that they were so, as the parganas were divisions of the country made for revenue purposes, and each of them was probably originally in the hands of a single individual or family. The most irregular are the parganas which were composed chiefly of taluqs, such as Buzurgumedpúr. The absence of maps and the want of local knowledge among the officers of the distant courts of Delhi and Dacca of course prevented the divisions from being quite regular. Much of Bákarganj also was in old times covered with jungle, and determinate boundaries were therefore impossible. Thus the great pargana of Buzurgumedpúr appears to have been very vaguely defined towards the south, and was considered to comprise many of the lands which are now classed as the Sundarbans. It has been said that Jeradkhana and Muradkhana were the old names for the Sundarbans, but as regards the Bákarganj Sundarbans, it appears to me that it would be more correct to say that they were included in Buzurgumedpúr. Some of the present irregularities of the parganas are interesting as showing the physical changes which have taken place in the district. Thus, when we find the parganas of Uttar Shahbázpúr, Ramnagar, Nazirpúr, and Ratandi Kalikapúr on both sides of the Títulia and Ilsa, some portions being in thanas Mendiganj and Baufal on the mainland, and some on the island of Dakhin Shahbázpúr, we are reminded of a time when that island was only separated from the mainland by a narrow channel. So also we have an illustration of the action of the rivers in the parganas of Srírámpúr and Idilpúr, one of which has almost disappeared, while the other is neither so large nor so fertile as in old times. It should be noted that the land revenue shown in the list of parganas does not represent the revenue of the whole district. It only shows that of the parganas and of the taluqs separated from them, and does not include the revenue from the Sundarban grants, from Government estates (*khas mahals*), from resumptions, or from fisheries. The list only shows a revenue of about ten lacs, but the total revenue of the district is upwards of thirteen and a half lacs (Rs. 1,367,770).

LIST of the PARGANAS, &c., in BÁKARGANJ, showing the Revenue of each, and the Proportion in which that is paid by the Zamindaries and by the Taluqs.

No.	Name of Pargana, &c.	Revenue of Zamindaries.	No. of Taluqs.	Revenue of Taluqs.	Total Revenue.	Remarks.
1	Chandradwip	82,562 14 4½	73	58,104 10 8½	140,667 9 1	
2	Gird-i-Bandar	...	1	53 5 4	53 5 4	
3	Buzurgumedpúr	34,546 8 11¾	407	265,894 14 5	300,441 7 4¾	The Buzurgumedpúr zamindari consists of the farm (No. 1406), the Dari char (No. 1447), and the Chakran (No. 1437). The fractions are chiefly the result of the conversion of sicca into Government rupees.
4	Selímábád	98,227 0 1	20	4,798 4 1½	103,025 4 2½	
5	Tappa Havili Selímábád	11,055 11 5	9	3,323 0 6	14,378 11 11	
6	Tappa Havili	644 8 10	5	480 0 1½	1,124 8 11½	
7	Idilpúr	65,904 4 11	119	8,637 5 9	74,541 10 8	
8	Tappa Nazirpúr	28,783 1 4½	4	14,687 9 11	43,470 12 3½	
9	P. Ratandi Kalikapúr	25,237 11 4	6	3,314 1 6	28,551 12 10	
10	Uttar Shahbázpúr	7,645 12 9½	294	10,899 9 10½	18,545 6 8	
11	Dakhin Shahbázpúr	44,413 15 5	4	15,531 10 6½	59,945 0 0	
12	Kistodebpúr	816 0 0	...	...	816 0 0	
13	Alinagar	1,578 5 5	...	...	1,578 5 5	
14	Ramnagar	5,187 6 6	15	3,676 12 5½	8,864 2 11½	
15	Ram Hari char	...	1	119 4 6	119 4 6	
16	Kalmi char	...	1	1,846 10 8	1,846 10 8	
17	Sultanábád	21,128 13 5	10	5,646 13 1	26,775 10 6	
18	Kasimnagar joár Dáspára	1,633 9 11	...	...	1,633 9 11	
19	Khanja Bahadur Nagar	64 8 6½	59	6,598 11 6	6,663 4 0½	
20	Srírámpúr	441 4 1½	84	4,797 9 4½	5,238 13 6	
21	Tappa Abdulapúr	3,551 11 6	1	798 0 0	4,349 11 6	
22	Tappa Kadirábád	962 15 10½	1	598 9 3½	1,561 9 2	
23	Tappa Azimpúr	2,749 6 8½	41	7,732 10 0½	10,482 0 9	
24	P. Jahapúr	853 11 10	2	42 15 11½	896 11 9½	
25	Idrakpúr	3,278 11 10	52	2,060 7 10½	5,339 3 8½	
26	Rasulpúr	...	47	984 0 9½	984 0 9½	
27	Bangrora	365 6 9½	939	20,724 2 9	21,089 9 6½	
28	Birmohan	...	69	272 13 9½	272 13 9½	
29	Tappa Birmohan	13 5 4	27	295 7 10	308 13 2	
30	Habibpúr	878 14 11½	...	...	878 14 11½	
31	Maizardi	345 0 6	23	427 6 10½	772 8 4½	
32	Jalálpúr	365 6 4¾	1	1,113 0 1½	1,478 6 6¼	
33	Shaistábád	1,040 14 0½	5	991 15 0	2,032 13 0½	
34	Shaistanagar	1,537 1 6	161	14,927 14 10½	16,495 0 4½	There is also a pargana called Amrapúr, but as it is represented only by a khas mahal with a revenue of Rs.7-2, I have not included it in the list.
35	Shahzádpúr	6,897 3 3½	26	850 4 6½	7,747 7 10	
36	Tappa Bahadurpúr	4,913 1 1	2	304 0 0	5,217 1 1	
37	P. Arangpúr	14,364 7 6	22	9,604 12 9½	23,969 4 3½	
38	Syedpúr	6,570 13 9	4	21,341 3 3	27,912 0 0	
39	Baikanthpúr[1]	...	32	7,216 10 11	7,216 10 11	
40	Tappa Lakshirdiya	...	27	1,251 3 6	1,251 3 6	
41	Rajnagar	...	9	471 1 10	471 1 10	
42	Tappa Safipúr Kala	...	62	877 1 11½	877 1 11½	
43	Amirábád	...	1	336 0 0	336 0 0	
44	Bikrampúr	...	1	34 3 8	34 3 8	
45	Gopalpúr	...	5	4,675 0 0	4,675 0 0	
46	Durgapúr	...	1	4 14 11½	4 14 11½	
47	Kasimpúr Selapati	...	27	731 12 8½	731 12 8½	
		478,654 0 2	2700	507,714 6 0¼	986,368 6 2¼	

[1] Baikanthpúr is remarkable for its lands being so much scattered. There is part of it in Dakhin Shahbázpúr.

I now proceed to describe each pargana separately, and begin with Chandradwip, which is at once the oldest and the most interesting in the district.

1. Chandradwip.

(a.) *Its History.*

Chandradwip was one of the four mahals or parganas into which sarkár Bákla was divided at the time of Todar Mal's settlement. At that time it seems to have been known by the name of Ismáilpúr or Bákla, and it appears from Professor Blochmann's work that Abul Fazl uses the term Bákla as synonymous with Chandradwip. The zamindar of Bákla, who had in 1583 a son called Parmanand Rai, was evidently one of the Chandradwip Rajahs, and probably was Rajah Krishna Ballab.

It appears from traditions, and from official records, that Chandradwip belonged from early times to a Hindu family of the Kayast caste, and that they enjoyed the title of Rajah. The name Chandradwip appears to mean the island of Chandra, whether Chandra be taken as the name of a man, or in its literal signification of the moon. The name, therefore, appears to date back to a time when a great part of the district was covered by the sea. According to tradition, much of Bákarganj was formerly the bed of a large river called the Sugandha or Sunda; and the name of Sugandha, or "the Fragrant," is, as already stated, said to be derived from the fact that when the goddess Bhagabati was cut in pieces, and the fragments scattered over the earth, her nose fell into this river. The name Sugandha is still applied, I believe, to the upper part of the Kalijiri river, and the name is perpetuated, under the abbreviated form of Sunda, in the name Sundarkúl, or bank of the Sunda, which is borne by, I think, two villages, one near Panchakaran, and another near Nalchiti.

The following romantic story is told in connection with the name Chandradwip: There was once a Bráhman in Bikrampúr pargana of the name of Chandra, whose tutelary deity (Ishtodebta) was Bhagabati or Kali. He married a young Bráhman lady, but it was not until he brought his bride home that he knew what her name was. He then found out that she bore the same name as his patron goddess, and was greatly distressed by the coincidence, "for," he said to himself, "how can I pray to the goddess in my wife's name? It will seem as if I were worshipping my wife. Or again, how can I treat as my wife one who bears the name of my goddess? It were better that I should kill myself than that I should run the risk of committing acts of impiety." Under these feelings of perplexity he got into a boat and resolved to sail on until he was lost. It was then all open sea to the south of Bikrampúr, and he sailed on for a day and a night without meeting any one. Next morning, however, he was surprised to observe a little boat, rowed by a solitary fisher-maiden. He addressed her, and asked her how she had the courage to be there all alone. "Oh," she said, "I am following my trade, and I have no fear; but how do you, who are a Bráhman and a landsman, come to be in such a place?" Then he told her of the perplexity which had befallen him. The girl gave a scornful laugh, and said, "O Bráhman, how foolish and ignorant you are! Do you not know that the goddess Bhagabati dwells in every woman, and that every woman is a part of her? Why, then, should you be startled to find that your bride bears her name?" The Bráhman was amazed to receive such a reproof from a simple fisher-girl, and at once felt sure that she was other than she seemed, and was a goddess in disguise.

Leaping into her boat, he clasped her knees, and adjured her to tell him who she really was. In vain she reminded him of his caste, and bade him not sully it by contact with a fisher-maiden. He refused to let her go, and she was constrained to acknowledge that she was his goddess Bhagabati. The Bráhman was not slow to take advantage of the confession, and forthwith supplicated the goddess to bestow a boon upon her worshipper. She assented, and told him that the sea on which he then was would one day become dry land, and that he would possess it, and call it Chandradwip, after his own name.

Another story is, that there was a great ascetic, of the name of Chandra Sekhar Chakrabarti, who used to travel about accompanied by his disciple, Ram Nath Dhanaj Mardan Dé. One night, when he was asleep in his boat, the goddess Kali appeared to him in a dream, and told him that there were some images lying under water near his boat, and that he should secure them. Next morning he made his disciple dive twice into the water. Each time a stone image was brought up. Unfortunately, the disciple did not dive a third time, or he would have brought up Lakshmi, the goddess of Fortune. The two images he found were Katayani and Madan Gopal. They are sculptured in black stone, and are still worshipped in Madhabpásha. Chandra Sekhar then predicted to his disciple that the sea at the place where they were would one day be dry land, and that he would be the Rajah of it. He also bade him call it Chandradwip, after the name of his master.

The first seat of the family was at Kachua, a village on the right or west bank of the Títulia river, and in the Baufal thana of the Patuyakháli subdivision. According to one tradition, the Rajahs were forced to leave Kachua on account of the incursions of the Mugs — *i.e.*, the Burmese — and according to another story, they left it on account of the encroachments of the river. There is no doubt that much diluviation has taken place near Kachua, and indeed it is still going on. The local tradition is that the Títulia was once a very narrow stream, and that the main course of the Meghna flowed on the east side of the island of Dakhin Shahbázpúr. This view is supported by the circumstance that the same parganas are to be found on both sides of the river—viz., Ratandi Kalikapúr, Nazirpúr, and Uttar Shahbázpúr. The traveller Ralph Fitch describes a visit he paid to Bákla in 1586. There is no town or village of the name of Bákla now in existence, nor have I ever heard any tradition of there having been such a town. I presume, therefore, that Bákla must be the same as Kachua, though if so it must have been a much larger place in Fitch's time. Probably much of the old town has been washed away. Fitch describes the country as being governed by a Hindu prince who was of a good disposition and fond of shooting. I visited Kachua in the end of 1874, and found that the only remains of old building were a lonely and deserted temple standing on a high mound overlooking the river, and a series of vaulted chambers of very strong masonry, which are said to have been the *rajbari* or palace. The temple is conical in shape and is double storied, which is, I believe, not commonly the case in modern Hindu temples. It is evidently of considerable age, for there is a large tree (a *pakour*) growing on the top, which is so branching as almost to conceal the temple underneath.[1] The rajbari is a little farther inland, and is surrounded with jungle.

[1] Perhaps this was the very temple in which the Rajah's son is said to have taken refuge. It certainly was a natural place to run to in case of an inundation.

The genealogy of the Chandradwip family is told by their descendants with one or two variations, but the most correct account appears to be as follows: Ram Nath Dhanaj Mardan Dé was, as we have seen, the founder of the family. He lived at Kachua, and was succeeded by his son Ram Ballab. Ram Ballab was followed by Sri Ballab, Hari Ballab, and finally by Krishna Ballab, who had no sons, and with whom therefore the direct male line became extinct. Krishna Ballab, however, had a daughter named Kamala, who has left her mark on the district, and deserves a passing remembrance. I have said that Kachua is on the bank of the Títulia; the work for which Kamala is famous is the excavation of a large tank at a place not far from Kachua, and near the mouth of the Kalaia river. The tank is now in ruins, but enough remains to show that it was larger than any tank, not excepting Durga Sagur, which has since been dug in the district. The tradition is that after Kamala dug the tank the water would not rise in it, and that the people reproached her family, saying that on account of the Rajah's sins the water would not come in. Thereafter Kamala, being warned in a dream, went and stood in the middle of the tank, and the waters rose up and closed round her, and she remained in their midst under the guise of a water-lily. According to another tradition, she floated out to the great river by a stream which still flows through the tank. The tradition goes on to say that Kamala had an infant child, and that when her husband saw the waters closing round her, he called to her to come out. She replied that she could not, as the waters were drawing her down; and then he asked her who would nurse her child if she did not return. Under instructions from the goddess Ganga, Kamala answered that if her child were placed every morning on the steps of the *ghât,* or landing-place, she would come and nurse him, but no one else must see or touch her. The child was accordingly set down on the ghât every morning, and Kamala rose out of the water and nursed him. But the Rajah, being disconsolate for her loss, resolved to try and get her back; so he hid himself near the ghât, and attempted to seize Kamala as she was giving milk to the child; but she escaped from his embrace, disappeared in the water, and never again emerged. There is a Bengali song about these occurrences, which is still sung in the neighbourhood of the tank. A few verses of it have been recovered for me by Babu Chandra Kumar Ghose, the police sub-inspector of Baufal. They are printed in the Appendix. Another part of the tradition is, that when Kamala set about making the tank she resolved that it should extend as far as she could walk without turning round. She had walked about four *druns* (three druns and thirteen kanies), when her servants, being alarmed lest she should walk too far, induced her to turn round by smearing her heel with the blood of a pigeon, and calling on her to stop as her foot was bleeding. Labourers were brought from Dakhin Shahbázpúr to dig the tank, and Kala Bhadranath and his twenty-seven sons and thirteen grandsons made the *kodals* or spades for them. The digging cost nine lacs of rupees. According to one account, Kamala was the wife of Rajah Jagadanand Bosu; and according to another (unless the two names refer to the same person), she was the wife of the Kala or Black Rajah, whose name still survives in the Kala Rajah bíl, an extensive swamp in the Baufal thana.

The tank is no longer full of water, but Kamala's good

deed has not been unfruitful, for its bed now yields a rich harvest of rice, and its lofty walls or sides support forty or fifty homesteads, luxuriant in tamarind-trees, gáb-fruit trees, and bamboos. It is pleasant to see these homesteads raised high above the surrounding swamps, and to think that their inhabitants owe their comforts to a forgotten Bengali princess. We are reminded of the noble language used by Burke when speaking of the tanks in the Carnatic: "These are the monuments of real kings, who were the fathers of their people; testators to a posterity which they embraced as their own. These are the grand sepulchres built by ambition, but by the ambition of an insatiable benevolence which, not contented with reigning in the dispensation of happiness during the contracted tenure of human life, had strained, with all the reachings and graspings of a vivacious mind, to extend the dominion of their bounty beyond the limits of nature, and to perpetuate themselves through generations of generations the guardians, the protectors, the nourishers of mankind."

Krishna Ballab is said to have been succeeded by his daughter's son, Sib Nand, *alias* Parmanand Rai. He was the son of Balabhadra Bosu, and with him commenced the Bosu family. Parmanand was succeeded by Jagadanand, who was drowned in the Ganges, and whose son, Kandarpa Narain, removed on this account from Kachua and settled at Madhabpásha, about seven miles west-north-west of Barisál. There is a tradition that an astrologer foretold to Jagadanand that he would be drowned, and that to guard against this he shut himself up in his palace at Kachua. But at the appointed time the river swelled and rose up to the level of the balcony, and as the Rajah looked out upon the flood the goddess Ganga rose out of the water and stretched out her arms and beckoned to him to come. The Rajah, seeing that his fate was inevitable, yielded to it, and sinking into the arms of the goddess, disappeared into the river, which immediately afterwards returned to its old bed. This tradition appears to be a poetical reminiscence of the great storm which overwhelmed sarkár Bákla in 1583 or 1584. It appears from Professor Blochmann's work that the son of the zamindar of Bákla in 1583 was called Parmanand Rai, and this may have been Jagadanand's father.

Rajah Kandarpa Narain was succeeded by Ram Chandra Rai, who married a daughter of the famous Rajah Pratápáditya. It is said that when Ram Chandra Rai went to his father-in-law's house to bring away his bride he was accompanied by a favourite jester called Ramai Bhar. This man dressed himself up as a woman, and so gained admission to Pratápáditya's zenana and conversed with his queen. This came to the ears of the Rajah, and he resolved to revenge the insult by killing his son-in-law. His queen told this to her daughter, who communicated it to her husband, and he contrived to escape from the palace in disguise. On coming to his boat, however, a new difficulty presented itself, for Prátápáditya had felled trees and made a barricade in front of the boats in order to prevent his son-in-law's escape. But a famous athlete, named Ram Mohan Mal, who was in the Rajah's company, surmounted the difficulty. Though the boat was one of sixty-four oars, Ram Mohan lifted it over the barricade and launched it into the river. Afterwards Pratápáditya relented, and sent his daughter to Ram Chandra, and the place where she landed, near Madhabpásha, is still called Bodhu Mata Hát, or the Bride's Market, as a market was established there in her honour. It may be mentioned here that Ram Mohan Mal is said to have been the founder of the old family known by the name of the Raies of Ujirpúr, and it is a curious circumstance that the present Rajah of Chandradwip is a scion of this family, he being an adopted son. Thus Ram Mohan Mal's descendants have attained the dignity which their ancestor helped to preserve. Unfortunately, however, the glory of the Chandradwip family has long since departed.

Ram Chandra Rai is mentioned in Harish Chandra Tarkalankar's history of Rajah Pratápáditya, but the story of his escape is told somewhat differently. Ram Chandra, it is there said, was Pratápáditya's son-in-law, and had left his country and fled to his father-in-law's house. Pratápáditya resolved to have him assassinated, and to take possession of his kingdom.[1] Pratápáditya's daughter heard of the plot, and warned her husband, who called in the aid of Udai Aditya, his brother-in-law. Udai Aditya said he was going that night to Jessore to a *nách,* and suggested that Ram Chandra should disguise himself as a linkman and accompany the palanquin. Ram Chandra did so, and escaped; and then Pratápáditya sent his general, Kamal Khoja, to take Ram Chandra's country.

This Ram Chandra is in all probability the boy-king of Bákla whom the Jesuit Fonseca speaks of, and who was son-in-law of the King of Chandecan. Du Jarric says he was driven out of his country by the Arracanese, which agrees with the statement above that he had fled to his father-in-law's house (see below, in chapter on Sundarbans).

Ram Chandra was succeeded by his son Kirti Narain, who is reported to have been a great warrior, and who,

[1] Tarkalankar speaks of Ram Chandra as being only a zamindar, but this is a mistake (see the original life of Pratápáditya by Ram Ram Bosu).

according to a tradition common to several Hindu families, lost his caste by smelling a Masalman's dinner. He lost his rajahship from the same cause, and was succeeded first by his younger brother Bashodeb, and then by his son Pratáp Narain. Pratáp Narain was succeeded by his son Prem Narain, with whom the Bosu dynasty became extinct, and was replaced by the Mitra family. Prem Narain was succeeded by his son-in-law, Gouri Charan Mitra, who had two sons, Udai Narain and Raj Narain. Udai Narain was expelled by two Mahomedans of Chakar, called Mendi Mozamdar and Sarafaddin Mozamdar, who had found favour with the ruling Nawab by giving to him in marriage their sister, who was famed for her beauty. Udai Narain went to plead his cause with the Nawab, but was told that he must first exhibit his prowess against a tiger. An arena was prepared. Udai Narain killed the tiger in the presence of the Nawab, and then craved a boon. The Nawab's beautiful wife was present, and as she favoured her brothers, and was vexed at Udai Narain's victory, she flung him the rind of a plantain fruit, and scornfully told him to take that as a gift. The rind of a plantain is called *bákla*, which also, as we have seen, was another name for Udai Narain's zamindari. So the ready-witted Hindu quickly picked up the plantain skin, and gratefully thanked the Nawab and the lady for having given him Bákla. The Nawab was pleased with his wit, and restored his zamindari to him. It may add some confirmation to this story to mention that it appears from a report of Mr Massie's, dated 18th June 1801, that the Chandradwip family had at one time possessed three firmans or grants of the time of King Mahomed Shah, bearing the seal of Nawab Murshid Kali Khan—*i.e.*, Nawab Jaffar Khan—confirming Udai Narain in the zamindari, *hissajat*, and *nánkar* lands of Chandradwip. In these papers he was described as having succeeded Indra Narain, who had died without children, and as being the grandson of Pratáp Narain.

Udai Narain's brother, Raj Narain, did not get any share in the zamindari, but he got a taluq called Rajmata, and established himself at Pratappúr, two or three miles north of Madhabpásha. Udai Narain was succeeded by his son Sib Narain, who became insane, set fire to his house, and destroyed many old papers (see enclosures of Mr Massie's report of 18th June 1801). Sib Narain was succeeded by his eldest son, Lakshmi Narain, who died shortly before 1780 (see enclosures to above report), and was succeeded by Jai Narain, also called Durga Kuar Narain. During Jai Narain's infancy, his servant, Sankhar Bakshi, got possession of the zamindari, but Jai Narain's mother recovered it with the help of the famous Ganga Govind Sing. Perhaps it was on this occasion that the sanad of 24th November 1780 was given, which bore the seal of the Provincial Council of Dacca and the signature of Mr Holland, the Chief of Dacca, and of which a translation is appended to Mr Massie's report aforesaid. The getting of the sanad is said to have cost the Rani a good deal of money, and this, and the digging of a large tank near Madhabpásha, which is called after her, Durga Sagur, are said to have impoverished the estate. Probably it was the expense of feeding the Bráhmans, and of the other religious ceremonies attending the construction of the tank, which weighed more heavily on the estate than the mere cost of the manual labour. Jai Narain, *alias* Durga Kuar, was the last zamindar, as in his time the Chandradwip pargana was sold by the Collector for arrears of revenue in 1799. Jai Narain was succeeded by his son, Nar

Sing Rai, who was famed for his personal beauty. He had no son, but each of his two widows adopted a son, and these are now the representatives of the family. Their names are Bir Sing Narain Rai and Dabendra Narain Rai, and they are popularly known as the Bara and Chota Raja. They live at Madhabpásha, but are in poor circumstances, as they have nothing to support them except the lands round about Madhabpásha, which are *lakhiraj*, or rent-free, and some dependent taluqs. Most of the lakhiraj belongs to what is called the *khanabari* or homestead, locally called *Srinagar*. An attempt was made to resume it, but it was finally released. The khanabari is of considerable extent, and is bounded on the west by a stream called Rajar Ber, or the Rajah's Moat, which commences on the east of Rahamatpúr, and which is said to have been made by one of the rajahs as a defence to his palace. Madhabpásha is connected with Barisál by a road made many years ago by a Hindu lady named Parvati Chaudharine. There are many ruins of old buildings about Madhabpásha, but none of them are at all remarkable, and the finest thing about the place is undoubtedly the large tank called the Durga Sagur. There is a brass cannon lying near the bazár, and there is a small old tank in the neighbourhood called Kamantolla. Some have professed to read the name Kandarpa Narain on this cannon, and to connect it with the Rajah of that name, but the inscription is, to say the least, very indistinct, and it seems to me not improbable that the gun may have been brought by Rajah Durga Kuar Narain from the Mahomedan fort of Sujábád. There is a petition among the records from him asking leave to bring away some cannon from that place.

(*b.*) *Financial History of Chandradwip.*

In the Settlement of Todar Mal the revenue of sarkár Bákla is put down at Rs.178,266, and this is larger than the revenue at that time of Khalífatábád—*i.e.*, Jessore. In 1135 B.S. the revenue of Chandradwip pargana was only Rs.6608 (Grant, p. 365). This small amount only represents the *khalsa,* or exchequer revenue, and is evidently the result of the greater parts of the pargana having been held as a *jaghir*, or fief, on the condition of the zamindar's furnishing boats and crews to the Dacca flotilla. In 1165 (Grant, p. 367) the revenue was Rs.68,509, of which only Rs.1170 were khalsa, and Rs.58,581 were jaghir, the remaining Rs.8758 being apparently composed of *abwabs* or cesses. At this time the pargana stood in the name of Adi (Udai ?) Narain of the Ganges, and is described as consisting of one zamindari and twenty-two mahals—*i.e.*, apparently parganas. This circumstance, that the zamindari consisted of twenty-two subordinate mahals, is very interesting, as it helps to explain a curious fact in the topography of the district—*i.e.*, that there is one village in the district the lands of which belong to no less than twenty-two parganas. The village is Nohalia—a large village in the Baufal thana of the Patuyakháli subdivision, and therefore not very far from Kachua, the ancient seat of the Chandradwip rajahs.

The following parganas are to be found in this village:

1. Buzurgumedpúr.
2. Bangrora.
3. Khanjabahadurnagar.
4. Arangpúr.
5. Shaistanagar.
6. Bahadurpúr.
7. Fadainagar.
8. Uttar Shahbázpúr.

9. Azimpúr.
10. Ramnagar.
11. Idrakpúr.
12. Khorda Shafipúr.
13. Shahzádpúr.
14. Kasimpúr Selapati.
15. Rasulpúr.
16. Shaistábád.
17. Farokhábád.
18. Tappa Birmohan.
19. Nazirpúr.
20. Sultanábád.
21. Shafipúr Kala.
22. Pargana Birmohan.

All the lands of these parganas are now traceable in the village except those of Farokhábád, Kasimpúr Selapati, Khorda Shafipúr, and Rasulpúr, which, however, are said by the villagers to be still in existence, but to be hidden in the jungle which covers the outskirts of the village. On account of this grouping together of twenty-two parganas, the place is popularly called Gachani—*i.e.*, the bundling or tying together. The word is also used to mean the forcing a person to accept something against his will, and hence in revenue parlance *gachani* means the compelling a proprietor or farmer to take the settlement of several estates—*i.e.*, the good and the bad together.

Two things are deserving of note in this list. The first is, that the name Chandradwip is conspicuous by its absence; and secondly, that the large pargana of Ratandi Kalikapúr is not mentioned. Now, it is known that Ratandi Kalikapúr was formed out of part of Nazirpúr and other parganas in 1149 B.S., and therefore we may reasonably conclude that the gachani took place before that period. This circumstance and the omission of Chandradwip give countenance to the following tradition: Rajah Udai Narain's brother, Raj Narain, did not take any share of the zamindari, but in order to keep alive the memory of his rights, and also of the fact that Chandradwip was composed of twenty-two parganas, he made the village of Nohalia into a taluq, and aggregated in it the names of all the parganas. It is a fact known from other sources that most of the parganas in Bákarganj have been formed out of Chandradwip; in revenue parlance they are *kharija*, or excluded from Chandradwip, and the above list is an additional proof of this.

In 1169 B.S., as appears from a report by Mr Massie, dated 25th November 1800, the revenue of Chandradwip was Rs.71,042; and in 1194—*i.e.*, 1787—it was Rs.85,725. Mr Day, in his proposals for the Permanent Settlement, recommended that this assessment should be increased by Rs.15,000, in consideration of the Hissajat or stipendiary lands held by the zamindar. The Board of Revenue approved of this proposal, but expressed a hope that it would not cause distress to the zamindar or his family, or to the ryots. On 6th April 1790 Mr Douglas reported that Rs.3000 of the increase was obtained in 1195, and Rs.1000 more in the assessment for the current year (1196). He added, "The proprietor of the pargana is a youth of seventeen years of age, but as no attention has been paid to his education, he remains in total ignorance of the minutiæ of the Mofussil collections; his time is wholly spent in the luxuries of a zenana, and these his mother, wishing to continue in the management of the pargana, supplies him with the means of gratifying." On 29th April the Board replied by directing the Collector to make the Decennial Settlement of Chandradwip on the revenue of 1196—viz., Rs.89,725. On 4th October 1791 Mr Douglas reports that he called on the zamindar to enter into engagements on the terms proposed by Mr Day, and that he positively declined to do so. Mr Douglas adds, that some of the lands had suffered much from the inundation, but that he thought the estate could bear the increase if it were well managed, and if the Hissajat lands were resumed.

Eventually Mr Douglas proposed that the revenue for the remaining years of the Decennial Settlement—viz., from 1200 to 1206—should be fixed at Rs.87,652-1-8, and this was approved by the Board and the Governor-General. It seems that a *tahsildar*, or native collector, of Chandradwip had been appointed, owing to the Rajah's having defaulted; and on 26th October 1791 Mr Douglas reports that the owsh or early rice crop had been much injured by crabs, and that he had therefore suspended the payment of an instalment of the revenue. The zamindar did not agree to Mr Douglas's proposals, and on 21st October 1795 the Collector (Mr Armstrong) reports that the zamindar of Chandradwip is not under engagements to Government, and that he gives as a reason for not being so, that some taluqs had been separated from his zamindari in 1198 which were not entitled to separation, and that others had been separated at a much inferior rate of rent to that which he used from time immemorial to receive from them. Mr Armstrong considered that there was some truth in the latter assertion; but apparently Mr Armstrong was not a sufficiently active Collector, for he was called upon by the Governor-General in Council to explain why the revenue in his time was invariably in arrear, whereas under a former Collector it was realised with the greatest regularity. In his defence he pleads that the low price of grain, and the protracted suits which the zamindars had to bring against their under-renters, prevented them from paying the revenue (25th July 1795). Meanwhile the affairs of the Rajah of Chandradwip went from bad to worse, and on 11th November 1799 Mr Massie reports that the whole of the Rajah's lands have been sold by public auction, and that there was still a balance due of upwards of Rs.35,000, and requests that he may be allowed to put the Rajah in the Dacca Civil Jail, if he can succeed in apprehending him. "He has distinguished himself very much," writes Mr Massie, "by his refractoriness, and the making an example of him would, I am confident, be attended with very beneficial effects in this district." The Board replied on the 22d idem by approving of this proposal. The Rajah was never actually imprisoned, but Mr Massie attempted to carry out his proposal, for there is a petition from the Rajah's mother (called by Mr Massie, the old Rani of Chandradwip), dated January 1800, in which she says that a *piada* has come to summon Rajah Jai Narain—*i.e.*, Durga Kuar. "How shall I describe to you how sick the Rajah is? The whole of the zamindari has been sold. I am a widow, and the only son I have is on the point of death." In a subsequent petition, dated March 1800, the Rani begs that the Collector will pass an order for the recall of the piada deputed to summon the Rajah. "The whole of the zamindari has been sold, and the Rajah is sick, and therefore I am distressed beyond measure; you are master of the country, and I am hopeful that, taking compassion on a poor widow, you will remit the fine, and by whatever means I can I will pay the money." It may be noted here, in explanation of Mr Massie's apparently harsh proceedings, that the preamble to Regulation 3 of 1794 states that "from the earliest times the rulers of these provinces have exercised a discretionary power of confining proprietors of land who have failed in the discharge of the public revenue." The Regulation took away the power in ordinary cases, but section 14 retained it for instances in which the proceeds of the sale of the defaulter's land did not cover the arrears, as was the case with the Rajah of Chandradwip.

Chandradwip pargana was sold at Dacca in 1206 B.S. (1799), and was bought by two Greeks, Messrs George and Alexander Panioty, by one Dal Sing of Dacca, and by several others, of whom the chief appears to have been Ram Manik Mudi. It appears to have been sold in three shares, as follows:—

	A.	Gandas.	Krants.
Ram Manik Mudi and others . .	8	12½	2
Messrs Panioty	5	10	0
Dal Sing	1	17¼	1
	16	0	0

Soon after the purchase the pargana was attached because the purchasers fell into arrears, and an amín was sent to collect the rents. Another amín was also sent to make a partition of the pargana, in accordance with a request of the purchasers. The difficulties of the Collector and the purchasers lasted for some time, and in one petition Messrs Panioty pathetically observe that "what we intended as a purchase of lands has only been the purchase of disputes in the Faujdari and Diwani Adâlats." On 15th April 1800 Mr Massie writes, "It is extremely unpleasant to me to be so very troublesome to your Board with regard to the affairs of pargana Chandradwip, but really the parties concerned are so clamorous and harass me so much with their petitions and representations of one kind or another," &c.

Messrs Panioty represented that they were the only real purchasers, and that Ram Manik Mudi was only a *benamidar* (man of straw) for the Rajah. Unfortunately for the Chandradwip family, this was not the case. According to the story now current in Bákarganj, Ram Manik was a *mudi* or petty shopkeeper in the Madhabpásha bazár, but he was also the Rajah's agent or *gomasta*, and he pretended to him that he was only buying the estate on his behalf. Afterwards, however, he turned round and claimed to be the real purchaser. Ram Manik's descendants are still in possession of the zamindari, and live at Madhabpásha side by side with the representatives of the old rajahs. They are still contemptuously spoken of as the Mudi Bansa or family, and I am sorry to say that though some of them are rich, they have done very little to wipe out the discredit which rests on their ancestor's name.

The difficulties experienced by the purchasers in getting possession arose partly from the claim of the Rajah to hold certain lands rent free. These were called Hissajat lands, and are thus defined by Mr Massie in a statement submitted to the Board on 5th November 1798 : "It seems that in the time of the incursions of the Mugs, the zamindars of this part of the country held certain lands exempt from revenue on condition of their furnishing boats and men to oppose those people. And the lands so held were termed Nowara lands. Some, if not all of the principal zamindars, exclusive of furnishing boats, &c., engaged to go in person in these expeditions against the Mugs, and in such cases they were allowed to hold a still greater proportion of land exempt from revenue, in consideration of their own personal services. And the lands, though included under the general term Nowara, were distinguished by the specific term Hissajat, of which latter description are the lands alluded to." Durga Narain Kuar petitioned about these lands, and Mr Massie submitted a report thereon on 18th June 1801. He states that Durga Narain produced among other papers a *parwana* signed by Mr Holland, the Chief of Dacca, dated 24th November 1780. The preamble to the parwana is worth quoting. "To the matsaddies that are employed at present, or that may be employed hereafter, the chaudharies, zamindars, kanangoes, taluqdars, ryots, and all other inhabitants of pargana Chandradwip, &c., sarkár Bákla, Mahal Nowara, &c., dependent on Chakla Jahangirnagar, in the souba of Bengal, the paradise of kingdoms,—be it known that the aforesaid pargana, &c., is a zamindari of forty-two cosas [a kind of boat], of thirty-two mullahs [boatmen] each, and that Hissajat has been allotted to Udai Narain, the zamindar." On 21st July 1801 the Board rejected Durga Narain's claim to the Hissajat lands.

The partition papers of Chandradwip, which are in the Collectorate, bear the date of 1210 B.S. (A.D. 1803–4), but apparently the partition was not completed then, for Mr Battye, in a letter of 8th June 1807, speaks of the extraordinary delay which has taken place in completing the partition, and mentions that at last the zamindars had applied, under section 22 of Regulation 25 of 1793, for permission to make the partition by private arrangement. The Board had approved of this proposal, and Mr Battye submitted the partition papers, with the letter aforesaid. The Board confirmed the partition on 21st July 1807. A portion of the Paniotys' share is still held by their descendants, and another portion has been bought by Babus Rajendra and Mohima, of Chaudharassi, and a third portion belongs to the Kallowas family. Dal Sing's share is still held by his descendants.

In closing this account of Chandradwip, and of the ancient family which once possessed it, it is impossible to avoid the conclusion that the ruin of the rajahs was inevitable. Mr Massie may have been somewhat harsh, and our settlements and our sale laws somewhat rigid, and Ram Manik may have behaved to the Rajah after the fashion of Glossin in his dealings with the Laird of Ellangowan, but, after all, what hope was there for a youth like the Rajah, who had spent all his life in the zenana? If none of the other adverse influences had existed, he must still in time have gone to the ground from sheer incapacity to manage his affairs; and if it were possible now to restore Chandradwip to the present representatives of the family, they would be unable to keep it. The elder or Bara Rajah is intelligent, and of fair character, but he is devoid of energy, and the demon of discord has taken possession of him and his brother, so that cases between them, and these, too, of no very reputable character, not unfrequently come before our criminal courts.

It is a remark of Mr Helps in his life of Mr Brassey, that families seem to be like certain plants which take long to come to maturity, and then flower and die; and the remark is probably even more applicable to Bengal than to Europe. I could enumerate many native families which, after being long obscure, have shot up during a single generation, have exercised much power and influence, and then have sunk back into insignificance with the death of the one leading spirit. The great Narail family of Jessore is a case in point, for it does not appear to have produced a single man of mark before or after Ram Ratan Rai. The Tagores of Idilpúr, the Ghosals of Selímábád, and the Biswases of Jolabari are also instances; and if we look at men who are now flourishing—such as Khajah Abdul Ghani, C.S.I. of Dacca; Gholam Ali Chaudhari of Haturia; Raj Ballab Rai of Madhabpásha; or Boroda Kanth Rai, the present energetic zamindar of Arangpúr—we must feel it to be very doubtful if they will leave successors who will be able to walk in their footsteps. Apart from questions of climate and race, I think there are two circumstances which make such declensions more common in Bengal than in Europe. One is, that, as a general rule, a man of rank in India gets no training worthy of the name. If he becomes great, he does so by the pure force of his own abilities, and by breasting the blows of his surrounding circumstances. But as genius is always rare, it is not likely that it should show itself in two successive generations; and there is no external aid in the shape of good teaching, &c., to supplement deficiencies, and to enable a man of only average ability to fill a difficult position. Another circumstance, I think, is that, owing to the institution of caste, it is not so easy to get a new strain into a family as it is in Europe. In Hindu families the practice of adoption might be supposed to have some influence in this respect; but not only is the liberty of choice in adoption restricted by the rules of caste, but also, unfortunately, adoption must take place at a very early age, and therefore before anything can be known of the capacities of the adopted child.

The present revenue of the Chandradwip zamindari is Rs.82,562-14-4½. There are also seventy-three separated taluqs in it, the revenue of which is Rs.58,104-10-8½; so that the total land revenue is Rs.140,667-9-1. The Chakrabarties of Rahamatpúr, said to be descended from the Rajah's dewan or minister, are among the largest taluqdars in the pargana. The pargana is situated chiefly in thanas Kotwali, Mendiganj, and Baufal. In old records it is described as Chandradwip, &c., and the &c. is said to refer to two obsolete parganas, called Jaffirábád and Rafianagar. The Sundarban portion of Chandradwip belonged to these two parganas. The lands of Chandradwip are in general fertile and well cultivated. It is, along with Kotwalipara and one or two other parganas, remarkable for the number of Bráhmans who live in it. Many of them hold rent-free lands, though the quantity in each case is generally small. The town of Barisál is situated in this pargana. The land measure in use is the *kani.* It is divided into gandas, cowries, and krants, there being twenty gandas in a kani, four cowries in a ganda, and three krants in a cowry. Sixteen kanies make one drun. The kani is measured by a nal or rod eight cubits and eight fingerbreadths in length. Twenty-four nals by twenty make a kani, and as the eight fingerbreadths are reckoned as equal to six inches, a nal is twelve and a half feet long (the cubit being of eighteen inches); so that twenty-four by twenty nals are equal to 300 by 250 feet, or 75,000 square feet. The standard bigha used in the measurement of Government estates, &c., is in area, 14,400 square feet, or 1600 square yards; so that the Chandradwip kani is equal to about five bighas, four kathas, and two chittaks—*i.e.*, to about five and one-fifth bighas, or about one and three-fourths of a statute acre. The same measurement is in use in parganas Azimpúr, Bangrora, Buzurgumedpúr, Gird-i-Bandar, Idilpúr, and tappa Havili. There is, however, occasionally some confusion about the size of the Chandradwip kani, one being sometimes referred to in which the nal is only eight cubits long, the fingerbreadths being omitted. This is the kani referred to by Mr Hunter in his letter to the Board of 9th December 1818, in which he describes the Chandradwip kani as being 288 by 240 feet, or 69,120 square feet. It is thus equal to four bighas and sixteen kathas, or upwards of one and a half acre. I may mention here that it is almost impossible to state all the land measures in use. There is an old list in the Collectorate, and on this Mr Reilly, when

Deputy-Collector, constructed a table, which is referred to in cases of doubt, but it does not appear to be exhaustive.

One of the principal families residing in Chandradwip, though their property lies in pargana Azimpúr, &c., is the Raies of Lakutia, about six miles from Barisál. They are a Bráhman family, and their ancestors are said to have been originally the cooks of the Rajah of Chandradwip. But, whatever their origin, they can boast of at least one member who would have done honour to any family. This was Raj Chandra Rai, the father of the present owners. He was a pleader and an enlightened zamindar, and made one of the best roads and canals in the district (the Lakutia road and khál) entirely at his own expense. The estate at present belongs to three brothers, who have become Bráhmos and have thrown aside their sacred thread.

The following papers connected with Chandradwip appear in a volume in the India Office Library, called General Appendix to Judicial Papers, 1774:—

To the Honourable Warren Hastings, &c.

We beg leave to refer to your consideration a petition which has been laid before us by the vakil of Raghanandan Chaudhari, security for the pargana of Chandradwip. We understand the two Europeans there mentioned are officers of the Supreme Court of Judicature; and we transmit this petition to you as an instance of the inconveniences which attend this jurisdiction's being exercised on the persons employed on the collections. In the present case we presume the zamindars are not amenable to the power of the Supreme Court, not being servants of the Company or any European.

(Signed) Rouse, Purling, &c.

Dacca, 30*th Oct.* 1775.

The petition of Khosal Chasat, vakil of the security for the parganas Chandradwip, Jaffirábád, and Rafianagar.

Showing—That Odal San (?), the former Naib, having preferred a complaint for debt against Sib Narain, zamindar, and Ram Sankhar Bakshy, Naib of aforesaid parganas, in Calcutta, has brought from thence two Europeans to the said zamindar's house, seized and confined the Naib. . . . If the zamindar and Naib are carried to Calcutta on account of an old debt, the business of the collections cannot be carried on, &c.

2. Gird-i-Bandar.

Though called a pargana, this is merely a small portion of Chandradwip, which has been excluded from it in order to form the bazár of Barisál. It consists of one village (Barisál), and this a very small one, and is altogether comprised in one taluq, called Hari Radha Nath Dass, of which the revenue is only Rs. 53-5-4. The town of Barisál now includes much more than the village of that name. The civil courts and the collectorate and the magistrates' cutcheries are built on the aforesaid taluq, the sites being held by Government as an under-tenure. The taluq belongs to Babu Chandi Charan Rai, and is a very profitable one.

3. Buzurgumedpúr.

This is an old pargana, and was formerly included in sarkár Bazuha. It is said to derive its name from Buzurg Umed Khan, son of Shaista Khan who governed Bengal in the latter half of the seventeenth century. Some account of him will be found in vol. liii. of the "Calcutta Review" for 1871, article "Feringhies of Chittagong." Buzurgumedpúr belonged to Aga Bákar, and the mart of Bákarganj, which gave its name to the district, is situated within it. On Aga Bákar's death, Buzurgumedpúr became the property of Rajah Raj Ballab, the Naib of Shahamat Jung, nephew and son-in-law of Aliverdi Khan. He was also the Peshkar of the Nowara or Fleet lands. Grant refers to Buzurgumedpúr as a petty zamindari, which in the space of five-and-thirty years anterior to 1170, improved in its rental from Rs.6000 to two lacs, chiefly through new acquisitions of soil, though doubtless partly from amelioration of the uncultivated wastes of the Sundarbans, increased manufacture of salt, and growth of betel-nut. In 1135 the revenue of Buzurgumedpúr is put down as only Rs.4647. At present it is upwards of three lacs—that is, including the revenues of the permanent taluqs and of the temporarily settled estates. The zamindari cutchery of Buzurgumedpúr was at Golabari, near Bákarganj. There are still some ruins of buildings there, and the remains of a road which connected it with Bákarganj. The name Buzurgumedpúr is older than that of Bákarganj, and it appears from an official order published in vol. i. p. 185, of Seton-Karr's Selections, that Buzurgumedpúr was at one time considered important enough to be managed by a European Collector, and that Mr Henry Lodge had charge of it previous to 1787. A petition from the vakil or agent of the zamindar of Buzurgumedpúr (Rajah Raj Ballab), dated 1764, is printed at page 408 of Mr Long's Selections. It is full of complaints against the English traders. "By reason of the oppressions of the factories of the Company and many other English traders, all the inhabitants are fled: the people of the factories take from the merchants what they please at half price; cut down bamboos and trees belonging to the inhabitants, and take them away by force; if any one complain, they punish him for it. They press the inhabitants, and carry them in the woods of Sundarban, paying them only half their wages. They take possession of land in the Sundarban and make *tafalls* of salt, for which they pay no rent. They seize the salt of the tafalls of the pargana and of the inhabitants. They force the inhabitants to take tobacco, salt, and other articles, and refuse to pay the legal duties on the trade which they carry on. If we demand a sight of the Company's *dustak*, they beat us with bamboos. Some of them pretend that they have been robbed and insist on our making restitution, placing peons upon us, and putting us to a good expense. They judge causes, impose and exact fines. They send peons and seize the Naib of the pargana, taking for *talabana* (peons' fees) one rupee every day. They grant guards to many of the taluqdars and mahajuns in the country, by which means we are prevented from collecting the King's revenues; and many inhabitants take shelter in the factories, and thereby avoid paying the rents. There is little chunam made within the distance of four days' journey from hence, the whole quantity made within the pargana not exceeding 2000 maunds. Notwithstanding, Mr Dobbins has established two factories within my pargana, committing every species of injury and oppression, and violating the women of the inhabitants, and erecting factories in places where none ever were before, drives away the inhabitants, and, upon the information of many people, he takes upon him to recover debts of five and ten years' standing."

The early records are full of reports about the Buzurgumedpúr pargana, and of petitions by its proprietors. Rajah Raj Ballab, who lived at Rajnagar, in the Mulfatganj thana, and was the most conspicuous native in the Dacca division in the middle of the last century, got possession of the pargana on the death of Aga Bákar. He had it measured in 1167 B.S. (A.D. 1759), and an assessment was made according to this measurement in the following year. Raj Ballab's history rather belongs to Dacca and Farídpúr than to Bákarganj, but I may mention here that he held the office of *peshkar* of the *nowara* or fleet, and that he was also, I believe, the dewan of the Naib of Dacca. He was a Baidya by caste, but was of humble origin,[1] and only got into good society by dint of his wealth. He is said to have bought for the Baidyas the privilege of wearing the sacred thread. The buildings erected by him at Rajnagar have all been washed away by the Padma, but the large tank which he dug there is still in existence. He had seven sons. Kissen Dass, one of the seven, is famous as having been the person who fled to Calcutta in Surajah Daulah's time, and whom Governor Drake refused to give up—a refusal which led to the war between the Nawab and the English, and to the battle of Plassy. Kissen Dass escaped on this occasion only to die a violent death some years afterwards, for he and his father were seized by Mir Kassim and drowned in the Bhagireti at Monghyr.[2] Rajah Gopal Kissen, another son, thereon succeeded to the charge of the property. He died 24th Ashar 1194 B.S. (6th July 1787), and his son Pitambar Sein, and Raj Ballab's

[1] I believe it is correct that Raj Ballab was not of good family, but the evidence of the Serishtadar Mritanjai Mukti, when examined before Mr Thompson in the proceedings about Rajnagar on 20th September 1791, seems to show that Raj Ballab inherited some wealth, and was not altogether a self-made man. The Serishtadar's words are, "I have served in the zamindari from the age of fifteen or sixteen years, and am now sixty-two. My father served before me, in the time of Raj Ballab's father, and we were both employed as the head Serishtadars of the whole zamindari."

Raj Ballab is referred to by Orme, who says that he was the dewan of Nowazis. Nowazis died in 1756, and Raj Ballab's influence continued during the time of the widow, with whom Raj Ballab was said to be improperly intimate (Orme, vol. ii. p. 49).

[2] In a petition of Pitambar Sein, dated June 1798, he says, "We are the descendants of Maharajah Raj Ballab, who was a wellwisher of the Company, in consequence of which Kassim Ally Khan drowned him and his son Kissen Dass Bahadur in the Ganges, and having deputed Aka Reza, confiscated to the State his house and property."

other grandchildren, inherited the estate. They quarrelled among themselves, and in 1790 Mr George Thompson, assistant to the Collector of Dacca, was deputed to make a partition of Rajnagar and Buzurgumedpúr. It appears that the first application for the partition was made to the Civil Court by Kali Sankhar, one of the partners, that he got a decree in 1189 B.S. (1782) in the Dacca Court, and that this order was confirmed on appeal in Baisak 1194 B.S. (1787). Mr Day accordingly attached the parganas of Buzurgumedpúr, Rajnagar, and Kartikpúr Sujábád, but through the intrigues of Pitambar Sein, no partition was made until afterwards. Mr Thompson accomplished it. It was Gopal Kissen, the father of Pitambar, who appealed against the decree of division given by Mr Duncanson in the Dacca Court.

I have heard it said that Gopal Kissen had his cutchery at Sutaluri, near Jhalukátti.

It also appears that the munsiff, acting, I presume, under Mr Thompson's superintendence, was the authority who directly made the partition. The partition, however, generally goes by the name of Mr Thompson's Batwara; and he is stated in the official papers to have completed the partition of Rajnagar, &c., Buzurgumedpúr, &c., and Kartikpúr Sujábád on 2d May 1792. The estate was divided into five shares, and the five partners cast lots for their shares, the lots being drawn by two boys of the Bráhman caste, one of about ten years and the other of eight years. The engagement was made for eight years, ending 1799. As there was much jungle in Buzurgumedpúr, Mr Thompson did not measure the pargana, but only made a division of the revenue and rent of it. He also did not include the Sundarban lands, much of which was considered to be part of Buzurgumedpúr, in the assessment, and therefore they were afterwards resumed by Government on the ground that they had not been included in the Decennial Settlement. In the original engagement the partners said as follows: "The Sundarban forest-lands, as well as the cane and reed jungle-lands appertaining to the pargana Buzurgumedpúr, our zamindari, not being included in the division now made between us, but continue as heretofore our joint property in equal shares, we therefore write and deposit this as our engagement that the duties and revenue forthcoming therefrom, and collections under the Mahal Bhashan Gorekátti, shall be divided and received by us severally in equal shares, and that the same mode of division shall be observed between us with regard to all revenue or profits to be derived from taluqdari grants made, or which may hereafter be made, of the aforesaid jungle-lands."

It appears from the record that there were three ranís or widows of Raj Ballab living at the time, and it was a stipulation of the partition that each of them should receive Rs.100 sicca monthly. The revenue payable by the zamindars, according to Mr Thompson's partition of 1792, was sicca Rs.181,107, 5 anas, and that payable to them from the taluqdars was *bhari* or *arcot* Rs.237,496, 8 anas, 17 gandas, equal to Rs.2,30436-14-3 sicca, Rs.7059,10-14 being deducted as batta. (The bhari or Company's arcot rupee was coined at Calcutta, and was in value 3½ per cent. less than the sicca rupee.)

Mr Thompson received the thanks of Government for his work, but the zamindars complained that he had over-assessed them, and they were certainly never able to pay the revenue. Both Rajnagar and Buzurgumedpúr had suffered severely from the inundations of 1787, and it is probable that Mr Thompson did not make sufficient allowance for this circumstance. There was also much controversy about the *nij* taluqs or private tenures held by each shareholder subordinate to the zamindari, and as the partners were at bitter enmity with one another, it is probable that their *zidd* and envy led to the over-assessment of each of them. Buzurgumedpúr was a taluqdari mahal—*i.e.*, most of the land was held by taluqdars, and as the lands were not divided, to each shareholder in the zamindari was assigned one-fifth of the revenue of each taluq; and on the same principle each shareholder who held a taluq had to pay four-fifths of its revenue to his co-sharers.

Mr Thompson considered that he had discovered that a great fraud had been committed by Rajah Gopal Kissen when he was manager of the estate, in that he had reduced the assessment on the estate by Rs.17,500, and had then concealed the deficiency by adding to the paper assets of the estate Rs.17,500 as the proceeds of a sayer mahal which had formerly been abolished, and therefore could not really yield anything. The sayer mahal was called the *Phanri Malwa*, and seems to have been a transit duty, as the word *phanri* means a station or outpost, and is still in use to designate a police outpost. The discovery has been endorsed by Mr Sutherland in his description of Bákarganj, but Mr Douglas's letter of 6th April 1791 shows that there was another side to the question, and that probably Gopal Kissen had been authorised by the Government to make the deduction in the assessment.

In a petition from Pitambar Sein, the son of Gopal Kissen, and one of the parties to the batwara, there occurs the following significant allusion to Sir Elijah Impey: "Mr Hastings having inspected these [certain proceedings of the Superintendent of the Khalsa], referred them to the decision of Sir Elijah Impey, the Judge of the Court of Appeal. The said Sir Elijah having received from me a considerable sum on account of commission, received my petition for the two parganas, and having issued his summons and *parwanas* in the Mofussil, investigated for a length of time the cause, and leaving his proceedings, departed for Europe without passing a decision on it."

Buzurgumedpúr soon fell into arrears, and it was no easy matter to recover them, although there was a *tahsildar* or native collector stationed at the *golabari* or zamindari cutchery of Buzurgumedpúr, near Bákarganj, for several years after the Permanent Settlement. This officer used to clear his balance in part by paying the salary of the Judge-Magistrate of Bákarganj, who in this way was saved the trouble and expense of sending to Dacca for money. In April 1801 the tahsildar reported that the buildings at the golabari had been destroyed by a storm, and in 1802 he reported that he had engaged spearmen at the rate of Rs.2-8 a month to protect the treasure against dacoits. On 16th November 1796 Mr Armstrong, the Collector of Dacca, reported that he had put up the pargana to sale by auction for three successive days, and for two hours each day, and that nobody had made a bid for it. This was in consequence of its consisting almost entirely of dependent taluqs. These taluqs were of the description called *Jangalburi* taluqs, and it appears from a letter of Government to the Board of Revenue (13th July 1821) that the rules about Jangalburi taluqs, contained in section 8 of Regulation 8 of 1793, had been framed with reference to this very pargana of Buzurgumedpúr. Jangalburi taluqs—*i.e.*, jangal-cutting taluqs—were generally granted on a rent-free tenure for a number of years, with a provision that thereafter the cultivation should be measured and assessed at certain rates specified in the lease. They were common in Buzurgumedpúr, because about three-fourths of the pargana were formerly Sundarban jangal, and could only be cleared by the granting of improving leases with a condition of permanency. Under the Government orders of 10th October 1799, Mr Massie, the successor of Mr Armstrong, bought in for Government in November of that year the whole pargana of Buzurgumedpúr (see his letter, 29th November 1799), and Government has ever since been the zamindar of the pargana. Government was, of course, the creditor at whose instance the estate was brought to the hammer, and all that it paid for the acquisition was the nominal price of one rupee.

The sale of the zamindari was followed in 1801 by the sale of the dependent taluqs. There were then 594 of them (28th November 1801). There are now 407. It had been held by Government (Resolution of Governor-General of 31st December 1790), and afterwards declared by law (Regulation 8 of 1793), that Jangalburi taluqs were not entitled to separation. When, however, Government acquired the zamindari, it was found expedient to allow the separation of the taluqs, as in that way the expense of collecting the rents was saved, and also the arrears were more speedily and regularly collected. In making the separations the Board adhered to the rentals shown in Mr Thompson's Batwara papers; but a letter of Government, dated 13th July 1821, and written by the famous Holt Mackenzie, shows that Government by no means approved of this step, and also that the Board had exceeded their powers in granting the separations at all. "It appears to have been hitherto assumed," he writes, "that the rent demandable by Government, on converting the taluqs into independent tenures, was necessarily to be fixed at the rate specified in the Batwara jama adjusted by Mr Thompson; but although that rate might justly be taken to show the amount demandable by the zamindar, and consequently by Government, until a fresh *Jamabandi* should be made, yet, unless in the case of taluqs holding under *mocurrari* tenures, it is not apparent why it should be assumed as constituting the ultimate limit of Government demand; and after the period fixed by Regulation 1 of 1801 for the separation of taluqs, no taluqdar could of course claim to become hazuri as a matter of right. Under these circumstances Government would be justified in annulling the whole of the separations made by the Board without reference to Government." He then adds that the great length of time, &c., prevented Government from taking this course. In 1799, the year of the sale of the pargana, the arrears due to Government were Rs.171,346; and so little had the sale improved matters, that the arrears had increased in 1801 to sicca Rs.386,574. It was then that the sale of the taluqs was resolved on. The separation, however, of the taluqs did not take place until several years after their sale, and was only accomplished gradually. A notification was issued on 27th January 1812, inviting all the Buzurgumedpúr taluqdars to become hazuri—*i.e.*, independent. It was after the experiment of khas management had been tried and had failed that separation was had resort to. There was great confusion in the accounts of Buzurgumedpúr when it was under khas or direct management; and indeed this might be anticipated, when we consider the extent of the collections, the fact that there was no Collector of Bákarganj at the time, and that the only control over the tahsildar was situated so far off as Dacca. Kali Prasad was about the last Naib or tahsildar. He was guilty of embezzlement, and fled in December 1812 to his home in Birbhum, where he shortly afterwards died. He was succeeded by Radha Nath, who remained in charge till Asar 1219 (1813), when, in place of the direct mode of management, the taluqs were separated off, and the remainder of the estate was farmed. There is a full report by Mr Prinsep, the Legal Remembrancer, on the embezzlement and mismanagement in connection with Buzurgumedpúr, and in it he refers to the state of the Dacca Collectorate, and observes that "the state of the *amla* of Dacca has long been notorious" (24th March 1817). In 1822 the revenue of Buzurgumedpúr was sicca Rs.244,867; of this, Rs.217,295 were collected from the separated taluqs, and Rs.27,571 from the dependent tenures included in Tilak Chandra Rai's farm. This farm apparently consisted of such under-tenures, howalas, and the like, as were not considered entitled to separation, or the holders of which had not applied for it. It probably also contained any lands which had been the khas or direct property of the former zamindars, or which had been their nij or private taluqs. At present there are 407 separated taluqs, and their united revenue is Rs.265,895. Each of these taluqs bears a separate number on the Revenue Roll, and the holders of them pay in the revenue direct to Government. But besides these separated taluqs there are three mahals, or estates, belonging to Buzurgumedpúr, and numbered respectively on the Revenue Roll 1406, 1437, and 1447. No. 1406, which goes by the name of the farm or *izara*, contains a great many properties, and is apparently the portion of the pargana of which Government acquired the direct possession when it bought the pargana in 1799. There is, however, some obscurity about its history, and I am not able to state positively that it is the property which was known in 1822 as Tilak Chandra Rai's izara. There is no doubt, however, that it corresponds to it in some measure.

There are in No. 1406 149 estates of which the revenues are permanently fixed, and there are 47 temporarily settled estates, or altogether there are 196 estates in No. 1406, each one of which ought to bear a distinct number in the Revenue Roll. Owing to this not having been done as yet, the full number of the estates in Bákarganj is not shown in the books, and the true amount of the work in the *Taujih* or Revenue Department is not exhibited. Of the 47 temporarily settled estates, four are ferries, so that they may be considered as relics of the old sayer duties. They have been leased for terms of years. They are the ferry on the Bishkháli (revenue, Rs.40); the Kumarkháli ferry, on the Nalchiti river (revenue, Rs.46); that between Bishkháli and Tulatuli (revenue, Rs.9); and that on the Srimantapúr. The total revenue annually derived from them is Rs.115. I once proposed to make them public ferries, and to transfer them to the Road Committee, but the proposal was negatived by the Commissioner. The 43 other temporarily settled estates are let in farm to various persons. No. 1437 is let to Mr Brown. It consists of resumed *chakran* or service lands, and is scattered over no less than 45 kismats or hamlets. It was bought at a sale for arrears of revenue in 1840. No. 1447, also called the Dari char, consists chiefly of resumptions. There were 77 estates in it, but there now only remain 28 temporarily settled estates, and 4 permanently settled estates. The rest have been sold.

The revenue of No. 1406 is Rs.29,413, and of this,

Rs.26,196 belong to the permanently settled estates, and Rs.3217 to those temporarily settled.

The revenue of No. 1447 is Rs.3935-4, of which Rs.3850 belong to the farm, and Rs.85-4 to the permanently settled estates.

It is reckoned that there are 431 estates in Buzurgumedpúr—viz., 407 separated, 11 khas mahals, and 2 zamindaries, Nos. 1406 and 1447. Altogether, and with inclusion of the revenue of No. 1437 (I do not know accurately its present rental), Buzurgumedpúr yields to Government in round numbers Rs.337,000 annually. It thus yields by far the largest revenue of any of the parganas. Large sums also were obtained when Government sold the khas mahals or Government estates belonging to it, and there still remain some to be sold.

Buzurgumedpúr is remarkable for the number and value of its taluqs. The most interesting as regards its origin is the taluq Padrian or Mission taluq of Sibpúr. It is said that it was originally granted by Raj Ballab Sein to some Christians from Bandel. The tradition is that he wanted to coerce his tenantry, who were inclined to be disobedient to him, and that he judged that Christians would be well fitted for the purpose, as mere contact with them would be sufficient to destroy the ryots' caste, and that the latter would therefore gladly come to terms in order to avoid the visits of the Christian servants. He accordingly applied to the Portuguese Mission at Bandel for some Christians, and four were sent to him. They afterwards applied to him for a priest, in order to perform their religious ceremonies. He procured one from Bandel, and assigned him four pieces of land or howalas for his maintenance. The four Christians were put in charge of the property, but in consequence of their dissensions the howalas were formed into a taluq, and made over to the priest in trust for the mission. The first priest was called Fray Raphael das Anjos, and the date of his *patta* or lease for the taluq was 9th Phalgun 1171 B.S., or A.D. 1764. In the decision of the Sadr Diwani Adâlat, dated 18th April 1856, it is said that the lease was granted by Rajah Pitambar Singh (Sein ?), zamindar of Arangábád, but from the date it appears more probable that the lease was granted, as is the tradition, by Pitambar's grandfather, Rajah Raj Ballab. It was renewed by Mr Thompson in 1790 or 1791, when he was making the partition of Raj Ballab's estates among Pitambar Sein and the other heirs. The first church at Sibpúr is said to have been built by one Pedro Gonsalves, but it has been superseded by a larger edifice built with money left by Domingo de Silva. The first priests were Augustinian monks; and they, acting in subordination to the Prior of Bandel and to the Bishop of Meliapore, from the year 1764 down to the year 1836, were in uninterrupted possession of the Sibpúr taluq, and administered the duties of priests of Sibpúr. But in 1836 an attempt was made to bring the exercise of the clerical office at Sibpúr and the management of the property thereto attached under the immediate control of the Vicar Apostolic, Dr St Leger, who, with a view to the organisation of the Roman Catholic hierarchy for the first time in Bengal, by the Pope's brief of 18th April 1834, had been appointed to that office. Dr St Leger dismissed Fray Jos das Neves, and appointed in his room Ignatius Xavier Mascarhenas to be the incumbent at Sibpúr, and this Mascarhenas managed to get himself substituted for Fray Jos das Neves as decree-holder in a rent suit, and so got possession of the taluq, &c., by a summary order of the Bákarganj Civil Court (S. D. A.

decision). The real fact, I believe, was that the Roman Catholic inhabitants of Sibpúr quarrelled with their pastor because he refused to perform the burial service for a parishioner who had died without making confession, and that, like true Bákarganj ryots, they placed themselves under the *zimba* or protection of Dr St Leger. In consequence of the quarrel the Sibpúr incumbent left the place, and for several years there was no service in the church. A protracted litigation followed on the appointment of Mascarhenas. The Portuguese priests sued for recovery of possession of the church and lands; and as Mr Loughnan, who was the Judge of Bákarganj, was a Roman Catholic, the suit was at his request transferred to the court of the judge of the twenty-four parganas. The Augustinians were successful both in that court and in the Sadr Diwani Adâlat, and the litigation ended in 1857 with their recovering possession of the taluq, and with their getting a decree for mesne profits, which, however, was not enforced. The decision of Mr Robert Torrens, the judge of the twenty-four parganas, dated 9th December 1847 (published in the decisions of the Zila Judges for that year), gives a full account of the suit. It states that the taluq had been in possession of Fray Raphael das Anjos previous to 1171 B.S. (1764), and that in that year, on the 9th Agrahan, the rent payable by him was reduced from Rs.2234-3 by Rs.533-3, making the yearly rent Rs.1701.[1] The patta was granted to Fray Raphael by Lakyi Narain Rai,[2] and after the death of the former, Pitambar Sein, the zamindar, confirmed the grant by a written

[1] The present rental is Rs.1761-8-10, being the equivalent in Government rupees of Rs. 1701 sicca.

[2] Lakyi Narain is a name of Vishnu, and was the name under which Rajah Raj Ballab recorded his zamindari of Rajnagar and Buzurgumedpúr.

declaration on 25th Phalgan 1198 to Fray Raphael's successor.

It also appears from Mr Torrens' decision that the first church was built by Pedro Gonsalves, and that afterwards, in accordance with the will of Domingo de Silva, his son Manuel pulled down the old church and built in 1823 the present enlarged edifice, which the De Silva family have continued to repair (see also decision of 31st December 1853). Since the termination of the litigation, the Sibpúr incumbent has been appointed by the Archbishop of Goa. The revenue of the taluq used to be paid to the zamindar of Buzurgumedpúr, but in 1808 it was separated, and made an independent taluq. The agreement with the Collector, dated 1215 B.S., and stipulating for payment of revenue in eight instalments, is in the Collector's record-room. The taluq yields a profit of about Rs.700 or Rs.800, which are spent in supporting the mission. The priest also receives the fees on marriages, funerals, &c.; and these, I believe, amount to a considerable sum. Sibpúr was once a very flourishing place, and there are the remains of many large houses in it. It is situated on the Srimantapúr khál, and is about five miles from Bákarganj, with which it is connected by a road (now in disrepair), in which there are several masonry bridges. Its prosperity was owing to the rice and betel-nut trade, but now Bákarganj and Kaliganj have taken its place. The most conspicuous resident of Sibpúr was Domingo de Silva, who made a large fortune in the rice trade. He came to Sibpúr (I believe from Goa) at the end of the last century, and died in 1821. By his will, dated 7th October 1821, he left money for the building of the church, and also ordered that Rs.500 should be distributed in charity every year on the anniversary of his death (21st November 1821) to poor Christians and needy and helpless orphans, "together with such poor, be they Mahomedans or Hindoos, as may be present on that day" (at Sibpúr).

The charity still exists, and the money is paid to the priest by the Administrator-General of the High Court. The existence of the charity is well known to the faqirs and the rest of the begging population of Bákarganj, and they flock down to Sibpúr on the appointed day.

The Feringhies of Sibpúr, as they are called, are less numerous and less prosperous than they were half a century ago. They support themselves chiefly by going about to Mahomedan marriages and firing off *feux de joie*. They are also employed by the villagers to kill pigs, and some hold appointments in the police. They are indisposed to agriculture or other regular industry, and they are about as ignorant and superstitious as their Bengali neighbours. The only thing for which I can heartily praise them is the great neatness and cleanliness of their homesteads. Probably, however, the want of cattle or agricultural implements has something to do with this. They have adopted the Eastern notions about the seclusion of women, and do not like to give their daughters any education. Their numbers are about 800—the census giving 785 Christians in Bákarganj, and 43 in Mirzaganj. Sibpúr is by far the largest settlement; but there are a few families at Kalada, also in the Bákarganj thana, and at Maitbhanga in the Mirzaganj thana.

The largest taluq in Buzurgumedpúr is that called joár Ramna-Bamna, which is now in possession of the Bamna Chaudries. The revenue is Rs.19,487-10-8. It is situated on the west bank of the Bishkháli river, in the subdivision of Perozpúr, contains forty-three villages, and is very profitable. It was originally entered in the name of an Armenian named Khajah Michael, and is described in the old records as Mudafat Khajah Michael. One Mahomed Shuffee, the ancestor of the present proprietors, got a settlement of the taluq from the Board in 1809. The popular tradition is that he was originally only a salt-piada, and this is supported by the fact of his being styled in the official papers Mahomed Shuffee Jamadar. At the time of Mr Thompson's Batwara the land was waste, and was entered as Mudafat Khajah Michael. It seems to have been originally included in pargana Shahzádpúr, six anas of which were transferred to Buzurgumedpúr (see Mr Battye's letter of 19th February 1807). The property was at one time in the possession of one Sadasib Mozamdar, who was Naib of the former zamindar of Buzurgumedpúr. Sadasib's sons disputed Mahomed Shuffee's claim to it, and said that he was only *ausat* taluqdar, and that their father held a patta for it, given in 1188 by Rajah Lakyi Narain Rai. They, however, lost their cause; and Mahomed Shuffee got the settlement on the ground of his former possession, which, it appears, dated as far back as 1202 (1795). The settlement made with him in 1809 was for seven years, and the annual rent was Rs. 1165.

The leading taluqdars in Buzurgumedpúr are the Rahamatpúr Chakrabarties, the Narainpúr Chakrabarties, Khajah Ahsanoolah, Rassik Chandra Newgi, Chandra Kanth Mukharjya of Bara Mozamdar, the Messrs Brown, who own a taluq with the curious name of Bagdeshwar (a mistake for Balthazar) Johannes, Prosunno Kumar Sein, the Ghosal family, Thomas Gomez, the De Silvas, Bhagabati Debya, the heirs of Dr Clement of Dacca, the Banarjis of Koulipara.

One Ainaddin Sikdar, who lived at Chamta, near Niamati, and was a notorious dacoit, had taluqs in Buzurgumedpúr. In 1789 he was banished, and his property confiscated. There is extant a vast amount of correspondence about this man's property, and about that of Mahomed Hayat, which was confiscated under similar circumstances. It was found very difficult to discover their properties, as the zamindars did their best to conceal them; but eventually some were found, and were gradually disposed of by sale.[1]

The most remarkable incident in the history of Buzurgumedpúr is perhaps that by which many thousand acres of land in it were given away in perpetuity for a quit-rent of Rs.372 a year. I refer to the famous grant of the villages of Aila Tearkháli and Phuljhuri, which led to a long litigation between Government and the purchaser from the original grantee, and which terminated adversely to Government on 26th January 1870, by the Privy Council's upholding the decree of the High Court.

The first mention of the lease occurs in a letter dated 18th March 1805, sent by Mr J. Battye, Collector of Dacca, to the Board of Revenue, and in which he forwards a copy and translation of a petition from one Ram Dhan Chattarji applying for a taluqdari lease of some jungle-lands in Buzurgumedpúr. Ram Dhan Chattarji applied for a rent-free grant for seven years, and offered to pay afterwards a fixed rent of Rs.349 sicca. He described the villages as Aila Tearkháli and Phuljhuri, and gave a specification of their boundaries. Mr Battye, in forwarding the application, said that the offer was

[1] For a full report about these taluqs, see Mr Massie's report, 19th August 1800. A full report on Buzurgumedpúr generally will be found in a letter of Mr Collector Phillips of 20th December 1822.

the highest among those which he had received, and that the land had not been included in Mr Thompson's partition of the pargana; and that from the information he had been able to gather through his officers, the land did not appear to be able, when brought into a state of cultivation, to bear a much higher assessment. Unfortunately, Mr Battye depended for his information on the Naib of Buzurgumedpúr, who was, it seems, the real applicant for the lease, Ram Dhan Chattarji being merely a *benamidar*. The Board sanctioned the proposal (with the authorisation of the Governor-General) on 9th April 1805, and on the 17th idem Ram Dhan executed the necessary engagements and was put into possession (Mr Bird's letter, 5th November 1807).

One Surjya Narain Bannarji, who had also applied for the lease, petitioned Mr Battye and Mr Fortescue his successor, alleging that the Naib of Buzurgumedpúr had himself obtained the pottah in Ram Dhan's name, and that the Naib had accepted his (Surjya Narain's) petition, and promised to report it to the Collector, but had afterwards not done so. Mr Bird, the Collector, adds that "repeated parwanahs were issued to the Naib in consequence of Surjya Narain's petitions, but that the Naib had denied every charge." Mr Bird trusted, therefore, that the Board would deem Surjya Narain's petition worthy of no further consideration! It appears from a report of Mr Hunter, dated 5th August 1818, that two other persons—namely, Ram Rattan Bosu and Chandra Sekhar—petitioned the Collector of Dacca, and made the same allegations against the Naib. The name of the Naib was Kali Prasad Mozamdar, and it appears that there were certain sums which he had not accounted for, and that the petitioners alleged that Kali Prasad had spent the money in cultivating the jungle-lands, and offered to prove this by the evidence of Domingo de Silva, Mahomed Shaffi, and others. However, says Mr Hunter, no final orders appear to have been passed on these petitions, nor was any investigation made into the truth of the assertions. Ram Dhan's lease was dated 6th Baisak 1212, and the agreement was that he should begin to pay rent from 1219. On 14th Chait 1213, however, he sold his rights to Nand Kumar Rai Sarm *alias* Ganga Nand Rai Sarm, alleging that he was unable to cultivate the land. Ram Dhan's name was struck out in 1216 B.S. Nand Kumar was the Naib's brother, and he purchased the property from Ram Dhan in the name of Krishna Govind Charan Rai, and the transfer in the Collector's books was made in this name. The name Krishna Govind Charan Rai was said by the petitioners to be a junction of two names—namely, Krishna Kishor Rai, the son of Kali Prasad, and Govind Charan, the son of his brother Nand Kumar. Kali Prasad, as we have already seen, took flight in order to escape arrest, and his brother, Nand Kumar, afterwards sold Aila Phuljhuri to Hafizoolah of Dacca, who, I believe, was the grand-uncle of Khajah Abdul Ghani, for Rs.21,000 on 27th Chait 1219, or 8th April 1812. Mr Hunter goes on to observe, "The strongest presumption may be formed that Kali Prasad [the Naib] was the real proprietor of the taluqs until his death, as the transfer of it in 1216 to Krishna Govind Charan Rai, the son and nephew, proves. It must, in fact, have been only a deception, he being well aware that claims would be brought against him for the balance of his unaudited accounts of 1214–15, and that it would be an easy matter to prove at that time that the original jangalburi patta was *benami*, although now, from the lapse of time and late transfer of records, as well as change of *amla*, I am much puzzled to get at the real state of the case. This is corroborated by Nand Kumar Rai, his brother's, subsequent sale of the property without explaining in his *kawala* (deed of sale) further than that the taluq is his benami, Kissen Govind Charan Rai. I have not a doubt, though I might find it difficult to prove in a court of justice, that Hafizoolah was well aware of the impending cloud over the heirs of Kali Prashad at the time he bought the taluq, as he is an inhabitant of Dacca, and a landholder and *mahajan* in that zilla."

Mr Hunter's object in writing this report was to make Hafizoolah, as owner of Aila Phuljhuri, responsible for the amount which might be decreed against the Naib's heirs in a suit which Government had brought against them for embezzlement, and which was valued at upwards of Rs.70,000. I do not know what steps were taken on this letter, but it is curious that no attempt appears to have been made by Government to impeach the original patta on the ground of fraud. Hafizoolah afterwards granted three anas of the land to Mir Gholam Imam of Shaistábád, and the estate is now held by Khajah Ahsanoolah and the Mirs of Shaistábád. It is a very large and valuable property, and is said to yield Khajah Ahsanoolah a profit of about one lac of rupees. The question in the suit between Government and the proprietors turned on the construction of the boundaries stated in the patta of Ram Dhan Chattarji. These consisted of rivers, and it was not easy to say what was meant by the terms used. The litigation began as early as 1830. In the latter stages of the proceedings the Government abandoned all claim to the resumption of Phuljhuri, as the boundaries given of it in the patta were precise and indisputable. The contest thus became confined to Aila Tearkháli, and the great question about it was the determination of the western boundary. Khajah Abdul Ghani claimed under his patta not only Phuljhuri and Aila Tearkháli, but also three *chucks* or plots called Dhallooa, Bargona, and Naltona, and which lay to the south of Phuljhuri and Aila. His contention was that his boundary went down to the sea. He instituted a suit for the recovery of the possession of these three southern chucks in 1857. Afterwards, in 1860, he was dispossessed from chucks Aila and Phuljhuri by Mr Reilly, the Commissioner of the Sundarbans, who resumed them, and whose proceedings were confirmed by the Commissioner of Nạdiya in the following year. After the resumption, Mr Reilly made a settlement with the ryots, and appointed the Messrs Morrell tahsildars or collectors on a commission of twenty-five per cent. Khajah Abdul Ghani then instituted a suit for the recovery of possession of Aila and Phuljhuri, and this suit and that instituted in 1857 were tried together, as both were based on Ram Dhan Chattarji's patta. The suit for the three southern chucks was dismissed by the High Court, and that for the Aila and Phuljhuri chucks decreed, and these orders were upheld on appeal to the Privy Council. Afterwards, Khajah Abdul Ghani instituted a suit for recovery of mesne profits, and this was compromised in May 1871 by Government's paying him the sum of Rs.272,348. In addition to this I believe that Khajah Abdul Ghani indirectly profited by his dispossession, owing to the howaladars and other under-tenure holders on the estate giving him an increase of rent on his recovering possession, and I believe that the increase was given in the shape of an extra rupee of rent on each kani of land held by them. This was given by them in acknowledgment of Khajah Abdul Ghani's services in fighting their and his battle in the courts, for thirteen years, in India and in England; for when he was dispossessed the under-tenure holders were dispossessed also, the settlement being made by the revenue authorities with the *karsadars* or simple cultivators. When therefore Khajah Abdul Ghani was restored to possession, the under-tenure holders were restored also, and that without their having borne the expense of the litigation.

Khajah Abdul Ghani, or rather his son, Ahsanoolah, in whose name the property is now entered, has a cutchery at Phuljhuri, which is a bazár, and is also the seat of a police outpost, subordinate to the station at Gúlsakhâli. Phuljhuri is a place of some trade, as sundari wood is brought there for sale. It is reputed to be the place where the first clearing in the Bákarganj Sundarbans was effected. There is no doubt that the grant of the Aila Phuljhuri lease to Ram Dhan Chattarji was most improvident, and deprived Government of a very large revenue. It may be thought that it at least had the good effect of encouraging cultivation, and that the public have been in this way indemnified in some degree for the loss of revenue. However, whatever has been the result in subsequent years, it appears that the grant did not for a long time give an impetus to cultivation, but rather was a hindrance to it. The very magnitude of the grant prevented cultivation, for there was too much land to be managed by one lessee, and the vagueness of the boundaries, &c., deterred other cultivators from settling in the neighbourhood. It is true Aila Phuljhuri is well cultivated now, but so also is Ramna-Bamna, which pays a considerable revenue to Government. On 16th December 1818 Mr Hunter reports that "the two mozahs, or, more properly, girds of Aila Tearkháli and Phuljhuri are almost entirely jungle. A portion of Phuljhuri is at present in a state of cultivation, the produce of which would, even now, admit of an increase of revenue in a quadruple proportion, and the cultivation is at present being extended. Aila Tearkháli is so extensive that it occupied me more than a tide to pass it on the east side; if it were all cultivated, which I have reason to suppose it capable of being, the revenue derivable from it would be very considerable; but at present no person will commence on the cultivation while the pattadar holds it along with Phuljhuri, from the fear of being dispossessed by him." In a letter written one day previously, Mr Hunter had said that he had visited Ramna-Bamna, and had found only a very small portion of it under cultivation. On 20th December 1822 Mr Phillips writes, that if the whole tract of Aila Phuljhuri were brought into cultivation it might yield Rs.25,000. The revenue received by Government for it is Rs.372-4, this being the equivalent in Government rupees of the Rs.349 sicca. There is a market at Aila, and endeavours have lately been made to establish a *mela* or fair.

4. SELÍMÁBÁD.

This is a very large pargana. It comprises most of the land in the west central part of the district, and even extends across the Baleshwar into the Baghahát subdivision of the Jessore district. According to Professor Blochmann, this pargana was originally called Sulaimánabád, after Sulaiman Shah of Bengal, and he suggests that the name may have been changed to Selímábád in honour of Akbar's son, Prince Selim, afterwards known as Emperor Jahángír. I have, however, never seen it designated by any other name than Selímábád. It belonged to sarkár Fathábád.

Its history is given by Mr Collector Thompson in a report to the Board, dated 28th December 1793. He states that the whole pargana was taken possession of by Aga Bákar at the time he was *wadadar* or farmer of it. In 1156 B.S. the dispossessed proprietors complained to the Subah, and were restored to 4½ anas of it. This 4½ anas were some time afterwards divided into ten shares. Aga Bákar remained in possession of 11½ anas till 1160 B.S., when he was put to death for rebellion, and Rajah Raj Ballab was appointed to attach his property. Rajah Raj Ballab managed to retain possession of the 11½ anas up to 1164 B.S., when Sheo Narain, a son of Jai Narain, one of the original proprietors, recovered the estate in the time of Mr Verelst. Sheo Narain was assisted by the influence of Gokal Chandra Ghosal, Dewan of the Provincial Council of Chittagong, to whom, as a reward for his services, Sheo Narain gave half of the recovered property—*i.e.*, 5 anas 15 gondas. This share was entered in the name of Bhowani Charan, which is said to have been the esoteric or astrological name of Gokal Ghosal (Massie, 12th April A.D. 1798), and the 11½ anas were held by him and Sheo Narain jointly till 1179 B.S., when at their request a partition was made by Mr Barwell, who was then Chief of Dacca. A copy of the partition papers, dated 1180 B.S., exists in the Bákarganj Collectorate. In Grant's "Analysis," Selímábád is described as belonging to Jai Narain, Bhowani Charan, and others in 1170 B.S., and as consisting of four zamindaries bearing a revenue of Rs.40,190. On 14th January 1791 Mr Douglas refers to the decline in the assets of the pargana, and states that this was chiefly owing to the misconduct of Bhowani

Charan, who used to live in Calcutta and let the office of his agent or land-steward to the highest bidder. Thus there had been as many as four *gomastas* or agents in one year. Gokal Ghosal, as I find from an elaborate report of Mr Money, dated 2d September 1847, died in 1779, or 1186 B.S., and ten years afterwards—namely, on 6th July 1789—his share was sold for a private debt under a decree of court, and bought by Kashi Nath Chaudhari for Rs.29,100. Kashi Nath, however, was merely the ostensible purchaser, the real buyers being the Ghosal family. A few years before this, Sheo Narain had fallen into arrears, and one-half of his share, or 2 anas 17½ gandas, was bought by Jai Narain Ghosal in the name of his son, Kali Sankhar. This was in 1189 B.S. In 1796 Kashi Nath's share was sold by a decree of the Supreme Court to Rajah Raj Kissen, and ten years afterwards his son, Noba Kissen, resold it to Kali Sankhar Ghosal. Thus the Ghosal family became possessed of 8 anas 12½ gandas 2 krants of the whole pargana—namely, 5 anas 15 gandas, and 2 anas 17 gandas 2 krants—and these shares they still retain. They reside at Bhukoilas, near Calcutta, and have enjoyed the title of Rajah from the time of Kali Sankhar Ghosal, who was made a Rajah and a Bahadur in 1825 (Government letter, 15th July 1825). The Ghosal family were famous for many years for the excellent way in which they kept their accounts, and for the quietness with which they managed their zamindari. They never were in the criminal court, and they collected their rents chiefly through the Collector's office (Act 10 of 1859). They are still reported to be easy landlords, but dissensions have broken out among them, and their affairs are now in the hands of a receiver. One of their ancestors, I believe, left a will, or made some other arrangement to prevent that subdivision of property among heirs which has pulverised so many large estates. Their head cutchery or office is at Jhalukátti, about twelve miles west of Barisál. Rajah Satya Charan Ghosal built three houses there, laid out some gardens, and made some roads through and near the bazár. It was in consequence, I presume, of these improvements that Jhalukátti, which literally means the clearing of the fisherman, received the more dignified appellation of Maharajganj. Jhalukátti is one of the largest marts in the district, and is the seat of most of the wood trade.

The descendants of Jai Narain live at Raikátti, in thana Perozpúr, about four miles from the subdivisional headquarters. The name Raikátti means literally the clearing of the Raies, and points to a time when the country was covered with jungle. According to tradition, one Satrujit Rai, an inhabitant of Deganga, near Calcutta, was the founder of the family. The goddess Sidheshwari is said to have appeared to him in a dream and directed him to proceed to Selímábád and settle there. The family is one of the oldest in the district, and there is a Sanskrit inscription on a temple of Kali at Raikátti to the effect that the idol was set up by Radu Narain Rai in 1050 B.S., that the temple for it was erected in 1144 B.S., and that Jai Narain Rai inaugurated it on 30th Paus 1162 B.S.

Selímábád was at one time a chief seat of salt manufacture, and on this account much of it lay waste. In the Ninth Report of the Committee of the House of Commons, dated 25th June 1783, it is stated that an Armenian merchant, named Khaja Kaworke, had the salt farm of Selímábád in 1773. In 1774 Mr Barwell, the Chief of Dacca, held the salt estates of Selímábád.

He relet them to Khaja Kaworke in consideration of a present; for this he was censured by the Court of Directors. The collections of Selímábád gave the Government officers much trouble for many years. On 20th June 1792 the Governor-General ordered the whole zamindari to be held khas—*i.e.*, to be managed directly by Government officers. The arrears of land revenue were borne on the books of the Dacca Collectorate for a long time, and were even transferred to Bákarganj when it was made a district in 1817. Thirty years afterwards Mr Money wrote a long report about them, and suggested that they should be realised from the Ghosal family.

The present revenue of Selímábád is Rs.98,227, of which Rs.59,982-2-6½ are paid by the Ghosal family. The remainder is divided among fourteen sets of shareholders, some of whom reside in Jessore. The Ghosals are Bráhmans and the Raies of Raikátti are Kayasts, and among the most respectable of that caste. The most prominent members of the Raikátti family are Raj Kumar Rai, and the two brothers Madhab Narain and Nar Narain. Madhab Narain is a gentleman of considerable ability, and is possessed of a good estate, though I believe he does not hold a bigha of land in his own name. Nar Narain has distinguished himself as an author, and as the supporter of an Anglo-vernacular school at Raikátti. His wife also has published some poems. Nowhere is the benami principle carried out further than at Raikátti, nearly all of the shareholders holding their lands in the names of their servants and relatives. This is owing to most of them being in debt. Among the principal taluqdars in Selímábád are Prosunno Kumar Sein of Kirttipásha, near Jhalukátti, who is also a small shareholder in the pargana; the Mahullanavises of Basanda, where they have a large school; the Biswases of Jalabari, and the Datts of Amrajhuri. Prosunno Kumar Sein's ancestor was the Dewan or Naib of Satrujit Rai, and the Mahullanavises were formerly servants of his family. Most of Selímábád is now highly cultivated, and produces much rice, supari, and pán. It lies chiefly in thanas Jhalukátti, Surapkátti, and Perozpúr. One of the most important places in it is Banaripara, which, with the neighbouring villages of Gabha, &c., is inhabited by numbers of Kulin Kayasts, such as the Thakurtas, the Guhas, &c. The land measure in general use is the bigha. The nal is small, being only five cubits, but these cubits are more than eighteen inches long, for the nal is equal to eight feet seven and a half inches. Twenty nals by twenty make one bigha, which is equal to about two bighas and one katha of the standard bigha measurement. The same measurement appears to be in use in Arangpúr, Kotwalipara, and Telihati.

5. Tappa Havili Selímábád.

This is a small pargana, lying chiefly in thana Nalchiti, and has evidently been formed out of pargana Selímábád. The word *havili* implies that the tract was the stipendiary or demesne land of the zamindar—that is, it was the land appropriated to his own use. It thus corresponds to the word *nankar*, which literally means bread-making. It is a peculiarity of this pargana that it consists of seven anas instead of sixteen. The other nine anas have been included in Selímábád, as is shown by the partition papers of 1180 B.S., already referred to. Four anas out of the seven belong to Khajah Ahsanoolah, and the remainder to the Panabalia Chaudharies and others. Panabalia is a little below Nalchiti, and was formerly the headquarters of the zamindar of the pargana. The Sugandha or Sunda river is said to have flowed past it in old times, and hence a village in the neighbourhood bears the name of Sundarkúl or shore of the Sunda. There is an ancient image of Siva at Shamrail, near Panabalia, and it is fabled that Bhagabati's finger fell here. The Panabalia Chaudharies belong to an old Baidya family, but they are now in impoverished circumstances, and, moreover, the different members are at enmity with one another. The pargana of Syedpúr is said to have been formerly included in Havili Selímábád, and to have been separated from it through the influence of Bhagirath Singh, who was a kanungo. Gupta Chaudhari was the first zamindar. His son Ram Bhadra Rai is said to have fought with the Mahrattas or Bargis, and to have defeated them near Panabalia. Curiously enough there is an entry in Mr Long's Selections under date 1748, that the city of Dacca was much alarmed on account of the approach of the Mahrattas, who were coming by the Sundarbans, and had advanced as far as Sundarkúl.

6. Tappa Havili.

This small pargana appears also to have been formed out of Selímábád. Its lands lie, I believe, in thanas Nalchiti and Bákarganj. It is divided into two shares, a ten-ana and a six-ana. The ten-ana share is possessed by Asmat Ali Khan and Fazal Ali Khan of Charamadi, and by the Ghoses of Bakai; also by the Bosus of Bamrail. The six-ana share belongs to the Charamadi family above noted, and to some Bráhmans of Pinglakátti, in Gournadi thana.

7. Idilpúr.

Professor Blochmann states that the real name of this pargana is Adilpúr, from *adil*, "just." It is one of the four parganas originally included in sarkár Bákla. In Grant it is described as having belonged in 1170 B.S. (1764) to one Ram Ballab, as situated at the confluence of the Ganges and Meghna, and as consisting of three zamindaries and eight mahals. The revenue was Rs.106,270. Perhaps no pargana gave more trouble to the early collectors than Idilpúr. The Chaudharies of Idilpúr, as they were called, were Hindus of the Kayast caste, and did not bear a good character, as they were accused of harbouring dacoits. Doubtless the jungly condition of the pargana encouraged bad characters to resort to it.

On 23d June 1795, Mr Armstrong writes: "In the Bengal year 1184, during the existence of the Provincial Councils of Revenue, the settlement of Idilpúr was adjusted and jama fixed at Rs.83,506. Some animosities, however, taking place, the proprietors tendered up a *darkhast* to the Council, requesting their estate might be divided. An amín was accordingly deputed, the estate divided, and they entered into separate engagements for the payment of their revenue at the rate of Rs.81,115, on which terms they continued holding it until the year 1188, when, declining it, it was given in farm to Manik Bosu for seven years. In 1195 it was held khas and fell in balance Rs.30,541. In 1196 the assessment was reduced to Rs.80,000, and the Chaudharies again undertook the management of it, but finding it was not equal to the payment of such a high revenue, relinquished it at the close of the year. In

1197 it was accordingly held khas, when the collections did not exceed Rs.63,346, out of which the sezawal's salary (Rs.2640) and the zamindar's mashahara (Rs.5936) being deducted, the net collections appear to be Rs.54,769. In the year following the taluqdars were separated at Rs.13,547-2-13 (which the zamindars assert was only half what they used to pay before), which being deducted from what the estate yielded the preceding year (Rs.63,346), the remainder is Rs.49,798-13." The Chaudharies did not accept the terms offered to them at the Decennial Settlement, and afterwards, when the estate was sold for arrears of revenue, they made this a ground of appeal. The pargana was held khas at various times, but this did not much mend matters. There is a long report on the pargana by Mr Armstrong, dated 9th February 1797. He ascribes the balances to encroachment of the river (the pargana lies chiefly in the Mendiganj thana, on the west bank of the Meghna), contumacy of the Chaudharies, and interference of the Civil Court. Another reason, probably more powerful than any other, was that many chars had formed in the Meghna, and that the ryots had deserted the mainland for them. "The land of the pargana is high, and as there are few khâls in it, the soil is no longer fertile." I think it proper to observe here that it is precisely the highest and most valuable lands which suffer most from river action in Bákarganj. *A priori* it might be supposed that the low lands would suffer most, but this is not so; for the evil done by the rivers is not the mere overflowing of the land, which in a rice country, and where there are so many khâls and other channels to carry off the water, is not of so much consequence, but the carrying away of the land bodily. A high bank is always the sign of diluviation, for there the stream runs deepest and strongest, and therefore cuts away the land most, while on the shallow side its force is broken by the shoals. This is well known to native boatmen, who, in towing or rowing up against the stream, always prefer the side of the river where the bank is low.

Mr Armstrong goes on to say, "The ryots of the high land pay twelve rupees a kani (1645 square yards), which seldom produces more than ten maunds of grain, and the land takes much trouble to cultivate, not only from its being a hard soil, but from the prevalence of underwood and jungle. The low land, on the contrary, is easily cultivated. The first year the ryot pays nothing, the second only one rupee, the third two rupees, the fourth three rupees, and the fifth the full jama, which only amounts to four rupees per kani, which, after the third year's cultivation, always produces twenty maunds of paddy. The consequence of which has been that, instead of the pargana's being in the flourishing state of cultivation it was in in 1177 B.S. (1770), when the sezawal realised in it one lac and sixteen thousand rupees, the lands have been neglected, the ryots have deserted, and the pargana has become in many parts an impenetrable jungle, and its cultivation reduced to one-eighth. . . .

"The great plenty which has been felt in the pargana these last three years, and particularly in the present, has also affected the realisation of the revenue in a very great degree. Paddy that used to sell for three maunds the rupee, and then considered very cheap, now sells for eight maunds the rupee, eighty-two sicca weight. Red pepper that used before to bring two and a half, and sometimes three rupees per maund, now is so plentiful as not to pay for the expense of bringing it in, and when sold never yields more than eight or ten anas a maund. Molasses that formerly sold from four to seven rupees per maund, is now sold for one rupee, and sometimes twelve anas." In a letter of 20th December 1796, the Collector says that if the river does not take a turn, no part of Idilpúr pargana will be left in two years, and also reports that there is a plague in the pargana which carries off hundreds of the inhabitants daily.

This plague is also referred to in the letter of 9th February above quoted. Mr Armstrong writes, "The mortality has likewise been of infinite injury to the welfare of the pargana. In the house of Sarbeshwar Pal, in particular, a grain merchant, who by his trade has supported many of the poor families, seventeen lives were lost in the space of eleven days; and I make no doubt, from the account I have received, that 400 or 500 lives have already fallen a sacrifice to the plague, which is not yet subsided."

I do not know if these explanations proved satisfactory, but I am afraid that Mr Armstrong was not very successful in such matters. In another letter he writes that the sentiments expressed by the Governor-General concerning him have weighed heavy on his peace of mind, and concludes a long letter by begging the Board to have the goodness to make allowances for a mind not at ease, from the idea of having risked the censure of the Governor-General in Council as well as of the Board. He appears to have been superseded by an officer of a different stamp (Mr Massie). In 1198 B.S.—*i.e.*, at the time of the Novennial Settlement—Ram Ballab Rai, Kista Ballab Rai, and Nar Sing Rai were among the principal proprietors. In a report dated August 1797, it is stated that the pargana is subdivided into nine distinct shares, and that there are numerous partners in each of them.

The Board instituted a suit against the Chaudharies for the arrears due by them, and gained a decree. Afterwards, in July 1804, the Board ordered the Chaudharies to be put in possession of their estate, they having agreed to pay up the arrears within ten years from the beginning of 1214 B.S. Here we appear to have an instance of the authorities trying to bolster up the old families; but the experiment failed, and in 1812 the zamindari was put up to sale, and bought by Mohini Mohan Tagore, in whose family it still remains.

The revenue is Rs.65,904-4-11, but there are also 119 independent taluqs, the revenue of which is Rs.8637. The revenue of the zamindari is still paid into the Bákarganj treasury, but a considerable part of the pargana has been transferred along with the Burirhát outpost to Farídpúr. Serious affrays took place in 1815 between the auction purchaser and the old proprietors. Such contests are, or at least were, frequent in Bákarganj on the occasion of any large property's changing hands; and as a general rule, it is the *mazul* or old proprietors who are in fault, as they try by force or fraud to deprive the purchaser of his legal rights. However, it would appear from Mr Sage, the Magistrate's, letter of 23d September 1815, that in the case of Idilpúr the auction purchaser was to blame. The Naib of Mohini Mohan Thakur found that some lands claimed by the Nawab of Dacca as a jaghir had been let to the taluqdars, and he tried to get hold of them. An affray, in which a man was killed, took place on 8th September 1815. At that time the pargana was under the district known by the name of the City of Daccà; and it was on account of such affrays, and of the difficulty of managing the pargana from a place so distant, that it was transferred to the Bákarganj magistracy.

The portion of Idilpúr which remains in Bákarganj lies chiefly, if not entirely, in the Mendiganj thana. It is a well-wooded pargana, and the land is high and well adapted for riding over. It suffers from the want of khâls, and there are as yet no made roads in it. The whole pargana being in the hands of one zamindar, he, or rather his agents (for he himself is an absentee) have considerable power, and the ryots are not forward with complaints. The thana is at present at Patarhát, although it has been proposed to remove it to Allyganj. There are a rural registrar's office and a bazár in Patarhát. The best *kós* boats are made in thana Mendiganj, near a place called Debaikháli. There is a large betel-nut cultivation in the pargana, and it also produces a few oranges. It was in Idilpúr that the copperplate inscription elsewhere referred to was discovered. There are some old villages in the pargana, and indications of forts and battles. There are many Bráhman families in Idilpúr.

8. Tappa Nazirpúr.

This pargana is described in one document as a tappa dependent on pargana Kasimnagar, sarkár Bazuha. Mr Douglas, on 27th May 1790, reported that there were thirteen claimants to this pargana—namely, the widow and legitimate son of Imamuddin, the late proprietor, and eleven illegitimate sons. It appears to have been held khas for several years.

Tappa Nazirpúr is somewhat scattered, part of it being in Gournadi and part in the south and east of the district. This pargana or tappa is a very old one, and Professor Blochmann thinks that it is marked on the maps of De Barros and Blaev opposite the group of islands called the Don Manik Islands. I doubt, however, if this be the Bákarganj Nazirpúr, as the map seems to place it north of the city of Dacca. Char Kalmi, one of these islands, was claimed by the zamindars as part of Nazirpúr, and was afterwards settled by one of the family. Portions of Dakhin Shahbázpúr belong to Nazirpúr and to Ratandi Kalikapúr, which was formed out of it. There is a full report on the early history of Nazirpúr by Mr Massie, dated 6th December 1797. It was sold for arrears of revenue, and bought by the Tagore family in 1819. Fourteen-sixteenths were purchased then, and the remaining two-sixteenths were acquired by the Tagores by private purchase from Mr Panioty and others in 1830. The Tagore family are thus the largest zamindars in Bákarganj, as they hold two entire parganas (Idilpúr and Nazirpúr). Some interesting facts regarding Nazirpúr will be found in a Privy Council decision of March 1865 (Gopal Lal Thakur, appellant, Moore's Appeals, vol. x.) In 1704 (1111 B.S.) Syed Shamsuddin Mahomed was the zamindar; Syed Imamuddin Mahomed was his descendant, and died in 1785 (1192 B.S.) The family is now represented by Mir Mamtazuddin, who lives at Nalchira, where the old family mansion was. He is very poor, and the family has become degraded by misalliances contracted for the sake of gain, but it still enjoys some respect on account of its great antiquity. According to the family papers, Alfat Ghazi of Ghazipúr was the founder of the family. He was vizier of one of the Delhi emperors, and came to Dacca in the time of Jahangír. Possibly the old village of Uzirpúr (the city of the vizier) is named after him. His son Syed Jan obtained the zamindari and settled at Tero char, and the grandson of Syed Jan removed the family residence to Nalchira. His name was Ainuddin, and he was succeeded by Shamsuddin, who created a taluq in his own name, which was afterwords bought by Mr Gill, grandfather of Mr Brown of Barisál. The zamindari was sold in the time of Shamsuddin's son Hoseinuddin.[1]

9. RATANDI KALIKAPÚR.

This pargana was formed in 1149 B.S. by a sanad from Aliverdi Khan. The sanad, a copy of which has been filed in a recent lawsuit, states that the pargana is formed out of Nazirpúr tappa and other places, that it is to be called Ratandi Kalikapúr, and that Krishna

[1] The name of Imamuddin figures in some complaints of the Provincial Council of Dacca against the proceedings of an attorney named Peat, who settled himself at Dacca, and used the processes of the Supreme Court against the zamindars. On 18th September 1777, Mr Rous and the other members of the Provincial Council wrote to the Governor-General (Warren Hastings) as follows: "For instance, the zamindar of Nazirpúr, which pays an annual revenue of about Rs.40,000, is seized by a warrant, in order to be carried away to Calcutta, at the instant he was proceeding to his lands to take measures for discharging the revenues for which he has bound himself. Thereby he may be absent for many months, the collections will be ill-conducted during the master's absence, the revenue of the Government will fall short, and at last his pargana is sold to make good the deficiency. It will be a poor compensation to the zamindar in the end to be informed that he was unjustly arrested."

Lall Rai, the zamindar of Uttar Shahbázpúr, had been arrested in like manner.

See "Observations upon the Administration of Justice in Bengal, occasioned by some late Proceedings at Dacca."

Imamuddin's petition is printed in an appendix to Judicial Papers for 1774 (India Office Library). He says, "Char Tengra Colla, under tappa Nazirpúr, formed by the inundation of the river, is in my possession, but is contested with me by Mahomed Radák, taluqdar of pargana Bangrora," &c.

Ram, the son of Rataneshwar (who thus gave his name to the pargana), is to be the chaudhari of it. It is stipulated that the zamindar shall pay the revenue (Rs.1777), treat the ryots well, assist in suppressing evil-disposed persons, root out dacoits and thieves, encourage the cultivation of the land, keep the roads and ghâts in good order, so that the public may travel about without impediment, prevent the drinking of intoxicants, and at the end of each year file his papers signed by himself and the kanungo. The kanungo also entered into a covenant that he would be security for the zamindar and cause his attendance when required, and that if the latter absconded he would take possession of the estate and collect the revenue, &c. The descendants of Krishna Ram reside at Uzirpúr, in the Gournadi thana, and still retain a share in the zamindari. They are much reduced in circumstances, and the greater part of the pargana has passed into the hands of other persons—viz., Sarup Chandra Guha, Brindaban Chakrabarti, Chandra Nath Sein (these three have five and a half anas), Abhai Charan Nazir of the Judge's Court, &c. As I have mentioned elsewhere, the family is said to be descended from Ram Mohan Mal, a servant of one of the Chandradwip Rajahs. It is one of the four old Hindu families in the district, the other three being the Chandradwip Rajahs, the Raikátti family, and the Arangpúr and Shaistanagar zamindars (Kalaskátti).

10. Uttar Shahbázpúr.

This pargana has suffered much from diluviation, and is now of small extent. It is situated chiefly in thana Mendiganj, but there are portions of it in the island of Dakhin Shahbázpúr. It is said to derive its name from one Shahbáz Khan, a Mogul general in old times. A Shahbáz Khan Kumboo is mentioned in Stewart's "History of Bengal" as a general of Akbar, and as having been employed in the subjugation of Bengal; but Professor Blochmann informs me that the name Shahbázpúr is older than the date of this officer's expedition. The pargana is held in ten shares. The proprietors are chiefly Hindus, and Kali Nath Rai and Rashamani Chaudharine are among the principal of them. Some of the shareholders have held their lands for several generations, but most have acquired them by purchase in recent times. It is curious to find the pargana extending down into the island of Dakhin Shahbázpúr, and the explanation commonly given is that in old times the channel separating the island from the mainland to the north was much smaller than it now is. On 10th July 1794 the Collector reports that the zamindars of this pargana had not given tahút—*i.e.*, had not agreed to the settlement.

The zamindar of Uttar Shahbázpúr was one of those who suffered from the aggressions of Mr Peat, an attorney, who had been Mr Justice Hyde's clerk. Among other things, he shot a native for trying, as he said, to resist his authority. The unfortunate Provincial Council of Dacca seem to have been driven to distraction by Mr Peat and his English law, and so tried to turn the tables on him by unearthing a statute of Henry V. They remark, in a letter dated Dacca, 22d September 1777, "We take this occasion to notice a very important circumstance in the present discussion, that Mr Peat has been acting contrary to law during the whole time of his residence at Dacca, by holding a very active practice as attorney-at-law at Dacca, proved by his original letters already sent you, and at the same time acting as Deputy-Sheriff, contrary to a statute of Henry V., which enacts 'that an Under-Sheriff cannot execute that office and practise as an attorney at the same time.' . . . Mr Peat's threefold capacity—Master in Chancery, attorney, and Deputy-Sheriff—in a situation so far removed from the Supreme Court, gives him an influence and advantage in the suits he engages in, and leaves little chance of equality to the poor native against whom he may be employed."

The following paper is published in the Proceedings:

"Translation of a petition from the vakil of Lall Ram, zamindar of Uttar Shahbázpúr.

"Your petitioner, Anand Ram, vakil of Lall Ram, the Chaudhari of Uttar Shahbázpúr, represents that Bhangesh Chaudhari, partner of his constituent, having falsely charged him with plunder and devastation in the cutchery of the Supreme Court of Mr Peat, has had your petitioner's constituent, together with his gomasta, arrested and confined in the gaol. Your petitioner's constituent has never been employed by the Company, or in any English service. He is hopeful for justice."

11. Dakhin Shahbázpúr.

This pargana belonged to sarkár Khalífatábád, which was also called sarkár Fathábád. It was only annexed to Bákarganj in 1869, or rather it was reannexed in that year, for it had belonged first to Dacca Jalalpúr and then to Bákarganj up to 1822, when it was transferred to the newly-established district of Noakháli. It appears from a petition of Khajah Aratoon, forwarded on 1st October 1795, that the pargana formerly belonged to Mirza Jan, and that in 1187 B.S. (1780), seven anas of it were sold for arrears of revenue, and bought by Khajah Michael, an Armenian merchant in Dacca, and the father of Khajah Aratoon. In 1193 B.S. (1786), the remaining nine anas were sold, and were also bought by Khajah Michael; but in 1195 B.S. Mr Douglas restored 3 anas 1½ gandas 1 krant to Mirza Jan, and this share still belongs to his descendants—*i.e.*, the Mirza Sahibs of Dacca. It is separate from the 12 anas 18 gandas 1 cowrie 2 krants share. The latter is held by many proprietors, some of whom are descendants of Khajah Michael, and some of whom have obtained their shares by purchase. Among them are the Stephenses of Dacca, Mr Harney, Mr Lucas of Barisál, Mr Bagram as executor for the Gaspar family, and the Baisakhs of Dacca. All the zamindars of Dakhin Shahbázpúr are absentees, and there is hardly a *pakka*-house on the island. According to tradition, the first zamindars of Dakhin Shahbázpúr were Aman Ula Sikdar, Bijai Narain Mozamdar of Bhulua, and four other persons from Dacca. The villages of Amani and Bijaipúr are called after the two first-named individuals, and the zamindari cutcheries of several of the shareholders are still at Amani, which is a few miles from Daulat Khan. Before this time the island seems to have been held by the Arracanese, and by the famous Portuguese pirate Gonzales, who had a fort on the neighbouring island of Sandwip. Aman Ula and his party did not pay the revenue, and so the pargana was made over to a faquir named Abu Syed, who took it in the name of one of his wives, Sartaz Bibi.

Abu Syed and his dewan Krishna Ram Chakrabarti, who came from Srírámpúr in Bákarganj, succeeded in cultivating the island by letting out portions to howaladars and others on permanent tenures, as no one would undertake the clearing of the jungle on other terms.

Mirza Jan, or Mirza Ahmed Jan, was Sartaz Bibi's grandson, and it seems that it was the disputes between him and his stepbrother, Khuda Baksh, which led to the sale of the larger share of the property, and its purchase by Khajah Michael. In Grant, Dakhin Shahbázpúr is entered as having belonged in 1165 (1759) to one Bushan Ula, to whom also the old pargana of Srírámpúr appears to have belonged.

The revenue of Dakhin Shahbázpúr is now upwards of Rs.44,000, but it was formerly greater, being Rs.54,000 (sicca) at the time of the Permanent Settlement. A deduction of Rs.12,208 (sicca) was allowed as *khalari* suspension—*i.e.*, as compensation for land occupied by the salt manufacture. In a statement of the Board of Revenue, 8th May 1808,[1] this deduction is divided as follows among the two shares in the pargana :—

	a.	g.	k.	Revenue.			Khalari Suspension.		
Khajah Aratoon's share	12	18	1	Rs.43,487	4	15	Rs.9858	10	10
Mirza Jan's share .	3	1	3	10,358	12	15	2349	5	10

There were then two salt agencies, one at Rai Mangal, which appears to have been the same place as Jhalukátti, and another at Bhulua (Noakháli). The Dakhin Shahbázpúr manufacture belonged to the latter agency. Khajah Michael and Khajah Kaworke were at one time the lessees of the salt-farm, and we find a reference to Dakhin Shahbázpúr in the Ninth Report of the Committee of the House of Commons. The place was then known under the not infelicitous corruption of Savagepore; and the notorious Mr Richard Barwell, the Chief of Dacca, had the salt-farm in 1774, he having engaged for it, as he said, "in the persuasion of its being a very profitable farm." It seems that Mr Barwell held the lease both of the Selímábád and the Shahbázpúr salt-farms, and that he relet them to two Armenian merchants, Michael and Kaworke, on condition of their paying him Rs.125,000, exclusive of their engagement to the Company. Mr Barwell's engagement with them was benami—*i.e.*, it was in the names of Basant Rai and Kissen Deb Sing, as it was not thought consistent with the public regulations that the names of any Europeans should appear. Khajah Kaworke complained that after Mr Barwell had let him the farms, and taken a lac and Rs.25,000 from him on this account, he dispossessed him, and relet the farms to another person for another lac of rupees. When Mr Barwell was first called upon to explain his transactions with these Armenians, he candidly confessed that the salt-farms of Selímábád and Savagepore had been taken by him, and bursting into a fine train of sentiment, he exclaims, "If I am mistaken in my reasoning, and the wish to add to my fortune has warped my judgment in a transaction that may appear to the Board [of Directors] in a light different to what I view it in, it is past; I cannot recall it, and I rather choose to admit an error than deny a fact." In another letter he said, "To the honourable Court of Directors I will submit all my rights in the salt contracts I engaged in; and if in their opinion those rights vest in the Company, I will account to them for the last shilling I have received from such contracts, my intentions being upright; and as I never did wish to profit myself to the prejudice of my employers, by their judgment I will be implicitly directed."

Upon these expressions of Mr Barwell the Committee caustically observe, that "the extraordinary caution, and the intricate contrivances with which his share in this transaction is wrapped up, form a sufficient proof that he was not altogether misled in his judgment; and though there might be some merit in acknowledging an error before it was discovered, there could be very little in a confession produced by previous detection." The Board of Directors ordered a prosecution, but it never took place. Meanwhile, Mr Barwell withdrew from his offer to abide by the judgment of the Directors, though he still indulged in a fine flow of sentiment, but in a new vein. His compliance (with the demands made on him) would be urged as a confession of delinquency, and as proceeding from conviction of his having usurped on the rights of the Company. Rather than do this, he resolved "to appeal to the laws of his country in order to vindicate his fame." Like draws to like, and it seems that Sir Elijah Impey became the guardian of Mr Barwell's children, and was the trustee for his affairs.

When the manufacture of salt in Dakhin Shahbázpúr was discontinued, it was proposed that the Rs.12,000 of khalari suspensions should be readded to the revenue at the zamindari, but the proposal was negatived at the instance of Mr Ricketts, who was then Commissioner of Chittagong, and who pointed out that the zamindars had suffered much by diluviation. In fact, the pargana is by no means very profitable to the zamindars. Much of the land has been washed away by the Meghna, and though there have been many re-formations, these were for the most part resumed by Government as island chars. At that time the law of re-formation on the old site, as since expounded by the Privy Council, was not understood. Some lands also appear to have been resumed by the Sundarban Commissioners in rather an arbitrary manner. For instance, the island of Manpúra was taken possession of by them, though it is entered in the papers of the partition of the pargana which was made before the Permanent Settlement. Only a small part of the island of Dakhin Shahbázpúr now belongs to the pargana of that name, and the south of the island consists mostly of chars resumed by Government. The most valuable interests in the land are held by the howaladars and other middlemen, and the zamindars have not been able generally to enhance their rents. On the other hand, most, if not all, the shareholders in the zamindari have also subordinate holdings in it, and are their own and their co-sharers' taluqdars, howaladars, &c., and probably these are among the most valuable of their rights in the pargana. It seems that formerly Dakhin Shahbázpúr pargana was bounded on the west by a large river called the Betua; that west of this river were the lands of Ratandi Kalikapúr, Uttar Shahbázpúr, Shaistanagar, and Baikanthpúr, &c.; and that west of them was the Ilsa or Títulia, which was then a small river. Now the Betua has been dried up, and much of the land in the centre of the island is situated in its old bed, and was resumed by Government, while the Títulia has become a very large river. The river between Hattia and Dakhin Shahbázpúr was also small in old times, and there is still a small portion of Dakhin Shahbázpúr pargana in Hattia. It is, I believe, a taluq, and bears a Portuguese name (das Anjos ?), so that it seems to be a reminiscence of the days when the Portuguese of Chittagong had possessions in these parts. There are no descendants of the Portuguese now in Dakhin Shahbázpúr, though there were a few till lately in the island of Hattia.

The zamindar of Dakhin Shahbázpúr, who then, I presume, resided at Dacca, is mentioned by Mr Mill as one of the victims of the usurpations of the old Supreme Court, his house having been broken open, and even the apartments of his women rudely violated, on pretence that he had been arrested and afterwards rescued.

The large or *shahi* kani is in use in this pargana. It is four times the size of the ordinary kani, and is equal to 19⅛ bighas.

Some copies of the partition effected in 1188 B.S. (1781) are in the Collectorate record-room. They bear the signature of Mr Day, who was formerly Collector of Dacca.

The book in the India Library, already quoted, contains some correspondence about Dakhin Shahbázpúr. One case is that of Sarup Chand Khazanchi. He, it seems, had been imprisoned by the Provincial Council for not paying the revenue of the pargana, and had sued out his Habeas Corpus in the Supreme Court. In a petition by him, included in the Proceedings of the Dacca Provincial Council, 18th August 1777, he says, "At the time of the Committee's *bandobast*, my father, Nitai Anand Dás Khazanchi, was security for the pargana of Dakhin Shahbázpúr; and I, to the year 1182, borrowed money and discharged the Government revenue," &c. In Chait 1183 Mr Purling demanded the balance to the end of the year, and confined his gomasta. The zamindars objected, alleging "the plunder and oppression by the invasion of the Mugs." Sarup Chand was released by the Supreme Court. In his examination before the Supreme Court he mentioned that several gentlemen of the Provincial Council were privately indebted to him in large sums. The case seems to have excited a good deal of attention, and Mr Justice Le Maistre recorded a long judgment on it.

A more important case, however, probably was that mentioned above of the zamindar of Dakhin Shahbázpúr. The papers are in the volume above quoted.

The zamindar was Mirza Jan, and he was sued by one Elias Abraham. A bailiff of the Supreme Court came to arrest him, and in trying to do so a tumult took place, and a slave-girl was wounded with a sword. This occurred on 1st February 1779.

I may note here that in the list of members of the Provincial Council, given in General Appendix No. 30 of the above-mentioned volume, the name of W. M. Thackeray[1] (father of the novelist?) appears as third member of the Dacca Council. His pay was Rs.500 (sicca) a month, exclusive apparently of the allowances according to the rank he would have held in Calcutta —viz., a senior or junior merchant, factor, or writer.

In Appendix No. 36 of the same volume a list of the

[1] If this be the father of the novelist, then he is probably the person who was the Company's Resident at Sylhet, and who was severely censured by the Court of Directors. It seems that he had taken under a fictitious name an elephant-farm in Sylhet, and that he had supplied elephants which were in such bad condition that only sixteen out of sixty-six arrived at their destination. The elephants had previously been passed by the Patna Council, and the Company applied to Mr Thackeray to know how this had been done; but he refused to tell, because, having given his word and honour that he would not divulge particulars, "he would be breaking his promise, forfeit the character of a man of principle and honour, and suffer in the opinion of his friends." The Directors observed that "these reasons appear to us very extraordinary when urged by a man whose duplicity has just been manifested, who had, to use the Governor-General's words, been convicted of having secretly obtained the farm of Sylhet under fictitious titles, and punished for that offence; nor are we able to reconcile the Governor-General's tenderness for Mr Thackeray's honour and delicacy with his own further declaration that from the above transaction Mr Thackeray had been unanimously and justly condemned." Mr Thackeray appears to have sued the Company in connection with these transactions, and he got a decree in the Supreme Court for Rs.29,600 and costs. Warren Hastings and Mr Barwell allowed the case to be decreed *ex parte*, and General Clavering is quoted in the Court of Directors' letter as having said that the cause was lost by "a most shameless desertion" on the part of the defendants. See India Papers, vol. i. 1787, and also vol. i. of Appendix to Parliamentary Proceedings against Warren Hastings, p. 175. The Court's letter is dated 28th November 1777.

zamindaries of the Dacca division and their revenues for the year 1777-78, &c., is given.

12. Tappa Kistodebpúr.

This tappa is situated on the west side of the island of Dakhin Shahbázpúr, about half way from its north and south extremities. It is said to have been formed out of Uttar Shahbázpúr, and to be named after a Bráhman called Kista Deb Bidyabagish, who got a sanad for it through the influence of Rajah Ganga Govind Sing, in whose house he was a pandit. The revenue is only Rs.816, but the pargana has so increased by alluviation that it now contains more than a lac of bighas. It is at present under partition, and has been so for many years. Part of it has been sold to the Shahs of Baliatti, and the Bráhman descendants of the original owner have made over the remainder in *patni* to a Mymensing zamindar. The estate is highly cultivated, but it is full of under-tenures, so that the profit to the zamindar is less than might be expected.

13. Tappa Alinagar.

This is another tappa of Uttar Shahbázpúr. It is situated in the northern part of the island of Dakhin Shahbázpúr, and belongs to Mr John Courjon. The revenue is only Rs.1578, but the collections from the ryots amount to about Rs.14,000.

14. Pargana Ramnagar.

This was once the property of Rajah Raj Ballab. It also was formed out of Uttar Shahbázpúr. Balia and Gangapúr belong to it, and it is now chiefly owned by a Dacca family, the Koulipara zamindars. They have twelve anas, and the Madhabpásha zamindars, who are descended from Ram Manik Mudi, hold the other four anas.

15. Taraf Ram Hari Char.

This consists of one taluq called Dordana Khanam. It was created by Mr Henckell in 1785 under the same conditions as char Kalmi, and was granted in favour of Dordana Khanam, which was another name of Etimonissa. The amount of land conveyed was 313 bighas; and the taluq was composed of chars Patti, Maya, and Nangla, the last two of which, at all events, are a little to the north of char Kalmi. The history of this taluq is given in Mr Fortescue's report of 9th May 1806. See also the Board's reply of the 16th idem.

16. Kalmi Char and Taraf.

Char Kalmi is an island in the estuary of the Meghna. It was originally let on a jangalburi tenure by Mr Tilman Henckell in 1192 B.S. (1785) to Baidya Nath Sein and others, who, it appears, were merely bēnamidars for Serajuddin, the son of Syed Imamuddin, zamindar of Nazirpúr. The conditions of the lease were that no rent was to be paid for three years; that the rate was to be two anas a bigha for the fourth year, four anas for the fifth, six anas for the sixth, and eight anas for the seventh. This last rate was to be perpetual. The agreement was for 245 bighas, and a deduction of one-ninth, or of 200 bighas out of 1200, was allowed for *malikana*, &c. There is an unauthenticated copy of the original lease in the Collectorate. Mr Henckell granted this and other leases as Superintendent of the Sundarbans. He was Collector of Jessore, and figures largely in Mr Westland's account of that district. Mr Westland has chronicled Mr Henckell's disputes with the Salt Department, and his endeavours to prevent their oppression, and it is pleasant to quote in this connection a newspaper extract of 24th April 1788, published at page 253 of Seton-Karr's Selections, which in all probability refers to Mr Henckell. "It is a fact," says the newspaper, "that the conduct of Mr H—— in the Sundarbans has been so exemplary and mild towards the poor *molunghies* or salt manufacturers, that, to express their gratitude, they have made a representation of his figure or image, which they worship among themselves. A strong proof that the natives of this country are sensible of kind treatment, and easily governed without coercive measures." Mr Hunter, the first Collector of Bákarganj, visited char Kalmi in 1818 or 1819. He found one Matioolah in possession of the greater part of the island as *ausat* taluqdar under Etimonissa, who was the widow of Serajuddin. Under the Board's orders he made the settlement with Etimonissa at a rent of Rs.1731-4 (sicca), being at the rate of eight anas a bigha on the land then in cultivation, after deduction of 16¼ per cent. (see Mr Hunter's letters of 25th May and 31st July 1818, of 17th March and 12th June 1819, and the Board's letter of 6th April 1819). This rent still holds good, the difference between it and the present amount (Rs.1846) being caused by the conversion of sicca into Government rupees. The island is now held by Imdad Ali Munshi, who resides on it, and a Ghose family resident in the Twenty-four Parganas. The former holds seven and the latter nine anas. I visited the island in the end of 1874, and found it well cultivated, though rice was almost the only product. The survey area is about 3300 acres. There are about 635 inhabitants, all of whom are Mahomedans except one or two Hindu washermen and barbers.

Kalmi taraf is marked on the survey map as a distinct char, but it seems now to have diluviated. The river at Kalmi appears to bear the name of the Bura Gouranga. Kalmi is said to have been first cultivated by one Badan Ali Khan.

17. SULTANÁBÁD.

This pargana is chiefly situated in thana Baufal, but there are portions of it in thanas Barisál and Bákarganj. In 1797, Kalab Ali, one of the zamindars of the pargana, is described as being a lunatic. Khajah Ahsanoolah is the chief proprietor, as he holds 7 anas $10\frac{1}{2}$ gandas $1\frac{1}{2}$ krants. The oldest proprietor seems to be Syed Abdalla Chaudhari of Dacca, who is said to hold 6 anas $3\frac{1}{2}$ gandas; but this, again, is divided into six shares, which are held in various names. Meharanissa Khanam, a lady who lives in Barisál, holds 1 ana $15\frac{1}{2}$ gandas $2\frac{1}{2}$ krants. Ahsan Mir and Mir Tajammal Ali, Deputy-Magistrate, have also shares. The pargana has been undergoing partition for many years, and the division is to be into ten shares. It is said to contain a lac and thirty-six thousand bighas. A char named Sanyasi has lately accreted to the pargana, and added a new difficulty to its partition. The zamindari assets are reckoned at half a lac, and as the Government revenue is Rs.23,000, the pargana is not a very profitable one to the landholders. There are many undertenures in Sultanábád, and these are in numerous instances held by the zamindars.

18. Kasimnagar Joár Dáspára.

This is a small estate situated at the ancient village of Dáspára, and near the Baufal police station. It is registered in the name of Hamidonissa Khatun.

19. Khanja Bahadur Nagar.

This is another small estate in Baufal thana. There are lands belonging to it in the village of Govindpúr. Whether its name be connected with the famous Khanja Ali I know not. Maulavi Mahomed Fazil, formerly police inspector, holds a share in this pargana.

20. Pargana Srírámpúr.

This is an old pargana, and has been nearly all washed away by the Meghna. It belongs to the Mirza Sahebs of Dacca, the family who own a portion of Dakhin Shahbázpúr, and who have held their lands for many generations. A famous riot took place in this pargana in 1869. It is situated in the Mendiganj thana. Government holds several chars which have been resumed from this pargana. As a proof of its deterioration from diluviation and other causes, I may mention that Government has acquired, by purchase at sales for arrears of revenue, fifty-two estates in Srírámpúr, and that their total revenue is only a little over Rs.200 (227-9).

21. Tappa Abdulapúr.

This appears to have been formed out of the four and a half anas of Selímábád. Its lands chiefly lie in

Mendiganj, but there are some in Jhalukátti. It belongs to a Baidya family (Har Nath Rai and others) who reside at Japsa in the Mulfatganj or Palang thana. Their ancestor was one Gopi Raman Sein.

22. Tappa Kadirábád.

This small pargana belongs to a Bráhman family who reside in the district of Dacca, and are known as the Koulipara Banarjis. Its lands are situated in Mendiganj.

23. Tappa Azimpúr.

This is a scattered pargana, and appears to have suffered from diluviation. It is situated in thanas Gournadi, Barisál, and Bákarganj, and there is part of it also in Bikrampúr in Dacca or Farídpúr. It belongs to the Piprakátti Shamadars, a Bráhman family, who reside near Palardi, in the Gournadi thana; to the Jahapúr Datts, to Asmat Ali Khan of Charamadi, and to the Lakutia Raies. The last-named shareholders have acquired their share recently by purchase. The Collectorate register of estates being arranged alphabetically, Azimpúr is the first on the list.

24. Pargana Jahapúr.

This is an old pargana, and has been nearly all swept away by the Arial Khan. It is situated in the Mendiganj thana, on the east bank of the Dakaitia river—*i.e.*, the Arial Khan. Char Jahapúr has probably formed on the old site of lands belonging to this pargana, and it too has lately been much washed away. The pargana belongs to an old but greatly reduced Hindu family called the Jahapúr Datts.

25. Pargana Idrakpúr.

The land of this pargana appears to be *ijmali* or joint with that of Rasulpúr, there being many holdings in it of which eight anas or one-half of the rent is paid to Idrakpúr and the other half to Rasulpúr. It is situated in the northern part of the district, on both sides of the Arial Khan, in thanas Gournadi and Mendiganj. Three anas have been purchased by a family of traders called the Kundas of Lohajang, and the remainder belongs to a Dacca family, of which the present representatives appear to be Amiranissa Khatun, Abedanissa Khatun, and Karimanissa, and who have long been fighting in the civil and criminal courts. Their offices are at Sarikal and Gachua. A part of the pargana has been purchased by Nazimuddin Chaudhari of Kartikpúr. From a letter dated 10th July 1794 it appears that the pargana was bought in 1190 by one Imamuddin Chaudhari.

26. Pargana Rasulpúr.

There is no zamindari belonging to this pargana in Bákarganj. It suffered a great deal from the inundations of 1787. It appears also in old times to have suffered from mismanagement, for the Collector writes of it as follows: "The general mode of realising the revenues when the settlement was concluded with the three proprietors, was for each to appoint a Mofussil manager with equal powers. The consequences were that the ryots were constantly harassed, and frequently peons were placed on them at one time by the three managers for the same demand, thus it often happened that three rupees were extorted from the ryots when the original demand was only for one."

27. Bangrora.

This pargana is remarkable for the large number of its separated taluqs, there being nearly a thousand in it. Many of them are very small, and their lands are greatly intermixed, so that frequent disputes arise among the owners. The zamindari is registered in the name of Hayatonissa Khatun. The principal taluqdars are the Datts of Batajor, the Dasses of Goila, and the Bakshies of Barthi. The large village of Goila is situated in Bangrora, which lies in Gournadi thana in the northern part of the district. Most of the land is very fertile, but some of it is marshy. The land revenue of the taluqs is Rs.20,724-2-9.

28, 29. Pargana Birmohan and Tappa Birmohan.

These are situated in thana Gournadi. In old times Birmohan was infested with tigers, and the Collector writes in July 1790, that he had endeavoured to induce the tiger-killers to repair to it, but without success. It appears that the tigers had increased in consequence of the desertion of the pargana, and its consequent relapse into jungle, after the inundations of 1787. It belongs to a Bráhman family known as the Birmohan Chaudharies, and to the Narail family (Jessore). It is at present undergoing partition, but the work is being carried on at Farídpúr, as the pargana has been transferred to that Collectorate.

30. Habibpúr.

This pargana is in the Gournadi and Sarupkátti thanas, and belongs to Lakya Kanth Bhuia and others of Bikrampúr, and to a family of Ghoses (one of them was formerly sub-inspector of Gournadi). There are many dependent taluqdars in the pargana, and the chief profit from it is received by them.

31. Maizardi.

This is a small pargana, situated in Mendiganj. It belongs to the Mirza Sahebs of Dacca, the Srinagar zamindars, and Dinu Bandhu Chakrabarti of Tunghibari (Bikrampúr). Gholam Gafur was the original proprietor, and he still holds a small share. Maizardi has suffered much from diluviation, like all the parganas in Mendiganj. Part of it was at one time bought by Government at a sale for arrears of revenue, but most of the purchase has been resold. In March 1793 the Collector reported that Maizardi had to be held khas on account of the zamindar's refusing to engage.

32. Jalálpúr.

This pargana chiefly belongs to Farídpúr, but there are portions of it in the north of Bákarganj and in Dacca. It is remarkable for the number of its taluqs. Mr Thompson (5th February 1794) wrote that there were about 2000 in the pargana, that many of the taluqdars were in extreme distress, and that upwards of 100 of them had fled, from inability to pay their revenue dues. The pargana suffered much in the inundations of 1787.

33. SHAISTÁBÁD.

This is a small pargana formed out of Chandradwip. Syed Hassad Ali states, in a petition forwarded in February 1793, that he is the zamindar, and that the property had formerly belonged to his maternal grandfather, Mahomed Hanif Chaudhari. It once belonged to Mendi Mozamdar of Chakar, and the present Shaistábád family obtained it by marriage, their ancestor Mir Salimuddin having married Mendi Mozamdar's granddaughter. Mir Salimuddin came from Mokimpúr in the Dacca district. According to a paper given to me by Syed Mozaffar Hoosein, one of the present proprietors, Shaistábád derives its name from Shaista Khan, who was Governor of Bengal in the reign of Arangzeb. It belonged to sarkár Khalífatábád, and was included in chakla Jessore. The lands of the pargana are a good deal scattered. The zamindari residence is near Charaman, in the village of Aicha, about eight miles north-east of Barisál. Phultolla, Mírganj, and Karimganj are the chief trading-places. It is said that one Eerach Khan, a soldier or servant of the Nawab, obtained the pargana as a jaghir, and bequeathed it to his daughter Omdatanissa, also called the Bahu Begam, from her having married into the Nawab's family. She leased the pargana on a fixed rent to Mahomed Hanif Chaudhari by a sanad dated 25th Safar, 5th jalus (the chronological year cannot be deciphered). On the death of Mahomed Hanif, his widow, Amina Khatun, gave her only daughter in marriage to Mir Salimuddin, and made over the estate to their son, Mir Asad Ali, by a deed of gift dated 21st Asar 1171. Asad Ali left the estate to his three sons, Abbas Ali, Imdad Ali, and Gholam Imam. Ábbas Ali left no son, and

Gholam Imam's two sons died without issue, hence the property devolved on the four sons of Imdad Ali—viz., Mir Tajammal Ali, Mir Abdul Majid, Mir Moazzam Hoosein, and Mir Abdullah. The family are Syeds, as descended from the Prophet. The gentleman who has obliged me with the above information has given me his genealogical tree, which seems to me to be interesting, and I therefore subjoin it (see p. 159). The family is the most considerable Mahomedan one in the district, and is remarkable for the number of officers whom it has given to the public service. It holds a share in Sultanábád, and three anas of the very profitable Sundarban estate known as Aila Phuljhuri.

34. Shaistanagar.

This is a small pargana, situated chiefly in thana Bákarganj. It belongs to a Bráhman family known as the Garuria Chaudharies, to the Narail family, and to Babu Chandi Charan Rai of Barisál, and others. The Garuria Chaudharies live near Kalaskátti, and belong to the same stock as the Arangpúr zamindars. They are a very old family, but are much reduced in circumstances.[1]

35. Shahzádpúr.

This is a small pargana, situated chiefly in thana Nalchiti. The principal owner is Durga Gati Rai of Siddhakátti, though Har Nath Datt of Amrajuri and others have also shares. Durga Gati belongs to a very good family, and is what is called a Kulin Baidya. The

[1] This Shaistanagar is distinct from the Shaistanagar in Dakhin Shahbázpúr, the revenue of which is paid into the Noakháli treasury.

pargana is an old one, but the most important thing about it at present is that the Nalchiti bazár is situated within it. In a petition of 12th May 1791, Pitambar Sein of Rajnagar claims the merit of having established the Nalchiti market. He says, "Receiving pottahs for lands belonging to Shahzádpúr and other parganas, and expending a large sum of money, I erected a hát at Nalchiti." In reply, Keval Ram and his other co-sharers say, "In regard to the exclusive claim which Pitambar Sein makes to the hát Nalchiti, we have to observe that the land upon which it is erected was received by him from the parganas of Shahzádpúr and Shaistanagar in exchange for others given by him to the proprietors of those parganas from that of Buzurgumedpúr, our joint property and estate." It will be noticed that the co-sharers hereby admit Pitambar's claim to be the founder of the market. Pitambar was the son of Gopal Kissen, and grandson of Raj Ballab, as has been elsewhere stated. There is an old temple of the goddess Tara at Nalchiti, which is said to have been founded by Gopal Kissen.

36. Tappa Bahadurpúr.

This is a valuable property, situated chiefly in thana Bákarganj. It belongs to the Messrs Pogose of Dacca, who inherited it from their grandfather, Khajah Nikus.

37. Pargana Arangpúr.

This pargana was formed out of Chandradwip. Professor Blochmann supposes that it derives its name from the emperor Arangzeb, but it seems unlikely that a comparatively small and obscure pargana should have been named after him.

The pargana still belongs in part to the Bráhman family who held it at the time of the Permanent Settlement, though now there are many other shareholders. The former reside at Kaloskátti, near Bákarganj. The Shaistanagar (Garuria) and Arangpúr families were originally one, and Gopal Rai is said to have been their common founder. He obtained the zamindari of Shaistanagar, and died, leaving several sons. Among them was Janaki Ballab. He, I suppose, was the youngest, and his brothers would not give him any share of the zamindari. Though he was only eight years of age, he went to Dacca to the Nawab, and succeeded in getting pargana Arangpúr from him. It was composed of three parganas—viz., Arangpúr, Raghanathpúr, and Itmadpúr, the last being given to the boy by Itmad Khan, a servant of the Nawab. Up to a recent date the zamindari continued to be entered in Janaki Ballab's name. A large part of the south of the district is included in the pargana, and it extends down to the line of the Sundarbans. The headquarters of the Patuyakháli subdivision, and much of its jurisdiction, are included in Arangpúr. The largest shareholder in the zamindari is Boroda Kanth Rai, who is reputed to be the wealthiest man in the district. According to a story current in Bákarganj, he owes part of his wealth to the circumstance of his having been fined Rs.30,000. He had given recognisances in this amount for the preservation of the peace, and on the occurrence of a riot, in which he was considered to be implicated, his recognisances were estreated, and the Rs.30,000 levied. Boroda paid the money, but immediately lodged an appeal, and at the same time recouped himself by taking Rs.30,000 from his ryots. On appeal the fine was remitted, and so Boroda got back his money, but he did not return to the ryots what he had levied from them. A story somewhat similar to this is told of one of the Bamna chaudharies. He subscribed Rs.10,000 to the patriotic fund which was raised at the close of the Crimean war, and received the thanks of Government for so doing. Afterwards it came to light that he had not paid the money from his own coffers, but had screwed it out of the ryots. The Governor-General indignantly ordered that the money should be returned to him, but as he did not make restitution to the ryots, he made a profit of Rs.10,000. Although I narrate these stories, I must say that I think they are rather apocryphal. The second is of very dubious authenticity, for I do not think Government would be so foolish as to give back money which, according to the hypothesis, had never belonged to the ostensible donor; and as for the first, though I believe there is a foundation of truth in it, yet the fact of Boroda's having been put on Rs.30,000 recognisances implies that he was already a wealthy man. Boroda Kanth is a type of the conservative Hindu, being very strict in his religious observances, seldom or never wearing anything which has been sewn, and very chary of visiting the officials, or of subscribing to schools or dispensaries. He is remarkable as a benamidar—*i.e.*, he holds a great deal of property in other people's names. Thus all his zamindari is held in the name of his wife, Muktakeshi Debya, but this is so openly admitted by him and his agents that I can hardly think it has been done for the sake of fraud or concealment. Probably there was some notion of luck involved in it. He also holds numerous howalas and other under-tenures in Arangpúr under fictitious names. Arangpúr is divided into two shares, called the nine-ana and the seven-ana. This division was made by private arrangement in 1197 B.S. (1790), and the ryots of the two shares are still separate. Each of these shares is, however, now subdivided among many people, and a batwara or partition of them has long been going on. This partition is one of the opprobria of the Bákarganj administration, it having been commenced more than fifty years ago, not long after the passing of the Batwara Law of 1814, and not yet being finished. Owing to disputes among the proprietors the seven-ana share of Arangpúr was attached by the Civil Court many years ago, and is now managed by Mr Scott, the Sarbarakar or Manager of Attached Estates. Khajah Ahsanoolah has a share of Arangpúr, and so also have the heirs of certain Banarjis. The seven anas were once sold for arrears of revenue. Durga Prosunno Rai had a share in the zamindari, but he has now given it in patni to Boroda Kanth Rai, and I understand that Khajah Ahsanoolah has done the same thing with his share.

38. Pargana Syedpúr.

This pargana is in the south-west of the district. Ten anas of it belong to Lalla Mitrajit Singh of Dacca, and six anas to the heirs of Briju Ratan Das. It was the disturbances between them which led to the famous Singhkháli cases some twenty years ago. Bhagirath Singh, who is said to have been a kanungo, was the founder of the Singh family. The Permanent Settlement was made with one Lalla Jeyt Singh. There is a report by the Collector on the pargana, dated 27th December 1809. Syedpúr was to a large extent a Sundarban pargana, and the Government estate of Tushkháli was resumed from it, and is described as *lakt*, or adjacent to Syedpúr. The Táki Babus, as they are called, a family of Kayasts residing at Táki, in the Twenty-four Parganas, have a large *abád* or tract of country called the Debnathpúr abád in this pargana. It is held on a permanent lease, and contains about thirty thousand bighas. They had a law-suit with Government (when Tushkháli was measured and settled), and succeeded in recovering possession of some nineteen thousand bighas. The family is descended from Kachu[1] Rai, whose father was killed by Pratápáditya.

[1] The name is said to be derived from the circumstance of his having, when a child, been hidden by his nurse in some *kachu* or *arum* jungle in order to save him from his father's fate. See the "Kshitisha Bansavali Charitam" or "Chronicle of Krishnagur," Berlin, 1852. There is an analysis of this work in the Calcutta Review for December 1855.

MOHUMMUD, THE PROPHET.

FATIMA (daughter).

1. Hosein (son). — Hasan (son).
2. Syed Zainolabideen (son).
3. Syed Mohummud Baker (son).
4. Syed Mohumud Emam Jafer Sady (son).
5. Syed Sha Ahmud Bulakhy (son).
6. Syed Abulunam (son).
7. Syed Anwarol Huq Bulkhi (son).
8. Syed Addlul Huq Bulkhi (son), buried in Samarkand.
9. Syed Sha Alum Bulkhee, who afterwards died at Samarkand.
10. Syed Sha Abdul Khalaque Bulkhee, lying buried there.
11. Syed Abdul Razzak (son), of Samarkand.
12. Syed Abdul Quader (son), of Samarkand.
13. Syed Godool Huq (son).
14. Syed Shah Sultan (son).
15. Salar Samarkandi (son).
16. Quorer Samarkandi (son).
17. Shah Bukhsee (son).
18. Shah Amanuth (son).
19. Shah Zukuriah (son).
20. Shumsuddeen (son).
21. Shah Mohummed Wallee (son).
22. Shah Adam (son), Walee Scindh.
23. Mortaza (son).
24. Hasamuddeen (son), came from Scindh.
25. Shamsoddeen (son).
26. Salimuddeen Chowdhri (son).
27. Assad Ali Chowdhry (son).

Sons of Assad Ali Chowdhry:

- Syed Abbas Ali, died without issue.
- 28. Mir Emdad Ali.
- Meer Gholam Imam (left two sons, who died subsequently).

Children of Mir Emdad Ali:

- Meer Tujummol Ali.
  - Meer Tufuzzul Ahmed (son).
- Meer Abdul Mujeed.
  - Meer Abdul Hameed (son).
  - Abdul Waheed (son.)
- Meer Moazzum Hosein.
  - Meer Mozuffer Hosein (son).
  - Meer Abdur Rub (son.).
  - Meer Mohumed Hosein (son).
  - Mir Mohmood Hosein.
  - Mir Mothalin Hosein.
- Meer Abdullah.
  - Meer Mohumed Israil (son).
  - Meer Obeidullah (son).
- Three daughters.

CHAPTER V.

SUNDARBANS.

I. GENERAL DESCRIPTION.

THE different explanations of the origin of the name Sundarbans have already been given. The lands known under this name were not included in the Permanent Settlement. It was directed by Regulation 9 of 1816 that a special officer should be appointed to the charge of the Sundarbans, who should be styled Commissioner in the Sundarbans. Regulation 23 of 1817 (repealed by Regulation 2 of 1819) in its preamble describes the Sundarbans, and refers to Bákarganj and Jalálpúr.

The Sundarbans were surveyed by Lieutenant Hodges in 1830. Those belonging to Bákarganj are small in comparison with those of Jessore, or of the Twenty-four Parganas, but are much more cultivated, owing to their higher level and to the large quantity of fresh water brought in by the Meghna and Bráhmaputra. The Commissioner has his headquarters at Alipúr, near Calcutta. Most of the estates in the Sundarbans are managed by him either directly or through farmers, and the Collector of Bákarganj has no connection with them further than that their revenues are paid into his treasury. There are, however, some estates—such as Ramna-Bamna, Halta, Sonakháli, Aila Phuljhuri—which have been permanently settled, and are no longer under the control of the Commissioner. These estates are, I believe, seventy-one in number, and are arranged in the Collectorate papers according to the parganas to which they are lakt or contiguous. Their united revenue is Rs.134,098. (The seventy-one include eleven in Buzurgumedpúr and Nos. 1437 and 1447.) The estates of Ramna-Bamna and Aila Phuljhuri have been described in the account of pargana Buzurgumedpúr. Halta and Sonakháli belong to Messrs Morrell. At Schillergunge, on the banks of the Sapleza, Mr Casperz has a property of about 12,000 acres, which he has called Casperábád, and which is for the most part rent free. Dhallooa, Bargona, and Naltona lie to the south of Aila Phuljhuri. They were claimed by Khajah Abdul Ghani, but his claim was rejected by the Privy Council, and they are now under khas management. Kolaran Chandipúr is a Sundarban taluq situated in the Perozpúr subdivision, but the revenue is paid into the Jessore treasury. Its history is given by Mr Rocke in a letter to the Collector of Dacca, dated 21st August 1790. He says that in 1192 B.S. one Kanye Ghosal applied for seven chucks as a taluq. Three of them—viz., Kolaran, Chandipúr, and Baleshwar—were granted to him, and he then sold them by patta to Bijai Ram Sha (the ancestor of the Shas of Dattapara). The amount of land stated in the patta is 500 bighas. Mr Rocke mentions that Bijai Sha complained that the zamindar of Selímábád had imprisoned his son for rent.

The boundary line of the Sundarbans is irregular; and we find estates, such as Baisdia, Rangabali, Kázal, &c., which are the property of private individuals, and were so at the time of the Permanent Settlement, in the middle of the Government Sundarbans. This is especially the case in the south-east of Bákarganj, where the kharija or separated taluqs of Chandradwip extend to the seaboard. It is curious that the islands of Kúkri Múkri, or, more properly, Kukuria Mekuria—*i.e.*, Dog-and-Cat Islands—belong to the Sundarbans, while the neighbouring island of Chopa does not.

The Sundarbans proper chiefly occur in the Gúlsakháli and Perozpúr thanas. Their general aspect is that of lonely forests traversed by sullen streams. The trees are seldom allowed to grow to any great height, as they are cut down by the woodcutters, or *bawalis*, as they are called. These people go down in the cold weather to cut wood, and in spite of their taking faquirs to charm them away, are often carried off by tigers. There were formerly two sayer holdings in the Sundarbans, called Gore Katta and Takta mahals, consisting of tolls levied from the woodcutters. They were abolished by the Board's orders, 8th May 1818. The chief wood-marts are Amtolli, Gúlsakháli, Jhalukátti, Phuljhuri, Bákargânj, and Nalchiti. Charcoal is made in the Sundarbans, but in a rude way without pits. The chief supply for Europeans is brought from Moidapúr, near Nalchiti, where the Mahomedans manufacture large jars, and afterwards sell the charcoal which remains in the kilns. The Sundarbans are much used for the pasturing of buffaloes, which are swum across to Kúkri Múkri, Chopa, &c. At Dhula char, near Chapli, the wind has heaped the sand into low dunes or sand-heaps. Boats cannot track in the Sundarbans, and have to depend entirely on the tides. According to Mr Gomess, about one-half of the Bákarganj Sundarbans has been cleared. It appears from a statement of the same gentleman in the Census Report, that 276,804 square miles (177,152 acres) were cleared between 1830 and 1872.

In early times the Mugs used to commit depredations in the Sundarbans, and in Rennel's map a large tract is marked as depopulated by them. They have been in the habit of trading in betel-nut from an early date, and there is a letter of Mr Battye, dated 31st December 1812, about some Mugs who had come over from Ramu, and whom he had arrested under the idea that they were adherents of one Kiobering. They were afterwards released, and Rs.326 were paid by Government for their keep (see letters of 17th January and 11th March 1812).[1]

The Mugs at the present time occupy many parts of the Sundarbans, but there is no reason to suppose that they have been there since the time of their early depredations, and probably none of their settlements are more than seventy years old. On 24th March 1824, Thungari Mug petitioned the Board of Revenue, saying that he had brought 230 families of settlers at a great expense from Chittagong and Ramu, and that he had been dispossessed by Domingo de Silva. He added that he was a native of Arracan, and that he had abandoned his country when its monarch was dethroned, and had availed himself of the asylum offered by the British Government. He had brought over the settlers, he said, on the faith of an encouraging letter which he had received from the Collector of Dacca, dated 31st July

[1] Mr Sutherland remarks that he could not say who this Kiobering was. I have found a description of him in Mr Paton's account of Arracan, vol. xvi. of "Asiatic Researches," p. 368, where the name is given as Khyng-berring. It seems that he attempted a rebellion in the Mug era, 1173 (1811 ?). Along with other Sardars, he formed a resolution to expel the Burmese; and having collected 500 men, invaded Arracan in twenty-five boats. He was defeated by the King of Arracan, and after making various other ineffectual raids, he died in exile. According to Sir Arthur Phayre, A. S. J., vol. x. for 1841, the correct name is Khyeng-byan, literally Khyeng-return; and he was so called because he was the first-born after his father returned from the Khyeng Hills. A son of Khyeng-byan died at Akyab in 1840.

1816.[1] The Mugs now in the district state that they were driven from their country by war. It appears that they came from Arracan, which was annexed to Burmah in 1787. In 1798 30,000 Arracanese took refuge in Chittagong, and it is probable that some of them came to Chapli. The principal seat of the Mugs is at Khaprabhanga, near Chapli, in thana Gúlsakháli. They are also numerously settled at Chapli, Nishanbari, and Maudhobi. Khaprabhanga is a little further inland than the place usually visited by Europeans. When I visited it in October 1874, I found a priest and a small *kaioung* or monastic school. The Mugs are all Buddhists. They are very good clearers of jungle for a time, but seem wanting in persistent energy. During the five years I was in the district, they had made no noticeable extension of cultivation. Many, indeed, seem to have returned to Arracan, and the number and energy of those who remain are not sufficient to make much impression on the vast jungles by which they are surrounded. The number of Mugs in the district, according to the census, is 4049, of whom 2140 are men and 1909 women.

The Mugs are well spoken of by Bengalis for their truthfulness. As a general rule, they are inoffensive, though I am sorry to say that they have been losing their good reputation, and that some dacoities and other crimes have lately been committed by them. I cannot say that I have been favourably impressed by them. They are a dirty people, and have not the art of making their houses look pretty or comfortable. They only know how to clear jungle and to plant rice, and for their

[1] The Mugs at Chapli informed me that Thungari was not the first settler, and that Anju Chaudhari was the first to come. One Mirasat Chaudhari told me that Anju Chaudhari and Amparit Chaudhari were the first settlers, and that Boro Baisdia was the first settlement.

dhulat—*i.e.*, cold-weather crops—they rely upon their Mahomedan tenants and neighbours. Some Mugs settled in Kúkri Múkri, but their rice crops suffered extremely from the Sundarban rats, which are there large and numerous. The Mugs speak and write their own language, but have also picked up a colloquial knowledge of Bengali. They are generally addressed by Bengalis by the title of Chaudhari—a title which seems to have originated with Chila Chaudhari, a Mug who made a good deal of money, and was well known to the Government officers.

The Mugs live in houses raised on piles, and thatched with the *golpati*. They make ropes of the *banpát*, a species of hibiscus, and the women weave cloth. They are addicted to the use of opium. They have a great objection to the payment of rent, and often desert their clearings when it is demanded. They are quite omnivorous, and regard as a great delicacy the turtles' eggs, which they collect on the chars.

As Kúkri Múkri is seldom visited by Europeans, I append here an account of a visit which I made to it in October 1874 :—

"Next morning we left Kalmi, and sailed down to Kúkri Múkri. In doing so we left the *maij*—*i.e.*, middle char—and the wooded island of Chopa on our left, and the reedy and swampy island of Nalua on our right. This island of Nalua is not marked on the maps, as it formed only about four years ago. At Kúkri Múkri we moored in a khál near the sheds of some buffalo-herdsmen. The island is large, and covered with dark tree jungle. It lies athwart the stream, and at a distance it looks like a huge black alligator stretched out on the water. The buffalo-herdsmen, who were Mahomedans, told us that they came from Kalmi char, that they kept their buffaloes at Kúkri Múkri up to December and January, and that they then removed them, as the water got salt, and the herbage became unfit for food. To my surprise the water both on the south and east side of Kúkri Múkri was perfectly fresh on the occasion of our visit, and I believe it remains so till December, or even later. Such a fact as this, I think, gives a very strong impression of the immense volume of water which must be brought down by the rivers, for a reference to the map will show that Kúkri Múkri is almost in the Bay of Bengal. We learned from the herdsmen that the only permanent inhabitants of the island were a few Mugs or Burmese, who lived on the banks of a creek to the eastward. We went off to visit them, and in doing so passed through the dōn or channel—called the Daiar dōn—which divides Kúkri from Múkri, or rather Kukuria from Mekuria. The sides of the dōn were thickly clothed with wood, and the creepers, with which the trees were often festooned, had a very pretty appearance. There was no sound, however, in the wood, except the occasional short whistle of a bird, and almost the only life to be seen was a kingfisher flitting with his brilliant plumage over the muddy water. It seemed almost a profanation that so beautiful a bird should have his home by a sullen creek fit only for alligators and their like, instead of dwelling by the crystal waters of a mountain stream. But such is nature; and we need perhaps not wonder to find a kingfisher and mud together, when we reflect that the most brilliant dyes are extracted from a substance so nasty as coal tar. We found the Mug settlement to consist of seven households. They had been on the island for four years, and had tried to grow rice, but had failed on account of the great number of bandicoot rats. I am afraid that Mugs do not in the long-run make good settlers. They are very energetic for a year or two, and clear a lot of jungle, but they seem to relapse into lazy habits after a time. Khela, the principal Mug, spoke favourably of the island. He said the climate was cool and healthy, the soil rich, and that there were no tigers. If the rats could only be kept down—and surely this might be done with the help of poison—the island might become highly cultivated. I suppose it has an area of about seven thousand acres. There is another island to the east of it called Phul Kachia, and to the east of it again there is a small island with trees on it, and which is not marked on the map. I did not go to it, but Khela informed me that the Mugs occasionally visit it in quest of turtles' eggs. The trees at Kúkri Múkri grow to the height of fifty or sixty feet. The chief tree is called the kerua. I did not see any sundari-trees on the island, and the Mugs told me that there are none. The sundari is rarely met with on the chars, and is indeed by no means so common in the Sundarbans as one would expect. In Chopa, which is a little to the north of Kúkri Múkri, I saw only two or three young trees of sundari. The kerua was the prevailing tree. Another tree which is very common on the chars is the *bolye*. This tree does not seem to be so well known as it deserves. Its inner bark yields a strong fibre, which the herdsmen twist into tethering ropes for their buffaloes, and which is also largely used instead of rattan or string in the roofing of houses. The tree is bushy, with large leaves, and seems to affect especially the sides of khâls. It grows so abundantly that possibly the bark might have a commercial value. When burnt it yields an ash which is used by the washermen as a substitute for soap. I questioned Khela Mug about the curious phenomenon known by the name of the

Barisál guns. He said that he heard them often in the months of Jaist and Ashar—*i.e.*, in the beginning of the rains. He described the sound as being exactly that of the discharge of a cannon, and said it appeared to have no connection with the tide, and that the noise was quite different from that of the bore or of the coming in of the breakers. The noises appeared to come from the north, south, and south-west. This statement, that they are sometimes heard from the north, is important, for hitherto we have supposed that no one ever got to the south of them. It is because they are always heard from the south that natives poetically represent them as caused by the shutting and opening of Ravan's gate in the island of Lanka (Ceylon). Khela's statement seems conclusive against three hypotheses for the origin of the sounds. These are—1st, that they are nothing but the guns fired at marriage processions; 2d, that they are caused by the falling in of the river-banks; 3d, that they are the sound of the breakers. But there are no marriage processions and no high river-banks north of, or anywhere near, Kúkri Múkri; and as the breakers come in on the south side of Kúkri Múkri with great force in the stormy season, Khela must be well acquainted with the sound they make. When, therefore, both he and the Mugs at Chapli say that the Barisál guns are not the sound of the breakers, I do not see how we can refuse to believe them. The conclusion, therefore, which I come to is that the sounds are atmospheric, and in some way connected with electricity. In conclusion, I should mention that there are no deer on Kúkri Múkri or the neighbouring island of Chopa, but there are wild buffaloes and wild pigs. On Kúkri Múkri there are also wild cattle, which are said by some to have been carried there by an inundation, and by others to be the remains of some cattle employed by former cultivators."—*Bengal Times*, November 7, 1874.

II. WERE THE SUNDARBANS INHABITED IN ANCIENT TIMES?

This is a question which has excited a great deal of attention. The Bengali mind, as being prone to the marvellous, and to the exaltation of the past at the expense of the present, has answered the question in the affirmative, and maintains that there were formerly large cities in the Sundarbans. Some persons also have suggested that the present desolate condition of the Sundarbans may be due to a subsidence of the land, and that this may have been contemporaneous with the formation of the submarine hollow known as the "Swatch of No Ground." It seems to me, however, to be very doubtful indeed that the Sundarbans were ever largely peopled, and still more so that their inhabitants lived in cities or were otherwise civilised. As regards the eastern half of the Sundarbans—namely, that which lies in the districts of Bákarganj and Noakháli, and includes Sandwip and the other islands in the estuary of the Meghna—it seems to me that the fact of so much salt having been manufactured there in old times militates against the view of an extensive cultivation, for the salt could not have been made without a great expenditure of fuel, and this of course implies the existence of large tracts of jungle. Du Jarric speaks of Sandwip as being able to supply the whole of Bengal with salt, and it seems evident that in old times salt was reckoned as the most valuable production of this part of the country. How inimical this must have been to a widespread cultivation of the neighbouring tracts may be judged of from the fact that in modern times the Government salt manufacture was a great obstacle to the clearing and colonising of the chars and islands in Bákarganj and Noakháli. The Government officers used to insist upon the jungle being maintained for the supply of the tafals, and the disputes between them and the lessees of waste lands and other settlers led to much correspondence. The tendency of the salt manufacture to keep land out of cultivation is shown by the circumstance, elsewhere mentioned by me, that the zamindars of Dakhin Shahbázpúr annually obtained a large reduction of their land revenue on account of some of their lands being taken up for the salt manufacture.

Sandwip was, it is true, cultivated in Cæsar Frederick's time (1569), but so it is now, and there is no reason to suppose that its civilisation was greater then than it is at present. It may have had at that time, as it certainly had some thirty or forty years later, one or more forts, but these were marks of insecurity rather than of prosperity, and they do not now exist simply because there is peace in the land, and the Arracanese and the Portuguese pirates are no longer formidable.

Ralph Fitch visited Bákla in 1586, and describes the country as being very great and fruitful. He does not expressly say that Bákla was a city, and it is possible that he found the people of the country living, as they do now, in detached houses, and not crowded together in large towns. But even if we take the words, "the houses be very fair and high builded, the streets large," to mean that there was a city of Bákla, and give full credence to Fitch's statements, the next clause of his description—viz., "the people naked, except a little cloth about their waist"—does not suggest the existence of much civilisation or refinement. Moreover, it appears to me that Fitch was not a very observant or satisfactory traveller. His descriptions of places are meagre, and his itinerary not distinct. I think, too, that if he had kept his eyes and ears open he must have been able to tell us something about the great storm which had devastated Bákla only a twelvemonth or so before his arrival. It is hardly possible that a storm which is said to have drowned 200,000 people could have left no physical marks behind it which Fitch might have seen, and, at all events, its moral effects must have been still existent, and Fitch could hardly have had any intercourse with the inhabitants without hearing of it. I think, therefore, that we must not press his statements too far. It is not likely that he stayed long at the place.

However, the question of Fitch's credibility and intelligence is not very material, for there is nothing to show that Bákla was situated in the Sundarbans. It probably was the same as Kachua, which, according to tradition, was the old seat of the Chandradwip rajahs. But Kachua is in thana Baufal, which is at this day one of the most fertile and best cultivated parts of Bákarganj, and is the only thana in the south of the district which contains a large Hindu population. No doubt there has been a great amount of diluviation near Kachua, and the river between the mainland and Dakhin Shahbázpúr has become much wider than it was in old times. In this way the old city of Bákla and much of its territory may have disappeared, and to this extent there probably has been a decay of civilisation. I have no doubt also that many settlers in the south of the district, especially the Hindu portion of them, left their homes when the Chandradwip rajahs removed to Madhabpásha, and when the Mug inroads became troublesome, but I do not believe that these settlers were very numerous, or that they were civilised and dwelt in cities, &c.

Another thing which indisposes me to believe in the early colonisation of the eastern Sundarbans is the terrible hardships which the crew and passengers of the ship "Ter Schelling" suffered on this coast in 1661. The "Ter Schelling" was a Dutch ship which sailed from Batavia for Angueli (Hijlí), in Bengala, on the 3d September 1661, and which was wrecked off the coast of Bengal on the 8th of the following month. The narrative of the shipwreck, and of the sufferings and adventures of the crew and passengers, was written by one of the latter named Glanius. He was, I presume, a Dutchman, and his account was first published at Amsterdam, and afterwards, in 1682, at London, under the title of "A Relation of an Unfortunate Voyage to the Kingdom of Bengala." The shipwrecked men seem to have landed on an island near Sandwip, and their sufferings from hunger were most terrible. They were compelled to live on most disgusting objects, such as a putrid buffalo, a dead tortoise, a small quadruped called by the natives a *legane*, and which the sailors found eating the buffalo, serpents, snails, &c. A chief part of their sustenance was derived from eating the leaves of the jungle trees, and they even tried eating grass, but this they could not manage. Their only drink was salt water. They saw very few inhabitants, and those whom they did come across were in almost as wretched a plight as they themselves, and appeared to have been driven out from more civilised regions. They were several times on the eve of resorting to cannibalism, but eventually they got to Sandwip, where they were kindly treated by the Governor and sent on to Balwa (Bhalloah). The Prince of Balwa was also kind to them, and sent them on to

Decka (Dacca), where they were impressed, and made to serve under Mir Jamla in the war against Assam. Eventually they got their release and made their way to Hijlí, but Glanius did not return to Europe for several years. Unfortunately, he does not clearly mention the site of his shipwreck, but it was apparently somewhere on the sea-coast of the Sundarbans. The people whom he met, or at least some of them, were Mahomedans, for they used the expression *salam.*[1]

I do not wish, however, to lay too much stress on Glanius's description, for his shipwreck took place in 1661, and it may be that "the depopulation by Mugs" noted in Rennel's map occurred at an earlier date. Indeed, we know from Du Jarric that the King of Arracan conquered Bákla in the beginning of the seventeenth century, and it may be that the desolation of the country dates from this time.

I may also notice here that the copperplate inscription found at Idilpúr in Bákarganj, and described by Babu Pratáp Chandra Ghose in the Asiatic Society's Journal (1838), seems to indicate that the inhabitants of that part of the country belonged to a degraded tribe called the Chandabhandas,[2] a fact which is not favourable to the supposition of the Sundarbans having been at an early period inhabited by a high-caste population.

By far the most interesting account of the Sundarbans is contained in the letters of the Jesuit priests who visited Bákarganj and Jessore in 1599 and 1600. They were addressed to Nicholas Pimenta, a visitor of the order stationed at Goa, and were forwarded by him,

[1] In Professor Blochmann's "Contributions to the Geography, &c., of Bengal," p. 18, reference is made to Van den Broucke's map in Valentyn's work, as showing the place where the "Ter Schelling" was wrecked.

[2] Babu P. C. Ghose compares the Chandabhandas to the Molunghies.

along with some remarks of his own, to Claude Aquaviva, who was then general of the order. The letters seem to have been originally written in Italian, and were first published at Venice in 1602 or 1603, and were afterwards translated into Latin and French. I was indebted for my introduction to them to my friend Dr Wise, who told me that they were quoted in "Purchas's Pilgrimage." Extracts from the letters and the subsequent history of the mission will be found in Pierre du Jarric's "Histoire des Choses plus memorables advenues aux Indes Orientales," &c., Bordeaux, 1608–14.

It appears from Pimenta's account that he sent the priests Fernandez and Sosa to Bengal in 1598, and two others—namely, Melchior da Fonseca and Andrew Bowes—in the following year. Fernandez and Sosa sailed from Cochin on 3d May 1598, and arrived in eighteen days at the Little Port (Porto Pequino). From thence they sailed up the river to Gullo or Goli, where they arrived in eight days after leaving Porto Pequino. From here they seem to have gone on to Chittagong. While at Gullo they received an invitation from the King of a place called Chandecan (in Italian, Ciandecan) to pay him a visit. They did not go then, but as Fernandez afterwards heard that the King was angry at their not coming to him, he sent Sosa to Chandecan sometime in 1599, and he met with a very favourable reception. Afterwards Fernandez himself went to Chandecan in October 1599, and got letters-patent from the King authorising him to carry on the mission. In December 1599 Fernandez was at Sripúr, and on the 22d of that month he wrote a letter to Pimenta giving an account of the mission; and on 20th January 1600 Fonseca wrote a similar letter from Chandecan. Fonseca's letter is most interesting, and has been quoted at p. 31.

For my present purpose it is only necessary that I quote the following passage: "The King [of Bákla], after compliments, asked me where I was bound for, and I replied, 'I am going to the King of Ciandecan, who is to be your Highness's father-in-law.'" These words are extremely important, because they help us to identify both the King of Bákla and the King of Chandecan. Chandecan, as I hereafter will show, is identical with Dhumghát or Jessore, and the boy-king of Bákla (Fonseca says he was only eight years old) can be no other than Ram Chandra Rai, who, we know, married a daughter of the famous Pratápáditya. Before, however, going into this matter, I wish to draw attention to Fonseca's description of the journey from Bákla to Chandecan (see p. 31). Now, though the good father evidently had an eye for natural scenery, and was delighted with the woods and rivers, it is evident that what he admired so much must have appeared to many to be "horrid jungle," and indeed was very like what the Sundarbans now are. In fact, Fonseca's description of the route from Bákla to Chandecan might almost be used at the present day to describe the route from Barisál to Kaliganj, near which Pratápáditya's capital was situated. The chief difference is that the progress of civilisation has driven away the herds of deer and the monkeys from the ordinary routes, though they are still to be found in the woods, and the herds of deer have given their name to one of the largest rivers in the Sundarbans (Haringháttá). The faithfulness of Fonseca's description seems indicated by his modestly admitting that he had never seen a rhinoceros, while stating (quite truly) that there were such animals in the woods. Had Fonseca come upon any town on his journey, it is reasonable to suppose that he would have mentioned it; and my point is, that his description shows that the Sundarbans were in much the same condition in 1599 as they are in now.

I may add that the missionaries speak of dacoits as infesting the rivers, which certainly was a marked feature of the Sundarbans up to the last fifty or sixty years. Fonseca arrived at Chandecan on the 20th November 1599, and there he found Fernandez' companion, Dominic de Sosa. The King received Fonseca with great kindness, so much so that he says a Christian prince could not have behaved better to him. A church was built at Chandecan, and was formally opened on 1st January 1600. It was the first church in Bengal, and was on this account dedicated to Jesus Christ. Chittagong was the second, and Bandel the third. The last was built about this time by a Portuguese named Villalobos.

In reply to the questions, Where was Chandecan, and who was its King? I answer, that as I believe Chandecan to have been identical with Dhumghát, or at least in the same neighbourhood, it must have lain in the Twenty-four Parganas, and near the modern bazár of Kaliganj, and that its king was no other than Partápáditya.

My reasons for this view are, firstly, that Chandecan[1] or Ciandecan is evidently the same as Chand Khan, which, as we know from the life of Rajah Pratápáditya, by Ram Ram Bosu (modernised by Haris Chandra Tarkalankar), was the name of the former proprietor of the estate in the Sundarbans which Pratápáditya's father

[1] Chandecan does not appear to be marked on any of the old maps, and as far as I am aware Bernouilli is the only other person besides the priests who refers to it. In the article on the Feringhies of Chittagong, in "Calcutta Review," Bernouilli is quoted as speaking of *Kandecan*, an old name for the province of Satigam, which included Hughli, &c.

Bikramaditya got from King Daoud. Chand Khan Masandari had died, we are told, without leaving any heirs, and consequently his territory, which was near the sea, had relapsed into jungle. Bikramaditya saw that King Daoud would be ruined, as he had taken upon himself to resist the Emperor of Delhi, and therefore Bikramaditya, who was his minister, took the precaution of establishing a retreat for himself in the jungles. King Daoud was killed in 1576, and Bikramaditya, though he had prepared a city beforehand, seems to have gone to it in person about this time. His dynasty had been only about twenty-four or twenty-five years in the country when the Jesuits visited it, and it would have been quite natural if the name of the old proprietor (Chand Khan) had still clung to it. Moreover, we know that Pratápáditya did not live always, at least, at his father's city of Jessore. He rebelled against him, and established a rival city at Dhumghát. In so doing he may have selected the site of Chand Khan's capital, and this may have retained the name of Chand Khan for two or three years after Pratápáditya had removed to it. Nor is there anything in this opposed to the fact that one Khanja Ali formerly owned Jessore; Khanja Ali died in 1458, or about 120 years before Bikramaditya appeared on the scene, so that Chand Khan may very well have been the name of one of Khanja Ali's descendants.

But there is still more evidence of the identity of Chandecan with Dhumghát.

The fair prospects of the mission, as described by Fernandez and Fonseca, were soon overclouded. Fernandez died, on 14th November 1602, in prison in Chittagong, in consequence of injuries which he had received in a tumult there, and the other priests took refuge in Sandwip. In consequence, however, of a war with the King of Arracan, they soon left the island and took refuge in Chandecan. But the King of Chandecan was cruel and treacherous (traits which agree with the description of Pratápáditya), and was desirous of making his peace with the King of Arracan, who was then very powerful, and had, as Du Jarric informs us, taken possession of the kingdom of Bákla. Carvalho, the gallant captain of the Portuguese, was at Chandecan, and the King of Chandecan, who was then at "Jasor,"[1] sent for Carvalho, and had him murdered in order to ingratiate himself with the King of Arracan. Du Jarric adds that the news of Carvalho's murder at Jasor reached Chandecan on the following midnight, which may give us some idea of the distance between the two places.

This ended the Bengal Mission, for the King of Chandecan destroyed the church and ordered the priests out of the country. We are glad to think that this king, if he was, as we believe, Pratápáditya, shortly afterwards expiated his crimes and died in an iron cage at Benares. That Pratápáditya was a cruel monster, and quite capable of directing the assassination of a brave man like Carvalho, we have proof enough in the work of his admiring biographer, who tells us that Pratápáditya cut off the breasts of a female slave who had offended him.

There are two other slight pieces of evidence in support of the identity between Pratápáditya and the King of Chandecan. One is that Du Jarric tells us that the

[1] *Jasr* means "bridge" in Arabic, and General Cunningham derives the name Jessore from this word, and observes that the appellation indicates the nature of the country. He also states that the old name of the Ganges delta was Samotata. Murali was an old name for Jessore; query, was this connected with Muradkhana, which we know to have been an old name for the Sundarbans?

young King of Bákla was absent when the King of Arracan overran his territory, and we know that Ram Chandra Rai was for awhile a prisoner in the city of his father-in-law, who wished to assassinate him. Another is that when Fernandez came to Chandecan in October 1599, and got the King's signature to the letters-patent, he took the precaution of having them also signed (with the King's permission) by the King's son, who was then about twelve years old. This may have been Pratápáditya's son Udai Aditya, whom we know to have been a great friend of his brother-in-law Ram Chandra Rai, and to have succeeded in saving his life. The two young princes must, from the accounts of Fonseca and Fernandez, have been of nearly the same age, and this makes the story of their friendship all the more probable.

I must not omit to point out that the fact that Bikramaditya chose Jessore as a safe retreat is the strongest possible evidence of the jungly nature of the surrounding country. It is true it had been cultivated in the previous century by Khanja Ali, but the experiment had proved a failure, and the land had in the time of his successor, (?) Chand Khan, relapsed into jungle.

To sum up, it seems to me that the Sundarbans have never been in a more flourishing condition than they are in at present. I believe that large parts of Bákarganj and Jessore were at one time cultivated, that they relapsed into jungle, and that they have now been cleared again; and I have also no doubt that the Court of the Kings of Bákla and of Chandecan imparted some degree of splendour to the surrounding country; but I do not believe that the gloomy Sundarbans, or the sea face of Jessore and Bákarganj, were ever well-peopled or the sites of cities.[1]

[1] The following interesting description of the Sundarbans, as they appeared in 1712–13, is given by Père Barbier in vol. xiii. of "Lettres edifiantes et curieuses," ed. 1781. Père Barbier accompanied Bishop Laynez when the latter made a visitation to the Bengal portion of his diocese, and this is what they saw on the journey from Chandarnagore to Chittagong: "Pour nous y (Chittagong) rendre nous eûmes à tenir une route affreuse. Huit jours entiers, quoiqu'on ramât dix-huit heures chaque jour et que le courant et souvent la marée fussent favorables, suffirent à peine pour nous faire trouver une habitation; jusques là nous ne vîmes que des bois épais, des bras de rivières par où le Gange se dégorge, tantôt d'une étendue prodigieuse, tantôt si étroits qu'on ne le pouvoit ramer que d'un côté. Les bords garnis de grandes arbres dont les branches s'avancent fort avant dans l'eau et pardessus tout l'appréhension continuelle où l'on est des tigres dont on voit des vestiges de temps en temps par des pieux plantés aux endroits où il y a des personnes dévorées à terre ou bien enlevées jusque dans leurs bateaux. Dans l'eau se trouvent des crocodiles longs de vingt et trente pieds qui engloutissent hommes entiers. Enfin on y est souvent à la merci des voleurs qui rôdent incessament dans ces parages montés sur des *panceaux* (pansways) qui vont comme un trait." From Chittagong they went to Bhulu (Noakháli), where there was then a Christian settlement, and from thence to Dacca and Rangamatti, passing on the way Hooseinpúr in Mymensing.

The literature of the Sundarbans is very scanty. Ritter has collected the principal authorities in his "Erdkunde." Williamson, in his "East India Vade Mecum," gives some account of the state of the molunghies or salt-makers in the Sundarbans. See also Forbes's "Oriental Memoirs." Other authorities are Gastrell's Report, Westland's "Jessore," Hooker's "Himalayan Journal," vol. ii., Pogson's "Tour to Chittagong" (Serampúr, 1831), "Calcutta Review," March 1859, article "Gangetic Delta." A map of the Sundarban grants has been made by Mr Gomess, and I believe he has also written a memorandum on the Sundarbans. Lloyd's memoir, on his survey of the coast from Calcutta to Chittagong, is still in MS. (see Markham, Indian Surveys).

The Lieutenant-Governor considers that the reclamation of the Sundarbans has been carried sufficiently far for the present, and that there is a danger of the woods being too much cut down. No more clearing grants are to be made, and the tract has been placed under the management of the Forest Conservancy (B. A. Report for 1873–74, p. 36).

CHAPTER VI.

GOVERNMENT ESTATES, ETC.

THE number of Government estates in Bákarganj was at one time very large, and though many of them have been sold, a considerable number still remain. There is probably no other district in Bengal Proper where Government has so many and such valuable estates, and therefore we may say that there is no other district in which Government has so large and direct an interest.

We have seen that Government is the zamindar of Buzurgumedpúr pargana, but besides this, it owns a great many islands and chars. This is a natural consequence of the fact that the district is an alluvial formation. The rivers continually throw up islands and chars, and under the resumption laws these were taken possession of by Government. Of late years, however, resumption proceedings have nearly ceased, and Government now only takes possession of islands in navigable rivers. The existence of these is brought to light by Government officers in their tours, or more commonly by some one reporting that a sandbank has formed in such and such a river, and asking for a settlement of it These petitions are generally referred to a deputy-collector for inquiry, and if the formation is found to be really an island—*i.e.*, if the water between it and the shore is not fordable at any time of the year (Regulation 11 of 1825, sec. 4, cl. 3)—he takes possession of it by sticking up a bamboo on it. Such inquiries are more protracted than they were in former days, for now private individuals are more alive to their rights and better skilled in maintaining them, and the decision of the Privy Council in the famous Lopez case has enabled many persons to raise with success the plea of reformation on an old site. The apparently simple question of fordability is not always easy of determination, for the rivers vary much in depth, according to the season and the state of the tide. According to the rule now in force, the question of fordability is decided when the rivers are at their lowest—*i.e.*, in or about the month of February. The number of islands in Bákarganj which are now the property of Government appears to be 133. Many of them belong to the Dakhin Shahbázpúr subdivision, and were transferred along with it to Bákarganj in 1869, from the district of Noakháli. The most interesting of the island-estates, or *jaziras*, as they are called, is Manpúra, an island situated to the south-south-east of Dakhin Shahbázpúr. It was resumed by the Commissioner of the Sundarbans in 1833, though it seems doubtful if the resumption was justifiable, for the island is an old formation, and was included in the partition of the Dakhin Shahbázpúr zamindari, which took place in 1188 B.S. (A.D. 1781)—that is, nine years before the Decennial Settlement. It is said to owe its name to one Man Ghazi, who got a lease from the Dakhin Shahbázpúr zamindars, and was the first to break up the soil. At the time of the resumption the island was in the hands of the zamindars, and there were 536 acres under cultivation. According to the papers of the partition already referred to, the amount of cultivation in 1781 was thirteen kanies—that is, about 250 bighas or 160 acres, as the kani in use in Manpúra is the large or shahi kani, which is four times the size of the ordinary one. Manpúra is diluviating at the north-east, and alluviating at the south and west, where a large char called Kista Prasad has formed. The area of Manpúra is about fourteen square miles, and its population 4500. Three-fourths of the inhabitants are Hindus, so that the island is an exception to the general rule that the inhabitants of the islands and chars in Bákarganj are Mahomedans. The Hindus are all low-caste men, and are called Dasses or Halia Dasses—*i.e.*, Dasses who hold the plough, as distinguished from the Dasses who follow clerical pursuits, or who are fishermen. The Dasses are a quiet and well-behaved set of men, and are very hard-working. It is a Bengali saying that the Dass and the *bhaish*—*i.e.*, the buffalo—are equally strong and laborious. They have two customs which are looked upon with abhorrence by the stricter Hindus—they eat pigs, and they marry widows. The remaining fourth of the inhabitants are Mahomedans, and they too are quiet and inoffensive, and do not seem to be tinctured with any Ferazi notions. There are a schoolmaster, a post-master, a pound-keeper, and nine chaukidars on the island, but there is no magistrate nor any regular police. The island is well raised, and is very fertile, though rice is nearly the only product. There is no jungle on it except a belt which surrounds it, and which is preserved by the inhabitants because it breaks the force of the waves and keeps out the salt water from their cultivation. A few deer and a good many pigs live in this jungle, but there are no tigers or leopards. For everything except rice, milk, and firewood, the inhabitants have to depend on the markets in the adjacent island of Dakhin Shahbázpúr. During the cold weather boats come from Dacca, and from the bazár of Bákarganj, &c.,

and export rice from the island. During the rains the island is not easily accessible, and is seldom visited by boats from a distance, though a ferry-boat regularly plies between it and Tazamuddin in Dakhin Shahbázpúr. I have referred in the chapter on under-tenures to the curious fact that four different classes of proprietors have sprung up in the island. The late settlements have been made with the *abádkárs*, but the rate of rent payable to them by the howaladars has been fixed at eleven anas three pies a bigha. The old rate prevalent in the island was Rs.2-8 the small or *karsha* kani, or eight anas four pies a bigha. No expenses of collection were allowed to the abádkárs or howaladars in former times; but, on the other hand, they were allowed a deduction on account of *ails*—*i.e.*, the limits or ridges separating the fields—and for *matan*, as it is called—*i.e.*, a deduction allowed to a tenant as his profit on condition of his bringing the adjacent lands into cultivation. The rate of rent actually paid in former times was, after deduction of matan and for ails, seven anas three pies a bigha. The above rate of Rs.2-8 a kani was the general one in all the Noakháli chars, and was adopted by Mr Ricketts in his settlements. Manpúra is divided into eight estates, the net revenue from which to Government is about Rs.8500. In 1844 the revenue was only Rs.1311. The first settlement was made in 1837, when Mr Ricketts was Commissioner of Chittagong. The holdings of the ryots under the howaladars and nim howaladars are called *jotes*. These inferior ryots are divided into two classes—viz., *khudkast* and *paikast*, the khudkast being those who cultivate lands on the estate on which they reside, and the paikast those who cultivate lands on other estates. The same person may be both a khudkast and a paikast ryot—

i.e., khudkast with regard to the land he cultivates near his homestead, and paikast with regard to that which he cultivates at a distance. There are 226 khudkast ryots, and 179 of them have rights of occupancy. Sixty-six paikast ryots have similar rights. The total number of ryots is 566; so that if we reckon five to a family, the ryots number 2830, or more than half the population of the island. The other inhabitants are howaladars and nim howaladars, but they for the most part cultivate their own lands. The ryots pay Rs.16 to Rs.24½ per shahi kani, according to the nature of their lands. They have also to work two days in the year on the lands of their titular superiors, or to pay eight anas in lieu of this service. The island originally contained only one estate, which was divided into blocks under orders of Mr Ricketts in order to facilitate cultivation. When Mr Garrett, the Deputy-Collector of Noakháli, reported on the island in 1841, there were only two classes of residents—namely, howaladars and jötedars. Six out of the eight estates have been settled up to 1907 B.S.

The incidents in the history of Manpúra are not numerous. In 1218 B.S. (1811) the manufacture of salt was introduced, and caused so much oppression that 350 homesteads had been deserted by 1225 B.S. (1818). In 1229 B.S. (1822) a cyclone swept over the island and drowned most of the inhabitants, and another inundation took place in 1850, and led to a remission of one-fourth of the revenue. Four or five years ago a whale was stranded on the island, and some of its bones were afterwards brought to Barisál and placed in the public library. I have said there are no tigers or leopards; there are not even any jackals; but there are snakes, and cases of death from snake-bite occasionally occur. I have referred to Mr Ricketts in connection with Manpúra, and I may take this opportunity of noticing that this officer (now Sir Henry Ricketts) is famous all over Dakhin Shahbázpúr and Noakháli, and, I believe, throughout the whole Chittagong division, for his settlements, and that there is no name more frequently or more honourably mentioned either by ryots or by old native servants of Government. His letter of 22d May 1841 is the most important one in the history of the settlements of Manpúra, and is that in which the title taluqdar is applied to the abádkárs.

There is a very full and excellent report about Manpúra by Babu Anand Chandra Sein, Deputy-Collector, dated 3d December 1873, and to this reference should be made by all who wish to know more about Manpúra and its settlements. The Babu made the settlements, which have lately been confirmed by the Board and by Government.

It would take up too much space if I were to describe the other islands belonging to Government, and I am not aware that there is anything specially interesting connected with them. Many of them have ceased to be islands, owing to the silting up of the intervening channels; and it is probable that at no distant date Manpúra will also cease to be an island, and be joined on to the Dakhin Shahbázpúr mainland. Many of the islands show by their names the periods at which they were formed, or at least at which they were taken possession of by Government. Thus we have Lord Hardinge char and Lawrence char (spelt Lallon on the map, and situated in Noakháli), which point to the period of the Sikh war; while Falcon char, Alexander char, Drummond char, Price char, Hankey char, Brown char, Ram Kanye char, Henderson char, &c., point to the time when the officers whose names they bear were collectors of Noakháli, or otherwise employed in that district.

Besides the islands, there are ninety-four or ninety-five Government estates included in parganas, which have chiefly been acquired by purchase at sales for arrears of revenue. Such estates are not generally of much value, for it is almost always owing to their deterioration that Government has to put them up to sale for arrears of revenue, or that Government is enabled to purchase them at the upset price of Rs.1. Fifty-two of them belong to the pargana of Srírámpúr, forming part of an old estate called Gokul Mukarjya (see p. 147).

With the addition of Nos. 1406, 1437, and 1447 (described under pargana Buzurgumedpúr), the khas mahals—*i.e.*, Government estates (exclusive of the islands)—may be reckoned as numbering ninety-seven estates, and as bearing a revenue of about Rs.115,000.

There are also resumed or *bazyafti* estates. These are the property of individuals, but are managed by Government, either directly or through farmers, owing to the owners not accepting the terms of settlement offered by Government. Such resumptions were made under Regulation 2 of 1819 and 9 of 1825, and are to be distinguished from resumptions under Regulation 11 of 1825, whereby islands become the exclusive property of Government. There are 111 bazyafti mahals, and the Government revenue from them is about Rs.84,000. The owners receive *malikana* or proprietary allowance. Some bazyafti mahals not included in the 111 have been permanently settled with their owners. The bazyafti mahals are chiefly *taufirs—i.e.*, lands which have accreted since the Permanent Settlement, and which were not included in it. They are numerous in Dakhin Shahbázpúr, where the collections from resumptions amount to about Rs.50,000. The largest is Jainagar, which is managed directly by the Collector through a tahsildar, and which yields about Rs.15,000 a year. It belongs to the heirs of the notorious Sibkissen Banarji. The bazyafti mahals were let by Government to abádkárs or improving tenants, and now that the lands have been cleared the owners are coming forward and claiming them.

The large estate of Tushkháli in the Perozpúr subdivision is the exclusive property of Government, and should have been mentioned among the khas mahals. The rental is about Rs.78,000, and the estate is at present undergoing settlement with a view to enhancement. The rate of rent hitherto prevailing was Rs.1-4 a bigha. It was farmed to the Morrells for twenty years, but their lease has been cancelled, and it is now under direct management. Tushkháli was resumed from pargana Syedpúr, and was first cleared by the De Silva family. It was once sold to the Ghosal family, but the sale was cancelled in consequence of the lawsuit referred to at p. 158.

FISHERIES.—It might be supposed that there would be many fisheries in Bákarganj belonging to Government. There are, however, only four, and the total revenue derived from them is very little more than one thousand rupees (1029). They are the Jahapúr Fishery, the Meghna Jhap Fishery, the Bishkháli Fishery, called Surjya Narain Chakrabarti or the Buzurgumedpúr Bishandi Jál, and the Bhashan Títulia. The first of these is a resumption, the second is a part of the Gokul Mukarjya taluq already referred to as lying in Srírámpúr pargana, and the third and fourth belong to pargana Buzurgumedpúr. There was a lawsuit about the Bhashan Títulia Fishery in 1858, and there is a full account of it in a letter of Mr Collector Dalrymple to the judge, dated 11th December 1858. It appears that *bhashan*, or floating, means the right to collect rent from fishmongers who within certain limits in the Títulia buy fish from the fishermen. Bhashan Títulia was originally an under-tenure of Buzurgumedpúr, and was separated at the application of its owner in 1803, and registered as bearing a revenue of Rs.97-7-15. It was held that the right to such an estate was not affected by Regulation 27 of 1793. The taluq is now in the hands of the Chakrabarties of Rupatolli, who have given an ausat taluq of it to certain *nikaries* or fishmongers.

It appears that altogether there are 3232 estates on the Bákarganj revenue roll, but fifteen of these do not bear any revenue.

COURT OF WARDS AND ATTACHED ESTATES.

The number of these is very small, and none of them possesses much interest or importance. The largest is the seven anas of Arangpúr pargana, which was attached by order of the Civil Court, and is under the charge of Mr Scott, the Sarbarakar or Manager-General. The most important ward's estate is that of the lunatic Jagat Narain Chakrabarti, who is a small shareholder in the Selímábád pargana, and resides at Raikátti. The estate is managed by his son.

CHAPTER VII.

LAND TENURES.

I. TENURES-IN-CHIEF.

THE tenures-in-chief of Bákarganj have been described in the chapter on financial history, and in the account of the different parganas, but before proceeding to describe the under-tenures it seems desirable to say a few words more about the zamindars.

The number of zamindaries in the district is reckoned to be 101,[1] but the number of zamindars is at least four or five times this number.[2] No notice is taken in the official registers of subdivisions of estates which have not been announced by the owners to the Collector, and there are many estates entered in one name, but which really belong to several families. In looking over the list of proprietors of zamindaries and independent taluqs, we find that most of them are Hindus of the Bráhman caste, and that there are comparatively few Mahomedans. The principal Bráhman family resident in the district is

[1] According to a return in the Bengal Administration Report for 1872–73, p. 74, there were forty-six large estates in Bákarganj, 664 of moderate size, and 4618 under 500 acres apiece. This includes the estates of the Mádaripúr subdivision, and I think exaggerates the number of large estates. At least it must not be supposed that each of these forty-six estates is in the hands of one man, or even family, for nearly every one of them is divided among several families. *N.B.*—The word "estate" includes all lands paying rent direct to Government, whether they be zamindaries, taluqs, or farms.

[2] According to census, there are 1963 zamindars (males only).

that of the Arangpúr zamindar, for the Tagore and Ghosal families are absentees. Some country-born Greeks, Armenians, and Eurasians have properties in the district, but no one of European birth and parentage holds land in Bákarganj.

The dearth of old Mahomedan families in a district which is so full of Mahomedans, and where so many of the parganas and villages have names of Mahomedan origin, is not a little remarkable. Khajah Ahsanoolah of Dacca is a stranger to the district, and his possessions in it have all been acquired by purchase in comparatively recent times. Even the Shaistábád family, though commonly considered the best in the district, has not been long settled in it, the present family having acquired the estate by marriage, and having originally belonged to Farídpúr. The Mahomedan families of Charamudi, Bamna, and Gyanpara are of no great standing, and do not enjoy much respect. The family which is really the oldest, is, I believe, that of the Mozamdars of Chákár; but they, as well as the old family who once held Nazirpúr pargana, have long ceased to be zamindars. It appears certain that Mahomedan families are less able to keep up with the age than Hindus, and that they decline more rapidly. Even those which still keep a footing in the district are for the most part in insolvent circumstances. It would be difficult and invidious to discuss minutely the causes of this difference between Mahomedans and Hindus, but I think something must be attributed to the practice of polygamy among the former. At least this seems to have led to the ruin of the Nazirpúr family, the last zamindar before the Permanent Settlement having left twelve sons by different mothers to dispute his succession. It is also a fact admitted by Mahomedans themselves that the wealthy professors of their creed are more prone to idleness and dissipation than are Hindus.

II. UNDER-TENURES.

Bákarganj is famous for the number of its under-tenures. It has been supposed that this is due to the litigious and intriguing character of the inhabitants, and no doubt this cause has not been without effect; but even the people most prone to litigation and intrigue seldom act from the mere love of these things, and we must, I think, search deeper for the efficient cause of so much sub-infeudation.

Undoubtedly the first cause is the physical characteristics of the district. This has acted in two ways: firstly, it has made the principal landholders absentees, and has thrown the direct management of the soil into the hands of the under-tenants; and secondly, it has made the latter insist upon permanency of tenure.

Bákarganj has never been a favourite residence of the wealthier classes. Its remoteness from Calcutta, its large rivers and the banditti who infested or were supposed to infest them, and above all, the jungle and the salt air, have made the upper classes shy of living in it. The great zamindaries of the district are held by absentees, and by absentees of the most pronounced type, for I believe that the present holders of the three largest properties in Bákarganj—viz., Khajah Ahsanoolah and the representatives of the Ghosal and Tagore families—have never even set foot in the district.

The zamindars who do live in Bákarganj are generally too poor to have much influence, and besides, even they live a long way off from portions of their estates, and owing to difficulties of communication, &c., seldom visit them. In the cold season, when the *aman* harvest has been gathered in and the ryots are flush of money, the zamindars and taluqdars are in the habit of making progresses through their estates, and of collecting rents and presents. But for nine months in the year the under-tenantry are left to themselves and the land-stewards. Even the latter are not always present, for as they are generally Hindus, they do not like to live in the midst of a Mahomedan population. They go to their homes at the time of the *durga puja*, and do not return for two or three months. As, therefore, the zamindars cannot, or do not, live on their estates, they are forced, in Burke's phrase, to govern with a loose rein, and to allow the under-tenantry to create or acquire transferable rights. But apart from this, it is plain that when a country is covered with jungle, people will not settle in it, or undertake the cultivation of it, unless they get permanency of tenure. Therefore, as in old times, much of Bákarganj was covered with Sundarban jungle, and as also much of it consisted of newly-formed land, which could not be made productive until several years after occupation, the Government and the zamindars found it necessary to grant improving leases carrying permanent rights. Hence arose the system of jangálburi taluqs, *abdas,* &c. The pargana of Buzurgumedpúr was entirely composed of such taluqs, and it is chiefly by the instrumentality of the holders of them that the revenue of the pargana has been raised from a few thousand rupees to upwards of two lacs. It is a common stipulation in improving leases that no rent is to be paid for the first two or three years, and that there is to be a progressive rate, or *rasad,* as it is called, until the full rate (*pura dastúr*) has been attained. The technical name for a reclaimer of jungle in Bákarganj is *abádkár*

—*i.e.*, clearer or cultivator—and his tenure is called *abádkári* or *abádi.* But the freedom from rent for several years is such a general incident of the tenure that the word *abda*, which seems to be a corruption of abádi, has come to mean rent free. Thus, to hold land abda, means in Bákarganj to hold it rent free, though the term is only applied to lands held temporarily rent free for purposes of cultivation.

As a proof that the system of under-tenures is the growth of circumstances, and is not to be ascribed to the chicanery of the Bákarganj ryots, I may refer to the island of Manpúra, which is a Government property, and which, up to the last five years, belonged to the district of Noakháli. Government acquired possession of this island about forty years ago, under a decree of the Resumption Commissioner. It was then nearly all covered with jungle, and the few cultivators who inhabited it appear to have been all of one class, and to have borne the name of jotedars. At present there are about 4500 inhabitants on the island, and there are four classes of persons possessing distinct rights in the soil. There are first the abádkárs or taluqdars, who pay the Government revenue; secondly, the howaladars; thirdly, the nim howaladars; and fourthly, the karshadars or simple cultivators.

"It is a natural consequence of hereditary benefices," says Hallam, "that those who possess them carve out portions to be held of themselves by a similar tenure." This result, which appeared in the feudal system in Europe, has not failed to show itself in India, for human nature is the same everywhere. The existence of a right generally leads to the exercise of it, and persons who acquire permanent and transferable interests in land soon begin to alienate them in whole or in part.

Another cause of sub-infeudation is that tracts of uncultivated land are often let out to several persons who club together to clear them. Thus the lease of a howala is often in the names of ten or twelve persons. At first they all cultivate the land together, and generally one of their number has a certain representative capacity, and is the man to whom the landlord looks for rent. But as cultivation advances, the lands become marked off into aliquot parts, two anas, four anas, &c., or portions of them are granted to inferior tenants, as nim howalas, karshas, &c. A ryot cannot cultivate more than a certain amount of land—say forty or fifty bighas at the outside—and if, therefore, he get a grant of jungle which is double or quadruple that size, he is obliged in time to let out a portion to some one. It is a mistake to suppose that the cultivation of jungle in Bákarganj has been accomplished by squatters. Mugs squat in the Sundarbans, and occasionally a Bengali may take possession of an uncultivated bit of land, but such instances are rare. Neither has the reclamation been accomplished by the zamindars or other large proprietors of land. As a rule, these men are absentees or indolent, and the main stress of the work of cultivation has fallen on the under-tenure holders or middlemen. It is the howaladar and the nim howaladar who have brought the Sundarbans and the chars of Dakhin Shahbázpúr into cultivation.

In consequence of under-tenures, we often find three or four persons holding different rights in the same piece of ground. It has been said that the number sometimes amounts to eight or nine, but I have never come across an instance of so many. It is quite common, however, to find three or four; and it is this complication which makes the taking up of land for public purposes such a thorny piece of business in Bákarganj. At the top we have the zamindar or independent taluqdar, who pays the revenue to Government, and who is thus the tenant *in capite* of feudal law. After him come the ausat taluqdar, the howaladar, the nim howaladar, and the karshadar or tiller of the soil. The karshadar is the lowest in the scale, unless we add the borghadar; but there is more than one description of karsha-tenure. There is the *miras karsha*, or *miras malguzari*, as it is also called, which is a hereditary and transferable tenure, and is often underlaid by the *miadi* or temporary karsha. The incidents of a karsha are different also in different parts of the district. Thus in Dakhin Shahbázpúr a karsha is by local custom transferable by sale, and is sold in execution of decrees accordingly, whereas in Bákarganj Proper karshas are generally looked upon as not saleable. All over the district, however, ryots are in the habit of selling their holdings, especially their homesteads, and in practice these transfers are generally recognised by the superior landlord. The rent is commonly paid to a gomasta or tahsildar, and he is glad enough to get it, for often he has contracted to pay a certain sum to his master, whatever his collections may amount to; and if the transferee pays him the rent, and also gives him a *nazzar* or present, he seldom objects to the change of name.

It must not be supposed that because there are a great number of under-tenures in Bákarganj, there must be at least an equal number of distinct persons who hold these separate rights. It often happens that one and the same person holds three or four classes of rights in the same piece of ground; and thus, though it is common enough to find four or five gradations of rights in one field, it is not so common to find that each of these rights is held by a distinct person. Thus the same person is often both ausat taluqdar and howaladar; and nearly all zamindars and taluqdars possess subordinate rights in their estates, and are their own ausat taluqdars, howaladars, and even karshadars. The existence of each of these rights is carefully kept up in the zamindari accounts, and leads to a very intricate system of debit and credit, or *jama kharach*, as it is called. Thus a zamindar will be found crediting himself with rent payable to him as zamindar by himself as howaladar, and again debiting himself as howaladar with the rent due to himself as zamindar. Nor is the system so superfluous or irrational as it at first sight appears. It arises in a great measure from the subdivision of property, and from the fact of many estates being held jointly—*i.e.*, *ijmáli*. Thus a person may have a two or three-and-a-half ana share in a zamindari, and under this there is a taluq or howala, the rent of which is payable to all the shareholders in the zamindari—that is, in the case under illustration, the person gets two or two and a half anas rent of the taluq or howala; but if this taluq or howala is sold by decree of court or otherwise, and the shareholder in the zamindari buy it, he acquires a new right, and one which may be very valuable to him. If the whole right in the taluq or howala—*i.e.*, the sixteen-ana right, as it is called—is sold, he becomes full proprietor of the lands comprised in it, and pays fourteen or thirteen and a half anas of the rent of it to his co-sharers in the zamindari, and pays the remainder to himself. It does not follow that because he has bought the taluq or howala, he gets khas or direct possession of the land; for there may be a nim howala or a karsha below the right he has purchased, and if he wishes direct possession, he may have to go on purchasing the other rights in the land. It is the contests between shareholders in zamindaries about the buying or otherwise getting possession of under-tenures in their joint estates which lead to so much fighting amongst them in and out of the courts. Though we may deplore the circumstance, we can hardly say that it is absurd or unnatural. It is also this system which makes it so very difficult to carry through a batwara or partition in Bákarganj, or indeed anywhere in Bengal. At first sight it seems simple enough to divide a zamindari into three or four shares, but when we find that the zamindari share is by no means the only, or even the most valuable right which each shareholder possesses, the problem becomes much more complicated. The shareholders in a zamindari often make a rough kind of division of their shares, or a Mofussil batwara, as they call it — that is, their zamindari lands are often distinct, and their ryots are distinct also. There are often ryots who pay the whole, or the sixteen anas, of their rent to one shareholder, and who have nothing whatever to do with any of the other shareholders, and this although no legal partition of the estate may have taken place; but the relation of ryot and zamindar is never the only one which exists in a joint estate. Each share is dovetailed into the others by an intricate series of under-tenures, and it is the separation and consolidation of these subsidiary rights possessed by the shareholders which constitutes the difficulty of making a partition. The outside public cannot be expected to know much of such matters, and may therefore be excused when they denounce the delay in making partitions, and ascribe it to the trickery of the amíns and *insouciance* of collectors. But I have known a Commissioner who was no better informed, and who gravely observed that all which was required for the partition of an estate containing some thirty thousand acres was to make a map of it, and then to divide it off into three or four blocks, according to the number and extent of the shares. Truly this seemed simple enough; but suppose that one block had consisted of under-tenures paying a low and unenhanceable rent, and that another had consisted of ryotwari land paying the full pargana rate, and the tenants of which could be evicted, where would be the equality in value of the two blocks?

Although the system of under-tenures has mainly arisen out of the physical characteristics of Bákarganj, I do not mean to say that their number has not often been multiplied unnecessarily by the subtlety or tenacity of the Bengali. One use frequently made of the large number of under-tenures is to enable a man to retain his hold on a property after one or more of his rights has been sold. Thus we may say that the sale-law is one cause of sub-infeudation. Suppose, for instance, that a zamindar's right and title in his zamindari are sold for arrears of revenue, or in satisfaction of a decree, it might be imagined that this would terminate his connection with the estate; but, as a general rule, this would be far from the case. The *mazul*—*i.e.*, quondam zamindar—does not surrender his hold on the land so readily. If he cannot in any way impeach the sale by showing that he did not get notice of it, that the estate was sold below its value, that the decree was fraudulent, &c., or that the property did not belong to him, but was his wife's or his brother-in-law's, he proceeds to another battle-field, and claims to hold a nij taluq—*i.e.*, a taluq belonging to the zamindar—or a howala, or other under-tenure. Indeed, the Bengali, and especially the Bákarganj Bengali, holds on to his land with a persistence which reminds one of the Athenian soldier who grasped the Persian ship with his right hand, and who, when that was cut off, seized it with his left, and when that too was lopped away, clung to it with his teeth. The last fight of all made by a dispossessed proprietor is generally that for the *khanabari* or paternal homestead, and is literally a fight *pro arâ et foco.* The most serious riots in the district have their origin in disputes between the auction purchaser and the old proprietor, and the *casus belli* is then generally a dispute about an under-tenure. Such a riot occurred in the early part of this century, when the Tagores took possession of Idilpúr, and also when Ali Khan, the grandfather of Khajah Ahsanoolah, took possession of his share of Selímábád, &c.

ZIMBA.—A practice which gives rise to much subinfeudation, and to many breaches of the peace, is that called *zimba*, and which seems, in name at least, peculiar to Bákarganj. Zimba literally means charge or protection, and the system of zimba, as it is understood in Bákarganj, means a practice by which a ryot, or other subordinate holder of land, transfers his allegiance from his proper landlord to a third party. This third party is called his *zimbadar*. Thus A. B. is a ryot having a right of occupancy in his land. He is oppressed by his landlord or is discontented with him, and so he goes to another proprietor and offers to come under his zimba. If this offer be accepted, he generally transfers his holding to his protector by deed of sale, and receives it back again by another deed. Thus the possession of the land does not actually pass, the ryot continues to hold his house and land as before, but pays his rent to his zimbadar, who in turn pays it to the real landlord. Should the latter refuse to receive it, it is deposited in court, or simply withheld till a suit is brought and a decree obtained. In the deed by which the ryot gets back his land he is generally described as getting the tenure next below that which he sold. Thus if he be a howaladar, he sells the howala and becomes the nim howaladar; if he is a miras karshadar, he becomes an ordinary karshadar. If in reality he have no transferable right, and be merely an occupancy-ryot, or even a ryot without the right of occupancy, he will still describe himself as an under-tenure holder of some kind—*i.e.*, a nim howaladar—and so get over the difficulty of his position. The system of zimba is especially common in ijmáli or joint estates, and the reason for this is intelligible enough. When a ryot has several masters he is often oppressed or harassed by them. He therefore finds it his best plan to come under the zimba of the most powerful or the most troublesome among them, as thenceforth he has only one man to conciliate. The system is a bad one, and nothing gives rise to more disputes. I am sorry to say, too, that it appears to have received a fresh impetus from the passing of the Registration law, and that many deeds which are pointed to as proofs of the increase of sub-infeudation are in reality merely paper transfers, and do not express any substantive change in the tenancy of the land. I may note here that the purposes of the Registration law are often perverted by persons who want to take possession of land which does not belong to them. The Bengali cannot get rid of the idea that a registered *kabuliyat* is evidence against third parties; so when two parties are fighting about, say, the possession of a newly-formed char, each of them takes a troop of his dependents to the register office, and makes them register kabuliyats or leases for land which they have not possession of. It is by no means easy to punish such proceedings, for as between the parties there is no fraud or deception, and if no action is taken after the registration, it is difficult to prove that a third party has been injured. There is, I think, a defect in the Registration law on this point.

When a ryot gives his land in zimba he generally gives a present or *salami* to the zimbadar, and, I believe, he defrays all the conveyancing expenses—*i.e.*, the stamps, registration fees, &c. The proper landlord of the ryot, of course, opposes the zimbadari process as much as possible, for not only does he lose prestige by his ryot being no longer "his man," so to speak, but he loses certain incidents of homage. In fact, he henceforth gets merely the bare rent of the land, and loses the cesses paid by the ryot, such as marriage presents, fines for cattle trespass, &c., as all these are paid to the zimbadar. In Hallam's "Middle Ages" mention is made of the system of commendation, which he describes as a personal relation between lord and vassal, resembling that of patron and client in the Roman Republic. I think that this system must have closely resembled the Bákarganj zimba, and I would suggest that the word "zimba" might be translated "commendation."

Perhaps the description of one or two actual cases of zimba will put the matter in a much clearer light. I shall take the first illustration from the subdivision of Perozpúr, which, by the way, is the most troublesome part of the district, and is to the other subdivisions of it what Bákarganj is to the rest of Bengal. There is a village called Kal Megha in the Matbária thana, in the Sundarban estate of Gyanpara, and away down at the mouth of the Bishkháli river. The land had long remained as a Sundarban forest, but some years ago the wealthy Hindu family of the Seins or Mahallanavises of Basinda acquired certain rights in the place, and set about reclaiming the jungle. For this purpose they brought in ryots from other villages and settled them at a considerable expense. Here I must make a digression in order to explain the process by which jungle is reclaimed, when done not by the middlemen or under-tenure holders acting independently, but by a zamindar or moneyed man. It then becomes a regular case of colonisation. The zamindar does not, as might be supposed, hire a number of labourers to clear the ground, but he acts somewhat as the New Zealand Government acts with emigrants. He induces ryots to come and settle by making them advances for the removal of their houses and cattle, by giving them rice, by establishing a convenient market for them, &c. In many cases he has to purchase cattle for them, and to build their houses. Further, he takes no rent from them for three or four years, and he promises them permanency of tenure at a moderate rent. When a ryot accepts such terms and comes down to the jungle, he generally leaves his wife and family behind him for a year or two, and puts up a small house where he and one or two of his brothers or friends can sleep. In this *doala* homestead—*i.e.*, subsidiary or second home—he lives during the working season, and only occasionally revisits his home. If he find the place unhealthy, or too much infested with tigers, or otherwise unsuitable, he abandons it; but if he think that it will suit him, and elect to remain, he gradually plants fruit-trees, &c., and eventually brings away his old house (roof and all being carried on boats), and settles in the new place with his family. In making such arrangements regular leases or pattas are not given at first. This would be too expensive, on account of the registration and stamp fees; and besides, neither party can precisely say what the land is worth until after two or three years' trial. The practice, therefore, is that either no documents are given at all, or only a preliminary one on unstamped paper, and not hard and fast in its terms. This is given to the ryot, and is called an *amilnama*.

This practice was followed by the Seins in Kal Megha, but after the ryots had been settled for some years, and had cleared a good deal of land, the Seins delayed or refused to give them permanent leases. The excuse given by them for not giving them was that the ryots were threatening to be rebellious, and that they were afraid lest, by giving them permanent, and therefore transferable rights, they should be putting weapons into their hands, which might be used against themselves by the transference of their rights to a zimbadar. Disputes arose between the Seins and the ryots about this, and as the quarrel was fomented by one Sidam Mia, a Mahomedan taluqdar of the neighbourhood, a number of the newly-settled ryots went over to him and under his zimba, saying that they were nim howalas and not simple ryots.

The Seins seeing this, and fearing lest they should be suddenly dispossessed and deprived of the fruits of their labours and expenditure, hired clubmen, and endeavoured to bring the ryots back to their allegiance, and to keep Sidam Mia out of the village. The result was several affrays, in which firearms were used and one or two persons killed.

It might be thought that this was a dispute which could have been easily settled by the authorities, as Sidam

Mia was manifestly a usurper, and was trying to reap what he had not sown. But in fact the matter was not so simple. It is true that neither he nor the ryots could say that he had spent any money in improving the property, or could deny that the ryots had been brought in by the Seins, but Sidam Mia had, nevertheless, rights in Gyanpara. He was the superior landlord and paid revenue to Government, and he could and did say that the subordinate or under-tenure rights claimed by the Seins did not exist or were exaggerated, and that the clearings were part of his khas land—*i.e.*, were included in the land of which he had direct possession. For these reasons an attempt made by the magistrate to quiet the dispute by prohibiting Sidam Mia or his people from entering the village, failed before the Sessions judge, and the contest continued for several months.

At length Sidam Mia died, and though his claims were maintained by his family, they had eventually to yield to the longer purse of their opponents. Sidam Mia's share in Gyanpara was put up for sale in execution of a decree, and was bought by the Seins and others for some Rs.40,000, so that they have now both the superior and the subordinate rights in the estate.

An instance of zimba was nearly occurring the other day in the large Government estate of Tushkháli, which is also in the Perozpúr subdivision. This estate, which yields upwards of R.78,000 a year, was let in farm for twenty years to the Messrs Morrell. The ryots became discontented with the farmers because the latter wanted to raise their rent, and indeed had taken the farm at an advance of Rs.15,000 on the old rental, on the condition that they were to be allowed to enhance the ryots' rents. The ryots objected, urging that their dōls or leases were permanent, and refused to break them, as they phrased it, by giving any higher rate. When, therefore, the farmers issued notices on them, and took other steps to raise their rent, the ryots went to various zamindars in the district—*i.e.*, to the Raikátti zamindars, to Khajah Ahsanoolah, and to Har Chandra Chakrabarti of Kajlakátti—and offered to make over their dōls to them and to come under their zimba. As an inducement to the acceptance of this offer they were willing to pay salami, &c. Had their offers been accepted, a serious disturbance might have occurred, but the zamindars were afraid and held aloof.

It is a melancholy fact that the more energetic and able a zamindar is, the more is he disposed to create disturbances with his neighbours and to thwart the authorities. Such a person is always thrusting himself into the affairs of other estates, and is a centre of misrule and disaffection. Doubtless this is in a great measure the result of the exclusion of such men from legitimate careers; and it must be said, too, that his interference is not always unneeded, and not always quite spontaneous on his part. If a zamindar has a reputation for ability and courage, the ryots of other estates come to him and beg him to assist them against their oppressors. If interference of this kind was pardonable or commendable on the part of the ancient Romans, who built up their empire in this way, we cannot severely blame a Bengali zamindar for acting in a similar manner. I do not mean to defend the zimba system, but I believe that it often serves to protect the weak against the strong, and that it will last as long as the administration of justice is weak, uncertain, and dilatory. The knowledge that his ryots will, if driven to extremities, accept the protection of a zimbadar, will often prevent a tyrannical landlord from oppressing them too much. In other districts ryots run away when too much trampled upon; in Bákarganj they go to a zimbadar. If elsewhere zamindari management may often be described as oppression tempered by the fear of desertion, it may be described as being in Bákarganj oppression tempered by the fear of zimbadari. Oppression from their zamindar is not the only kind under which ryots have to suffer. They are often still more grievously oppressed by their fellow-villagers, and have resort to the zimbadari system to protect themselves against this form of oppression also. The following is an instance of oppression by fellow-villagers.

In the village of Phalaghar, near the Bákarganj thana, there was in 1871 a Hindu ryot who had a quarrel with his neighbours about a road. He was a boatbuilder as well as a cultivator, and required access to the khál, which flowed within a few yards of his homestead. When he and his neighbour were on good terms, the latter allowed him a right of way across his homestead, but when for some reason or other they quarrelled, his neighbour would not allow him to use the road any longer, at least not for his cattle; it became, therefore, necessary that the boatbuilder should find a new road. I have seen the place myself, and can therefore say that the road was a necessity for Kamal and Golab, the two owners of the more remote homestead. When their neighbour Chandra Dali inhibited them from crossing his homestead, they tried to make a new road, a little to one side of the old one. Unfortunately there was a small bit of waste land in the new line of road, which belonged to Chandra Dali, and which, though it was of no use to him, he would not let them have. Here I should explain that the homesteads both of Chandra Dali and of Golab and Kamal were included in a taluq belonging to a member of the De Silva family of Sibpúr. Kamal and Golab's homestead, however, was a nim howala, and included in the first instance in a howala belonging to one Raj Narain Bannerji, which again was included in the De Silva taluq. Chandra Dali was also connected with Raj Narain Banarji, as he was his karshadar; but I believe this was for lands other than his homestead. Kamal and Golab first tried to get the little bit of waste land from Raj Narain, but though they got a right in it, they could not dispossess Chandra Dali, who to make his position stronger, suddenly put up a small hut on the land and placed an old female relative in it to act as watchwoman. By the way, it is rather a favourite trick with Bákarganj people to make use of their poor relations as chaukidars and as signs of possession. They run up a hut in a night, put an old man or woman into it, add a few pots and pans, and then when the police come they are ready to swear that the hut has been on the spot and in occupation for several years. Kamal and Golab being unable to get their road amicably, went off some fifteen miles to a powerful zamindar at Madhabpásha, who had long been anxious to get a footing in the village of Phalaghar, and who was on bad terms with the De Silvas, and offered to come under his zimba. He agreed; a deed was executed, whereby the zamindar bought in the name of his brother-in-law, for Rs.25, a portion of Kamal and Golab's nim howala; and shortly afterwards the real consideration was paid by the zamindar's despatching a body of clubmen to the village. They arrived in the night, and early next morning (it was Christmas Day) they and a party of ryots proceeded to make a road across the waste land; but, unfortunately for themselves, Chandra Dali and his relatives heard the noise of the workers, and rushed out to oppose them. A fight ensued, in which, as might be supposed, the professional clubmen were victorious, and in which two of Chandra Dali's party were killed and one severely wounded. This case is an illustration of the anarchy which often prevails in a Bákarganj village. Had De Silva or the Madhabpásha zamindar been good landlords, they might have arbitrated in the matter, and have satisfied both parties; but they preferred to indulge their natural animosities, and the above was the result.

It might be expected that I should give statistics of the number of under-tenures in Bákarganj, but, in fact, no trustworthy figures are procurable. The inquiries in connection with the road cess will doubtless give some information on the subject, though I doubt if even they will elicit complete information.

III. LAKHIRAJ, OR RENT-FREE TENURES.

The number of officially-recorded rent-free tenures is only twenty-three, and of these several are of recent origin, having been created by the rule, which was for some time in force, of selling rent free the properties which yielded less than a rupee of revenue to Government. There are, however, 1143 lakhiraj sanads or grants in the Collectorate record-room, and these are probably valid, though their authenticity has never been formally recognised, and it is not known even whether the lands referred to in them are in existence or not. The number of rent-free holdings in Bákarganj is in reality very considerable, though in most cases the quantity of land is so small that the Government officials did not inquire into the validity of the grant. Many of these rent-free lands are Bráhmuttar—*i.e.*, they are lands granted to Bráhmans. They are especially common in pargana Chandradwip, and are said to owe their origin chiefly to the liberality of Rajah Sheo Narain, who was a great patron of Bráhmans, and who ended by becoming insane and setting fire to his palace. In his liberality to priests he resembled that Scotch king who was described by one of his successors as a sore saint for the crown.

None of the lakhiraj tenures seems to be of any interest except the Srinagar holding of the Chandradwip Rajahs, and that at Sujábád, formerly possessed by some Afghan soldiers. Both of these have been described elsewhere.

PART II.

CHAPTER VIII.

THE PEOPLE OF BÁKARGANJ.

I. GENERAL REMARKS.

THE population of Bákarganj, according to the census of 1872, and after deductions on account of the transfer of the Mádaripúr subdivision, is 1,878,144; of whom 1,254,429 are Mahomedans, 615,269 Hindus, 4049 Budhists, and 3264 Christians.[1] It thus appears that two-thirds of the inhabitants are Mahomedans. The Hindus are in a minority in almost every part of the district, but are especially outnumbered in the south and in Dakhin Shahbázpúr, where nearly the whole population is Mahomedan. The Hindus are most numerous in the northern and western thanas of Gournadi, Jhalukátti, and Sarupkátti.

Before proceeding to describe the inhabitants of Bákarganj according to the divisions made by their different creeds, it seems right to say something of their general characteristics, apart from the colouring which particular religions may have given to portions of them.

Carlyle says that the most important thing about a man is his religion; but he afterwards so qualifies this remark, so flattens out its point, so to speak, that it

[1] See note at p. 247.

becomes the mere truism, that the most important thing about a man is his character, or even the tautological statement, that the most important thing about a man is—what is most important about him. It seems to me that it would be truer to say that the most important thing about an individual man is the character of his parents, and about a people the race to which it belongs. Certainly I do not think, in looking at the Bákarganj people, that it would be correct to say that the most important thing about the majority of them is whether they are Hindus or Mahomedans. They were Bengalis before they were Hindus or Mahomedans: as regards the world in general, the most important fact about them is that they belong to the Bengali race; and as regards Bengal, that they are natives of Bákarganj. It is true that Bákarganj is not a natural division of country, and that it is not even an old artificial one. Still it is a large and tolerably compact tract of territory, containing nearly two millions of inhabitants, who must, from contiguity of place and other similarity of circumstances, have some characteristics in common. We find, accordingly, that by general consent of foreigners, whether Englishmen or inhabitants of other parts of Bengal, the people of Bákarganj have certain peculiarities which mark them out from the rest of their countrymen. These peculiarities are not, I am sorry to say, of an amiable description, and consist in the possession of superior craftiness and greater turbulence of spirit. Hence the frequency of remarks such as that every man in Bákarganj is a lawyer, nothing is impossible in Bákarganj, &c. It would be idle to attempt to deny altogether the truth of such remarks. Foreigners seldom or never abuse the people of any country altogether without cause; and it is better for the latter to accept external criticisms as partially true, and endeavour to profit by them, than to get angry, and regard them as entirely false. What especially strikes foreigners is the litigiousness of the Bákarganj people, and no doubt this is a marked feature in their character. Cases, both civil and criminal, are more numerous and more intricate in Bákarganj than in other districts. Bákarganj ryots, too, are a byword for turbulence, and for the readiness with which they combine to oppose their landlords. Forgery and perjury are of frequent occurrence; and such is the insecurity of the relation of landlord and tenant, that a practice has arisen which is, I believe, almost peculiar to Bákarganj. I refer to the practice of zamindars, and other receivers of rent, taking *chaláns* from their ryots on the payment of rent; so that there are always two documents drawn up on such occasions, one being the receipt given to the payer, and the other the chalán given to the payee. The origin of this custom is the anxiety to preserve a record of title, chaláns being always filed in suits about land to prove possession by receipt of rent.

There is a famous description of the Bengali character by Macaulay, in which he says that what the Italian is to the Englishman, what the Hindu is to the Italian, the Bengali is to other Hindus. Looking at the characteristics of the people of Bákarganj as described by foreigners, we might carry on Macaulay's illustration, and say that what Bengalis are to other nations, that are the inhabitants of Bákarganj to other Bengalis. I may add that a Deputy-Magistrate, who had been long in the district, once localised the climax still further by saying that what Bákarganj is to Bengal generally, that the subdivision of Perozpúr is to the rest of Bákarganj.

As far as the degrees of comparison go, I think the

illustration a good one. If Macaulay's estimate of the Bengali character be correct, the Bákarganj people may be said to be Bengalis of the Bengalis, for they excel the rest of their countrymen in the points noticed by the essayist. But Macaulay's description is much too neat and epigrammatic to be true, and there are a great many lights and shades of Bengali character which he has not noticed. Assuming, however, his estimate to be correct, I think we may say that the people of Bákarganj are typical Bengalis, and may proceed to inquire how they come to be so. I am inclined to think that the answer is to be found in part in the facts that Bákarganj has been chiefly peopled by emigrants from the rest of Bengal, and that emigrants are generally people of marked character. It is the listless and sluggish who remain at home, preferring to bear the ills they have than to fly to those they know not of, while the active and enterprising endeavour to better themselves elsewhere. Just, then, as we find the Americans exhibiting certain of the qualities of the English in an exaggerated degree, so we may expect to find the Bákarganj people exhibiting certain Bengali characteristics with peculiar prominence. Again, we find that the people of Bákarganj have been less controlled and less subjected to extraneous influences than Bengalis generally; hence their characters have developed more fully and completely. The district has always been somewhat neglected and despised, and has lain apart from the stream of events. The people have been left to themselves amongst their jungles and swamps, and have practically enjoyed much freedom. If we ask Bengali gentlemen why Bákarganj people differ from the inhabitants of Nadiya or other more civilised districts, they commonly reply that it is because there are so few of the upper classes in the district. No doubt this is a *vera causa.* Bákarganj landlords are nearly all absentees, and the professional, and even the trading and shopkeeping classes, are largely composed of foreigners. There is not a single resident in the district who has an income of £10,000 per annum, and I believe there are not ten who have an income equal to that of the district judge. Nothing shows more clearly the absence of the upper classes from Bákarganj than the smallness of the returns from the income-tax. Thus we find that when all persons who had less than Rs.750 a year were exempt, there were only 1567 assessable persons in the whole district; and that when the minimum was raised to Rs.1000, there were only 847. We find also that the scarcity of rich people was most marked in the south of the district, and that in the large subdivision of Patuyakháli, with a population of upwards of 400,000, there were only eighty-four assessees when the minimum was Rs.750, and thirty-four when the minimum was Rs.1000. In other words, out of 400,000 people there are only about thirty who are worth £100 a year. At the same time, there is probably less actual want and poverty in Bákarganj than in the rest of Bengal. The soil is fertile, and Bákarganj ryots are notoriously comfortable. They have plenty of rice, can catch fish in every ditch and water-hole, and have cocoa-nuts, betel-nuts, plantains, &c., in their orchards. There is little they need buy except salt, clothes, and tobacco. We may therefore apply Longfellow's description of Grand Pré to Bákarganj, and say, "There the richest is poor, and the poorest lives in abundance." This plenty, combined with the feeling of ownership and independence produced by the system of peasant properties, gives vigour and energy to the character. The effect of the inaccessibility of Bákarganj on the disposition of the people has already been touched upon, but the subject calls for further elucidation. Bákarganj is difficult of access from Calcutta, for though it is only 180 miles distant, there is no land route, and boats take six or even ten days on the journey. The route, too, is through the dreaded and inhospitable Sundarbans, which, in the minds of the timorous Bengalis, are still haunted by dacoits and wild beasts. Hence we find that Bákarganj has been little visited by the great of the earth. Besides this external inaccessibility, Bákarganj has very few roads, and it is consequently exceedingly difficult to travel rapidly or with comfort. The islands of the district are surrounded by large rivers which are really formidable during the rains, and they are seldom visited by strangers, except in the cold weather. The south of the district especially is intersected by rivers and creeks, and as its climate during and immediately after the rains is considered unhealthy, it is generally abandoned for the greater part of the year by every one who can get away from it. It is in this part of the district, where the people have been much left to themselves, that we find their peculiarities most strongly developed. Not only are they separated from the outer world, but they are also isolated from one another, so that each person's individuality gets full scope. Villages in Bákarganj, and especially in the south, are very different from villages in Behar or the north-west, or even in Bengal generally. The houses are much more scattered, and there is little of collective village life. Each house stands by itself on its mound, surrounded by a thicket of fruit-trees, and there is often no other house in sight or nearer than several hundred yards. The intervening space, too, is generally a swamp across which it is toilsome and difficult to walk. In such villages the system of village police is almost non-existent. Mr Reilly, in an interesting passage of his report on the Bákarganj police, has touched upon this peculiarity of life in the south of the district, and assigns to it the frequency of serious crime.

I have said that Macaulay's estimate of the Bengali character is not a correct or complete one. I may here briefly state how it errs, in my opinion. It does not do justice to some virtues possessed by Bengalis—namely, temperance, frugality, and patience. Neither is it quite just in the matter of courage, for though the Bengali is cowardly in some respects, he is not altogether timid. For example, he is probably more courageous with regard to wild beasts than most Europeans. The inhabitants of Bákarganj are hardy boatmen, and often cross rivers in rough and dangerous weather. The most serious charge of all brought against Bengalis is that they are liars. On this head I may quote from a lecture which I delivered in Scotland some years ago: "As regards the charge of the Bengalis being liars, people who abuse them of course make a great deal of what Lord Macaulay has said on the subject in his essays on Clive and Warren Hastings. Now Lord Macaulay was, as all the world acknowledges, a very brilliant writer, but his eloquence and love of paradox were apt to lift him off his feet. He was a Scotchman by origin, and therefore he had to a certain extent the Scottish intellect, which, like the French, is deductive and generalising, and apt to draw large conclusions from a scanty induction of facts. . . . At the same time, I am not here to-night to defend the Bengalis, but to tell the truth about them as far as I know it, and therefore I must admit that they are rather addicted to falsehood. I think that the extent of their lying propensities has been exaggerated, and that a great deal of what we are apt to consider deliberate falsehood on their part proceeds from nervousness, from a want of precision in thought and expression, and from our ignorance and impatience. Still it is not to be denied that lying is the great vice of the Oriental character, just as harshness and want of feeling are probably the most distinctive vices of Western nations; and it is possible that in both cases many centuries will elapse before such characteristics be obliterated."

The following remarks may also be quoted: "The charge of ingratitude brought against Bengalis hardly deserves a serious answer. In the first place, it is not true that they are destitute of a word expressive of gratitude; and in the second place, even if the dictionary did not give such a word, every one who knows the natives knows that they have the sentiment in their hearts, and that they show it in their actions.

"The general character of the Bengali is amiable. He has no large sympathies and little vigour of mind, but he is gentle and affectionate, and very charitable to the poor. He is particularly fond of children, and a Bengali servant makes a capital nurse for his master's children; he is so patient with them, and so willing and delighted to sit with them and amuse them all day long. Bengalis, indeed, are said to spoil their children by over-indulgence, and certainly they seem to indulge their whims to almost any extent. I remember to have seen a common Bengali peasant ploughing his field, which happened to be at the time under two or three inches of water, while his little child was perched on his shoulder. On my asking why he had the child with him, I was told that it cried at being left behind when his father went out to plough. So the father had taken him out with him, though he would have to bear his weight the whole forenoon in order to keep him out of the water.

"One of the charges most frequently brought against the Bengali is his fondness for litigation. A wealthy native, it is said, plumes himself on having two or three heavy law pleas on hand, much as a wealthy Englishman plumes himself on the possession of a yacht or a picture gallery. Nor is the poorer native backward in his liking for the same kind of sport; nothing seems to delight a Bengali peasant so much as the having an opportunity of stating his claim in a court of justice. The great subjects of the lawsuits are disputes about land; for, as a rule, the commercial classes keep out of the courts, and, moreover, the Bengalis are much more an agricultural than a trading people. Land in India is not the property of a few, as it is in this country, for the system of peasant proprietorship is in vogue, and, except in the case of the inhabitants of great towns, almost every householder has his small piece of land. Sometimes he holds the land rent free, but generally pays rent for it, either to the British Government or more commonly to some superior landholder, or zamindar as he is called. The amount of rent depends a good deal upon the custom of the district, and cannot be increased at the mere will and pleasure of the zamindar. Neither can the tenant, or ryot as he is called, be evicted from his holding as long as he pays the customary rent, unless the zamindar can prove that certain changes have taken place in the value of the produce, &c., which make the old rent too low to be fair and equitable. Such proof is rather difficult, and leads to tedious and expensive litigation, and so ryot and zamindar generally settle the matter amicably. For example, if land becomes much more valuable on account of a large bazár having sprung up in its neighbourhood, or of a railway passing through the district, the ryot will consent to an increase of rent; and, on the other hand, if the land becomes impoverished from overcropping, or from drought, the landholder will make a corresponding deduction from the rent.

"The system of agriculture undoubtedly appears very rude, but it seems to answer well, for the Bengalis get capital crops from their lands. They plough with bullocks, or occasionally buffaloes. The plough is a very light and ramshackle-looking affair, which the ploughman carries over his shoulders when going to and from his work. It is made of wood and bamboo, with a little iron at the point, and does not go more than a couple of inches into the ground. Some European indigo-planters have tried deep ploughing with steam-ploughs, but the result has not answered their expectations, the crops being no better than those produced by the surface-ploughing, while the expense is much greater. In fact, much of Bengal is so fertile that we may apply to it the saying of some one about rich land in other countries, 'Tickle it with a hoe, and it smiles a harvest.' The great crop is rice; but besides this the Bengali ryot cultivates sugar-cane, tobacco, jute, &c. All these latter are much more valuable crops than rice, and require more trouble and expense for their cultivation. The rice is cut with a short knife or sickle, and is threshed by being trodden by cattle. The threshing-floor is a circular space in the field, made bare and hardened by beating down. The cattle employed are never muzzled.

"I have no wish to enter into the merits of the

vexed question of the comparative merits of large and small systems of agriculture, or, in other words, of the system of large farms and that of small holdings. I can only say that the latter seems to work well in Bengal, and that I should be very sorry to see the Bengali ryot or cottier sinking into the condition of a hired labourer. There is no doubt that the feeling of being to a certain extent his own master is a great satisfaction to the Bengali peasant-proprietor, and fosters in him an honourable spirit of independence—makes a man of him, in short, and keeps him from many bad habits. As a general rule, the Bengali peasant is a sober, well-conducted, frugal man, fond of his home and his family, and contented with his lot. Indeed, the great fault that many people find with him is that he is too easily pleased, and they would like better to see him have more wants, so that he might be stimulated to greater exertion in order to satisfy them. The great majority are very poor, and their houses are dark, comfortless-looking places, with bare floors and no furniture, except perhaps a wooden bedstead and a stool or two. Their houses are, in fact, little more than sheds for sleeping and cooking; for they are out of doors nearly all day, and when they come home in the evening they are not long in retiring to rest. Instead of one house containing two or three rooms, as in this country, the Bengali peasant's house consists of one room only, so that he has generally two or three houses in his homestead—viz., a sleeping-house, a kitchen, and a cowhouse. The well-to-do ryots often have a fourth house, which they use as a parlour in which to sit and talk with their friends, or as a sort of chapel for worship. All these houses are constructed of bamboos, with a few wooden posts to support the thatched roofs, and are movable, the peasant always carrying away at least the roof of his house when he makes a flitting. Of course, the comfortless appearance of the Bengali's house is in part explained by the simplicity of his habits and the warmth of the climate. . . .

"Such money as the ryot has he expends in buying ornaments for his wife and children, or in marrying his sons and daughters. These ceremonies are the only times when he becomes thoroughly improvident and extravagant. Undoubtedly the thoughtless expenditure of money on such occasions is very foolish, but it has always been an Oriental custom to spend largely at marriages; and it appears to me that the Bengali who spends his savings upon his son's marriage is not much worse than the man who ruins himself by horse-racing or a contested election.

"Although the peasantry of Bengal are generally poor, yet, except in the case of a famine, there is hardly anything like actual destitution among them. The small piece of land which each holds supplies sufficient rice to keep his family from starvation, and the climate does the rest, for warm clothing and substantial dwelling-houses are not required. Hence it is in great measure that the country manages to get on without anything in the shape of a poor-law or organised relief, and that there are not many perpetual beggars except those who are either too idle to work or who are led by religious motives to subsist on alms. The above are in great measure the causes of the absence of destitution, but there is another cause, and that is the charitableness of Hindus. It is not the habit of the Oriental to devote large sums to the founding of hospitals, or to other great schemes of charity, but he is very open-handed in the distribution of food and clothing, and many rich men spend large sums yearly in relieving the poor at their gates. No doubt a great deal of this charity is indiscriminate, and must do harm; still it does some good, and often saves the lives of those who have become temporarily destitute from the failure of their crops or from other causes.

"In spite, or perhaps in some measure in consequence of the distinctions of caste, there is a considerable amount of sympathy between the rich and poor in India, and a mutual understanding of their respective trials and difficulties. I have said that this sympathy may in some measure be a consequence of caste, and though the statement seems paradoxical, it contains a truth; for it is plain that the very fact of the fixity of caste, the knowledge that a difference of caste can never be effaced, and that the Sudra can never marry the daughter of the Bráhman, or sit down at meat with him, must extinguish jealousy and make the high-caste man feel perfectly safe in being kind to those below him. The high-caste man in India has none of those fears which are said to haunt some of the great in this country; the fear, namely, lest the distinctions of rank and station become obliterated, and all persons be reduced to one common level. Moreover, there is no necessary connection between high caste and riches, and it often happens that a man of high caste is poor, while the low-caste Sudra is rich.

"Apart from all these causes there is also the fact that a feeling of sympathy and compassion for poverty and old age has always been a characteristic of the Oriental mind."

I may also quote from the same lecture some remarks on Bengali women:—

"Perhaps the most widely-known fact in this country about women in India is that of widows being obliged to burn themselves along with the bodies of their husbands. This horrid practice of *satí*, as it is called, was at one time prevalent all over Bengal, and there are still Europeans living in India who have witnessed the spectacle of a widow-burning, even in the neighbourhood of Calcutta. The custom is now strictly forbidden in British territory, and has become as obsolete as the practice of duelling among ourselves. The abolition of satí is one of the benefits which Hindus owe to Lord William Bentinck, and on the pedestal of the statue erected to that nobleman in Calcutta there is a bronze representing a Bráhman leading a young Hindu widow to the funeral pyre, but prevented from effecting his purpose by an officer of the British Government, while the mother of the dead man holds up her grandchild to her daughter-in-law and invites her to live for its sake.

"Nowadays Hindu widows are not only not burnt, but they are even allowed to marry again, and instances of widow-marriages are by no means uncommon. It is to be hoped that this reform will spread rapidly, for the lot of a Hindu widow is commonly a hard one. Often she is a mere child, for early marriages continue to be the rule, and a parent is thought to fail in his duty to his daughter if he does not get her married by the time she is eight or nine years of age. Soon after her husband may die, but she is bound by the laws of society to remain single, and to spend her days in perpetual widowhood for a husband whom she may never have seen. She must relinquish all her jewels and finery, eat only once a day, fast every new moon, and absent herself from every scene of festivity and social enjoyment. It is probable enough that many a young and childless Hindu widow, finding herself stranded almost before she has entered on the current of life, may curse the humanity which has preserved her, and wish in the bitterness of her heart that the sharp but short pain of fire might relieve her of the burden of existence.

"Widows, however, are not the only women in India who are unfortunate in their lot. All women are considered as inferior to men, and therefore as subject to their control. As one of the Hindu law-books expresses it, 'In every stage of her life woman is created to obey. At first she yields obedience to her father and mother. When married, she submits to her husband and to her father- and mother-in-law. In old age she must be ruled by her children. During her life she never can be under her own control.'

"The wife never eats with the husband, but waits until he has done, or, as the same law-book puts it, 'What woman would eat till her husband has first had his fill?' Speaking of other duties, the same authority says, 'When her husband sings, she must be in ecstasy; when he dances, she views him with delight: if he speaks of science, she is filled with admiration; when in his presence, she must be always gay.' So the poor woman must have occasionally a hard time of it; and one wonders what Mrs Caudle would have said to some of these regulations. Fortunately, the Bengali husband is not much given to joviality; and if he ever dance, he does not do so with young ladies; and if he ever sing, he is not likely to indulge in such strains as 'we won't go home till morning,' a ditty which it would be too much to expect any daughter of Eve to listen to with equanimity, far less ecstasy. As a curious instance of the reserve which a wife maintains with regard to her husband, I may mention that she is most unwilling to utter his name, and that when she is a witness in court, she generally fences with the magistrate a long time before she acknowledges whose wife she is. The Bengali husband has a similar delicacy in referring to his wife, and if he has occasion to mention her, generally describes her by some such circumlocution as 'the mother of my children.'

"'One touch of nature makes the whole world kin.' The Bengali matron resembles her British sister in her unwillingness to answer another question which the magistrate is sometimes obliged to put to her. She objects stoutly to mentioning her age, and generally takes refuge in the plea of ignorance. When addressing her husband in private, she calls him *náth*—*i.e.*, lord.

"The seclusion of women is a practice which does not appear to have been in force in early Hindu times, and which the Hindus are supposed to have learned from their Mahomedan conquerors. It is, however, almost universal now, and few Bengali women of respectability will consent to appear before strangers. The part of the house she inhabits is that farthest away from publicity, and is called emphatically the 'inner place.' In Scotch phrase, she spends all her time in the *ben*, and never appears in the *but*. When she is obliged to give evidence or to hold any communication with a stranger, she does so from behind a curtain or from within a covered palanquin. Some affect to be still more particular, and will not hold direct communication with any man, even though a curtain be hung between them. Such ladies insist upon the conversation being carried on through the intervention of a third party, generally a female servant, who carries the questions and answers from one to the other. The pomp and circumstance of an interview conducted with these formalities sometimes contrast ludicrously with the silliness of the questions.

"When a native lady has occasion to travel, she does so in a covered palanquin or litter, or in a boat. Sometimes she travels on an elephant, the howdah being carefully covered over. Many now make use of the railway, and I have heard bitter complaints from Bengali boatmen of the loss of custom sustained from this cause. 'Formerly,' they said, 'a gentleman taking his family to Benares or Allahabad, or other place of pilgrimage, would hire a boat, and would be weeks or even months on the journey; but now he engages a carriage in the train, and the whole distance is performed in one day.' Of course no native lady ever thinks of riding on horseback, and next to their dancing with other men than their husbands, nothing in the conduct of our countrywomen seems to surprise them so much as their riding.

"The only time when a native lady has a chance of seeing the world is when she goes on pilgrimage, and doubtless this is one reason why pilgrimages are so popular. It is by no means entirely or even chiefly from religious motives that women crowd to Hurdwar or to Púrí, &c., and I think our missionaries are wrong when they refuse to see anything in pilgrimages but the degrading superstition of the Hindu religion. It is, of course, foolish and pitiable that Hindu women should suppose that bathing in the Ganges or Bráhmaputra will cleanse them from their sins, but the change of scene and the novelty must do some good. I am persuaded that many rich old women go to the Ganges or to Kámrup for much the same reason that rich women in England go to Brighton or Homburg. When a Hindu widow has become advanced in years, and has either no children or they are settled in life, it is considered the proper thing for her to retire to the holy city of Benares, and to remain there till her death. Many old men do the same, and the good results of living and dying in Benares are said by some to be so great that even a Christian dying there has a chance of getting to heaven!

"Women in the poorer classes are of course unable to maintain the state of rigid seclusion I have described. They must go to the tank or the well to draw water, and they have to go on foot if they want to visit a temple or witness a religious ceremony. In all ranks, however, the marketing is done by men; the only women who are ever seen in the markets being poor widows who have no one to look after them or bring them home their food."

The following remarks on the subject of food I extract from the same lecture:—

"Speaking generally, the Bengali is one of the most temperate of men, and the large class of temptations to vice produced by strong drink have little hold over him. His chief drink is cold water, about the quality of which he is most fastidious; hence it is that the digging of wells and tanks is considered such a meritorious act. At the same time, the Bengali forms no exception to the general observation that every nation has some kind of stimulant, and he supplies the place of wine and spirits by tobacco and pán. Pán is a compound of lime, the leaf of the pán plant, and the nut of the betel or supari tree, with occasionally other ingredients in the form of spices. Both tobacco and pán are universally used by men, and all women chew pán, and not a few of them smoke also. These practices even enter into their religious worship; for with the daily food of rice, &c., with which they supply their gods, they offer also pán, and in some cases tobacco and a pipe in which to smoke it. A Hindu seldom eats flesh except what has been offered in sacrifice, and therefore when he wishes to treat himself to a meat dinner, the orthodox way of doing so is to offer a goat or a buffalo to the goddess Kali, a goddess who delights in bloody sacrifices. The animal is killed at her shrine by beheading, some executioners being so expert that they can sever the neck of a buffalo at a single blow.[1] Most Hindus eat fish without scruple, though some Bráhmans are so particular as to reject even this kind of animal food. Fish are abundant in the rivers and tanks of Bengal, and are caught either by nets or with the rod. Some scrupulous people draw a distinction between these two modes of capture, and will catch fish in nets but will not bait lines for them. The reason they give for the distinction

[1] There is, however, some trickery in the way this is done. Not only is the buffalo selected for sacrifice generally only a calf, but it is not standing loose or only tethered when it is decapitated. The unfortunate animal's neck is placed in an upright wooden fork, and there secured by a bolt. Several persons then pull the hind legs and others the head until the latter is almost torn from the body, and the neck becomes tight and drawn, and almost as thin as a knife-edge. It is after these preparations that the beheading takes place. They take some time, and meanwhile the poor beast bellows with fear and pain, and is almost dead before the final blow is given. I have never witnessed the sight myself, but it has been described to me as being a most horrid one, and as calling for the interposition of the Legislature. No doubt some fixing of the head is necessary, and such a mode of executing a bull as is shown in Raphael's cartoon is probably an impossibility. At all events, the real circumstances of a sacrifice in ancient times were probably much less graceful than the painter has represented them to be. Still, if buffaloes and goats must be sacrificed, some less painful mode of killing them might be adopted. If this were done, there would be comparatively little evil in the practice, for the victims are generally eaten, so that a sacrifice is only a roundabout way of procuring animal food.

is that rod-fishing implies deceit and treachery, the fish being deluded into being caught by the fisherman's putting on the mask of kindness and pretending to offer them food. Fowls are an abomination to the Hindu; so when a Mahomedan and a Hindu are next-door neighbours, it is a frequent complaint of the latter that the Mahomedan's fowls have flown into his courtyard or kitchen and defiled it. Fowls' eggs are also regarded as unclean, though, strangely enough, many Hindus will eat duck and goose eggs without scruple. The main food of the Bengali consists of rice, which is generally prepared by boiling. He cooks only once a day, dining about midday; and if he takes a second meal, it is eaten cold, and consists of the remains of his midday meal. The Bengali eats with his fingers, using the right hand only, and considering it improper to touch his food with the left. As rice is not a nutritious food it is necessary to eat it in large quantities in order to obtain the requisite amount of sustenance. The constant use of one kind of food cannot be wholesome, and Bengalis are in consequence often dyspeptic. In some parts of Bengal, where the evils arising from want of change of food are aggravated by the badness of the water, the pangs of indigestion occasionally become so great as to drive the sufferers to commit suicide. There were several instances of suicide from this cause in the district (Mymensing) to which I was first appointed, and in every case a *post mortem* examination showed a quantity of undigested rice in the stomach. Very few natives use tea or coffee except in illness, when they are very fond of a cup of tea, and in the case of fever consider it a good remedy. Corpulence is considered by Bengalis a sign of health, and of a man's being at ease in his possessions. They say that when a man is poor he is fretful and envious of the prosperity of others, and that these feelings keep him lean, but that when he gets on in the world his mind becomes tranquil and he grows fat. Certainly, whether from this cause or from want of exercise, wealthy Hindus are generally fat, and they take care to keep themselves so by consuming large quantities of melted butter, sugar, and sweetmeats."

The above remarks were written with reference to Bengalis in general, but they apply very well to the districts in Eastern Bengal, in which my experience has been almost exclusively gained. I shall supplement them with some further observations.

It is often said that drinking has become prevalent among the upper classes in Bengal, but I believe there is a good deal of exaggeration on this point. A desire to imitate the English has led some wealthy and indolent Babus to take to champagne and brandy, and the harder work, and change of hours for meals, &c., occasioned by attendance at our courts or by Government service, have led some lawyers and public servants to habituate themselves to the use of stimulants; but as a general rule, the educated classes are too poor to drink to any great extent, even if they felt inclined to do so. Those who do drink to excess generally confine their orgies to Saturday night, and they have then the whole of Sunday in which to recover from their debauch.

The Bengali professional men residing in Barisál have, I am sorry to say, rather a bad reputation for drinking. Formerly they drank rum, but several rum-drinkers having died suddenly, the topers have now taken to country spirit, which they consider more wholesome. This spirit is manufactured in the Public Distillery at Barisál, and there is also a distillery in each of the subdivisions. It is made from *gúr—i.e.*, native sugar—and is, I believe, a tolerably pure spirit, and is generally sold very weak. I believe some natives of Bákarganj excuse themselves for drinking on the ground that the salt air requires the use of stimulants; and all natives remark that Englishmen thrive better at places on the coast —such as Diamond Harbour, Chittagong, &c.—than natives. It is not improbable that a vegetarian diet is less suitable for the sea-coast than a meat diet. Women, I believe, never drink, except the prostitute class, which is a very large one in towns.

The excise system of the English Government undoubtedly tends to familiarise Bengalis with the subject of drinking, and to throw temptation in their way. In this respect our Government contrasts unfavourably with that of the Moguls, who seem never to have derived profit from an excise on liquor. The central distillery system is, no doubt, an improvement in many respects on the old out-still system, but it certainly mixes Government up more with the trade; and as natives are apt to believe that it is the duty of Government to teach morality, they may be led to think that Government approves of drinking, and this may have a prejudicial effect on their ideas. There is one way in which the central distillery system works badly, which has not, I think, been sufficiently noticed; this is the corrupting influence it exercised on the Government servants employed in it. The inferior excise officers are of necessity natives, and they are, I believe, always Hindus, for Mahomedans will have nothing to do with the liquor traffic. They are not very well paid, and have no prospect of rising to any lucrative or important employment. They are also looked down upon by their countrymen on account of their occupation. The natural consequences follow, that the excise department is officered by men of inferior ability and standing, who are less capable of withstanding temptations which are of a peculiarly seductive kind. They have to deal with a rather low class of men—namely, the vintners and *ganja*-sellers—and they have much opportunity for fraud. They have also the temptation to drink offered by its being possible to get liquor at little or no cost, and I fear that to many this temptation is too strong to be resisted. My experience has shown me that there is more drinking among excise officers than in any other class of Government servants.[1]

Ganja is consumed in considerable quantities by boatmen and others, and not unfrequently leads to the commission of crime and to insanity. It is imported into the district from Rajshye. The stricter sects of Mahomedans, such as the Ferazis, use little or no ganja, and as far as my experience extends, it is the Dacca boatmen who are most prone to the vice.

Opium is used medicinally and also as a stimulant by the Hindus, especially after they have passed middle age. They think that it is a preservative against rheumatism, and also that it is nourishing. It is sold at the Treasury in two-pound cakes at a cost of about £1, 3s. per pound; it is also sold in similar quantities at the central distilleries. It is of course only dealers who buy opium in cakes. They retail it in *tólas* (rupee-weights), or still

[1] The revenue in 1873–74 from country spirits in Bákarganj was Rs.17,910, against Rs.17,228 in the previous year. This is more than in Mymensing, another district of the Dacca division with which Bákarganj has several points of resemblance. On the other hand, ganja yielded in Bákarganj only Rs.28,457, against Rs.97,846 in Mymensing; spirits, Rs.18,364, against Rs.37,658 in Mymensing. The entire net revenue from excise in Bákarganj in 1873–74 was Rs.62,249, against Rs.154,095 in Mymensing for the same period.

smaller quantities, charging of course somewhat more than the wholesale price. Hence it is easy to see that opium is consumed only by the comparatively wealthy. I have already spoken of the almost universal use of tobacco by the male portion of the population. It is mixed with gúr, and smoked in the water-pipe or hookah, familiarly known amongst Europeans as the hubble-bubble. There is not much chewing of tobacco, nor is snuff largely taken, though pleaders and others who cannot always find an opportunity of smoking, occasionally carry snuff-boxes. Hardly any tobacco is grown in the district, and the wants of the people are almost entirely supplied from Kuch Behar and Rangpúr. Nalchiti is the principal mart of the trade. Tobacco is not allowed in the jail, and no provision in the jail code is more difficult to enforce than this. The prisoners have endless devices for procuring the drug, and it is probable that even in the best regulated jails they are occasionally successful. Even in jails in which discipline is most lax, the prisoners cannot however get their smoke regularly, and this is no doubt felt as one of the greatest hardships they experience in jail; it might therefore be a useful means of rewarding good conduct to grant permission to smoke. I may mention that I once knew the case of a native who had given up smoking altogether, because he lost the habit during a six months' imprisonment. Besides pán and tobacco, another form of stimulant is obtained from highly-spiced curries. Boatmen and others who are much exposed to the weather are notorious for the use of large quantities of red pepper in their curries.

There is in Barisál a large number of professional prostitutes, and there are some also in every bazár. They are chiefly Hindus. The destitute condition of many

Hindu widows no doubt often drives them to prostitution as a means of living, and when a Hindu woman has thus fallen there is no way open for her return to her home. On the other hand, among Mahomedans it is by no means uncommon for a man of respectable position to marry a prostitute, or, as the phrase is, to take his wife out of the bazár. Such an action is regarded as laudable rather than otherwise, as it restores a woman to virtue, and it is said that such women not uncommonly make very good wives. It is a singular illustration of native feeling that one of the most common words used to denote a prostitute is *peshagar*, which literally means a professional person, as if a woman's profession or trade must necessarily be an immoral one.

AMUSEMENTS.—The peasantry of Bákarganj have not many pastimes. As a rule, the Bengali is a sedate and somewhat melancholy personage, and even Bengali children seldom let their high spirits run away with them. The cares of a family, which so early fall on a Bengali, undoubtedly tend to steady and even sometimes to depress him, and his low diet and the relaxing nature of the climate keep him from boisterousness or horse-play. At the same time, he is easily pleased, and has a childish delight in fireworks, *tamashas*, or shows of every kind, and in kite-flying, which is practised with great assiduity at one period of the year. All, whether Hindus or Mahomedans, take more or less part in the durga puja processions, and in the *navanna*, or harvest-home. The durga puja, indeed, is quite the Bengali Christmas. Every one who can afford to do so, and even very many who have to borrow money for the purpose, go to their homes at this time and entertain their friends. There is very little drinking or other dissipation, but there is a vast amount of talking and eating and smoking, and very late hours are kept. A Bengali's power of sitting up at night on such occasions is wonderful, and he will listen with invincible patience to hours of monotonous singing. *Játras,* theatrical performances, *nátches,* are common at this season. Bengali women especially look forward to the coming of the durga puja, for the annual supply of clothes is bought at this time, and it is a pleasant sight to go into the villages and see men, women, and children in their new attire.

Boat-races take place at the durga puja and at the Bengali new year, and even the native Christians cannot resist the pleasure of joining in them. Curiously enough, horse or rather pony races are a favourite pastime in Bákarganj, especially among the Mahomedans of the south of the district. The ponies are ridden by boys across the wide open space left after the rice crops have been cut. I do not think that there is any betting on such occasions. Marriages take place chiefly in the cold season, and, except among the Ferazies, are celebrated with considerable pomp, firing of guns, beating of drums, &c.

At one time a gambling mania took possession of the people of Barisál, and this ancient and, so to speak, classic vice of Hindustan is still a good deal practised in the villages.

Professional men and Government servants generally make a holiday of the English Sunday, but the peasantry of course do not observe it. Neither, I think, do the Mahomedans particularly observe Friday, except perhaps that they say their prayers oftener and more publicly on that day. For Mahomedans, the great holiday is the Maharam, though the Sunies among them do not much regard it. The Maharam is a movable feast; a circumstance which often causes a good deal of inconvenience. The durga puja is also a movable feast, and sometimes comes too early in the season to be enjoyable, at least by Europeans. The Mahomedans are strict enough in observing the fast of the Ramzán, and as it too is movable, their sufferings are often very great; for example, it is no light thing for a Mahomedan boatman to work, as he often will, from sunrise to sunset in an exhausting July day without eating or drinking, or even smoking. On the other hand, the fast is over as soon as the sun sets, and before it has risen again the Mahomedan has made two and sometimes three meals—that is, he eats a little as soon as the sun goes down, makes an ample dinner at about midnight, and gets up again at three or four in the morning and has his food and his darling smoke before the labours of the day begin.

It is not without pleasure that one sees how human nature asserts itself during the Ramzán, and proves too strong for the curbing influence of superstition. The fast was undoubtedly intended as a means of mortifying the flesh, but many turn it into an occasion for feasting, and it is notorious that all the best dinners are given at this season. It is at this time too that the sweetmeat-sellers make their greatest profits, and as soon as the sun has set the Mahomedans make haste to gorge themselves with all the delicacies they can procure.

RIOTS.—Bákarganj used to be famous for its riots. The *lathials*, or clubmen, however, who fought in them were in many cases inhabitants of other districts, especially of Farídpúr, which was formerly as much noted for its lathials as Bikrampúr was and is for its clerks and *maharirs.* In many cases the riots were fomented by the zamindars and taluqdars, but many were also got up by the villagers themselves. This last circumstance has often prevented magistrates from nipping breaches of the peace in the bud, and thus helped to give Bákarganj its bad name. Before zamindars fight with one another, there are lawsuits and simmerings of various kinds before the actual outbreak, so that the authorities have time to be warned and to take preventive measures; but villagers break out into quarrels suddenly and unexpectedly. It is to the credit of the ryots that they are so independent and so prepared to assert their rights without seeking the aid of the zamindars, but the circumstance certainly damages the criminal returns.

It may be added that the definition of a riot in the penal code is so general that many comparatively trifling offences can be brought under it. Bengalis are gregarious in their mode of action; and their custom of two or three brothers, with their families, living in one homestead increases the number of persons interested in any quarrel. It takes only five persons to make a riot, and this number of men can be furnished from nearly every house in which two or three brothers live. The greatest and most notorious dispute in the district is that which culminated in the Singhkháli case, and as its history throws a considerable light on the genesis and development of riots, and on the state of Bákarganj some twenty years ago, I subjoin an account of it taken from official records.

Extract from the remarks of Mr Steer, Judge of Bákarganj, on the trial of Gogan Mia and others, 14th September 1854, and 5th January 1855:—

"The chief person who figures in this case is Gourhunoodin, commonly and extensively known as Gogan Mia. He is charged with being concerned in eight distinct cases, chiefly of plunder, riot, and arson. The rest of the prisoners appear in distinct calendars, some in some and some in others. It will be advisable to give a brief history of past events which led to these crimes.

"Pargana Syedpúr belongs in portions of ten anas and six anas to Lalla Mitrajit Singh and Babu Birja Rattan. The pargana has, as is usual in this district, several valuable dependent taluqs in it. The desire of each of the two sharers seems to have been to get exclusive possession of as many of these valuable properties as they could each manage. Summary suits were brought unknown to and against the taluqdars, and all the tenures purchased in for a song. In some cases the old proprietors fought the purchasers, in others the purchase by one of the zamindars led to disputes with his co-sharer, and thus things continued to go on. At length the ten-ana proprietor seems to have resolved on taking vigorous measures to put down opposition, come from what quarter it might. For this purpose he secured the goodwill of two brothers, indubitably the most notorious turbulent characters to be found in this notoriously lawless district. These brothers were Gogan Mir and Mohan Mir (since not inaptly named the Gog and Magog of these parts). The means employed to gain them over to the ten-ana interest was a lease on easy terms of certain desirable properties; but this compact was destined to be of short duration, from the bad faith of the ten-ana proprietor, who, after receiving a great part of the purchase-money of one of the taluqs transferred to the Mias, refused to complete the sale by the acceptance of the remainder of the purchase-money and the delivery of the deed of sale. The alliance before existing was thus cut asunder, and these parties became Mitrajit Singh's worst enemies. Innumerable were the *foujdari* (criminal) cases which these parties brought against each other; but the long purse of the Babu soon exhausted the small means of the Mias in this expensive and profitless warfare, and then the Mias changed their tactics. Leaving the Babu to the courts, the Mias gave him real cause to resort to them. They plundered the zamindar's cutchery, they robbed and oppressed all who professed to be favourable to him; and this course of life proved so tempting, from the plunder obtained, that the Mias were able, without any money of their own, to collect and keep together a force which Mitrajit's hired bands were not strong enough to cope with. Seeing that the Mias were such a match for his old opponent, Birja Rattan, the six-ana proprietor, moved by past wrongs, and hopeful that the utter ruin of his adversary would secure him from the like in future, joined hands with the Mias, who thereby felt so strong that they defied not only Mitrajit but the police. A fortified house was built, from which the rabble of that part of the country issued to plunder the inhabitants. Not a day passed that a report of some adventure did not reach the station; and at length the police, who made several ineffectual attempts to apprehend the Mias, reported that they were powerless, and entreated the Magistrate to take the field in person. And indeed it was time he should do so, for the district was in a state bordering on insurrection. The Magistrate, however, did not go in person, but he ordered three *darogahs* and the entire police of three thanas, with all their chaukidars, to attack the Mias' stronghold, and to capture them. The attempt made to do so hardly merits to be called an attempt. The cowardly police, so strong in numbers, hardly dared show their faces within sight of the Mias' stockade, and all fled on the first show of resistance. On the report of this discomfiture reaching the Magistrate, he determined to proceed in person to the spot. He did so, and found the fort deserted by its old defenders. Everything about the place gave evidence of the great concourse of men who had lately been assembled there. Weapons of various sorts, and gunpowder, and materials for making it, with remnants of plundered property, were found in plenty in and about the premises.

"The Magistrate having left the place, Gogan and Mohan of course soon returned, and the proprietors having in the meantime been induced to compromise their differences, the Mias no longer confined their depredations against the adherents of the ten-ana shares, but robbed and plundered every one without discrimination. A new species of toll, or rather black-mail, then first began to be heard of. This toll was called *luca* or torch salami; and if money commensurate with the demand was not paid by the owner, the torch was applied, and his house burnt down before his eyes. At length a high reward led to the capture of Gogan, one of the two Mias, and he has been made over in eight distinct cases, some of which occurred prior to the Magistrate's appearance before his house, and some subsequently to that event."

On this case coming before the judges of the Nizamat Adâlat, they severely remarked that the sobriquets of Gog and Magog, given to the two prisoners in the Sessions Judge's letter of reference, were quite out of place, and evinced a levity which was too indiscreet to be passed over without some notice. Mr Alexander, the Magistrate, was resisted in an attempt to capture Mohan and to destroy his fortification. His letter of 19th December 1854 thus describes the circumstances: "We had to walk, I should say, upwards of two miles before we reached a khál at the end of a long avenue that leads direct to Mohan Mia's house. Having crossed the khál without meeting with any resistance or even seeing any opponent, we marched on towards the house through an avenue some five hundred yards long and not more than twelve or thirteen feet broad, lined on both sides with tall cocoa-nut and other trees, thick jungle, and a deep ditch. As up to this time I had not seen the darogah return, I imagined he had hitherto met with no opposition, and must have arrived at Mohan Mia's house. My astonishment, therefore, was great when, without any previous intimation of an attack, from sixty to eighty *sulfiwallahs*, or spearmen, each armed with a spear of about twelve feet in length, and defended by a shield, gun-shot and sulfi-proof, capable of covering the whole body in a stooping posture, according to their mode of attack, came rushing down the avenue to oppose our farther progress. They were evidently well-trained and determined men, for they came down without flinching, even when they saw us three Europeans in front of our party with guns in our hands. Four abreast they advanced in an orderly and compact body. As soon as we saw them we called out to them to retreat and disperse, but not to attack us. Instead of retreating they came on the faster, each man advancing in a stooping posture, with the whole of his body covered by the shield in the left hand, and brandishing the spear in the right hand. We again urged them to retreat, but they were bent on an attack. Being most desirous of avoiding bloodshed,

I desired our party to retreat gradually, with our faces towards the enemy and our guns levelled. In this manner we retreated about ten paces, when the assailants approached still nearer. A third warning proved equally ineffectual; they persisted in coming on, and there was not the least doubt that they intended to kill us. They approached to within ten yards of us, and in another second their spears would have been into us, when, seeing no hope of keeping them off by any other means, we each of us fired our double-barrelled guns, which was loaded with shot, at the sulfiwallah directly in front of us. About six of them rolled over on the ground, but as they were mostly only hit about the left leg, they managed to get up and limp off. Those in the rear, however, were not checked by this discharge, but rushed on as before. We were therefore compelled to make use of our second guns, which were loaded with ball. In this second volley some five men must have been killed. Upon this the whole body of spearmen retired in confusion, but stopped and took up their stand at Mohan Mia's house, some thirty or forty yards in front of us, where there was a reserve force of spearmen and gunmen. Thinking at first they had fled for good, we followed them up for about twenty yards, within which distance I myself saw three men lying dead. I ordered their bodies to be carried off by my police, but the confusion was such that my order was not executed."

Mr Alexander was on this occasion accompanied by two of the Messrs Morrell from Morrellganj, and the tradition is that Mohan Mia's people did not know that the Magistrate was present, and mistook him and his companions for Sibpúr Feringhies, whom they thought the zamindars had hired to attack them. Mr Alexander retreated without securing any prisoners, and he mentions that some one in Mohan Mia's house had the audacity to fire a gun after them. Mohan Mia shortly afterwards surrendered himself to the authorities, and as he and his brother were each sentenced to fourteen years' imprisonment, the combination of rioters came to an end.

The visit to the house referred to in Mr Steer's judgment, was, I believe, one made by Mr Harrison, and took place before Mr Alexander's visit. Mr Harrison's letter contains an interesting description of the way in which the house was fortified. It is dated, I think, 28th February 1854.

FAIRS.—There are several fairs held in the district, but none of them is of great importance. I do not think that any of them is attended by the inhabitants of other districts, and there is certainly none of them which can at all compare in importance with the Kartik Barani fair in the neighbouring district of Dacca. Nearly all the fairs are held in the cold weather, and the result of this sensible arrangement is that there is very little sickness at any of them. The Perozpúr fair, which is held on the occasion of the Dol Jatra (March), is the only one which takes place far on in the season. By far the oldest of all the fairs is that called the Kalisuri Mela. It is held at Kalisuri, a small village on the borders of the Baufal thana (Patuyakháli subdivision), in the month of Agrahan (December). It is said to have been established some two hundred years ago by a Mahomedan saint named Syed Al Arfan, and his tomb is still shown at Kalisuri. It lies at the foot of a very old banyan-tree, and is visited by great numbers of believers, some of whom sacrifice oxen on the spot.

I am told, however, that the number of worshippers has diminished of late years owing to the spread of Ferazi tenets.

The tradition is that Syed Al Arfan was a holy man who had the power of working miracles, and that one day, as he was floating down the river on his magical carpet, he saw a Hindu girl come down to the bank to wash rice. He asked her to cook some food for him, and when she said that she could not cook for a Mahomedan, he bade her look into the vessel in which she had been washing the rice. On her doing so, she saw that the rice was already cooked—a miracle which made her at once become a convert to the Syed's religion. She besought him to grant her a boon, and in reply he promised that the place where she was standing should become the site of a great annual gathering, and that it should be called after her name. As the girl's name was Kali, and she belonged to the Suri caste, the village and fair received the name of Kalisuri.

Kalisuri fair is by no means a gay or animated gathering. There is a grave air of business about it, and it is very useful to the country-people, as they buy their winter clothing, &c., at it; but as a spectacle it is nothing, and the impression produced on the casual visitor is one of very great dulness. The booths are chiefly occupied by Barisál shopkeepers, and the goods exposed are for the most part the same as those sold in any ordinary bazár. The only frivolities allowed are a merry-go-round, and perhaps an exhibition of a *ban-manush* (ourang - outang) or a leopard. One most commendable feature in the management of this fair is that no prostitutes are allowed to practise their trade in it, nor do they visit it. In this respect Kalisuri offers a most edifying contrast to the other fairs in the district, where prostitutes abound, and immorality assumes its grossest and most disgusting form. No doubt the semi-religious character of the Kalisuri fair keeps away the prostitutes. I do not think that any drinking goes on at Kalisuri, and there is not much at the other fairs, although a good deal of ganja is sold at them.

The other principal fairs are those of Kalaskátti, Jhalukátti, Banaripara, and Lakutia.

II. MAHOMEDANS.

I have already said that the majority of the inhabitants are Mahomedans. This preponderance of Mahomedans is a feature which is common to all the districts of Eastern Bengal, and which becomes most marked as we approach the seaboard. *A priori* we might have expected that the proportion of Mahomedans would have been largest in the neighbourhood of the Mahomedan seats of Government, but Mr Beverley has pointed out in his report on the census that the facts of the case are otherwise. "In Dacca, which for a long time contained the seat of Government, Mahomedans are very slightly in excess of Hindus. In Maldah, which contained the city of Gour, the Mahomedans form only 46 per cent. of the population. In Murshidábád they are scarcely 45 per cent. In Patna they only form 12 per cent. of the inhabitants of the district. On the other hand, in Bákarganj, Tipperah, Rangpúr, and Mymensing they constitute two-thirds of the population; and in Dinajpúr, Nadiya, Jessore, and Farídpúr more than half. This circumstance seems to point to the conclusion that the existence of Mahomedans in Bengal is not due so much to the introduction of Moghal blood into the country as to the conversion of the former inhabitants, for whom a rigid system of caste discipline rendered Hinduism intolerable."

The causes of the preponderance of Mahomedans have been ably discussed by Mr Beverley, and he has pointed out that though the dislike of the Hindus to the sea may account for their being in a minority in some of the eastern districts, yet another explanation must be found for their numerical inferiority in such inland districts as Rajshye and Bograh. In Rajshye the Mahomedans are 77 per cent. of the population, and in Bograh they are proportionally more numerous than in any other district of Bengal, not even excepting Chittagong or Noakháli, and are upwards of 80 per cent. of the population.

Mr Beverley thinks that the preponderance of Mahomedans is chiefly due to conversion from the lower castes of Hindus, and that though in some cases persecution may have been employed, yet probably the low-caste Hindus were generally glad to change a religion of degradation for one which gave them independence and self-respect. In support of this view he refers to the fact that the Hindus who live in Bákarganj and other Mahomedan districts are chiefly of the lower castes, and observes with truth that these men are even now especially open to proselytising influences. It is among the Chandals of Farídpúr and Bákarganj that the Baptist missionaries have made nearly all their converts; and there are at this moment, I believe, more native Christians in Bákarganj than in any other district of Bengal, except Nadiya and the Twenty-four Parganas.[1] I may add also that the sup-

[1] It is probable also that many of the Christians in these two district have European blood in their veins.

position that the Hindus were forcibly converted to Mahomedanism appears to be negatived by the remarks already quoted about the paucity of Mahomedans in districts which contained the seats of Mahomedan Government, and more especially by the fact that the relative number of Mahomedans is less in Mahomedan cities than in Mahomedan districts. Thus in the Mahomedan cities of Murshidábád and Berhampúr we find that there are twice as many Hindus as Mahomedans; and in Dacca, which we habitually speak of as a Mahomedan town, and which appears to have been founded by the Mahomedans less than three hundred years ago, the Hindus slightly outnumber the Mahomedans (34,433 against 34,275 Mahomedans), although in the district as a whole there are more than a million of Mahomedans against less than 800,000 Hindus. Now, if persecution had been the agency employed in converting the Hindus, we should naturally expect that the result would have been greatest where the Mahomedan power and influence were most in the ascendant—namely, at the seats of Government.

One thing which we should not lose sight of in discussing this and other questions of a similar nature, is that our districts are for the most part artificial divisions of the country, and in many cases are of very recent origin. I am afraid that officials are apt to forget this, and that they endeavour to account for certain phenomena in a district as if it was an entity which had been separated off for as long a time as an English shire or parish. Bengal districts are subject to continual change, partly from diluviation and alluviation, but still more from the idiosyncrasies of their rulers. Thus within the last few years the proportion of Mahomedans in Bákarganj was increased by the transfer of the intensely Mahomedan thana of Mulfatganj from Dacca to Bákarganj, and then it was again increased in 1873 by the transfer of the Mádaripúr subdivision to Farídpúr.[1] Similar changes have occurred in other districts, and perhaps the abnormal number of Mahomedans in Bograh, for instance, may be accounted for by some disturbing cause of this kind.[2]

But in addition to the agencies of conversion and of the Hindu dislike of the sea, there is another potent cause of the Mahomedanism of Bákarganj—namely, that many parts of it were not inhabited until the Hindu religion and polity had fallen into decay. Much of the district is of recent formation, and even the older parts of it were probably covered with jungle till a comparatively recent period. The northern part is the oldest, as being the farthest from the sea; and here we meet with some ancient names, such, for example, as that of Gournadi.[3] Chandradwip, however, which was the name formerly given to much of the district, implies that it was in or near the sea; and Selímábád, the name given to the western part of the district, seems to imply that the country was not redeemed from the jungle till the time of Prince Selim, the son of Akbar, who was afterwards Emperor Jehangir.

[1] Mulfatganj was included in the transfer to Farídpúr, but still the effect was to increase the proportion of Mahomedans in Bákarganj, for Kotwalipara is essentially a Hindu thana, and the proportion of Hindus is also very large in Mádaripúr.

[2] Speaking of Jessore, Mr Westland remarks, "The district is now of course far from conterminous with Rajah Pratápáditya's territories; but that is only because since 1786, the date of its establishment, it has been made to suffer changes of boundary so violent that only half of what then was Jessore is within the limits of the district as it now stands."

[3] Although the name still exists, Gournadi village has long since been carried away by the Arial Khan.

The recent origin of much of the district is shown by the fact that salt was manufactured some fifty or sixty years ago at places which are now far inland, and where the water is now sweet for the greater part of the year. Thus we find tafals or places for making salt at Sibpúr, Niamati, &c. The former nature of the country is also indicated by the word *kátti*—*i.e.*, cutting or clearing—which we find affixed to the names of so many villages. Thus we have Raikátti, or the clearing of the Raies; Jhalukátti, or the clearing of the fishermen; Sarupkátti, or the clearing of Sarup; Kánudasskátti, or the clearing of Kánu Dass, &c.

It is probable that when the stream of Hindu civilisation came in from the north, it spread itself chiefly over Western and Central Bengal, and only slightly sprinkled the eastern tracts, which thus became Mahomedan by right of civilisation and conquest: by civilisation, namely, by the driving out of the wild beasts and by clearing the jungle; and by conquest, in north-east Bengal from the aboriginal tribes of the Koches and the Assamese, and in the south-east from the Burmese and Portuguese.

It is true that Ralph Fitch describes Bákla as being a large Hindu city in 1586; and Sripúr, Chandecan, and probably also the lost city of Bengala, were in the possession of Hindu princes. But on the other hand, though the island of Sandwip was not conquered by the Moghals till 1666, it appears to have had a Mahomedan population a hundred years before this; for Cæsar Frederick describes the people as being Moors—*i.e.*, Mahomedans—in 1569. The Jesuit priests, also, who visited Bengal in 1599, state that nine out of the twelve bhuyas of Bengal were Mahomedans. However, even if we suppose that most of the inhabitants as well as the Rajahs of Sripúr and Bákla were Hindus, and that also the Sundarbans had a much larger population formerly than they now have, it is clear that the original inhabitants eventually died out or left the country, which thereon relapsed into jungle, and was not cleared again till a comparatively recent period. Indeed, whatever was the condition of the Sundarbans some three hundred years ago, it seems certain that their present colonists have not been settled for more than fifty or sixty years. No doubt the great storm of 1584, in which we are told that 200,000 persons perished, did much to depopulate the country; and Grant, in a passage already quoted, ascribes the desolate condition of Bákla to this cause, and also to the subsequent ravages of the Mugs. Probably this last cause was more potent even than the inundation. The tradition is that it was the Mugs who compelled the Chandradwip Rajahs to forsake their ancient seat of Kachua, and we have already seen that Du Jarric describes the King of Arracan as having taken possession of Bákla in the beginning of the seventeenth century. Rennel's map also represents a large tract in the south of Bákarganj as depopulated by the Mugs.

It was only when a strong Mahomedan power was established at Dacca, and a fleet raised for the express purpose of combating the Mugs, that their inroads received a check. The Mugs were hardy and experienced sailors, and the Hindu princes were totally unable to contend with them. It is doubtful if they ever possessed any ships, and their notions about the impurity of boat-life, &c., were sufficient to deter them from the sea. Du Jarric says that the island of Sandwip belonged of right to Kedar Rai of Sripúr; but even if this were true, it is evident that he could not make good his right to it without the aid of Carvalho and the Portuguese sailors, and neither he nor the Rajah of Bákla were able to resist Gonzales when the latter chose to carve out for himself an independent principality. I may note also that Kedar Rai's right to Sandwip could not have been of very long standing, for it was in the hands of a Mahomedan king when Cæsar Frederick visited it.

When the Mugs began to give trouble, the more respectable—*i.e.*, the more inert and unwarlike—Hindus appear to have left the country, and Mr Westland (p. 220) describes Khalia in the Narail subdivision of Jessore as having been established by men of the upper castes who had left their homes in the south on account of the incursions of the Burmese. Most of the Hindus who remained in Bákarganj probably became voluntary converts to Mahomedanism, and there is little doubt that the process was hastened by the fact that the mere circumstance of their living side by side with Mugs, Portuguese, and Mahomedans was sufficient to tarnish their caste in the eyes of Hindus of other districts, and so to deprive them of the social advantages of Hinduism. It is not improbable that some mixture of races took place, and local traditions seem to countenance the supposition. Thus the Dasses of Ramzanpúr char in the Arial Khan say that they lost their caste owing to a Mug having touched one of their women with the humane intention of saving her from drowning. He was passing along the river-bank while she was bathing, and she seeing a stranger dived under water in order to elude his gaze. The Mug thought she was drowning, and jumped in and brought her to land, the result being that she and all her tribe lost their status, and were no longer regarded as respectable Sudras.

We find also that to this day the Hindus of Western and Central Bengal look down on the inhabitants of Eastern Bengal, and call them Bangals. This word, though etymologically it only means an inhabitant of Banga—*i.e.*, Eastern Bengal—has acquired an opprobrious signification, and is used to mean a rough or bungling person. It thus resembles in its use the adjective "Hieland"—*i.e.*, Highland—which, in spite of fine theories about the civilisation and superiority of the Highlanders, is still used by the common people in the neighbourhood of Glasgow as a synonym for anything stupid or awkward.[1]

The existence of such sentiments would, of course, predispose the Hindus of Bákarganj to embrace Mahomedanism. Still I have no doubt that the excessive preponderance of Mahomedans in the southern part of Bákarganj is not so much due to conversion as to colonisation. In the Patuyakháli subdivision the Mahomedans are 80·8 of the whole population, and in the Gúlsakháli thana of it they are as much as 86·4 per cent., whereas in the Sadr or Barisál subdivision they are only 64·8 per cent. It is the pressure of population in other districts, and also the protection against robbers afforded by the British Government, which have led to the colonisation of Southern Bákarganj; and when the process began, the Mahomedans easily outstripped the Hindus in the race for taking possession of the new country.

[1] A curious illustration of the opprobrious use of the word "Bangal" was given a few years ago by a lathial, or clubman, when he was dying from the effects of a spear-wound inflicted in a Bákarganj riot. Professional lathials have certain rules among themselves, and do not take unfair advantage of one another, or inflict deadly wounds on each other if they can help it. But a clodhopper had disregarded this rule, and had, like Nicole in "Le Bourgeois Gentilhomme," given a thrust not authorised by science, and so the lathial died regretting that a *Bangal* had killed him.

Mahomedans are not nearly such "stay-at-homes" as Hindus. They have fewer local superstitions, and no local gods, while the principle of the family is less strong among them. The joint-family system is unknown to them, and the practice of polygamy is unfavourable to fixity of residence. There is also no doubt that Mahomedans are more enterprising than Hindus; and that their more generous diet fits them better to endure an unhealthy climate, and especially the salt air of the eastern districts. Hence we find that the chars and islands are almost exclusively peopled by Mahomedans. Where, as in Manpúra, there is a Hindu settlement, it is of people of inferior caste, who eat meat, and have otherwise broken with Hindu practices.

The Mahomedans of Bákarganj are nearly all Sunis, and do not particularly observe the Maharam. They are altogether stricter in their religious notions than the Shias of the Dacca district. They do not drink spirits, and indulge sparingly in ganja and opium, as is shown by the comparatively small excise revenue of the district. Very many are Ferazis—*i.e.*, observers of the law or Ferz—and are thus followers of Dudha Mia. Dudha Mia was born in thana Mulfatganj (now transferred to Farídpúr), and his sect is particularly strong in that neighbourhood. It originated with his father, Shariyat Oolah. The Ferazis have often been identified with the Wahabis, and there is undoubtedly a resemblance between their creeds. Both appear to aim at a sort of primitive Church movement, or return to the doctrines of Mahomed, and to attempt to abandon the superstitious practices which have gathered round the earlier creed by lapse of time and by contact with Hindus and other infidels. It does not appear, however, that the Ferazis share the dangerous political views of the Wahabis, or that their revolutionary views extend beyond disputing their landlords' claims for rent. Hindu zamindars and alarmists generally are fond of representing the Ferazis as politically dangerous, but, I think, without sufficient reason. No doubt they are more vigorous and less tractable than ordinary Mahomedans, but this need not be a disadvantage in their character. They have no music at their marriages, they do not reverence saints, and they are distinguished somewhat from other Mahomedans by the arrangement of their *dhuti*, as they do not allow the end to fall down behind, but tuck it carefully up. They also, I believe, hold that it is not right to have mosques or places of public prayer in a country governed by infidels.

Many Mahomedans of Bákarganj call themselves followers of the late Karamat Ali of Juanpúr, but as far as I know, he had no distinctive theological tenets, being chiefly a preacher of morality.

The Mahomedans have adopted a number of Hindu customs from their neighbours. Thus they not only observe the *dusserah puja*, but keep the novanna, and are fond of talking of their caste.[1] There are several subdivisions among them. One class is called the *chákars*, or servants. They are the palki-bearers and punkah-pullers, and are in considerable number near Bari-

[1] Dr Taylor says in his "Topography of Dacca" that the boatmen worship a river-god named Budder. Budder or Badr is, I am told, a Mahomedan saint who is buried at Chittagong. The Bákarganj boatmen often chant the following Bengali verse :—

"Amra achhi pala pán,
Ulla hoilo nigahbán.
Gangar sire panch pír.
Budder, Budder."

The meaning being, "We are children, God is our guardian. There are five saints (sitting) on the head of the Ganges. Budder, Budder."

sál. They are somewhat looked down upon by other Mahomedans, who will not intermarry with them. The *nikáris*, or fishmongers, are another class by themselves. The largest class is that of the *bebajias*, or so-called gipsies. They live in boats or houses raised on piles, and subsist by selling fish-hooks, &c. They do not cultivate land, but keep ducks and poultry. Their largest settlements are at Amtolli and Bákarganj, but they are also to be met with at Jhalukátti, Kalaskátti, Sarikal, Dakhin Shahbázpúr, &c. They do not appear to be thieves.

Converts are occasionally made from Hinduism to Mahomedanism, but a love affair is commonly involved in the conversion. A Hindu widow perhaps, tired of her loneliness and poverty, adopts a neighbour's creed and espouses him; or a Hindu man falls in love with a Mahomedan woman, and changes his religion for her sake.

It has been said elsewhere that almost all the Mahomedans of Bákarganj belong to the lower classes. There are few families of distinction in the district. The great bulk of the Mahomedans are employed in the cultivation of the soil. Comparatively few are in the service of Government or belong to the professional classes. The pleaders, native physicians, traders, shopkeepers, barbers, carpenters, blacksmiths, potters, fishermen, and washermen are nearly all Hindus. The only quasi-literary occupation which Mahomedans much affect is that of the *mukhtar*, or attorney.

A striking feature in the character of the Mahomedan population is the frequency of cases of elopement amongst the women. The subject has attracted a good deal of attention, but, as might be expected, no legislative remedy has been adequate to cure the evil. It must be admitted that the sexual morality of Bákarganj Mahomedans is low. Many of them are boatmen,[1] leading wandering and solitary lives. Like most sailors, they are an immoral class; and their wives, from being left to themselves so much, often fall into intrigues.

The Mahomedans of Bákarganj are, generally speaking, very ignorant, and have an aversion to Government schools. They are especially averse to the education of their daughters in schools, and rarely send them. On the other hand, it must be said that girls belonging to the upper classes are generally taught at home, and that a knowledge of reading and writing is more common among them than among Hindu girls of similar position.

The Bákarganj Mahomedans have been described by Mr Sutherland and others as peculiarly bad specimens of their class. I have had experience in Dacca and Noakháli, and did not find the Mahomedans of those districts superior to those of Bákarganj. If there is any difference perceptible between them, it may be due to the fact that the latter, being of more independent character, show their good and bad qualities with less restraint.

III. HINDUS.

There is not, in my opinion, much which is peculiar or interesting about the Bákarganj Hindus. Most of them belong to the Nama Sudra or Chandal caste, which is especially prevalent in the northern and western parts of the district which border on Farídpúr. They are a strong and hard-working class, and are sought

[1] According to the census, there were 27,662 boatmen (males only).

after as roadmakers and diggers of tanks. They are ignorant and rather stupid, and are in general peaceable enough, but occasionally form combinations to resist their landlords. They practise widow-marriage, or at least often live in adulterous intercourse with widows.

There are comparatively few Bráhmans in Bákarganj; they are most numerous in Idilpúr and Kotwalipara, and the latter is noted for the number of its pandits. There are great numbers of Kayasts,[1] and this is partly due, no doubt, to the fact that the Chandradwip Rajahs were of this caste. To the same cause is also due the circumstance that many of the Kayasts are of very good family. There are what are called Kulin Kayasts; and the Kayasts of Banaripara and Gabha, &c.—viz., the Thakurtas, the Ghoses, and the Guhas—rank high in Hindu society both in Bákarganj and other districts. There are large numbers of the Baidya or doctor caste; hence the number and celebrity of the *kabirajes*, or native doctors, in the district. No doubt the large number of Baidyas is in some measure due to the prominence in the last century of Rajah Raj Ballab Sein.[2]

The distinctions of caste have become a good deal obliterated, but there are two points on which they are still immovable—marriage, and eating and drinking. It is still impossible for a Bráhman to marry a woman of any other caste, or to eat with a member of a different caste. Even within the same caste there are distinctions in this matter, some families

[1] According to the census, there are 27,395 Kayasts.

[2] I find there was another Rajah Raj Ballab, who held the office of Ray Royan, and was the son of Dulabram. Sir Elijah Impey refers to him in a letter of 20th January 1776, and says that he had always understood the Company was much indebted to Dulabram.

refusing to associate with others, though all may belong nominally to the same caste. Hence arise frequent squabbles, which occasionally come into court, men having been known to bring actions against their neighbours because they would not come to dine with them. The ground of action in such a case was that by the refusal the neighbours implied that the hosts were not of a good caste, and thereby libelled them. It is usual to speak of caste as an unmixed evil, but it has its advantages. If it represses originality and invention by compelling a man to adopt his father's trade, even although his natural aptitudes may lie in another direction; yet, on the other hand, it fosters hereditary capabilities, and checks undue competition. It may also be said to supply the place of national pride or patriotism. Undoubtedly, too, it chimes in with the natural temper and disposition of the Bengalis, and indeed if it did not, it would not stand a day. The Bengali, like every Oriental, likes to do everything just as his father and grandfather did it before him, and does not like new-fangled ways.

The Brahma Samáj was established in Barisál some fifteen years ago.[1] It has a church, but does not flourish as it did formerly. Many educated Hindus hold the opinions professed by the Samáj, but do not avow them or contribute to its funds.

IV. BUDDHISTS.

The Buddhists of Bákarganj all belong to the Mug race, and reside in the Sundarbans. An account of them has been given in chapter v.

[1] Ashar 10, 1268, or 1783 Sak = 1861 A.D.

V. CHRISTIANS.

The number of Christians in Bákarganj is stated in the Census Report to be 4852. The number, however, must be considerably less now, as the Christians were most numerous in the northern part of the district, and especially in thanas Gournadi and Kotwalipara. Nearly the whole of Kotwalipara and much of Gournadi have now been transferred to Farídpúr, and several Christian villages have been transferred with them. It is probable, therefore, that the Christian population of Bákarganj is now under 3000 persons. The number, however, is still very large for a rural district in Bengal, and shows that missionaries have been exceptionally successful in Bákarganj. About 800 of the number are accounted for by the existence of the Portuguese colony at Sibpúr. These Christians belong to the Roman Catholic faith, and have been described at p. 110.

The remaining 2200 or so reside almost entirely in the north and north-west parts of the district, and were originally, almost without exception, Chandals, or low-caste Hindus. I believe that there has not been a single instance of the conversion of a Mahomedan inhabitant of Bákarganj, so that the Masalman religion is as great an obstacle to Christian missionaries now as Fernandez and Fonseca found it nearly 280 years ago. Some have ascribed the success of the missionaries in the north of Bákarganj to the previous existence of a deistical sect known by the name of the Kartá Bhojás, or worshippers of the Lord. I believe, however, that it was the oppressions of the landholders and their agents which gave the chief impetus to the movement, and that Christianity recommended itself to the Chandals by its socialistic and insurrectionary doctrines, and by the fact that the Padre Saheb or missionary presented himself in some measure as a bulwark between them and their masters. It is at least certain that the landholders showed at one time great hostility to the movement; and as one of the most active among them was himself a Christian, it is not likely that religious bigotry had much to do with their conduct. This hostility reached its culminating-point in the abduction and subsequent confinement of some native Christian families about twenty years ago. This led to a trial, known as the Báropakhya case, which excited a large amount of attention in the district and in Calcutta, and also, I believe, in England. It was, I believe, true in the main, and I regret to say that the accused were acquitted by the appellate court.

The first preaching of Christianity in the district took place about 1830, in the time of Mr Garrett, who was Magistrate, and afterwards Judge, and who became a Baptist and was publicly dipped in a tank at Barisál. His Nazir or Sheriff, Mr Parry, was an active preacher for some time, and was afterwards a missionary in Jessore. He was succeeded, I believe, by a Mr Smith; and after Mr Smith came a Mr Sylvester Bareiro, who, I understand, originally came from Chittagong, and was schoolmaster in Barisál for some time. Mr Bareiro was greatly befriended by Mr Sturt (the Collector, who was afterwards degraded on account of defalcations in the treasury), and was made by him Superintendent of Stamps. He was a Baptist missionary for many years, but was at last removed on a charge of immorality. He then joined the Church of England, and set up an opposition mission, which still exists, and has a considerable number of adherents. It has been acknowledged and subsidised by the Bishop of Calcutta, although, according to the Baptists, most of Mr Bareiro's adherents are persons who have deserted from or been turned out of their Church. Mr Page was a Baptist missionary who long resided in Bákarganj and made many converts. The late Mr Sale also resided in the district for many years, and was greatly esteemed by every one who knew him.

The principal mission stations of the Baptists are at Ashkar and Dhánshar in the Gournadi thana. Mr Bareiro's church is at Dhándhoba. There are not many cases of conversion nowadays, and I do not think that the missions can be regarded as being in a flourishing state. The impulse which once led many to become Christians has died away, and the missionaries scarcely attempt to do more than keep together the converts they have already made. They have been unable to do even this, for many have relapsed into Hinduism. These men are known by the name of *pherti* or turn-aways, and I have met several in the bíls. One of them told me that he had abandoned Christianity because the ten commandments were too hard for him. I believe, however, that in most cases persons have apostatised in order to get back into society, and especially in order to have their daughters married. According to law, native Christian girls cannot marry until they are thirteen years of age, and as this is later than the ordinary age for marriage among the Hindus, parents complain much of the restriction.

There are very few Christians near Barisál, and none at all in the southern thanas. The movement, in fact, has been from first to last exceedingly local in its character, and has been confined to the swamps of Farídpúr and north-east Bákarganj.

I do not think that the native Christians are at all

superior to Hindus and Mahomedans of a similar class, but native gentlemen have told me that they are more truthful.[1] They are generally very ignorant, and have still a hankering after Hindu customs and amusements, such as boat-racing, &c. They are cultivators and fishermen, and in the cold weather they migrate to various parts of the district and work at road-making and the digging of tanks.

Since writing this account of the Christians, I have found in the India Office Library a volume of the "Calcutta Christian Observer" for 1856, which contains a full account of the Báropakhya case. It is in the form of a review of a pamphlet by Mr Underhill, who was Secretary to the Baptist body, and who afterwards took a leading part in the denunciation of Governor Eyre. The precise date of the outrage was 1st July 1855 (C. C. O., vol. xxv. p. 397, 1856).

The same volume contains (p. 408 *et seq.*) a very interesting account of the sects of the Kartá Bhojás and of the Satya Gurus, apparently from the pen of Dr Wenger, and as it incidentally describes the origin of Christianity in Bákarganj, I have taken the liberty of making the following extract:—

"The next sect is that of the Kartá Bhojás or 'worshippers of the Lord.' Many of its members were originally Mahomedans. All of them profess to repudiate idolatry and caste; but their moral principles are not so pure as was at first supposed. It was among adherents of this sect that the movement in Krishna-

[1] The Hon. F. B. Kemp was the judge who heard the appeal in the Báropakhya case. On being censured for releasing the accused he wrote a defence of his conduct, in which he gave some damaging particulars about the morals of the native Christians.

ghur in favour of Christianity originally commenced; and Krishna Pál, the first convert of the Baptist Mission, is believed to have belonged to this or a similar sect before he began to listen to the gospel. An opinion has repeatedly been expressed to the effect that the Kartá Bhojá sect owes its origin mainly to the diffusion of certain fragments of Christian truth. It would be difficult to produce any historical evidence in support of this idea, whilst on the other hand there is much in it that is probable. Is it not possible that some Christian ceremonies (such as might be noticed by any humble native observer) may have been blended with some elements of Mahomedanism and some Sháktya rites by the founder or founders of the sect?

"The following account of its origin is from the pen of an anonymous native correspondent of the 'Upadeshak,' and appears in that periodical in the number for November 1847. The writer says that it is based upon information derived from frequent personal intercourse with Kartá Bhojás and others. 'In the village of Ulá, on the western bank of the Ganges (Bhagirathi or Hooghly?), there lived a man named Mahadeb, a cultivator of pán (usually called the betel-leaf plant). He was childless; but one day on going into his plantation of pán, he found a weeping infant, and looking upon it as a gift of God, determined to adopt the child for his own, a resolution to which his wife gladly assented. The boy grew up, but being somewhat silly, the neighbours called him Oula. ' For some years he assisted his father in cultivating and selling pán; but after a time he ran away, dressed only in the tattered garment of a devotee. He reappeared on the eastern bank of the river, gave himself out to be a *mahápurush* (or "great man" who has completely subdued the senses), or at least a *guru* (spiritual teacher), and succeeded in gathering a company of twenty-two disciples.' (The names are all recorded, but need not be repeated here.) 'The *mantra* which he gave them was, "Satya bala, guru dhara, sange chala;" *i.e.*, "Speak the truth, cleave to the teacher, and come along with us." After this, he took them with him to the marshy district, near the Sunderbuns, where he set up as a worker of miracles, and succeeded in deluding many people.

"'After his death, some of his twenty-two disciples, imitating his example, began business on their own account. They would train some man to pretend deafness, until any sick person came to be healed, when, on receiving a blow, he was suddenly to speak. They would then strike the sick man also, and tell him, "You see this deaf man has been cured, but you have not yet sufficient faith, therefore you cannot be cured now. Eat some earth from under this tree, come every year to the master's house, and believe, then you will undoubtedly recover." In this way they have succeeded in deluding thousands.'

"At the close of this historical account the customary prayer of the Kartá Bhojás is given. As it is very interesting, and infinitely better than the preceding narrative would lead one to expect, we subjoin it here. After a brief invocation of 'the true one of Shiva and Rámballabh,' it goes on as follows: 'It is unreasonable to suppose that by studying any *shástra* a true knowledge of Thee can be obtained, for in the different shástras different religions are taught. Among this diversity of religions how can certainty be obtained? O Lord, we are ignorant and stupid; have mercy on us, and cause us to understand the truth, that we may be comforted. Further, great Lord, keep us from evil, and grant us willingness, courage, and ability to do good. If such be Thy pleasure, let it be accomplished.'

"A similar sect, though small, and confined to Eastern Bengal, is that of the Satya Gurus. It originated about the year 1804 with a native who read the gospel narrative, and even had some personal intercourse with the Serampore missionaries, but who was animated with the spirit of Simon Magus. Giving himself out to be a modern incarnation of the true teacher, Jesus Christ, and able to work miracles, he succeeded in obtaining a number of followers, and when he died transmitted his dignity to one of his chief disciples, who still carries on the work of delusion. In this case the origin of the sect can be clearly traced back to the indirect influence of Christianity.

"In other parts of the country, men rise up every now and then, who, professing to have discovered the true way, or to have been instructed by the true teacher, succeed in drawing a number of disciples after them. It is impossible to tell how much or how little floating rumours regarding the gospel of Christ may have to do with the origin of these sects. They are generally characterised by a repudiation of idols, of the ministrations of Bráhmans, and of certain restrictions of caste, and thereby in some measure pave the way for the reception of the gospel. The origin of the native Christian community in the Backergunje district supplies an illustration of this remark. Kángáli, the leader of the first band who openly embraced Christianity there, had for several years been such a *mahant* or spiritual guide of numerous disciples, who professed to obey the Satya Guru or true teacher. But he was evidently not satisfied with his own discoveries. The account which he himself gave afterwards of the way in which he was first led to Christianity, certainly shows a morbid state of the nervous system—probably the result of certain habits frequently found among Hindu ascetics—but it is nevertheless instructive. According to the impression left on his own mind, he once, whilst laid up with a dangerous illness, was favoured with a vision or visit from a resplendent person, who told him that he should recover if he called on the name of 'Eesoo.' Accordingly he did pray to the unknown being whose name was thus communicated to him, and recovered. Not only so, but the same result followed from such prayer in the case of a few other persons. Some time afterwards he met with a man who was returning from a market with a book in his hand. On inquiring after the contents of the book, he was told that it was only a book about 'Eesoo Christ,' and that he was welcome to it if he wished to have it. The coincidence of the name led him eagerly to accept the proferred tract, with the contents of which he made himself acquainted—as far as he could comprehend them—by means of one of his disciples who was able to read. The perusal of this tract proved to be the first dawn of Christian truth breaking in upon his dark mind. He succeeded from time to time in obtaining some fresh tracts, and at last felt a strong desire to seek out some one who could tell him more about the religion of Eesoo. In all these endeavours a number of his disciples sympathised with him. Their first impulse was to apply to the nearest European Government officials for instruction, but their courage failed them, and at length they were accidentally—or rather providentially—heard of and afterwards met with by itinerant native preachers from Barisál. Even after this long preparatory process nearly two years elapsed before they could make up their minds to embrace Christianity openly. Such is the statement made by Kángáli nearly ten years ago. Since then many of those who were first have become last, and the last first."[1]

VI. OTHERS.

There are a few Koches in the Perozpúr subdivision. They appear to have come from the Madhupúr jungle in Dacca, and are said to have been brought in by the zamindars to act as fighting men. Their weapons used to be bows and arrows.

Near Barisál there is a small colony of Bunas. They support themselves by agriculture, and by selling firewood. According to one account, they were brought in by the indigo-planters in old times; and according to another, they came when the new police system was introduced.

There are a few men from Hill Tipperah, in the jungles of Idilpúr (217, according to census).

At Barisál there are a few Greek and Armenian and other Eurasian families, and there is a Jewish shopkeeper. The Portuguese or Feringhies of Sibpúr have been described elsewhere.

VII. RESULTS OF THE CENSUS.

Unfortunately, the figures given in the Census Report cannot be fully made use of, because the area of the district and the arrangement of the thanas have been altered since 1872. The enumerators' books are now at

[1] "Bengal as a Field of Missions," by Mr Macleod Wylie, Calcutta, 1854, contains at p. 100 an interesting description of Bákarganj and the mission, written by Mr Page. Mr Page there states that Mr J. Smith was the first missionary, and that Mr Bareiro was sent four years afterwards from Serampore to succeed him in the management of the school. Mr Page joined the district in 1848. The movement seems to have begun in Ramsiddhi, which was Kángáli's village.

Barisál, and they are, I believe, being collated and their details brought into accordance with the new boundaries. When this has been done we shall know many interesting particulars regarding the relative numbers of the various Hindu castes, the occupations of the people, &c. Meanwhile I proceed to note a few general facts.

The most striking results of the Bengal census may be said to be three in number. The first is the discovery of the great populousness of Bengal as compared with former estimates.[1] The second is the discovery of the large extent of the Mahomedan element.[2] The third is the discovery of the almost total absence of large towns. Perhaps to these we might add a fourth—namely, the discovery of the quietness and ease with which a census can be taken.

With regard to the third of these results, I have pointed out in the chapter on Barisál that even the few towns which exist have a very sparse population, and are made up more or less of scattered villages.[3] The average number of persons per square mile in Bákarganj was 482, and I do not think that this has been

1 The total population of Bengal in 1872 was 66,856,859, and average per square mile 269, or more than double the average rate (110 per square mile) for Scotland (Census Report). In Bengal Proper the average is 389 per square mile.

2 "Total number of Mahomedans, 20,664,775." The vast majority of these—namely, 17½ millions—are found in Lower Bengal; in Behar they hardly number more than 2½ out of a total population of nearly 20 millions. In Assam, Chota Nagpúr, and particularly in Orissa, they are very sparse. In Assam, indeed, they are perhaps more numerous than might have been expected, owing chiefly to the inclusion in that province of the district of Goalpara, which formerly formed part of Rangpúr. Rangamati, in this district, was for some years a frontier station of the Moghals, and large numbers of the Koches and other aboriginal tribes seem to have been converted by them to Islám (Census Report).

3 It appears from Thucydides that the population in ancient Greece was at one time scattered over villages as it now is in Bengal, and that Lacedæmon adhered to this custom after the Greeks in other parts had gathered themselves into cities: κατὰ κώμας δὲ τῷ παλαιῷ τῆς Ἑλλάδος τρόπῳ οἰκισθεῖσα.

materially lessened by the transfer of Mádaripúr. The density of the population is greatest in the northern and central thanas, and least in the south of the district. The most thinly-peopled thana is Khalsakháli, which contains a large extent of Sundarban forest. In it the average per square mile is only 122. In the Patuyakháli subdivision (to which Khalsakháli belongs) the average is 287, in Perozpúr it is 581, and in the Sadr subdivision (Barisál) it is as high as 738. The lowest subdivisional average is in Dakhin Shahbázpúr, where it is 270. This at first excites surprise, for the greater part of the island is richly cultivated, and seems in the northern and central divisions to be one continuous garden of cocoa-nut and supari trees, and studded with homesteads. The explanation, however, is simple enough. Much of the south of the island is composed of newly-formed chars and of extensive plains where buffaloes are grazed, and which are almost uninhabited. If we could have a separate census of the northern half, I am persuaded that the population would be found to be as dense as that of almost any other part of the district. Here I should note that when the census was taken, Dakhin Shahbázpúr was divided into two thanas—viz., Daulat Khan and Dhaniya Maniya—and that their boundaries ran from north to south, the east side of the island belonging to Daulat Khan and the west to Dhaniya Maniya. Hence each had about an equal share of the cultivated and uncultivated tracts, and therefore we find that their populations were very nearly equal, Daulat Khan having a population of 114,262,[1] and Dhaniya Maniya one of 106,775,

[1] Even this slight excess may be accounted for by the fact that it includes the population of the town of Daulat Khan and that of the island of Manpúra.

the total population of the subdivision being 221,037. The island, however, has since been divided from east to west, Daulat Khan thana containing the northern and Barhanuddin Hát the southern half; and if the areas are made nearly equal, there can be no doubt that Daulat Khan will have much the largest share of the population.

Throughout the district the males are slightly in excess, the ratio being 50·7 to 49·3. In thanas Gournadi, Kewari, and Jhalukátti the women are in excess, but in all the other thanas which now belong to Bákarganj they are in a minority, except in thana Nalchiti, where the proportions of the sexes are equal. The disproportion of males is greatest in Patuyakháli subdivision, where the ratio is 52·6 to 47·4. In thana Khalsakháli, already mentioned, there are 56·2 men to 43·8 women. I think that these facts are very interesting, for they concur with what we should expect from considering the nature of the country and of native society, and therefore they tend to show that the census was correctly taken. The proportion of Mahomedans is largest in Dakhin Shahbázpúr, where there are 82·8 Mahomedans to 17·2 Hindus. In Patuyakháli subdivision the proportion is 80·8 to 18·2 Hindus. The remaining 1 per cent. consists of the Mugs, who are Buddhists. The most Mahomedan thanas in the district are Dhaniya Maniya and Gúlsakháli, where there are 86·4 Mahomedans to 13·6 Hindus. We thus see that the Mahomedans are most numerous in the south of the district and in the islands. The Hindus are most numerous in the north and west of the district. They are especially numerous in the west, where there is a large settlement of low-caste Hindus. This Hindu element extends into Farídpúr, and apparently there is something in the nature of the country, which consists for the most part of immense swamps, which has been peculiarly suitable for a Hindu population. Perhaps the large quantity of fish yielded by the swamps has attracted them, for this is the chief animal food of Hindus, and to this day most fishermen are Hindus. I am inclined, however, to think that no one would voluntarily occupy such a country. In the rains the country is almost one immense lake, in which the homesteads of the ryots appear as islands, and in April and May it consists of large treeless plains. The villages are never of very easy access; but things are at their worst at the beginning and at the end of the rains, for then there is neither enough water for boats nor sufficient dry land for foot-travelling. Add to this that the country swarms with mosquitoes, that there are numerous poisonous snakes, and that the ryots often lose their crops from overflooding, and it will be admitted, I think, that the country is not a desirable residence. It seems, therefore, probable that these low-caste Hindus, or Chandals, as they are called, were driven out from some other country, or that they left their homes in order to be free from oppression. The following account is given by Mr Wells, formerly Magistrate of Farídpúr, in a letter published in the Census Report: "The dreary and unwholesome swamps of the south are largely peopled by a highly interesting Chandal race. These Chandals were originally a complete Hindu community, consisting of persons of all castes from the Bráhman downwards, who, on having the misfortune to be cursed in a body by a vengeful Bráhman of unutterable sanctity in Dacca, quitted their ancestral homes and emigrated bodily to the southern wastes of Farídpúr, Jessore, and Bákarganj. There with great perseverance and toil they raised in the centre of the swamps large hillocks from twelve to twenty feet in height, whereon they built their homesteads in the dry weather, in order to preserve their cattle and goods during the high inundations. In this place they are located to the present day, cultivating the swamps with rice and jute, and carrying on the occupations of fishing and bird-catching, varied with mat and basket weaving, and the cutting of grass for thatching roofs and for the consumption of their cattle. In the dry weather they often suffer considerably from scarcity of water, and at times almost die from thirst. As they do not preserve water in tanks, they are often reduced to what little they may have kept by them in their earthen vessels, and not unfrequently drink it when it has become quite thick and green. In the rains the whole country becomes inundated; the water rises over ten feet, and leaves their artificial mounds like so many islands in a huge lake. Locomotion then becomes impossible except by boat, while they have to collect all their cattle and keep them in their homesteads, feeding them on what fodder they may have stored up during the dry season, and on a grass which, like the rice, grows with the rise of the water, and in appearance very much resembles paddy. These cattle have often to remain for weeks standing up to their necks in water, and as their food has to be stored up for them in the homesteads, they are fed on the minimum amount necessary to support existence. Consequently by the end of the rainy season they are reduced to skeletons, and very many die in the process. It is this that renders it impossible to introduce a larger and less hardy description of cattle. Notwithstanding all the difficulties this Chandal community have to contend against, however, they are strongly attached to the home of their adoption, and resist all inducements to abandon it. Efforts, for example, have been made to transfer some of them to the Sunderbuns, but with no measure of success. They prefer remaining in the region to which they have adapted themselves perseveringly and laboriously, where they are not likely to be envied their lot, and where they can dwell together a distinct community with their own Bráhmans, their own priests, castes, and traditions. Their occupations and their enforced practice of going about in boats during a great portion of the year have rendered the Chandals a hardy and muscular race, while they present a favourable contrast to their uncursed and therefore contemptuous neighbours in respect of ingenuousness and truthfulness."

The Hindu nature of the population of this part of the country is shown by the figures for Kotwalipara, a thana which has been nearly all transferred to Farídpúr. In it there were 59,582 Hindus against 23,122 Mahomedans. Kewari (now Sarupkátti) is the only thana in Bákarganj where the Hindus are in excess of the Mahomedans. In Jhalukátti they are nearly half the population.

In Patuyakháli subdivision the largest proportion of Hindus is found in thana Baufal, which was the site of the old capital of the Rajahs of Chandradwip.

There were in 1872 only twenty-seven Europeans in Bákarganj, and there were 127 Eurasians. There are other statements in the Census Report showing the numbers of the aboriginal tribes, and of the various castes, &c., but I do not think that the figures are correct, and therefore shall not make use of them. For example, I do not understand the entry of 2785 Nats. Nor do I think it likely that there were only 8989[1] Bráhmans in Bákarganj and 30,338 in Chittagong. The classification according to occupations is admittedly imperfect. The number of persons (males) engaged in agriculture or with animals is put down at 498,690, and 475,477 of them are said to be cultivators.

Vital Statistics.—Attempts have been made for some time to record the deaths all over the district, but the machinery employed (the village chaukidars) is altogether inefficient, and the results are totally untrustworthy. Although no official has ever pretended that the returns were even approximately correct, yet some have thought that the system should be kept up, as it could do no harm, and might prepare the way for a more perfect registration. This, however, seems an error. It cannot be said that the collection and tabulating of worthless statistics do no harm. Granted that nobody is deceived by them, still their collection involves some expense, were it only in postage, and a good deal of trouble, and it tends to demoralise every one who has to do with the work. Worst of all, however, it brings statistics into contempt, and will induce people to disbelieve our figures long after they have become trustworthy. Even now natives, as a general rule, do not believe in the results of the census, less, I think, because they know of inaccuracies in it, than because a long

[1] Especially when we find the number of priests or *purohits* in Bákarganj put down at 9450.

series of untrustworthy returns has made them regard figured statements of all kinds with suspicion. It is to be hoped, therefore, that Government will abandon the attempt to collect vital statistics for whole districts, more especially as the last Bengal Administration Report states that Sir George Campbell had come to the conclusion that the attempt was "hopeless at present" (p. 199 of Report for 1873–74).

The returns for the selected areas are more trustworthy, though even they are not yet quite satisfactory. There are four such areas in Bákarganj—namely, two town areas (Barisál and Daulat Khan) and two rural areas (Manpúra and Lakutia). The united population of the first two is given at 14,224, and the deaths in 1873 at 327, or 22·98 per 1000. The population of Barisál has however been increased since 1st January 1874 by the inclusion of additional area. The population of Manpúra and Lakutia is given at 13,652, and the deaths at 291 in 1873, or 21·31 per 1000.

Note.—The statistics of population given at p. 211 were prepared for me in the Collectorate, but the details leave 1133 unaccounted for, whereas the column "Others," in the Census Report, only gives 174. The fact is, I am sorry to say, that owing to changes of boundaries made since the completion of the census I am not able to state with accuracy the population of the district. The population of Bákarganj, according to Mr Beverley's Census Report, is 2,377,433, which are divided as follows:—

Mahomedans,	1,540,965
Hindus,	827,393
Christians,	4,852
Buddhists,	4,049
Others,	174
	2,377,433

Since then Mádaripúr subdivision has been transferred to Farídpúr. Its population, according to the census, is 663,043, which are divided as follows :—

Mahomedans, ...	360,085
Hindus, ...	299,540
Christians, ...	3,375
Others, ...	43
Total, . . .	663,043

But this total cannot be deducted, as parts of thanas Gournadi and Kotwalipara in the said subdivision were not included in the transfer. Moreover, a corner of Farídpúr, lying east of the Baleshwar and near the mouth of the Saldaha, was shortly afterwards included in Bákarganj. The population of this tract was, I think, about 10,000. The figures in the text professed to take account of these changes, but the above remarks show that they are still not quite accurate.

CHAPTER IX.

PRODUCTIONS.

RICE is the staple of the district of Bákarganj, and the variety of it which is most cultivated is that called *aman*. Aman rice is grown all over Bákarganj, wherever there is low land. In the Perozpúr and Patuyakháli subdivisions very little of any other kind is grown. The ploughing of the ground commences as early as the latter part of February in the northern parts of the district, and continues in the south as late as the beginning of September. These late ploughings, however, are of land into which the rice is to be transplanted. The chief ploughings take place in April and May. They begin earlier in the northern parts of the district, as it is the first to be flooded, owing to the lowness of much of the Gournadi thana, and its proximity to the Arial Khan. Cattle are generally used for ploughing, but in Dakhin Shahbázpúr and the south of the district buffaloes are often employed. Aman is generally transplanted, but in chars and other places it is sometimes sown broadcast. It is not unfrequent, especially in the northern parts of the district, to sow aman and owsh—*i.e.*, early rice—together. It is not usual to weed aman, and the crop gives little trouble to the ryot after it has been transplanted. The process of transplanting, however, is a very laborious one, and the ryot often "homeward plods his weary way" after his back has been almost broken from stooping for hours amidst mud and water, and after having been drenched with rain two or three times in the course of the day.

Irrigation is not regularly practised, and is seldom needed; but water-channels are frequently dammed across in order to keep the water in the paddy-fields. Also the water is often drained off when it is too plentiful, and to effect this the ryots do not scruple to dig trenches even across public highways. The putting up and the removal of the dams, or *bunds*, as they are called, are frequent sources of dispute among the villagers.

Rice is often damaged by insects, and loss from this cause appears to be especially common in Dakhin Shahbázpúr. Cloudy weather just before harvest is especially likely to breed insects, and is therefore regarded with great alarm by the ryots. Rice-fields near rivers are often injured by crabs and river-turtle, and brushwood and branches of the date palm are put round the fields at the water's edge to keep those animals out. In a report of 8th August 1791 special mention is made of the damage caused to the cultivated lands of pargana Buzurgumedpúr by an immense quantity of crabs being thrown upon them. Wild pigs do great mischief to standing rice, and unfortunately this is one evil against which the ryot is very helpless. He does not usually possess a gun, and the professional *palwáns* or *shikaries* (sportsmen) whom he sometimes employs find it difficult to carry on their handicraft, owing to the interference of the police and the stringent orders about licences for carrying arms. It is a common practice all over the district for the ryots to erect sheds, raised on a scaffolding of bamboos, in their fields about the time of harvest, and to spend their nights in them, in order to scare away the pigs. These sheds are called *túngis,* and are a very marked feature in the Bákarganj landscape, especially where there is any jungle in the neighbourhood. The ryots also make gigantic rattles by splitting a bamboo and attaching a rope to one of the limbs at the top of the cleft. In Dakhin Shahbázpúr these rattles may be heard at night and at the early dawn going off with a noise like the discharge of firearms. The noise is made by the ryots in the túngis pulling the ropes and then letting them go again. Buffaloes, wild and tame, often damage the crops, and cattle-trespass is a perennial source of dispute among neighbours. As there are no hedges or walls, and as no land is reserved as pasturage for the cattle, it can easily be understood how frequent cattle-trespass must be. Broad kh« áls and dōnes are not sufficient protection, for the cattle all take to the water readily, and can swim great distances.

Aman is generally reckoned as yielding twelve anas, or three-fourths of all the rice grown in the district. The other fourth is chiefly made up by owsh, which is grown on the high lands, and especially in the northern parts of the district. There is also a little *boro* grown in the chars and bíls in the north of the district. Gournadi and Kotwalipara (now transferred to Farídpúr) are the chief seats of this cultivation. Boro is sown at the end of the rains, when the waters are beginning to recede. It is sometimes sown broadcast, but is, I believe, as a general rule, transplanted like aman. The sowings take place in October, the transplanting in December and January, and the harvest in April. Boro is a coarse red grain, and is only eaten by the poorer classes. It is prized by them because it ripens earlier in the year (the Bengali year) than any other kind of paddy, and thus gives them food at a time when rice is scarce. Owsh is sown in Chait and Baisackh (March and April), and is reaped in July and August.

The bulk of the aman harvest takes place in Agráhan and Paus—*i.e.*, December and January—but there is some which ripens as early as Ashin, and hence it is called Ashini paddy. It is common to name rice according to the month it ripens in, and thus we have Ashini, Kartik, and Agráhani *dhan*, the last being by far the largest in quantity. In Dakhin Shahbázpúr and some other parts a kind of aman is largely grown which is called Lakhydigi, and ripens in October. It is said to derive its name from its being ready by the time of the Lakhy puja. On the occasion of the aman harvest there is a great festival called the Navanna or the new rice. It celebrates the first eating of the new crop. It is a movable feast, but commonly takes place in the month of Agráhan. The festival is primarily a Hindu one, but Mahomedans celebrate it also. It answers to the harvest-home or vintage feasts of other countries, and is a time when the scattered members of families and distant friends meet together. It is not peculiar to Bákarganj.

The average produce of rice per bigha (about two-thirds of an acre) is ten *mans* of paddy, representing about six mans of rice. In the southern parts of Bákarganj the ryot does not always, or even generally, cut his own rice. Bands of reapers come down from Farídpúr and other northern districts, cut the paddy and thresh it out for him. They are liberally paid, for they receive one-sixth, and more commonly one-fifth of the produce; formerly they received one-fourth. In the north of the district paddy is often threshed out by beating it against a plank, but in the south this is usually done by cattle. The cattle which tread out the corn are almost always unmuzzled, which shows that the practice of allowing the cattle to pull at the straws occasionally as they go round is general in the East, and that a divine precept was not necessary for its observance. The ryots also tread the rice out with their feet sometimes. When paddy is cut in the south of the district, the heads only of the grain are generally cut. The straw is left on the ground and cut at a later period. This is done because the load to be carried to the threshing-floor is hereby lightened, and because the straw would be damaged if trodden by the feet of the cattle. The Farídpúr reapers come down in Agráhan, or December, and return in Magh, or February. Early in December fleets of small boats may be seen sailing down with the north wind to the southern parts of Bákarganj; and two or three months after, they return loaded with paddy. Rice is sold by the ryots by measure, though in the bazár it is commonly sold by weight. When sold in the husk—*i.e.*, as paddy—the measure most commonly used in the south of the district is the *búdha*. This consists of four *káthis*, or baskets of thirty-two *sírs* each. This is *kachá* weight, and is equal to twenty-four sírs of *paká* weight. The káthi is a basket made of bent—*i.e.*, cane. In the north of the district rice is generally sold by the *katha*, or basket of twenty sírs. It thus appears that though rice be generally sold by measure, yet the measure is one founded upon weight. There is a weight in much use in the district called the Sahebganj or Bákarganj weight. It is larger than even the paká ordinary weight, as it contains ninety-six *tolas* to the sír.

Paddy is sold by the ryots chiefly to *paikárs* or middlemen, who come to their houses or to the local markets for it. The paikárs are of two sorts—large and small. The former, who are also called *aratdárs* or brokers, have their offices at the principal bazárs, and ship the rice from thence to Calcutta. The smaller paikárs are called *farias*, and their business *fariámi*. They go about to the villages and to the petty háts to buy paddy and rice, which they take to marts such as Bákarganj, Niamati, and Nalchiti. Thus these marts are not fed directly from the threshing-floors; all the little háts in the country are feeders to them, and the marts are chiefly entrepôts where the rice brought into the village markets is collected and eventually shipped off to Calcutta.

A good deal of paddy is disposed of by barter, and goes off in this way to supply the wants of less grain-producing districts. Thus in the cold weather boats come from Dacca laden with earthen pots. These the boatmen sell to the villagers for paddy, filling up their boat with it as their trade progresses; and eventually after a cruise of a month or two, they return to their homes with a cargo of paddy. The reason why this trade in pots is so brisk is that the Bákarganj earth is in general saltish and not suitable for pottery, and therefore the inhabitants have to depend on other districts for their supply of pots for household purposes, and for the making of molasses, &c. The price of a pot is generally its contents in paddy. The husking of rice is generally done by women, and is probably the most laborious task they have to perform. Women in Bákarganj do very little out-of-door work, for the bulk of the population is Mahomedan, and that too of a rather strait and fanatical sort. Except widows, and others who have no man to help them, no women, or at least no Mahomedan women, are ever seen marketing or working in the fields. I have scarcely ever seen women employed as reapers, and no doubt this is one reason why the Bákarganj ryot is obliged to have so much of his crop reaped for him. It is too much for him and his sons to reap and thresh out by themselves, and they will not allow their womankind to help them.

RICE TRADE.—The rice export trade begins in November and continues till March. The principal marts are Bákarganj or Sahebganj, Nalchiti, Jhalukátti, and Niamati. They present a most animated appearance during the rice season, for boats come to them from all parts of Bengal. There is a great demand for silver during the rice season, and the local treasury is soon cleared by the presentation of currency notes and supply bills.

It is a curious fact that though Bákarganj is a great exporting district, it also imports paddy (during the rains) from the districts of Tipperah, Mymensing, and Sylhet. The chief seats of this import trade are Jhalukátti, Babuganj, and Mirganj. It is owsh paddy which is thus imported, and it has a sale because it comes in at a time when aman is nearly out of the market. The Bákarganj rice is of superior quality, and is therefore exported to such an extent that a sufficient stock of rice does not remain in the country for local consumption, and owsh comes in from the eastern districts to supply the deficiency. The communication, too, between Bákarganj and Calcutta is so exceptionally easy, owing to the number and largeness of the rivers, that rice readily flows out of the district, whereas Tipperah and other eastern districts are in some measure shut out from the Calcutta market by their remoteness and defective water communication.

The price of rice is of course much higher now than it was in former times. On 9th February 1797 the Collector writes to the Board that paddy used to sell at 3 mans the rupee, but that in that year it was selling in the Idilpúr pargana at 8 mans the rupee. Paddy is generally reckoned nowadays as worth Rs. 1 per man. On 30th January 1875 rice was selling at Barisál at the rate of 17 sírs the rupee for best rice, and 21 sírs the rupee for common rice. A man of paddy, or 40 sírs, yields about 30 sírs of rice.

BETEL-NUT.—Next to rice, betel-nut is the most important staple of Bákarganj. It is grown extensively in Dakhin Shahbázpúr, and the northern and eastern parts of the district. Indeed nearly every homestead in Bákarganj has its few supari or betel-nut trees growing round it, and many a Bráhman or Kayast who is unwilling or unable to support himself by manual or mental labour gets his living by the produce of his betel-nut orchard. Betel-nuts are gathered in October, and the trade continues for a considerable part of the cold weather. The chief seats of the trade are Daulat Khan, Lálganj in Mendiganj, and Nalchiti. The Mugs and Burmese, and even a few Chinamen, come to Nalchiti in the cold weather to purchase betel-nuts for Arracan. There is a quarter of Nalchiti called Mugpara or Mug hamlet, because it is chiefly occupied by Mugs engaged in the betel-nut trade, and in the cold weather there is always a number of balam —*i.e.*, Mug—boats moored along the bank there. The betel-nuts are sometimes conveyed direct from Nalchiti to Chittagong and Arracan in balam boats, but more frequently, I believe, they are transported to Calcutta and shipped thence by steamer.

Betel-nuts are counted by tens or *gás*. One hundred gás—*i.e.*, a thousand nuts—sell for from three to four rupees. A betel-nut tree yields about a hundred nuts a year, and is reckoned as annually worth four anas. The annual value of a cocoa-nut tree is reckoned at one rupee. The wood of the betel-nut tree is used for planking, and it is also used for bridges, for handrails, and for posts. The gathering of betel-nuts is often a trade, and boys and men of light weight make a livelihood in this way. Many are so expert that they will gather the fruit of a grove of trees without ever descending. This they do by swaying the tree on which they are, and passing from it to the next one. The usual payment for gathering the nuts is ten nuts a tree, and for cocoa-nuts one nut a tree. If, however, the trees are exceptionally high, the payment has to be increased. The fruit of two hundred betel or of a hundred cocoa nut trees can be gathered in one day. Betel-nuts are prepared in three ways. 1st, The *Mugari supari*, so called because it is intended for the Burmese market. This is husked, steeped in water, washed, and dried. 2d, *Tátta suparis*. These are dried in the husk. 3d, *Maga suparis*. These are steeped in the husk. The freight for a cargo of suparis (betel-nuts) from Lálganj or Nalchiti to Calcutta is usually Rs.20 the hundred mans.

COCOA-NUTS.—A large quantity of cocoa-nuts are produced in the island of Dakhin Shahbázpúr, and most homesteads have two or three trees. The nuts are largely consumed within the district, but a considerable quantity is exported, and there is a local manufacture of cocoa-nut oil. In the cold weather sloops come over to Dakhin Shahbázpúr from Chittagong laden with earth-oil, and take away cocoa-nuts in exchange.

Sugar-cane.—Next to betel-nut, sugar-cane is, I think, the most important staple of Bákarganj. It is grown all over the district where there is high land. Hence, as the banks of rivers are generally high, we find that sugar-cane is largely cultivated on them. The cultivation of the sugar-cane is laborious and expensive. The ground requires to be prepared with great care; the plants have to be bought in the market, and it is many months before the outlay can be reimbursed. The landholders, too, generally claim an exceptionally high rate of rent for land cultivated in sugar-cane. The mill for expressing the juice and the labour for working it are also expensive. Hence it is very common for sugar-cane to be grown on the co-operative principle, several ryots joining in the speculation. Bákarganj sugar has a high reputation in Bengal, and Jabar Amal sugar is considered the best in the district. Jabar Amal, which is the chief seat of the sugar trade, is a market and village on the Kacha, in the Perozpúr subdivision. The raw fruit of the date-tree is eaten and the juice of the tree (*tari*) is drunk; it is also used as a sweetmeat when inspissated into the form of a cake, but it is not much used for making sugar.

Timber.—Next to rice, betel-nut, and sugar-cane, the most important products of the district are probably timber and firewood. These are chiefly obtained from the Sundarban tracts in the south. The sundari is the most valuable tree, as it is universally used for making boats. Even sálwood boats have the parts which are under water made of sundari, as it appears to be the only wood which resists the saltness of the water. The sundari, however, is by no means the most common tree in the Sundarbans. The kerua is the prevailing tree, at least on the chars and in the south-eastern part of the district, and the goma and bolye are also common. The kerua and goma are used for posts, &c., and the bolye is especially valuable for its inner bark, which yields a strong fibre. The bolye fibre is used by the ryots instead of string when making the roofs of their houses, &c., and it is also twisted in tethering ropes for cattle and buffaloes. The ashes of the bolye contain salt and potash, and are used by washermen in place of soap.

There are a large number of woodcutters in Bákarganj, though they generally combine agriculture with their trade. They are called *baülies,* and their boats *baüli*-boats. These are strong open boats, and the sundari logs are both packed into them and lashed alongside. Unfortunately, the sundari is so heavy that it will not float. It is unnecessary to describe the woodcutter's trade, as it has been fully done by Mr Westland. The chief seats of the timber trade are Jhalukátti *alias* Maharajganj, Gúlsakháli, Amtolli, and Nalchiti.

Bent or cane is brought from the Sundarbans, and is much used for making baskets, &c. The *gôlpatta* or wild cocoa-nut is an important plant, as the Mugs and the ryots generally in the south of the district thatch their houses with it. It is also said to yield excellent toddy.

The bíls and chars yield large quantities of reeds (*nal, hogla,* &c.), which are much used for mat-making, for the roofs of boats, &c., and are also largely exported to the surrounding districts.

A superior kind of mat, called the *sítalpati,* is made

from the outer covering of a reed called the *parita*. This reed has a branching and somewhat shrubby habit, and grows in damp places near homesteads. It does not appear to be really wild, at all events it is regularly cultivated by the ryots just as *san* or thatching grass is. The chief workers in sítalpati live at Rangasri and Helancha near Bákarganj, and it is there that the parita is most common. The workmen are called *paitiyas*.[1]

PÁN.—Pán is a good deal cultivated in the Gournadi and Baufal thanas, and in the Perozpúr subdivision. The Dacca market is to some extent supplied from Gournadi. Tarki, in that thana, is the chief mart. As it is necessary that the pán should arrive fresh at Dacca, pán-boatmen were long celebrated, and I believe are so still, for their dexterity as oarsmen. They are, I believe, all Hindus. Pán-gardens are only kept by Hindus—a curious instance of conservatism, for Mahomedans are just as fond of pán as Hindus. But we find the same thing in other trades, for most washermen, carpenters, and barbers are Hindus. The pán-gardens belong to the Baroi caste.

There is no indigo grown in the district. Some fifty years ago it was cultivated, and the remains of vats may still be seen at Panchakaran and Khagasura. These belonged to a Mr Nathaniel Monro, who was, I believe, originally employed in the Salt Department. It is said that the brackishness of the water prevented the success of the manufacture.

Scarcely any tobacco is grown in Bákarganj, and the requirements of the district are supplied from Rangpúr and Kuch Behar.

[1] A list of the principal Sundarban trees will be found in Gastrell's report.

(*Tíl sesamum*) is largely cultivated, and the amount of production appears to be increasing. It is grown for the sake of the seeds, from which an oil is expressed, which is used in cooking and also as a light. It is often mixed with mustard oil. It is grown in the northern parts of the district, and also in thana Mendiganj. It is not much grown in the south, as it appears to require high land, free from inundation.

Now that Mádaripúr has been transferred to Farídpúr, comparatively little jute is grown in the district. Some, however, is grown in Gournadi, Mendiganj, and Dakhin Shahbázpúr. The amount of cotton grown is inconsiderable, and is all consumed within the district. Thana Mendiganj and Dakhin Shahbázpúr are the principal localities for its cultivation.

COLD-WEATHER CROPS.—The cold-weather crops, the *dhulat—i.e.*, dry or sandy earth crops, as they are called —are not so important in Bákarganj as they are in the higher and drier districts of Western Bengal. Nevertheless, turmeric, melons, cucumbers, &c., are grown, especially on the high lands and chars. Linseed is grown to some extent in Dakhin Shahbázpúr. San, for making hemp, is grown on the chars in the Arial Khan, &c. It is stronger than jute, and is used for making nets.

FRUITS, &C.—Abundance of plantains, tamarinds, ják fruit, &c., are produced, but the plantains are generally of rather inferior quality. The same must be said of the mangoes, of which a great quantity are produced in thana Gournadi. A few limes and oranges are grown in Mendiganj. The *manjit* or Indian madder (*Rubia cordifolia*) is cultivated in Oozirpúr and Shikarpúr in the Gournadi thana, and the produce is exported to Calcutta. It is said to be a very profitable crop, and is locally known by the name of *malancha*.

GÁB-TREE. — The gáb-tree (*Diospyros embryopteris glutinifera*) is very important, as the fruit of it yields a juice which is used for caulking boats. It is a handsome tree, with dark green leaves, and a compact dome-shaped habit. It does not, I believe, grow wild in the Sundarbans, but is commonly seen on the banks of rivers and in homesteads, both deserted and occupied. The fruit is sold by the score or by the basket. Sometimes there is a scarcity, and then the price of the fruit is eight anas, or even a rupee per basket; generally the price is from two to four anas a basket. Gáb is applied to boats four times a year, except in the case of Balam boats, on which it is not used at all. The caulking of a *kós* boat with gáb costs from two to three rupees a year. About 1000 gáb fruits are required for the caulking of an ordinary-sized boat. Fishing-nets are steeped in gáb juice, and this gives them their black colour and also preserves them. The fruit, which is round, and when ripe, brown, is pounded in a mortar or *dhenki*, then water is added, and the mixture is heated over a fire. It is then put into a jar, closed so as to exclude the air and also the mosquitoes, which are fond of eating it. If it is to be applied to boats, the ashes of the gólpatti or of any jungle are mixed with it. It is customary to apply fire to the outside of boats before the gáb juice is put on, in order to kill the worms.

MINERAL PRODUCTS.—The only mineral product is salt; but the Government rules about salt, and the scarcity of fuel, do not admit of its manufacture. It is obtained from the sea, and can also be extracted from the earth. The soil of new formations in the district is impregnated with salt, and in some of the chars—for example, in parts of Dakhin Shahbázpúr—the salt efflorescence is sufficient to make the surface of the soil quite white, as if covered with hoarfrost. It has often been supposed that the illicit manufacture of salt is common in the district, and this has led to a stringent system of salt-passes, &c. It is, however, impossible that the manufacture can take place on a large scale, for, apart from all other difficulties, the want of a sufficient quantity of fuel must prevent this. It is on the chars that the soil is most favourable for salt-making, but these are now highly cultivated in most parts, and there is comparatively little jungle. For example, there is so little jungle now in the large island of Dakhin Shahbázpúr that there are no tigers in it, and hardly any leopards. In the days of the salt manufacture it was the jungle on the chars which supplied the fuel, and it was the necessity, imposed by the manufacture, of keeping so much land in jungle which retarded the cultivation of the chars for so many years. No doubt salt is illicitly manufactured for domestic consumption, but such proceedings are on so small a scale as almost to defy detection. A handful of earth from the chars will yield enough salt for a meal. The ashes of the branches of the cocoa-nut, of the plaintain, of the bamboo, &c., yield salt, and it is often said that widows and other poor people who live far inland get their salt from the cocoa-nut trees in their homesteads.

It appears strange that a country naturally so rich in salt as Bákarganj should have to depend on Europe for the supply of this necessary; and it is to be hoped that some day it will be found possible to manufacture it locally, or at least nearer home.

Fish.—Bákarganj has always been famous for the number and excellence of its fish, and fish is the chief form in which the bulk of the population obtain animal food. Fish is exported to Calcutta from the Kotwalipara bíls (now mostly transferred to Farídpúr), and this trade is the chief support of many of the inhabitants of those swamps. The fish are conveyed in wells at the bottom of the boats. They are small-sized fish, and belong chiefly to the species called the *koï* and the *singhi.* The *khalisa*, the *saül*, the *gázar*, the *fali*, the *magur*, and the *chang* are also caught in the bíls and exported to Calcutta. The Deputy-Magistrate of Mádaripúr once estimated the annual value of the export at between Rs.15,000 and Rs.16,000. Upwards of fifty species of fish are enumerated as being caught in the district and used for food. The best known are the *hilsa*, the *bhétki* or *koral*, the *ruï*, the *pangás*, the *boál*, the *kátal*, the *silon*, and the *mango* fish. This last is, however, only caught in the rains, and is smaller than, and in every respect inferior to, the mango fish of the Hughli. The hilsa has given its name to one of the largest rivers in the district (the Ilsa or Hilsa), between Dakhin Shahbázpúr and the mainland; and the pangás has a river named after it in the Gournadi thana. The hilsa is sometimes salted, but generally it is either eaten fresh, or dried in the sun without the use of any salt. The drying of fish is an extensive trade in parts of the south of the district, and boats come from Chittagong and Jessore every year and take away large quantities of *sútkis*, as they are called. In general, I believe, the drying and the exporting are done by the same people—viz., the boats' crews.

There is a small delicate fish called the *bánspata,* or bamboo leaf, from its resemblance to that leaf. The *puti* and the young puti, called the *titputi*, and the *isa* fish, are largely caught in the paddy-fields and ditches. Fish-fry or *pona,* which are chiefly the young of the *saul* and gázar, are also largely caught by herd-boys and others. *Chingris* or prawns are caught in abundance during the cold weather. The koï-fish,[1] already alluded to, is especially prized by Hindus, and there are many who do not care for any fish except the koï and the bíl-fish allied to it. It is made into soup, and is thought to be very nourishing. The koï is sold by number, twenty koïs fetching from three to four anas. Fish, when sold on the large scale, are sold by the man, and the price in Dakhin Shahbázpúr is about Rs. 5 per man. The *potka* deserves mention from the fact that it is a poisonous fish, and that several accidents have occurred from eating it. It is a thick and curiously-mottled fish, and is common in the bazárs, as it is prized by the poorer classes for its oily richness. It has sometimes been proposed to prohibit the sale of it, but such a measure would be of no avail, as it would not prevent people from catching it for their own use. The poison is contained, I believe, near the ventral fin, and this part should be cut out before the fish is cooked.

FISH OIL.—Many ryots make an oil for lighting their houses from decomposed fish, but the oil is not an article of trade.

Fish are caught by nets, by cages, and by hooks.

[1] This fish is able to propel itself a considerable distance across country.

According to the census, there are 17,607 fishermen (males only) in Bákarganj. Most of them are Hindus, and belong to the Jaliya or Kaibart castes. The fish-mongers—*i.e.*, those who buy fish from the fishermen and retail it to the public—are generally Mahomedans, and belong to a class called Nikaris and also Sikdars. There are several families of them near Barisál. They are a class by themselves, and are looked down upon by other Mahomedans, who will not intermarry with them. There is no close season in Bákarganj, and no precautions are taken to preserve the fish in the rivers. It is customary to stock tanks with fish, and the right of fishing in them is jealously guarded. It is common to see bamboos stuck here and there in a tank with the object of preventing night-poaching, the stakes preventing the throwing of nets. During the rains trenches are cut between the tanks and rivers, so as to allow fresh water and fish to enter the tanks. Tanks are often let for the sake of the fishing, and yield a considerable sum. There are several valuable tanks in Kewari thana, and the Barisál municipality have lately derived a small revenue from the letting of the rod-fishing in the public tanks. Fishing is a very favourite amusement of the Bengalis, and is dignified by them with the name of *shikar*. There are only four fisheries belonging to Government, and none of them is of much value.

Notwithstanding the apparently great abundance of fish, natives are frequently heard to complain of their scarcity and dearness. This is especially the case in the south of the district, though from the number and largeness of the rivers there, one would have thought that fish would have been most plentiful. This complaint is partially explained by the circumstance that professional fishermen, like other Hindus, are somewhat scarce in the south of the district. The best explanation, however, is that by far the largest proportion of the fish caught in the district is never brought to market, as it is taken by peasants and other amateur fishermen for their own consumption. Every ryot, young and old, is something of an angler, and his inexhaustible patience, and abundance of leisure at certain seasons, well fit him for the occupation.

CHAPTER X.

MANUFACTURES AND PRICES.

I. MANUFACTURES.

BÁKARGANJ is not at all a manufacturing district. There are no mills or other large works, and the great bulk of the people are engaged in agriculture. In old times the district was a very important seat of the salt manufacture; many descendants of the salt molunghees still reside in it, and the names Baipari, Góldar, Jamadar, have become patronymics in many families, especially in Dakhin Shahbázpúr, from their having been at one time connected with the salt trade. The introduction of Liverpool salt, and the cultivation of the islands and chars, have put an end to this industry. A few Mahomedan families in the village of Bilgaon, near Palardi police station, make a little country paper, but it is very coarse, and the trade is dying out. *Chalas* or *ghani* bags are made by the Kapali caste in Patihar and other villages of the Gournadi thana, and these have a good sale among the sugarmakers, &c. Opposite Nalchiti, at a place called Kalupara, or Oilman's hamlet, a good deal of mustard oil is made, the seed being brought from the north of the district. The production of sugar at Jabar Amal, &c., has already been referred to. Sítalpati mats are made at Chirapara, Rangasri, and Helancha; and hogla mats are made in great quantities all over the district. Cocoa-nut oil is made at Daulat Khan, Nalchiti, &c. Lime is made from shells at Chawalakátti and other places in the bíls, for home consumption only. Uzirpúr and its neighbourhood have a local reputation for the making of *dáos* and other iron implements. Large jars for holding rice, &c., are made at Madupúr, near Nalchiti, and pots and dishes are made by potters at various places in the Kotwali thana, &c. Nets are made at Ghanteshwar. Perhaps one of the most skilled crafts in the district is boat-making. This is carried on at Debaikháli and Shampúr in the Mendiganj thana, where the best kós boats are made; at Ghanteshwar, near Agarpúr, where the best *pansways* are made; and at Barsakátti in the Perozpúr thana. At this last place very large cargo-boats are made. A few canoes are hollowed out of kerua wood by the Mugs in the Sundarbans, and *dinghis* of sundari wood are made all over the district, but especially at Jhalukátti. Kaliganj, Bákarganj, Phalagar, are also boat-building places. There are weavers in the district, both Hindus and Mahomedans, but their trade is not a profitable one. The census gives the large number of 14,146 weavers (males only). Brick-making is carried on to a considerable extent in the neighbourhood of Barisál.

The largest workshop in the district is the Barisál Jail, but it does not produce anything worthy of much notice. It may be remarked that dexterity with the fingers is much more characteristic of the Hindu than of the Mahomedan population, and that as Bákarganj is pre-eminently a Mahomedan district, much artistic skill is not to be looked for. I have no doubt that the superior dexterity of the Hindu is in great measure to be explained by the doctrine of hereditary aptitudes, as the system of caste makes generation after generation follow the same trade.

II. PRICES, ETC.

The subject of prices is one about which it is difficult to give precise information. It is sufficiently established that there has been a considerable rise of prices within the last eighty years, and probably this rise has been most marked during the last decade, but I cannot exhibit it step by step. All I shall attempt to do will be to give a few facts, which I have collected from the official records and other sources.

In 1790 the average earnings of a blacksmith were reckoned to be Rs.3 a month, and in 1796 the *manjhis* of the patrol-boats received Rs.4, and the rowers Rs.3 per month. (It must be remembered that the rupees were sicca.) This was, I fancy, better than the ordinary pay of boatmen, and was given probably on account of the danger of the service. In the statement of the *dák* establishment, 30th August 1809, the pay of the manjhis is reckoned at Rs.3, and that of the rowers and the hire of the boat at Rs.2-8 a month. In 1802 the wages of spearmen (employed in the escort of treasure, &c.) were Rs.2-8 a month. In old times the prisoners in the jail did their own marketing, and received a certain amount of cowries daily for this purpose. In 1805 the daily allowance to each prisoner was three puns of cowries, equal to about three-fourths of an ana. Their monthly expenditure per head was reckoned at about Rs.1-6, of which 15 anas went for the purchase of rice. Of course this did not include the charges for guarding, for lights, for medicine, or for blankets. There is a letter from Mr Collector Armstrong, dated 9th February 1797, in which he says that in the Idilpúr pargana paddy used to sell at three maunds for the rupee, and was then considered cheap, but that at the time of his writing it was selling at the rate of eight maunds for the rupee. (The maund was of 82 sicca weight.) In 1807 bamboos sold at Rs.3 the 100, and in 1820 they sold at Rs.4 the 100. Lime was Rs.35 the 100 maunds, and iron was Rs.6 the maund.

On 19th March 1811 the Collector writes that "the price of rice has risen to a very unusual height; instead of one man for a rupee, it is now twenty-five sírs." On 27th March 1824 the price of salt is said to be Rs.4-8 per man when bought in quantities larger than a man, and Rs.5 a man for smaller quantities, so that the price was then about the same as now.

In a letter of 29th August 1799 it is reported that there was not a sicca rupee in Bákarganj. I presume there were Arcot and other rupees. The copper coinage was not introduced till 1814.

In 1861 paddy sold at one man and at 36 sírs for the rupee, and rice at 26 sírs for the rupee. Sugar-cane sold at 64 stems for the rupee, or about the same as now. Raw sugar sold at 10 sírs for the rupee, and milk at 12 sírs. In 1866 the price of rice rose on account of the Orissa famine, and was 15 sírs for the rupee in January, and even, it is said, as high as 8½ sírs in October. The average price for the year is given at 12 sírs for the rupee. On 30th January 1875 the price of good rice in the Barisál bazár was 17 sírs the rupee, and of inferior kinds 21 sírs for the rupee. At the same time salt was selling at 2 anas a sír, and firewood at 100 sírs a rupee.

Freights to Calcutta vary from Rs.20 to Rs.30 the 100 mans. Often goods are shipped on co-operative principle, the *mahajan* or shipper and the boatmen dividing the profit. When this is done, the mahajan generally gets 8 anas or one-half of the profit, and the other half is divided among the manjhi and his boatmen, he getting 10 anas and the boatmen 6 anas. When boatmen receive wages, they are also fed by the manjhi. It is very difficult to make any statement regarding the rates of rent paid by cultivators. A fact is always a difficult thing to lay hold of—it is so slippery, and has so many sides to it; but this is especially difficult when the question is one of prices, or of cognate matters, as so many theories and prejudices and interests are intertwined with it. However, I may state that the general rate of rent for rice-land seems to be about a rupee a bigha. Homestead-land and sugar-cane-land, or any land cultivated in a particular crop, generally lets at a much higher rate of rent.

PART III.

CHAPTER XI.

ENGLISH ADMINISTRATION.

THERE is no doubt that Bákarganj early attracted the attention of the English on account of its facilities for trade. It has always been productive of rice, and in the old days of the salt monopoly it was perhaps even more important in the eyes of the Government on account of the salt manufactured in it. Selímábád was long a chief seat of this manufacture, and I have elsewhere noticed Mr Barwell's (the Chief of Dacca) dealings with the salt-farm of this pargana and of Dakhin Shahbázpúr. There was also some exportation of lime from the district before the Sylhet lime quarries were worked, or at least before their produce was readily available for the Calcutta market. The lime was shell-lime, and was made by burning the shells found in the bíls and swamps. The rivers of the district were also then, as now, the highway of communication between Calcutta and Dacca and the other eastern districts. More than a hundred years ago the bazár of Bákarganj was spoken of as being a place of great trade; and as the letter in which this is mentioned gives an interesting, though rather painful, representation of the state of matters in the district in those days, I shall here give it in its entirety.

The letter was written by one Sergeant Brego from Bákarganj, on 25th May 1762, and was addressed to the Governor (Mr Vansittart). It is printed at p. 111 of vol. ii. of Vansittart's "Narrative" (London, 1766).

"The situation of affairs at this place obliges me to apply to your Honour for instructions for my further proceedings.

"My instructions which I brought here were, that in case any Europeans or their servants committed any disorders, they were to be sent to Calcutta, notwithstanding any pretences they shall make for so doing.

"Notwithstanding the rigour of these orders, I have ever made it my business (when anything trifling happened) to endeavour by gentle means to persuade the gentlemen's several gomastahs here to act in a peaceable manner, which, although repeated several times, has had no effect, but, on the contrary, has occasioned their writing complaints of me to their respective masters that I obstructed them in their business and ill-used them; and in return I have received menacing letters from several gentlemen, threatening, if I interfere with their servants, to use such measures as I may repent; nor have the gentlemen only done this, their very gomastahs have made it public here, that in case I stop them in any proceeding, they will use the same methods; for the truth of which I have good proofs.

"Now, sir, I am to inform you what I have obstructed them in. This place was of great trade formerly, but now brought to nothing by the following practices. A gentleman sends a gomastah here to buy or sell; he immediately looks upon himself as sufficient to force every inhabitant either to buy his goods or sell him theirs, and on refusal (in case of non-capacity) a flogging or confinement immediately ensues. This is not sufficient even when willing, but a second force is made use of, which is to engross the different branches of trade to themselves and not to suffer any persons to buy or sell the articles they trade in, and if the country-people do it, then a repetition of their authority is put in practice; and again, what things they purchase, they think the least they can do is to take them for a considerable deal less than another merchant, and oftentimes refuse paying that, and my interfering causes an immediate complaint. This and many other oppressions, more than can be related, which are daily used by the Bengal gomastahs, is the reason that this place is growing destitute of inhabitants. Every day numbers leave the town to seek a residence more safe, and the very markets, which before afforded plenty, do hardly now produce anything of use, their peons being allowed to force poor people, and if the zamindar tries to prevent it, he is threatened to be used in the same manner.

"Before, justice was given in the public cutchery, but now every gomastah is become a judge, and every one's house a cutchery; they even pass sentences on the zamindars themselves, and draw money from them by pretended injuries, such as a quarrel with some of their peons, or their having, as they assert, stole something, which is more likely to have been taken by their own people; but allowing they were robbed, I believe no gomastah's authority extends so far as to take his own satisfaction on the Government.

"Having thus far acquainted your Honour with the behaviour of the gomastahs here, I am to request your Honour's interest, that in case I am to put your orders into execution, I may be borne harmless therein. Now I beg leave to conclude, being, with all respect," &c.

An extract from this letter is given in a note to Mr

Mill's "History of India," vol. iii. p. 330 (ed. 1830); but Mr Mill wrongly describes it as a letter written to the Nawab by one of his officers. In fact the letter was written to Mr Vansittart by an officer whom he had sent down with six sepoys to Bákarganj at the request of the Nawab, and in order to assist the zamindar of Bákarganj. This circumstance raises the importance of the letter by showing that its representations come from one holding a presumably independent position, and not from one of Mir Kassim's servants. The letter, however, not only shows the distracted condition of the country, but also the feebleness of the remedies applied. It almost provokes a smile to find Mr Vansittart unable to do anything more vigorous than to send a common sergeant (apparently, from his name, not even a European) with six sepoys to a large mart like Bákarganj, when such oppressions were going on. The orders, too, which were given to the poor sergeant—viz., to deport the Europeans and their servants to Calcutta—seem ludicrously out of keeping with the means of coercion placed at his disposal, and justify Macaulay's remark, that Vansittart, with fair intentions, was a feeble and inefficient ruler.

The following extract from a letter of the Nawab (Mir Kassim) to Mr Vansittart gives another picture of the state of matters. It appears to have been written on 26th December 1762, and is printed at p. 167 of the 2d volume of Vansittart's "Narrative:"—

"As the Company's gomastahs make salt at Sundeep, &c., I desire you will write to them not to make any more there, but, like other merchants, to purchase it from the molunghies at the market price. . . .

"In the parganas of Gopalpúr and Dakhanbárpúr [Dakhin Shahbázpúr], and other districts where salt is made, the people of the Company's factory work the salt-pans; and they take possession of all the salt which the molunghies of other parganas have made, by which means I suffer a very great loss. Moreover, they oblige the ryots to receive money from them for purchasing rice, and by force and violence they take more than the market price affords, and the ryots all run away on account of these oppressions. For many years it has been customary for the Cashmere merchants to advance money at Sunderbund, and provide molunghies to work the salt-pans there: they paid the rents for the salt-pans at the several parganas; and the duties on the salt, which were paid at Burry-saul Chokey, belonging to the Shahbunder, amounted to near Rs.30,000. At present the people of the factory have dispossessed the Cashmere merchants, and have appropriated all the salt to themselves."

In Long's "Selections," p. 55, there is an extract from the Government Consultations, dated 12th February 1755, stating that several boats loaded with rice had been stopped at Bákarganj by an order from Dacca (apparently issued by Rajah Raj Ballab), and that the stoppage had occasioned a great scarcity and dearness of grain in Calcutta. In consequence of this stoppage a Lieutenant Harding was sent with a small party of troops to clear the boats and take them under his protection. When the great famine of 1770 took place, help was sought for from Bákarganj,[1] just as in the

[1] It is mentioned in a memorandum by Sir George Campbell that a gentleman was despatched from Dacca to Bákarganj in 1770 to purchase grain. The fullest reference to the subject, however, is to be found in Hunter's "Rural Annals," Appendix B, p. 407, &c. Mr Sumner was the gentleman deputed (p. 419, Consultation of 3d April 1770). 33,913 mans had arrived from Bákarganj (p. 412). The rice from Bárkerganje (*sic*), Mr Becher observed, arrived at a most critical time; and "the Company has reaped a considerable benefit by the measure, which proved a general relief to the immediate dependants on the English here [Murshídábád],

famine of 1873–74 it was regarded as the chief source from which the distressed districts were to be supplied.

Probably the Portuguese were the first Europeans or quasi-Europeans who engaged in the Bákarganj trade. They came from Bandel and Goa, and settled at Sibpúr, about five miles from Bákarganj, towards the middle of the last century. As I have stated in another chapter, the Portuguese had dealings with the district of a less peaceful character—namely, in the beginning of the seventeenth century, when Sebastian Gonzales and other Portuguese pirates came from Chittagong and elsewhere, and in conjunction with the Burmese or Mugs, plundered the Sundarbans and the islands in the Meghna. The first British settler in the district was apparently a Scotchman, named William Robinson, who established himself at Madhupúr, in the neighbourhood of Baroikaran and Nalchiti, in 1766, and lived there for about thirty years. He described himself in 1794 as having embarked on board the ship "Falmouth" in 1765, and as having been cast ashore east of Saugor Sands in June 1766, from whence he had come up to Madhupúr by boat, and had been engaged in trade there ever since. His descendants still reside in the district, and his tomb is still to be seen in Barisál, in Mr Pereira's compound. There was also a Mr Frazer, who described himself in 1794 as having been for ten years at Baroikaran in the employment of Mr Gill.

In these days Nalchiti, which is now so large a mart, does not appear to have existed, or at least it was less

and tended to preserve order and regularity; otherwise the greatest confusion must have ensued." Rs.60,000 were given to the Dacca Council for the purchase of grain. If this were all the money spent at Bákarganj, the arrangement must have been very successful, for on 1st February 1771 the committee report that the sale of the Bákarganj rice produced a profit of Rs.67,593 (Appendix B, p. 419).

important than its neighbour Baroikaran, which is now almost deserted. Local tradition points to Baroikaran as the old headquarters of the district, and this is supported by a reference in the decree for the resumption of Baroikaran char to a piece of land therein which had originally been Mr Christopher Keating's cutchery. This is the Mr Keating of Hunter's "Annals," who, before he went to Birbhúm, was Civil Judge of Bákarganj in 1785. The ancient importance of Baroikaran is also shown by the fact that it was the site of the police station, which was not removed from it to Nalchiti until 1824.

DACOITS.—The great trade of Bákarganj, and the facilities for escape offered by its rivers and jungles, rendered it a favourite haunt of dacoits or gang-robbers, and the English Government was early obliged to take notice of their depredations. As far back as 1764 we find that an English gentleman named Mr Rose was murdered by dacoits near Bákarganj, and that the Nawab of Murshídábád was called upon to make the landholder refund the money and goods plundered, and to take such vigorous measures that the parts might be entirely cleared of robbers and murderers (Long's "Selections," p. 361. See also pp. 382, 383, and 385). The letter about Mr Rose given at p. 361 of Long's "Selections" is in answer to one from the Governor, dated 14th November 1764. The latter is interesting as a recognition of the practice of impaling, the Nawab being requested to order the Naib of Dacca to impale the robbers. I therefore quote it in full: "I have already by word of mouth represented to you, that as Mr Rose, an English gentleman, was travelling in a boat with some money and goods, the boat-people murdered him near Bákarganj and carried away the money and goods, and took shelter in the zamindari of Sitaram. In order to inquire into this affair, I sent an Englishman to the said zamindar, but he would not regard him. I have therefore enclosed for your observation an account of the money and goods that were plundered, and request that you will write an order to the Naib of Dacca to make the zamindar refund, and inflict such punishment on him as may prevent all such proceedings in future. The number of murderers and robbers in the neighbourhood of Báckerganje is daily increasing, insomuch that trading people are now afraid to pass backwards and forwards, wherefore I request that you will give orders to the Naib of Dacca to send some of the factory sepoys along with some of his own people to apprehend the said murderers and *impale* them, which will be very serviceable to traders." Mr Rose is elsewhere called Captain John Rose and also Mr Ross, and apparently it was his own boatmen who murdered him. The whole of his property, including Rs.5800 in cash, was estimated at Rs.13,000. Among his property were four slaves, who were reckoned altogether as worth only Rs.240. Other instances of the depredations of dacoits are given in Seton-Karr's "Selections," p. 269 *et seq.* In 1788 they killed a Mr Burgh between Kulpadi and Gournadi.

They also attacked Mr Willis, the Collector of Sylhet, on his way through the district, and he had to run his boat ashore in order to escape from them. In a private letter printed at p. 273 of Seton-Karr's "Selections" the writer says, "I am happy to tell you that most of the dacoits who attacked Mr Willis in the Sundarbans have been taken. It appears they have been roving about the Sundarban rivers for eighteen months without any settled habitation. They were chased by some armed boats, fitted out by Mr Day for the express purpose, below the island Sundeep, almost out at sea; and during the chase the pursuers and pursued were all nearly swallowed up by the high bore of the Meghna. There was skirmishing from time to time for a day and a half before the dacoits surrendered. They have since been brought to Dacca, and it is to be hoped that their fate will be an example and terror to others."

One Mahomed Hayat, a notorious dacoit, was sentenced by the Naib Nazim to perpetual imprisonment in 1790. The Governor-General ordered that he should be transported to the Prince of Wales Island. He returned in 1806.

I have noticed these dacoities here, because it was apparently in consequence of them that Government first took active measures for the administration of the district. An officer was appointed, called the Commissioner of the Sundarbans, who had his headquarters at Bákarganj. Unfortunately the Bákarganj magisterial records do not extend farther back than 1792, and I am unable to say at what date the office of Commissioner was established. Apparently Mr Lodge was the first Commissioner; he was succeeded in 1790 by Mr Hyndman ("Calcutta Gazette," 16th December 1790), and the latter by Mr Middleton.[1] At a still earlier date, however, there was a civil judge, first at Baroikaran and afterwards at Bákarganj. The first judge was

[1] The "Calcutta Gazette" of 6th December 1792 contains the following announcement: "The Governor-General in Council has been pleased to appoint Mr Samuel Middleton Commissioner in the Sundarbans for suppressing the depredations of dacoits, in the room of Mr William Hyndman deceased."

The same paper contains the announcement of the death of Mr Hyndman, "lately at Bákarganj."

apparently Mr Wroughton. He acted in 1782, and got into trouble with Mr Holland, the Chief of Dacca, about the execution of a process. The Governor (Warren Hastings) ordered him to be brought to trial about this, but I do not know what was the result. He was succeeded by Mr Keating, who was apparently succeeded by Mr Lodge. These facts are taken from some papers lent me by the Board of Revenue. Mr Lodge also held the office of Collector of Buzurgumedpúr, which was a zila or collectorate district long before Bákarganj. It appears from a letter of Mr Lodge, dated 12th August 1786, which is preserved in the office of the Board of Revenue, that the parganas of Chandradwip, Selímábád, Jaffirábád, Syedpúr, Arangpúr, and Azimpúr were attached to the zila of Buzurgumedpúr. Buzurgumedpúr apparently remained a separate charge till 1787, when it was annexed to the Collectorate of Dacca (Seton-Karr's Selections, p. 185).

CHAPTER XII.

REVENUE ADMINISTRATION.

I HAVE said that the magisterial records of Bákarganj do not extend farther back than 1792. The Collectorate records are not much older, the earliest being a letter dated 6th January 1790, which recommends the making of advances to the proprietors on account of the severe famine of 1787. It should also be noticed that the early Collectorate records are merely copies, the originals being at Dacca. The copies were obtained by Mr Hunter, the first Collector of Bákarganj, who came to Barisál in 1817 (see his letter to Board, 24th March 1819). They are not always perfect, and contain lacunæ as well as errors; but, on the other hand, they are probably in better preservation and more legible than the originals now are.

Next to the formation of the Permanent Settlement, the most important event in the history of Bákarganj during the last century was probably the famine of 1787. This appears to have caused a very great loss of life, especially in the northern parts of the district. It was the result of floods, not of drought; and indeed it may be said that the destruction of the crops by floods is the only possible cause of an extensive famine in Bákarganj. The country is so well watered that it is little in need of irrigation, and should the rain fail, enough water is brought into the southern parts of the districts by the tides in some measure to supply its place. I have not been able to find any detailed description of the famine, but the following reference to it is made by Mr Douglas in a letter to the Board of Revenue, dated 6th April 1790. The occasion of Mr Douglas's writing was his having to report on the proposals for the Decennial Settlement of the district. "However unwilling I am," he writes, "to animadvert on Mr Day's proposed plan of a ten years' settlement, yet a regard for my own character, and from a perfect conviction that I cannot conclude the Settlement with many of the mahals at the jama recommended by him, impels me to deliver my sentiments freely on the subject, relying on the Board's candour for putting a favourable construction on the motives by which I am actuated. It is necessary to observe that Mr Day did not send down his proposed plan of settlement for upwards of six months after this district [Dacca Jalálpúr, which included Farídpúr and Bákarganj] had been visited by the most dreadful calamity ever remembered by the oldest inhabitant of the district, and which deprived it (by Mr Day's calculation) of upwards of 60,000 of its inhabitants, who either miserably perished, or were reduced to the painful necessity of forsaking their habitations in search of a precarious subsistence. Mr Day visited some of the parganas when the famine raged with the greatest violence, and had ocular proofs of the extreme misery to which the wretched inhabitants were reduced. He saw the parganas inundated, whole crops destroyed, and cultivation totally neglected. He had the mortification of beholding hundreds of the poor wretched inhabitants daily dying without the means of affording them the smallest relief. After a local investigation of the cruel effects of the inundation, after a full conviction of the very heavy loss many of the principal parganas sustained both in their inhabitants and crops, and the consequent decline of cultivation, it is a matter of great surprise that Mr Day should, in many of the parganas which had suffered so materially by the inundation and loss of tenants, recommend an increase to be taken in the ensuing year's Settlement. That gentleman observes that his plan was founded on the 'Idea of a Ten Years' Bandobast.' Admitting of this, can it be supposed that districts which had been deprived of one-half of their natural resources, could in the short period of one year so far recover as to yield the customary revenue, much less bear an increase which would have added to the miseries they had already suffered, and in all probability have obliged the remaining ryots to desert their habitations and seek refuge in more favourable districts?"

Elsewhere the Collector reports of the pargana Idilpúr, that he has been told from respectable authority that the northern part of this zamindari lost three-fourths of its inhabitants in the dreadful calamity of 1194 B.S. (1787). It will be seen that Mr Douglas's words, "the most dreadful calamity ever remembered by the oldest inhabitant of the district," imply that Bákarganj did not suffer from the celebrated famine of 1770, which desolated so many districts in Bengal.

The famine of 1787 no doubt chiefly affected the northern and eastern parts of the district, and the more westerly and central portions probably escaped in great measure, for then, as now, the northern and eastern parts were especially exposed to being flooded. They are the first to feel the effects of the risings of the rivers, and they are full of low-lying lands and swamps. A great part of Farídpúr and of the Gournadi thana consists of swamps, and it is seldom that a year passes without their suffering some loss from floods.

The early Collectorate records are chiefly occupied with the preparations for the Permanent Settlement. I have inserted in the Appendix the most important of them. As a general rule, the correspondence is of an uninteresting character, and it is only rarely that one comes upon anything worthy of being quoted.

It is evident enough that the system of collecting the revenues before the Permanent Settlement was a very hand-to-mouth one, and that everything depended on the personal qualities of the Collector and his subordinates. Estates were let in farm from year to year, and if the farmers, as was often the case, fell into arrears, they were imprisoned, or their farms were placed under the management of a sazawal or other Government officer. The following extract from a Collector's letter, dated 8th October 1790, gives some hint of the state of matters: "The Board observing in almost all the accounts *jama kharach*, a charge made for diet to prisoners, desire to be informed of what description they are, and upon what grounds the charge is admitted into the sazawal's account. This is an allowance for diet made to ryots and others who, upon proving refractory or dilatory in paying their rents, are put under restraint or confined for a time in the sazawal's [house ?]. They have no other means of subsistence. It amounts in all the accounts to about Rs.10 or Rs.12 for the whole year." In another letter (14th July 1790) the Collector writes, "I have confined the farmer for the balance due on account of *mahai* [fish] and *bajantri* [music] mahals, and trust to recover the same in a few days." A letter of 19th July 1790 notices the depredations of wild elephants in Kassimpúr and Bhowal, and reports that Birmohan is infested with tigers, and that the Collector has in vain endeavoured to encourage the tiger-killers to repair to the pargana. On 9th August 1790 the Collector reports that he has, agreeably to the Governor-General's orders, done away with the gázar duty—*i.e.*, duty on washermen. It yielded only Rs.60 a year, which seems to show that washermen were even more scarce in the district in former times than they are now.

There were other mahals belonging to the sayer, such as the *dúmdari*, which was collected from bird-catchers, monkey and bear dancers, faqirs, snake-dancers, conjurors, &c. (9th August 1790). This farm yielded in one year Rs.1444, and the bajantri or music farm yielded as much as Rs.3102. There was another farm, called *mushrat kotwali*, which was composed of collections from artificers—*i.e.*, brickmakers, &c. *Púnya* charges, or the charges for the ceremonial of the first receipt of rent for the year, were disallowed by the Board, though the Collector says they were invariably incurred and included under the head of chakla expenses (12th April 1792). In another letter the Collector writes about the charge for guarding treasure: "Your Board deem the sum of Rs.550 on account *barkandazes* excessive, and expect I will considerably reduce them. I trust you will deem this sum indispensable, when you are informed that the barkandazes are entertained as guards over the Mofussil cutchery and treasure; that they always escort the revenues to my treasury; that for that purpose it requires a strong guard to prevent the boats conveying the treasure from being plundered by the dacoits who infest the Meghna river. Were not the barkandazes regularly kept at the Mofussil treasury, it would be liable to be attacked and robbed by the dacoits who inhabit the Sundarbans, to which Selímábád pargana is adjoining, and indeed forms part of the Sundarbans. The established rate of boat-hire from Selímábád to Dacca is Rs.9."

A letter of 16th February 1792 records an attempted insurrection of one Bolaki Shah, a faqir, who had collected an armed force, and proclaimed to his followers that the reign of the Feringhies or Europeans was at an end. He was said to have erected a fort at Subanredia; and a revenue peon who was seized by him reported that he saw at his place seven cannon, twelve ginjals, and five or six muskets, two spears, and two men employed in making gunpowder. A Naib and forty-eight sepoys were sent to apprehend him. I have been told that it was this faqir who removed the old cannon which used to lie in Sujábád Fort.

It was part of the arrangements of the Permanent Settlement that the zamindars should give their ryots pattas or leases, and Mr Douglas was called on to report what progress had been made in this matter. On 6th December 1792 he reports as follows:—

"Some zamindars object to giving pottahs. The zamindar of Nurallapúr says that, by the ancient custom of the country, pottahs are not granted to the old-established ryots, that they paid according to the rates fixed on their respective villages, or by a measurement. That any new ryots delivering in proposals for cultivating jungle-lands, to such ryots pottahs are granted, and they paid according to the quantity of land they annually cultivated. Others, again, do not take out pottahs for cultivating the jungle-lands, the demands from them are regulated according to the rates paid by other ryots who cultivate jungle-lands. That ever since the commencement of the current year he has been busily engaged in drawing out pottahs, framing accounts in conformity to the regulations; but his lands are much scattered. He finds it extremely difficult to carry into immediate effect the orders of Government. Besides, the old-established ryots obstinately oppose the receipt of pottahs, and threaten to leave their lands.

"The zamindars of Rasulpúr, Baikanthpúr, Sultanábád, Ratandi Kalikapúr, have delivered in similar representations with the above. As it appeared to me very extraordinary that any ryot should object to the receipt of pottahs which would secure him from any arbitrary demands, I called several of them before me to state their grounds of objection, which they did as follows: That they enjoyed the same lands possessed by their forefathers; that they cultivate the same, and pay the same revenue; that their ancestors never received pottahs; that their acceptance of them would be disgraceful, as it would betray a mutual want of confidence on their and the zamindar's part; that they should lose the honorary title of being called old-established ryots, and thereby become degraded by being styled new ryots. When I consider the prejudices of this people—how bigoted they are to old-established customs, and how extremely averse they are to any innovation which militates against former usage—I am the less surprised at the objection started by the ryots for receiving pottahs; but being convinced it will ultimately redound to their ease, comfort, and benefit, by carrying into effect the regulation, I have again issued peremptory orders to the landholders for granting pottahs to every description of ryots, and directed those who have not yet delivered to me forms of pottahs, to do so immediately. Many of the landholders have granted pottahs to their ryots, according to the forms approved by me."

There are a few letters among the records about the

weavers and the salt manufacture. One forwards a petition from some ryots in Rajnagar complaining that the Commercial Resident at Lakhypúr forces advances on them as weavers, although, in fact, they never had woven anything. Another letter, dated 2d October 1790, states that the ryots are seized by the agents of the Salt Department to act as smiths, and that not only were they seized, but they were made to pay *piadgan*, or the fees of the *piada* who seized them! This piadgan is a well-known zamindari charge in the present day, and is one which must strike even the apathetic Bengali with a sense of injustice. It seems so iniquitous first to drag a man away from his home, and then to make him pay for the outrage which has been committed on him.

Bákarganj was, as I have said, a great seat of the salt manufacture. The establishments on the islands of Hattia and Dakhin Shahbázpúr were managed from Noakháli, or Bhulua, as it is also called; but that in Selímábád, &c., was managed from Jhalukátti, which appears to be identical with Rai Mongal, and also with Jainagar. The last-mentioned place was situated near the Ghosal Rajah's seat at Gurudham. The name of Mr Ewart, who figures in Mr Westland's "Jessore," is still remembered at Jhalukátti. He had a large house there, and is said to have been so magnificent as to have had a European baker and a European barber.

As appears to have been the case everywhere, the salt manufacture in Bákarganj led to oppressions and lawlessness, and to consequent disputes between the salt officers and the Magistrates. In 1826 the Magistrate of Bákarganj was called upon by the Board of Customs, salt and opium, to state the result of the suits brought by and against the salt officers, and replied as follows:

"I beg leave to state that the issue of the suits since my taking charge of this district has been generally proved against the salt officers for atrocities and oppression of every description, and I do not hesitate in giving my opinion that the greatest coercion is had recourse to in order to force advances on the molunghies by the *baiparies* or salt contractors, many of whom have been found guilty and punished, and nine have been lately committed for trial before the Judge of Circuit, convicted, and sentenced to seven and six years' imprisonment, besides many who have been punished both by the former Magistrates and also by the Court of Circuit" (12th June 1826).

The remissions made to the zamindars of Dakhin Shahbázpúr and Selímábád and other places, on account of lands used for the salt manufacture, were a fruitful source of correspondence at various times (see an elaborate report by Mr Collector Sutherland, 13th June 1866).

The first Collector of Bákarganj was Mr Day. He was succeeded by Mr Douglas, who made the Permanent Settlement, and then followed Messrs Thompson, Armstrong, and Massie. All these, however, and their successors up to 1817, resided at Dacca, and scarcely ever visited Bákarganj. Mr Hunter, the first independent Collector of Bákarganj, received charge of his office on 8th December 1817. The Collectorate was established partly from an idea that the cultivation of the Sundarbans would thereby be facilitated, and apparently Mr Hunter was chosen on account of his supposed aptitude for such duty. (He was one of those who afterwards set about reclaiming Saugor Island.)

Bákarganj was not, however, entirely without resident revenue officers before Mr Hunter's arrival. In 1814 there was an Assistant-Collector at Barisál who had charge of the treasury, and who, I believe, also tried summary suits for rent. He was subordinate to the Collector of Dacca, but also corresponded directly with Calcutta. There was a similar officer at Farídpúr. The first officer appears to have been Mr E. Bagge. He was succeeded by Mr E. Lee Warner, and he in his turn was succeeded by Mr Pigou and by Mr Frazer. It was Mr Frazer who gave over charge to Mr Hunter. These Assistant-Collectors were also assistants to the Magistrate.

On 18th April 1818 Mr Hunter sent a list of the establishment proposed by him for the collectorship, and this was corrected by a subsequent letter dated 27th May. His pay was Rs.1500, and the cost of the proposed establishment was, including this, Rs.2458 a month.

Mr Hunter remained in charge of the Collectorate till 6th November 1819, when he made over charge to Mr Barlow, who was succeeded on 5th April 1820 by Mr Lara. Mr Hunter, however, took charge again on 30th October 1820, but finally made over charge to Mr Maxwell on 22d January 1821.

Mr Hunter was engaged actively in collecting information about the chars or alluvial formations which had been formed since the time of the Permanent Settlement, for this was the time of resumptions. He visited the remote parts of the district, including the island of Kúkri Múkri, and he employed a Mr Jackson to make a sort of survey of the Sundarbans.

After the Permanent Settlement was fairly completed, the work of the Collectorate became tolerably easy, and consisted chiefly in the trial of rent suits. After the passing of Regulation 11 of 1819, the work of resumption became considerable, and the number of islands and chars resumed in the district was very large. These resumptions also led to numerous Government suits, which the Collector had to look after. Notwithstanding this, it is probable that a Collector's work continued to be tolerably light until the passing of Act 10 of 1859, and the subsequent combination of the offices of Collector and Magistrate.

CHAPTER XIII.

PROGRESS OF THE CRIMINAL ADMINISTRATION AND GENERAL HISTORY.

THE Civil Judges of Bákarganj had, I believe, magisterial powers also. I do not know the exact nature of the office of Commissioner of Bákarganj, but I believe he had at first only preventive powers, and did not acquire judicial powers until 1794. These seem to have been conferred by the repealed Regulation 9 of 1793, the preamble to which gives a *résumé* of the various judicial systems. The same Regulation (sect. 40) makes Bákarganj one of the stations of the Dacca Court of Circuit. The office of Commissioner was abolished by Regulation 7 of 1797, which divided Dacca Jalálpúr into two divisions—"the northern to be denominated the zila of Dacca Jalálpúr [now Farídpúr], and the southern division the zila of Bákarganj." Section 1 states that one object of the Regulation is "to provide for the more effectual administration of justice in the Sundarbans and the district adjacent, heretofore included in the jurisdiction of the Commissioner of Bákarganj, who was invested with the powers of a Magistrate, but was not authorised to exercise any civil jurisdiction."

Mr Middleton is said to have removed the offices from Baroikaran to Bákarganj. Probably this was in 1792, when he was appointed Commissioner. Mr Middleton remained at Bákarganj till 1800, when he was succeeded by Mr Spedding, who again was succeeded by Mr Wintle who removed (1801) the offices to Barisál. Mr Middleton does not appear to have been a very efficient officer, and more than once incurred the censure of Government. Indeed, if he had been a good officer, it is not likely that he would have been sent to so disagreeable a place as Bákarganj, or kept there so long as eight years. One of Mr Middleton's most extraordinary proceedings was his sending one Alliar Khan, a notorious *goinda* or informer, to the island of Dakhin Shahbázpúr with a general warrant to arrest dacoits and suspicious characters. I believe this was done in consequence of a Mr Paliologus, the servant of a Mr Demetrius, a Greek salt merchant, having been speared and killed by dacoits while in the island. Alliar Khan brought in no less than 314 persons to Bákarganj (see letter of 22d January 1801), and Mr Middleton's successor was a good deal puzzled to know what to do with them. However, this happened near the end of Mr Middleton's tenure of office, and we must not be too hard on a man who had breathed for eight years an atmosphere which makes one feel as if only "half-alive" (letter of Mr Wintle). The Government of the day took a lenient view of the case, and ascribed Mr Middleton's action entirely to his zeal for the public service (5th March 1801).

In these early days ships came up to Bákarganj and traded there in rice. Mention is made in the records of the "Eliza," which was at Bákarganj in August 1794, and of the brig "Maria," which was there on 26th November 1808. The Civil Surgeon, Mr Harper, appears to have been in partnership with Mr Gill as a boatbuilder, and to have employed (in 1794) a Frenchman named Antoin Piaji. In consequence probably of the famine of 1787, Government took to storing rice at Bákarganj, and had fifty-two *golahs* or granaries there. It may be noted that in former times Government had no scruple whatever in carrying out a policy which was considered by many so monstrous in 1873-74, and that there are several instances in the official records, and in Seton-Karr's "Selections," of Government's stopping the exportation of grain.

Formerly it was the custom to execute criminals at the scene of their crime, and such an execution took place at Ram Prasad Hát on 7th July 1794. It seems also to have been the idea to make executions as public as possible, instead of, as now, hiding them from the public eye. I find an instance of a hanging which took place at Bákarganj at one o'clock in the day.

There is nothing in the records to show the kind of life led by the officers at Bákarganj. The society was very small—apparently Messrs Middleton and Harper were the only English officers of their day; and the only fact of interest that I have been able to discover is that Mr Middleton's wife resided with him at Bákarganj. On 8th April 1795 the Nizamat Adâlat sent Mr Middleton a cat-o'-nine-tails, and informed him that he would be furnished with a new cat whenever the one now sent to him became unserviceable.

The town of Bákarganj stands on a small river called the Srimantapúr khál. The situation can never have been very healthy or pleasant, and it became worse in consequence of the formation of a char in front of the cutcheries. Its advantages were that it was central, that it had a large market, and that it was near the Golabari, where the tahsildar of Buzurgumedpúr had his cutchery, and the Portuguese settlement of Sibpúr. Very few remains of the old buildings now exist. The cutcheries appear to have been situated where the thana now is, and there is still a brick terrace there. The jail was higher up the khál, and on the bank of a small stream which is still called the Jailkhana khál. There was a good deal of correspondence about the change of site. Mr Middleton recommended Mohanganj, but eventually Barisál was fixed upon. A letter of the Nizamat Adâlat, dated 1st May 1801, directs the Magistrate to remove to Barisál, which was the place recommended by the Dacca Court of Circuit. See also letter of 29th April 1801 to the Governor-General. It must, I think, be admitted that the new site was well chosen, and that it has stood the test of time very well, as Barisál is about the healthiest and most conveniently situated town in the district.

There are two orders of Circuit Judges preserved among the records, which are worth quoting for their singularity. One is an order of Mr Bayard, dated 26th December 1800, directing that three men should be imprisoned for fifteen days for "declining to come to my assistance in an embarrassing situation when required, and refusing me those attentions which as a Judge of Circuit I have a right to command from all descriptions of persons in travelling through this district." Another is a similar order of Mr Crisp, dated 27th July 1800, directing that some palki-bearers be imprisoned for fifteen days for contempt of court, in refusing to associate with other bearers who had carried him to the jail.

The great point looked to in the commencement of the Bákarganj criminal jurisdiction was the suppression of dacoities. There were fourteen stations and fourteen boats, and the river patrol was the subject of much correspondence. It is certain that the Magistrates had very daring dacoits to deal with. Two of them—viz.,

Mahomed Hayat and Ainudeen Sikdar—were men of property, and were ringleaders or *sardar* dacoits. They were transported and their lands confiscated—a measure which led to almost endless correspondence on the Collectorate side, as the zamindars and the dacoits' families concealed the ownership of the lands, so that it was exceedingly difficult to identify them.

I can find nothing remarkable in the early official history of Bákarganj. None of the Magistrates appear to have been above the average in point of ability. I am afraid, indeed, that Bákarganj has been from the earliest times what a friend of mine once called it, "the dust-bin of Bengal," and that no officer was sent to it except as a punishment, or because he was not thought good enough for a better district. Mr Garrett, writing to the Secretary to Government in 1827, says, "I scarcely think there is any need of expatiating to you on the circumstances of this district, its situation, the litigious character of the inhabitants, and the general dislike evinced by the gentlemen of the service to accept the situation of Judge and Magistrate of Bákarganj. The last confirmed Judge who joined this station was Mr A. Mackenzie. This gentleman quitted it in 1817, since which period there has been a succession of officiating Magistrates. Though no less than four gentlemen were fully appointed, none of them ever joined. The prejudice against this place is not without foundation; the duties are certainly laborious, and the climate bad." There is a report by Mr Gardner on the police system, dated 19th February 1805, from which it appears that the total annual cost of the police was Rs.33,360. At that time Gournadi was not under Bákarganj, it having been transferred in 1806, nor was Idilpúr pargana a part of the district. On the other hand, Kachua (now in Jessore) belonged to Bákarganj, and also Hattia and Dakhin Shahbázpúr. The latter islands belonged to Bákarganj up to 1822, when they were transferred to the newly-established district of Noakháli. Dakhin Shahbázpúr was retransferred to Bákarganj in 1869. In course of time various changes were made in police arrangements. Thus thanas Kotwalipara and Mirzaganj were established in 1812, the Kotwali or Barisál thana was established in 1820 (it had hitherto been part of Bakainagar thana), and the Baroikaran thana was removed in 1824 to Nalchiti.

In February 1812 there was a serious outbreak in the jail during the magistracy of Mr Battye, and twelve prisoners were shot before it was suppressed. Mr Battye was attacked on this occasion, and was only saved by the bravery and self-devotion of one of the sepoy guard. In September 1817 the Magistrate reports the occurrence of an epidemic (cholera ?), and on 28th February 1818 the *cholera morbus* is reported to have reappeared.[1] On 16th April 1820 the Magistrate asks for cholera medicines, and says that the disease is very prevalent in every part of the district. On 6th May 1822 cholera is reported to be prevalent. It again broke out in August 1825, and this was its most deadly manifestation; 24,960 persons are said to have died of it in the district, besides 90 who died in jail—total, 25,050. All these deaths are said to have occurred between 22d August and 10th September, within which short time twenty women performed satí. On 19th August 1820 the Magistrate forwards Rs.268, collected as a contribu-

[1] In the "Lettres edifiantes" there is a letter from a Père Papin, dated Bengal, 18th December 1709, in which he refers to the *mordechin* (?) or *cholera morbus* as being common in the country. He says the native treatment for it was to keep the patient from drinking water and to burn the soles of the feet.

tion towards a monument of Warren Hastings, late Governor-General of India.

The great event in the history of the district in this century was the inundation of the 6th June 1822, which is still well remembered by the people as the *banya* or flood of 1229 B.S. It was this inundation which swept over the island of Hattia, in the Noakháli district, and destroyed nearly every inhabitant. Mr Cardew was Collector of Bákarganj at the time, and on 9th June 1822 he reported as follows: "It is my painful duty to report, for the information of the Board, the dreadful state to which this district has been reduced by a most violent hurricane and inundation, which has extended its ravages through the whole district. This office was many feet under water, and I am sorry to say that a great part of the records have been swept away, including the whole of the kanungo's papers, the Bhulua papers, and the greatest part of the stamps. In fact, the mischief has been so great that as yet I am unable to state what has actually taken place. On the 6th I held a sale for arrears of revenue, which I was unable to complete." Mr Cardew adds that as the whole of the amlahs' property had been destroyed, he had advanced them two months' pay as *hawalat*. A *rubakari* or vernacular proceeding was drawn up about the affair. It recorded that "on the 6th June a sale of estates was fixed, and some mahals were disposed of. In the evening of that day it began to blow violently, and soon after the waters rose to a dreadful height, so that to escape with life became difficult. The destruction was terrible, &c.

"On the 9th June the hurricane became less violent, and the river subsided. A little after this time the *serishtadar*, &c., came into the Presence and stated what had happened in their offices. It was then impossible to hold cutchery; but the acting Collector proceeded with the above-named officers to the office, when he found that about four feet of water had risen in the cutchery, and that many bags of papers had been carried out of the office, while others were scattered about wet and covered with mud, and that some *almirahs* had been driven from their places." A rubakari, drawn up on the 18th July 1822, gave lengthy details of the papers which had been lost. Unfortunately, neither of the above rubakaris has been preserved, and I have only seen a condensed abstract of the first of them. 39,940 persons—namely, 20,125 males and 19,815 females—are said to have lost their lives in the inundation. In Khalsakháli thana alone 22,422 lives are said to have been lost, and 10,984 in Baufal; and according to my notes, the deaths in these thanas are not included in the total of 39,940. Also 98,834 cattle are said to have been lost, and Rs.1,326,691-11-8 of property are said to have been destroyed; but Mr Collector Phillips very reasonably objects to a list which professes to give even anas and gandas. A letter dated 9th July 1822 gives translations of the reports of the *darogahs*. The Baufal darogah's report was as follows: "At midday on the 6th June 1822 a storm commenced, and increased by degrees. After nine o'clock at night it was so violent that men, cattle, and property were washed away. Many persons were drowned, and some having got on *choppers* [roofs of houses], were driven from one village to another. Others ascended large trees and remained there all night. Next morning it decreased, but the storm continued for seven or eight days. Sir, having made inquiries in this thana, I have ascertained that there are sixty-three villages; in those situated in the eastern part, on the other side of the large river, many men, cattle, and property were destroyed. In the western side of the thana the inundation was less. It is difficult to find out the names in a short time, but by inquiries it has come to my knowledge that in the villages within this thana 4932 men and 6052 women—in all, 10,984 persons—and 9700 bullocks were drowned; besides which, the property of the population has been destroyed to an amount that is impossible to guess."

The notice that the storm began at Baufal at midday is interesting, as it shows how long the storm took to travel from Baufal to Barisál, where the storm commenced in the evening. Baufal is south-south-east of Barisál, and from the fact that it and Khalsakháli thana and the islands in the Meghna suffered most, it appears that the storm came from the south-east. "I am happy to say that the effects of the late inundation have not been so severely felt by the district in general as I had at first supposed. To the west and north-west there was very little water. The thanas of Tagra [now Perozpúr], Kachua [now in Jessore], Baroikaran, and Burirhát have suffered only from the violence of the wind. The chief brunt of the inundation appears to have fallen on the thanas Chandia [Dakhin Shahbázpúr,] Khalsakháli, Baufal, Bakainagar [in which Barisál was situated], and Mendiganj" (21st June 1822). The Collector also adds that he has great pleasure in being able to inform the Government that rice, which was a few days ago selling in the bazár at the enormous rate of ten sírs of sixty sicca weight per rupee, has been reduced to very nearly its former price, and that this has been occasioned by the meritorious and active exertions of Mr Dawes, the acting Magistrate of the city of Dacca, in inducing the merchants of the district to forward supplies. Government took notice of the catastrophe, and sent in rice through the great house of Palmer & Co. A committee was also formed in Calcutta, which despatched a Major Stewart to distribute relief. Rice was also received from Jessore, from the assistant to the salt agent. On 9th July the Collector reports that constant supplies of grain arrive from Dacca and elsewhere, and that the station and the neighbourhood continue healthy. On 11th August he reports that rice and other necessaries are procurable in Barisál and the neighbourhood at lower rates than those stated in the invoice from Messrs Palmer & Co. No details appear to have been ever given of the loss of life in Manpúra and the other islands, but the Collector writes that most of the inhabitants of Manpúra and the other islands had been swept into eternity. With regard to the jail, the Magistrate writes on 25th June 1822 that he had great difficulty in procuring food for the prisoners until the arrival of the very opportune supplies from Dacca and Narainganj, and that he had been obliged to feed the prisoners upon damaged rice. However, no evil effects had followed, and the jail had never been healthier, there being only one man in hospital.[1]

The following notice of the inundation appears in the "Asiatic Journal" for 1822, p. 620: "A most violent storm burst over Calcutta on the night of Friday last [7th June], which must have disturbed the sleep of the soundest. The furious peals of crashing thunder reverberating immediately overhead were truly appalling, and in the pauses between each peal of the 'artillery of heaven' the mind naturally reverted to the thousands who were exposed to the utmost terrors of the tempest on the great deep. Accounts from Dina-

[1] The Barisál gale is marked on Piddington's chart, vol. xvi. A. S. J., 1847; see also his "Sailor's Horn-Book," pp. 57, 59. The storm was too far at the head of the Bay to come in the track of ships.

púr mention that boats without number have been lost in the Ganges, and that the Patna shores were covered with wrecks. Several lives must have been lost, though no particulars have yet reached us. In the lower provinces the hopes of the indigo-planters have been bitterly disappointed. These, however, are but trivial effects of the late storm in comparison with the tremendous detail of devastation and misery which it is our painful duty to notice. What are we to expect from the next shipping accounts, when we are told that in one place on the land 100,000 lives have been lost? It is truly dreadful to think of such a terrible misfortune. The source of our intelligence upon this melancholy occasion is from the following extract of a letter from Jessore: 'Ten days ago my indigo prospects were promising beyond anything I could have calculated upon; since that period the most violent hurricane ever remembered in this quarter, accompanied with a deluge of rain, has destroyed full one-half of our plants, and rendered the recovery of a great part of the remainder precarious. The storm lasted forty-eight hours, and swept houses and everything before it. Many trees were torn up by the roots and carried to a distance of several feet. I never witnessed such a scene of devastation as this place presented. The rain continued almost without intermission for four days after the storm had ceased, so that the whole country is under water. I have just seen a letter from the acting Magistrate of Barisál, about 120 miles to the eastward of this station, detailing the effects of the late storm, which commenced there on the afternoon of the 7th. I scarcely ever perused a more melancholy account. Barisál is situated on the banks of the Meghna, which river, from the fury of the winds, broke over its boundaries in every direction, and inundated the whole country to an alarming depth. The river rose so rapidly that on the 8th, at night, they had upwards of five feet of water in their houses, and the current was so strong that the doors and windows were burst open, and a regular rush of water set in through the houses. This gentleman says he contrived to get two palanquins to the top of his house, and retreated thither with his wife and children as a last resort. The registrar and doctor's houses were carried away, or at least fell in from the violence of the storm. Nearly the whole property of the residents of the station was destroyed. Had this been the extent of the damage, however, it would have been of little consequence, comparatively speaking; but alas! the sufferings of the native inhabitants are not to be described. No fewer than one lac of lives are said to have been lost on this occasion, together with the whole of the cattle and grain of every description, both in store and what was on the ground. The dead bodies were floating in every direction, and carried with the current through the houses. The writer states that no rice was to be procured even for the prisoners, and that he felt he would be obliged to release them from jail, otherwise they must starve. From what information he could obtain, he believed that the district could not supply food for ten days' consumption to the inhabitants who had escaped this dreadful visitation. I should think the writer meant to include in the lac the lives of the cattle lost, although I should certainly infer from the letter that 100,000 human beings perished. I have not heard whether the storm reached beyond this district to the northward and westward.'"

A meeting for the relief of the distress in Bákarganj was held in the Calcutta Town Hall on the 19th of

June, and another on the 22d idem. A subscription was opened, and eventually upwards of Rs.18,000 were collected. (According to the latest reports of the committee, Rs.18,433 sicca.) Major Stewart volunteered his services, and was sent to Bákarganj to distribute relief. The "Calcutta Monthly Journal," speaking of his having finished the good work upon which he had entered with such philanthropic alacrity, says that the zeal and judgment displayed by him in its performance reflected on him the highest honour.

In the "Calcutta Journal" for 1822 (p. 192) the following curious incident is mentioned: "One of our correspondents mentions that at Ratandi he saw a child, who being only a few weeks old, his curiosity was excited to know how it had been preserved during the tempest and inundation. In reply to his inquiries, he was told that it was born in a tree when the whole surface of the country was covered with water; and its mother was then questioned, and corroborated this tale. The surprise of the inquirer was still further increased, however, when he came to learn that so far from this being a singular event, there were from thirty to forty females, some of whom having reached the period of natural delivery, but many more having the birth accelerated by terror and alarm, who gave birth to their infants in this dreadful situation, and yet so providentially is the wind tempered to the shorn lamb, that most of these individuals with their offspring lived, presenting a picture of misery and distress unprecedented, we believe, even in the imagination of the painter or the poet, and certainly without a parallel, as far as we remember, either in fable or in history. . . .

"The servant of a gentleman in Calcutta, whose family live at Hattia, says that out of four brothers and their families only one of the brothers was found after the storm and inundation, and he was blown across the river to the northward upon the top of a chopper" (roof).

The following appears in Sandeman's "Selections," dated Thursday, June 20, 1822: "On Sunday last we received an account of the awful calamity with which the civil station of Burrisol has been afflicted. It is brief, but the facts are of the most melancholy description, and require not detail to awaken feelings of the liveliest pity and commiseration. The sufferings of thousands—men, women, and children—during the terrible night of the storm must have been truly dreadful.

"The storm commenced on the evening of the 6th, and before midnight the body of water had overtopped the Bund, which runs along the margin of the river, and was approaching the gentlemen's houses rapidly. Mr Cardew, the Registrar,[1] had just sufficient time to send a palanquin with some food in it to the top of the house for his wife. Immediately after, his dining-room was three feet deep in water, the current carrying everything before it with irresistible violence. In another house there was five feet water in the dining-room, and dead bodies, washed from the native huts, floating about the room, in which only a few hours before dinner had been served. One thousand lives were lost in the bazár alone, and the loss throughout the district is not to be calculated. A famine was apprehended as inevitable. No provisions were procurable for the prisoners, in consequence of which they were released on the second day."[2]

It was probably the inundation which induced Government to build new cutcheries at Barisál. Formerly the Magistrate held cutchery in his own house, and received

[1] He was acting Collector and Magistrate.

[2] The criminal prisoners, at all events, were not released.

an allowance on this account. This arrangement continued to 1829. (See letters of May 25, June 20, 1826, &c.)

Mr Garrett appears to have been the first Magistrate who did much for the improvement of Barisál. He was Magistrate from 1827 to 1830, when he asked to be relieved, saying that he had been three and a half years at Barisál, and that he could not work so hard as formerly. He appears to have been the first officer who established a school (31st March 1828), and he also dug tanks and made other improvements. Government assigned to him Rs.1500, and Rs.925 were subscribed in the district for improvements at Barisál. In his time there were only three roads in the district—one of four miles, and two of two miles in length (5th June 1830). On 15th March 1828 he recommended the removal of the Gournadi police station to its present position at Palardi. Mr Garrett, I believe, left the district for a time, but he did not finally quit it till May 1832; so that he must have spent about five years in it. He acted as Judge as well as Magistrate. What partly led to his departure was, I believe, that he became a Baptist, and insisted upon being baptized in a tank in the station. His *nazir*, Mr Parry (he was dewani or judge's nazir), was one of the first to preach Christianity to the natives. Mr Parry afterwards became a regular missionary and went to Jessore. The practice of satí was abolished in Mr Garrett's time, and on 1st March 1830 he writes, "I am heartily thankful that the horrible practice of suttee has been put a stop to. It has been attended with no trouble, I am happy to say, in this jurisdiction. It must be a great ease of mind to all magistrates." In a previous letter, dated 17th August 1829, he writes, "The business is often harassing, but the subject most painful to me is the frequency of suttee. The number that have taken place this year up to the end of July amount to sixteen. I was induced the other day, thinking it my duty, to be present at one not very far from here, conceiving I might possibly do some good, but I regret to say it was not in my power, the poor creature appearing perfectly determined." For several years previous to the abolition of satí, Government had been endeavouring to check its occurrence; and on 14th December 1818, Mr Harrington, the Magistrate, reports that satís have diminished since the Government orders of 4th October 1814. It was the practice to have reports from the police of the number of satís in their jurisdictions. In 1825, the year of the cholera, there were as many as sixty-three; in 1824 there were twenty-three satís; in 1826, forty-five; and in 1827, twenty-nine.

Among the East India papers in the Indian Library there is a volume on the subject of Hindu widows, and it gives some curious statistics about satís. The details of the Bákarganj cases for 1824 and 1825 are given in it. Of the sixty-three cases in 1825, it is recorded that in twenty-three cases the husbands were rich, and that in the others they were poor. One case was what was called *anumaran—i.e.*, the husband died away from the wife, who burnt herself along with two strings of beads which had belonged to him. On an average, the widows in the sixty-three cases were middle-aged; one was over ninety, and only one was under twenty years of age. Satís were singularly few in Dacca. In Dacca city and Dacca Jalálpúr districts the numbers were as follows: Dacca city, 1823, fourteen; 1824, seven; 1825, eighteen; 1826, twelve. Dacca Jalálpúr, 1823, two; 1824, two; 1825, two; 1826, three.

The explanation seems to be that Mr Cracroft, the Judge of the Dacca Circuit, ruled that persons of the Baidya caste were not entitled to the privilege of satí. The relations of a Baidya widow appealed to the Nizamat Adâlat against this ruling, and the court ordered that the widow should be allowed to burn herself. (It was a case of *anumaran.*) However, I am glad to say that the delay had a good effect, and that the Magistrate (Mr Morrison) was able to report that the widow had changed her mind. The volume contains some curious correspondence between Mr Cracroft and the Judges of the Nizamat.

In 1845 there was a notable case of embezzlement in the treasury. Mr Sturt was then Collector; he appears to have been a careless and indolent officer, and to have left everything to his subordinates. The result was that in August 1845 he had to report that some Rs.50,000 were missing from the treasury, and that the treasurer had absconded. A lengthened investigation took place, first by the Commissioner, and afterwards by Messrs Ricketts & Samuells, of which the upshot was that Mr Sturt was degraded, and the treasurer brought to trial and sentenced to, I believe, seven years' imprisonment. A portion of the money embezzled was realised from the treasurer's securities, who were entirely ruined. I believe Mr Sturt was originally in the navy. He married a native lady, and used to give great entertainments, and even to have the swinging festival—*i.e.*, the *charak puja*—celebrated in front of his house.

A remarkable crime was committed in Bákarganj in 1847. Kali Prasad Kanjhi Lall, the gomasta or servant of an indigo-planter named Dunlop, whose factories were situated in the Mulfatganj thana, was attacked by the ryots and carried off in a boat to the south of the district, and finally murdered at Maudobi, in the south of Khalsakháli thana. It is said that the body was cut in pieces and thrown into the sea; hence the proverbial expression of making a Kanjhi Lall of one's enemy. (See Magistrate's letters of 20th February and 20th July 1847.) The reasons for Kanjhi Lall's being carried off were that Dudhu Mia, the head of the Ferazis, whose residence was at Sibchar, in the Mulfatganj thana, had disputes with Mr Dunlop, and that the ryots considered that Kanjhi Lall oppressed them. Mr Dunlop's factory at Panchchur was burnt at this time. Although Bákarganj was the scene of the murder, neither Kanjhi Lall nor his murderers were connected with the district. The circumstances of the attack on Mr Dunlop's factory, which occurred on 5th December 1846, are fully detailed in the printed report of the trial of the rioters. Dudhu Mia was tried before Mr Swetenham, Judge of Farídpúr, and convicted, but was acquitted by the Nizamat Adâlat. (See also Mr Latour's evidence before the Indigo Commission.)

The Indian mutiny had little or no effect on the district, and, as far as I am aware, the inhabitants showed no signs of sympathy with it.

As there are no indigo-factories in the district, there was no agitation at the time when the ryots of Nadiya and Jessore threw off the cultivation of indigo.

In 1865 cattle disease broke out very severely in Bákarganj, and some 40,000 cattle are said to have perished. The disease entered from Jessore, and was most severe in the Perozpúr subdivision. It is said that 13,199 cattle died in Tagra thana (Perozpúr) alone. (See Mr Sutherland's letter of 14th September 1865; also see Selections from Government Records (Bengal), No. 43, 1869.)

In 1869 an income-tax assessor was beaten in Dakhin Shahbázpúr, but I believe the attack was caused by his own misconduct.

Of late years the rent question has excited a good deal of attention, and there has been a considerable degree of bad feeling between the ryots and zamindars, but without any important outbreak.

The census of 1872 was taken without the least attempt at disturbance. It was commenced on the 15th of January, and nearly completed in twenty-four hours.

During the present century the district has undergone many changes in its administration and in its boundaries. In 1815 or 1816 its area was enlarged on the north by the addition of the Idilpúr pargana, which was then transferred to it from the jurisdiction of the city of Dacca. Lately this arrangement has been reversed, by the transfer of the pargana, together with the Mádaripúr subdivision, to Farídpúr.

In 1822 the islands of Hattia and Dakhin Shahbázpúr were transferred from Bákarganj and included in the newly-created district of Noakháli. In 1869 Dakhin Shahbázpúr was retransferred to Bákarganj, partly because the Títulia is a less formidable river than the Meghna, but chiefly because the civil and criminal jurisdictions were thereby made conterminous, for the Munsif of Dakhin Shahbázpúr had always been subordinate to the Judge of Bákarganj. For many years, indeed, the munsif held his court on the mainland, in thana Mendiganj; and it is only for about twenty years that his court has been held at Daulat Khan.

In 1863, or thereabouts, Kachua police station and that portion of Bákarganj which lay east of the Baleshwar were transferred to Jessore, and annexed to the newly-created subdivision of Baghahát.

In 1873 the area of the district was greatly circumscribed by the transfer to Farídpúr of the whole of the Mádaripúr subdivision, with the exception of thana Gournadi. On the other hand, a small portion of Farídpúr was transferred to Bákarganj, and included in Perozpúr. Unfortunately these changes were made after the completion of the census, and have thrown considerable confusion into its results.

At present the district of Bákarganj is divided into four subdivisions, as follows :—

Subdivisions.	Thanas.	Population of Subdivisions.
1. Barisál or Sadr . . .	Barisál, Gournadi, Nalchiti, Jhalukátti, Mendiganj, Bákarganj,	711,180 (?)
2. Dakhin Shahbázpúr . .	Daulat Khan, Barhanuddin Howaladar Hát,	221,037
3. Perozpúr	Perozpúr, Sarupkátti, Matbária,	363,426 (?)
4. Patuyakháli	Mirzaganj, Gúlsakháli, Khalsakháli or Galachipa,	418,747

The boundaries of the subdivisions are detailed in the "Calcutta Gazette."

Dakhin Shahbázpúr is the oldest of the four subdivisions, and indeed is one of the oldest in Bengal, having been established in 1845. It owes this distinction to its insular position, and to its importance in connection with the salt manufacture.

The Perozpúr subdivision was established in 1859. Its headquarters are somewhat unfortunately situated, as they are now on the extreme verge of the jurisdiction. Their position was more central before the transfer of Kachua and Morrellganj to Jessore.

Patuyakháli was established in July 1871. It includes the greater part of the south of the district.

STATISTICS OF CIVIL JUSTICE.

In 1873, 12,149 suits were instituted in the regular courts, and 12,746 were disposed of; 1185 were instituted in the Small Cause Courts, and 1201 disposed of. Value of suits instituted in 1873, Rs.1,152,451. The number of rent suits instituted was 7680, and of the Small Cause Court class of cases, 3675. Altogether there were 13,334 institutions, and 13,947 disposals in 1873. There were 49 suits for the enforcement of matrimonial rights. Of the 13,947 institutions, 3396 were withdrawn, compromised, &c.; 7401 were disposed of *exparte*, and 3150 were contested. 3540 decrees were wholly, and 8525 were partially, executed; and the total amount realised was Rs.427,233. 427 decrees were satisfied without execution, and Rs.25,113 realised.

There is a Civil and Sessions Judge at Barisál, and an additional judge visits it occasionally. In 1873 there were eleven munsifs employed in the district. The total cost of the Civil Courts for the year was estimated at Rs.128,525, and the realisations from stamps and court fees were 157,476, so that there was a surplus of Rs.29,000 (nearly). It must be remembered that Mádaripúr is included in all these statistics. There are generally two subordinate judges at Barisál. One or more munsifs are stationed at each of the subdivisions, and two or more at Barisál.

The average duration of contested cases before the munsifs is said to be three and a half months. (See High Court's Report on Civil Courts for 1873.)

STATISTICS OF REGISTRATION.

The number of deeds registered in Bákarganj is inordinately large, and in order to cope with it a number of rural registrars have been appointed. In 1873 there were altogether thirteen registration offices, and 25,200 deeds were registered affecting immovable property; 17,693 were deeds in which registration was compulsory, and 7517 in which it was approved. The total value of property transferred was twenty-three lacs, and the total amount of fees realised Rs.15,449. Of the compulsory deeds no less than 10,658 were perpetual leases, and 5123 were temporary leases. In the same year 2140 deeds affecting movable property were registered. The total receipts of the department were Rs.30,758, and the expenditure was Rs.19,625.

The above information has been taken from the Bengal Administration Report for 1873-74, and the tables there given show, moreover, that the receipts in Bákarganj were larger than in any other district, that the number of registration offices was greater than in any district except the Twenty-four Parganas, and that the number of compulsory registrations was greater than in any district except Chittagong. I must again remind my readers, however, that the figures include Mádaripúr.

SURVEYS.

The district has been trigonometrically surveyed, and there are now two towers in it—viz., one at Gangapúr in the Mendiganj thana, and another at Bháttra in Gournadi. There was a third at Khalishpúr, but it has been carried away by the river.

The revenue and topographical survey of the district was completed in 1863.

CHAPTER XIV.

POLICE SYSTEM.

THIS has already been touched upon in the chapter on the criminal administration. Bákarganj has been from the earliest times a troublesome district for the police; and the Magistrates' records are full of reports of crimes, and of the inefficiency of the efforts to stop them. It has been said in one account of the district that dacoity was put down in Bákarganj in 1814;[1] but this statement seems to have been premature, for later on a magistrate reports that there were at least thirty-one dacoities in the district in 1816. It is probable that our Hindu and Mahomedan predecessors had also trouble in putting down crime in Bákarganj, and indeed there are allusions to the prevalence of river-dacoity in the letters of the Jesuit priests who visited the country in 1599 and 1600. Two causes contributed to the existence and

[1] On 29th November 1814 the Government of India wrote as follows to the Court of Directors :—

"The Sunderbuns having been ordinarily regarded as the natural harbour of dacoits, it will be particularly satisfactory to your Honourable Court to observe the progress made in the suppression of gang-robbery in that part of the country. We cannot deny ourselves the gratification of transcribing the following passage from the letter of the Judge of Circuit on that subject: 'It does not occur to me as necessary to offer any further observations on the state of the Buckergunge district. It appears to be in that state of security from violent depredation which a few years back it would, perhaps, have been considered a vain hope that it could ever arrive at; and with respect to offences of other descriptions, they do not appear materially to prevail.'"—*Judicial Letter from Bengal, India Office Library.*

continuance of dacoity and other serious crimes in the district. In the first place, the district was in old times chiefly composed of jungle tracts such as the Sundarbans, &c., and it was therefore such an unpopular place of residence that almost no one resorted to it except criminals and men of bad character or desperate fortunes. Hence the district had to a certain extent a criminal population to start with; and these people continued and flourished in it, because the configuration of the country was eminently favourable to the commission of crime with impunity, and because it was at the same time the highway of communication between the eastern districts and Calcutta. In old times a strong force of patrol-boats was kept up in order to guard the rivers; and the records are full of suggestions from the Magistrates, the Courts of Circuit, and the Nizamat Adâlat about the best way of employing these boats, &c. In 1818 there were fourteen patrol-boats, with fourteen manjhis and 168 rowers—*i.e.*, there were one manjhi and twelve rowers to each boat. The manjhis got Rs. 4 a month, and the rowers Rs. 3, so that the monthly cost was Rs. 560.

In 1812 there were eleven thanas or police stations. The Magistrate's letter of 8th February 1812 refers to the establishment of a twelfth thana—viz., Mirzaganj—which shows that cultivation and population had been increasing in the south of the district. The same letter mentions that Gournadi was transferred to the Bákarganj district in 1807, and recommends that Nalchira—*i.e.*, I presume, the present Agarpúr outpost—be transferred to Mendiganj. In Mr Sutherland's account of the district an extract is given from a magistrate's letter, dated 20th February 1811, showing the names and positions at that time of the eleven thanas. The list there given singularly illustrates the changes which have taken place in the administration, for the sites of six of the thanas have been changed since then, and a seventh—viz., Kachua—has been transferred to Jessore and reduced to an outpost.

The old police stations were all placed on the banks of the large rivers, as the chief object had in view was the suppression of river-dacoities. Inland places were thought to be less in need of protection, and were left to shift for themselves. I do not wish to pass the least censure on this arrangement, which was undoubtedly the best possible, and was also recommended by the fact that it was necessary that the police stations should be on the banks of rivers, as these were then the only means of internal communication. I would only observe, that as there were then no subdivisions, and not even any village chaukidars,[1] the zamindars and ryots must have been left very much to themselves, and that it is to their credit that they seem to have managed to get on pretty well together.

At present there are fifteen thanas and ten (?) outposts in the district. In the Barisál or Sadr subdivision there are six thanas—viz., Gournadi, Barisál or the Kotwali, Nalchiti, Jhalukátti, Mendiganj, and Bákarganj. Gournadi has been lately transferred to the Sadr subdivision from Mádaripúr. Its outpost of Agarpúr had been some time previously placed under the Barisál thana. Nalchiti and Jhalukátti are too near one another, but it is difficult and expensive to make alterations of sites. Mendiganj has under it the outpost of Srírámpúr. The station of Mendiganj is now at Pátarhát, but it has been proposed to remove it to Alliganj. Bákarganj, which is by the

[1] Mr M'Neil tells us in his report that there were no village chaukidars in Bákarganj in 1818.

country-people often called Angaria,[1] from the circumstance of the station's formerly having been there, has an outpost called Niamati.

Perozpúr subdivision contains the three thanas of Perozpúr (formerly Tagra), Sarupkátti, and Matbária. Perozpúr has subordinate to it the outposts of Nazirpúr and Bhandaria. Sarupkátti is a new thana, and is in part composed of the old thana Kewaria.

Patuyakháli contains the thanas of Mirzaganj, Gúlsakháli, Khalsakháli or Galachipa, and Baufal. Gúlsakháli contains the outpost of Phuljhuri, and Khalsakháli contains that of Chalitabunia.

Dakhin Shahbázpúr contains two thanas—viz., Daulat Khan and Barhanuddin's Hát—and the three outposts of Ghazipúr, Tamizuddin, and Taltali. The first two outposts belong to Daulat Khan and the last to Barhanuddin. These statements must, however, be taken with reservation, for the thana arrangements of the district have long been in a confused state, and I do not know if they have yet received their final adjustment. The Daulat Khan thana was formerly at Chandia, and hence the thana is often called by that name.

In 1873 there were 626 policemen of all grades in the district, and the total cost of the police administration was Rs.119,438. The force consisted of 1 district superintendent, 1 assistant-superintendent, 6 inspectors, 24 sub-inspectors, 76 head constables, and 518 constables. Two of the force were Europeans, 3 Eurasians, and 621 were natives of India. Divided according to religion, there were 16 Christians, 170 Mahomedans, and 440 Hindus. The above cost of the police is much greater than it was in old times; for instance, in 1805,

[1] Angaria seems an old name, and appears to be marked on De Blaev's map.

when Mr Gardner could report that the total cost of the police was Rs.33,361. But in those days there were no district and assistant superintendents, and no inspectors, scarcely any travelling expenses, and no officer, I believe, receiving more than Rs.15 or Rs.20 a month. The figures for 1873 also include the jail and treasury guards and their pay, and are for the district before the transfer of Mádaripúr.

In old times the constables, or *barkandazes*, as they were called, got only Rs.3 a month, now they get Rs.6 and Rs.7 and upwards, and the superior officers receive salaries ranging from Rs.10 to Rs.200 a month. Still it is true, I regret to say, that it is almost impossible for a policeman to live on his pay. The expenses of living and travelling have greatly increased, and at the same time so much more is expected of the police.

Undoubtedly the police system is the opprobrium of our administration, and I fear that it will continue to be so. A larger expenditure of money would do much to improve matters, especially in the direction of supplying the inferior police with adequate means of locomotion; but even this would not do everything. The number of village chaukidars in Bákarganj in 1873 is said to have been 5172, and their emoluments to have been Rs.186,192. There are municipal police in Barisál, Nalchiti, Jhalukátti, Perozpúr, Baufal, Bákarganj, and Daulat Khan.

In 1873 there were 5793 cases cognisable by the police reported. 2952 were declared false, and only in 596 were convictions obtained. In the same year there were 8031 non-cognisable cases: processes were issued against 6077 persons; 3220 appeared, and 1910 were convicted. The proportion of convicted to the population was about 1 to 1244.

The number of arrests by the police in 1873 was 1504, and by orders of the Magistrate 1405. 1426 persons were convicted by the Magistrate, and 100 by the Court of Sessions. 1202 were acquitted by the Magistrate, and 108 by the Court of Sessions. Percentage of acquittals was about 46. In the same year Rs.28,765 worth of property was stolen, and Rs.6002 recovered.

There were twenty cases of murder.

The return of unnatural and accidental deaths in 1873 is as follows: Suicides, 61; drownings, 622;[1] snake-bite, 217; tigers, leopards, &c., 52; alligators, 48; other causes, 67:[2] total, 1042.

[1] The greatest number of cases of drowning are of children, and take place in the moats which surround the homesteads. Cases of drowning and also of snake-bite are most common in the rains.

[2] Of "other causes," 10 were lightning, and 28 falls from trees. There were also during the year 64 cases of homicide, and five persons were hanged.

CHAPTER XV.

THE JAIL.

THE jail was originally at Bákarganj, the old head-quarters of the district, and for some time was under the Naib Nazim, who managed it through a *faujdar.* The oldest letter in the Magistrate's office (27th October 1792) refers to the prisoners confined by the Naib Nazim, and the next oldest, dated 23d November idem, enjoins that the prisoners should be supplied with blankets. The jail was situated on the banks of the Srimantapúr or Bákarganj creek, a little higher up than the cutcheries, and a small stream which flows into the creek here is still known by the name of the Jailkhana khál. It appears from a petition of one Panchanand Datt of Rangasri, forwarded by the Board of Revenue on 17th April 1802, that Mr Lodge, the Judge, had built a jail on his taluq of Bista Narain Datt in 1193 B.S. (1786), but I presume this was only a civil jail. On 3d April 1793 Mr Middleton, the Magistrate, was called upon for a list of prisoners suitable to be sent to the Andamans. By this time the Magistrate had charge of the jail under the control of the Nizamat Adâlat. From a letter of the Nizamat Adâlat, dated 15th October 1795, it appears that the prisoners had been deprived of the use of tobacco, but that as the want of it had proved injurious, they were to be allowed to have it again. The jail at Bákarganj proved very unhealthy, and Mr Wintle mentions in a letter of 7th September 1801 that 242 prisoners had died in it in the last twelve months. He does not mention what proportion this bore to the number who were confined during the year, but it must have been about one-third, as he states that the number of the prisoners at the time he was writing was 750. The jail was a thatched one, and was of course insecure. There are two letters from the Nizamat Adâlat, dated 23d April and 15th May 1795, about the tattooing of prisoners, and directing that this should be done on the forehead. Only the life-prisoners were tattooed, and the object was to facilitate recapture in the event of their escape. The jail was removed to Barisál in 1801. A *kacha-paka* jail—*i.e.*, a jail with a thatched roof and brick walls—was erected there by the Magistrate, Mr Gardner, in 1804. It was flued, was surrounded by an outer wall, had a bomb-proof dungeon, and was calculated to hold 800 prisoners, and yet only cost Rs.2302-5-9. The amount sanctioned for its construction was Rs.3681-3-7. The lime with which it was constructed was brought from Sylhet. The following description of the jail is given in the estimate: "Account of expenses attending the erection of a foujdari jail at Barisál zila, Bákarganj, consisting of apartments for 800 prisoners, packa-walled, well raised and flued, an infirmary very highly raised, completely packa, beamed and terraced, a bomb-proof dungeon, and two guard-rooms, the whole enclosed with a surrounding packa wall twelve feet in height, and four packa sentry-boxes at the corners thereof." This jail, however, did not last long, or at least was found insufficient, for in 1812 the prisoners broke out and burnt the roof, and in 1817 the jail was replaced in whole or in part by a masonry building, erected under the superintendence of Mr Gardner, the

Civil Surgeon. The amount sanctioned for its construction was Rs.35,119. It was reported to be completed on 20th September 1817, and the surrounding wall was finished in the following year. In a report of Mr Lee Warner (the Magistrate), dated 18th April 1818, it is stated that the criminal jail was built in 1816, the surrounding wall in 1818, the hospital in 1811, and the magazine in 1802. The prisoners seem always to have been more numerous in the early days of our administration than they now are. Probably this was owing to the greater number of dacoities in those days, and to the more ready seizure of suspected persons. Something also was due to the delay in the jail-deliveries, owing to the Judges coming on circuit only once a quarter. In 1806 Mr Oswald writes that there are seldom fewer than from 800 to 900 prisoners in confinement. This was on 1st February, and on 12th July of the same year the Magistrate writes that the jail is not capable of containing more than 700 prisoners, and there are above 750. In the same letter he speaks of an additional jail which is to be built, and which, like the present, will have the walls of brick and mortar, and the roof thatched. The number of persons imprisoned for debt was much greater formerly than now, when indeed the civil jail is often altogether empty. In 1806 the Magistrate writes that there are seldom *more* than sixty or eighty persons in the debtors' jail. On 7th May 1807 an estimate is given for repairing the jail. Bundles of straw are estimated at Rs.4 a thousand, and bamboos at Rs.3 a hundred. On 15th May 1819 there were as many as 982 prisoners in the jail, and the Magistrate considered that it was capable of holding 2000. In 1873 the average strength of the jail, including the lockups, was only 520, of whom only 6½ were females. It must be remembered, however, that the number of prisoners in the Bákarganj jail is now systematically kept down by transfers, and that no life-prisoners are allowed to remain in it. Prisoners were occasionally transferred in old times, and I find that in February 1809 two hundred were sent to Dacca, but there were no rules on the subject, and probably they were only sent away when there was an unusual pressure. The prisons also were for a long time burdened with the life and long-term prisoners who had been sentenced by the Nawab Nazim, and as late as 25th June 1819 a list had to be made out of such prisoners.

The prisoners used to do their own marketing, and for this purpose they were paid in cowries, which were distributed by a *poddar* monthly, and for which he was reimbursed at the current rate of exchange (31st December 1811). He got a daily list of the prisoners before he distributed the diet-money. On 26th April 1820 the poddar is described as getting two puns of cowries per rupee as his remuneration. In 1805 the allowance to each prisoner was three puns of cowries, or about three-fourths of an ana, each day. Some remarks appear to have been made about the allowances to the prisoners being excessive, and on 15th August 1805 Mr Oswald writes as follows: "The observations of the third Judge of the Murshidábád Court of Circuit, regarding the cheapness of living and the low wages of labour in that division, do not appear to me applicable to this station, where the ordinary or average price of rice is fourteen anas a maund, of sixty sicca weight to the seer, and where the wages of the most common labour are in general six puns, and never less than five puns of cowries per diem. Allowing each convict one and a half seers of rice a day, of the above-mentioned weight, or forty-five seers a month, it will be found that his expenditure in the article of rice alone amounts to fifteen anas a month—rather more than two-thirds of his whole allowance. With the remaining third he has to purchase fuel and cooking utensils to dress his victuals, a little salt to season them, and to provide himself with clothing."[1] In the year 1811 the total cost for the prisoners' food was Rs.9253-15-4 (sicca).

From a letter written in 1809 in appears that previous to that date there was no separate accommodation for females.

Apparently the prisoners were chiefly employed in road-making, and in a letter written in 1815 it is said that prisoners were not formerly exempted from labour on the Sundays.

On 16th February 1812, at 11·15 A.M., there was an outbreak in the jail, in which Mr Battye, the Magistrate, nearly lost his life, and was only saved by the devotion of his subadar. (At that time both the jail and the treasury were guarded by a detachment of the Provincial Battalion.) The prisoners set fire to the thatched roof of the jail and attacked Mr Battye. The subadar flung himself in between the Magistrate and his assailant, and was cut desperately over the head. The subadar, the havildar, five sepoys, and one barkandaz were wounded, and twelve prisoners were shot before the riot could be quelled. In the newspaper account of the great cyclone of 1822, published in Mr Sandeman's "Selections," it is said that the prisoners were released on the second day afterwards for want of food. From the official reports, however, it appears that this statement is incorrect.

[1] In 1803 it is reported that 4000 kahuns of cowries were required each month for the prisoners, and that they had to be collected from all parts of the district.

The land originally taken up for the jail and for the Provincial Battalion, and which is still in the possession of Government, lies in the middle of the Barisál town, and amounts to about nine kanis, or between forty and fifty bighas. It is held on a permanent lease from the Rahamatpúr Chakrabarties, and the rate of rent is only Rs. 5 a kani, though the land is worth very much more at the present day. The Rs. 5 are sicca, and the old rent in sicca rupees was Rs. 45-5. It is now Rs. 48-5-4. The police lines are situated on this land, and another portion is let out to householders, and yields about Rs. 96 a year. Another small portion in a corner of the jail garden has been let to a shopkeeper as a woodyard for Rs. 48-5-4, so that in reality the jail site may be considered as rent-free.

The Barisál jail has always been damp and unhealthy. This is partly owing to its position, and partly to defects in its construction. It is nearly surrounded by a tidal khál, and the water is close to the surface throughout the jail compound. The amount of garden-ground is also very limited. It is a curious fact that the proper mode of building a jail for Bákarganj seems to have been best understood when the first one was built, and to have been lost sight of afterwards. At least the hospital, which was built in 1811, if not earlier, is by far the driest building in the jail, a circumstance which is due to its being raised on arches, through which the air can freely circulate. Of late a good deal has been done to improve the jail, and the erection of double-storied wards and of arched floors has been commenced. Some solitary cells have also been built. The jail has three lockups attached to it—viz., those at Perozpúr, Patuyakháli, and Daulat Khan, though the prisoners from the last have been temporarily sent to Noakháli.

The prisoners are employed in brick-making, in weaving, and in making mats and chairs, but there is nothing special in the industries of the jail. The great majority of the prisoners are Mahomedans.

In 1873 the average daily number of prisoners was 520. This, however, includes those in the subdivisional lockups. The average mortality for the ten years ending 1873 was 12·22 per cent., which of course is very high.

CHAPTER XVI.

EDUCATION.

I CANNOT pretend to treat of this important subject as it deserves, and must refer the reader to the educational reports, &c., for fuller information. The first attempt, I believe, to introduce English education into the district was made by the Magistrate, Mr Garrett, about 1830. Mr Sherring, however, in his "History of Protestant Missions," says that a school was established at Barisál by the Serámpúr missionaries in 1829. The lease for the present site of the Barisál school was obtained by Mr Sturt in 1842, and the school was made a Government institution a few years later. The school is what is called a higher English school, and is a very good one of its class. It has an average daily attendance of 278 boys. There is a vernacular school adjoining it. There is also a so-called higher class school at Basanda, but it does not really prepare boys for the entrance examination. Basanda is a small village about two miles from Jhalukátti; and it would be better if the school were removed to Jhalukátti, and the latter made the seat of a deputy-magistracy and of a munsif's court. There is a middle-class English school at the headquarters of each subdivision, but I do not think that any of these can be said to be in a very efficient condition. The best of them (and the remark is also applicable to the Barisál school) is still more or less of an exotic, for it is mainly attended by the children of professional men, who are only temporary residents in the neighbourhood. Altogether, there were in the year ending 31st March 1874, 365 schools under inspection in the district, and 12,110 pupils, so that about 7 per 1000 of the population were at school. The number of Hindus was, however, disproportionately larger, for though they only form about a third of the population, there were (in round numbers) 7500 Hindus at school, against 4600 Mahomedans. This, of course, is in great measure explained by the fact that the Mahomedans chiefly belong to the poorer classes, and are least numerous in the towns and bazárs. Something, however, is due to Mahomedan pride and apathy, and to their preference for a home education and Arabic studies.

Female Education.—This has made very little progress as yet. There is a pretty good girls' school at Barisál, and there are one or two in other parts of the district, but they have not yet taken firm root. In some of the primary schools girls and boys are taught together. Hinduism, Mahomedanism, and early marriage are commonly said to be the great obstacles to female education, and I have no wish to deny their influence. I am sorry, however, to say that the Feringhi Christians of Sibpúr are almost as unwilling to send their daughters to school as any Hindus are. No doubt the difficulty of getting about, especially in the rains, is a great drawback to the success of schools, and, physically speaking, the children are perhaps better at home. Of late years a great stir has been made about primary education, and many new *patsalas* or primary schools have been established, and many old ones have been subsidised. No doubt good has been done, and the very agitation of the subject has had a quickening effect on the bucolic mind; but in the south of the district, where 80 per cent. of the inhabitants are Mahomedans, the experiment has been a failure. The peasants do not care for education; and besides, they need their children to gather their betel-nuts, to row their boats, and above all to herd their cattle.

The worst of the change which has been effected is that in very many cases the villagers have given up paying fees to the village teacher, as he now gets paid by Government. In fact, therefore, the teacher's position has not been improved, there having been only a change of paymasters. The fact is, I believe, as I have stated it, and I confess that it is one for which it is not easy to see a remedy.

The accompanying table, which is taken from the inspector's report, gives many particulars of the state of education in the district in 1873-74. In the same year the receipts, including grants from provincial revenues and Rs.9872 of subscriptions, were Rs.44,941, and the expenditure was Rs.44,280.[1]

[1] The early state of Bákarganj in regard to education is described in Mr Adam's Report on Education in Bengal, 1835.

Return of Schools and Students in the Backergunge District for 1873–74.

Class of Institutions.	Government Institutions.										Aided Institutions.										Unaided Institutions under Inspection.										Grand Total of Institutions.	Grand Total of Students on the 31st March 1874.	Grand Total of—			
	Number of Institutions.	Number of Students on the Rolls on the 31st March 1874.	Average Daily Attendance.	Number of Students on the 31st March learning— English.	A Classical Language.	Vernacular only.	Religion of Students as on 31st March. Christians.	Hindus.	Muhammadans.	Others.	Number of Institutions.	Number of Students on the Rolls on the 31st March.	Average Daily Attendance.	Number of Students on the 31st March learning— English.	A Classical Language.	Vernacular only.	Religion of Students as on 31st March. Christians.	Hindus.	Muhammadans.	Others.	Number of Institutions.	Number of Students on the Rolls on the 31st March.	Average Daily Attendance.	Number of Students on the 31st March learning— English.	A Classical Language.	Vernacular only.	Religion of Students as on 31st March. Christians.	Hindus.	Muhammadans.	Others.			Christians.	Hindus.	Muhammadans.	Others.
Normal Schools—																																				
For Masters	1	22	14	...	...	22	...	15	7	...	...	...	...	...	...	...	...	...	...	...	...	...	...	...	...	...	...	...	...	...	1	22	...	15	7	...
For Mistresses ...	...	...	...	...	...	...	...	...	...	...	...	...	...	...	...	...	...	...	...	...	...	...	...	...	...	...	...	...	...	...	...	...	...	...	...	...
Schools of Art.																																				
Other Technical Schools.																																				
Schools for Boys—																																				
Higher English ...	1	381	278	381	81	...	6	349	26	...	1	56	40	56	29	...	...	56	...	...	...	...	...	...	...	...	...	...	...	...	2	437	6	405	26	...
Middle English ...	...	...	...	...	...	...	...	...	...	...	14	1071	778	511	91	486	...	1015	56	...	4	233	153	100	...	133	...	203	30	...	18	1304	...	1218	86	...
Middle Vernacular	3	112	82	...	...	112	...	41	71	...	27	1446	1070	16	1	1429	...	1319	127	...	4	179	149	...	...	179	...	163	13	3	34	1737	...	1523	211	3
Lower Vernacular	...	...	...	...	...	...	...	...	...	...	235	6678	4548	...	513	6492	8	3203	3464	3	69	1852	1155	...	57	1842	...	1047	805	...	304	8530	8	4250	4269	3
Schools for Girls—																																				
For Natives	...	...	...	...	...	...	...	...	...	...	3	35	26	...	...	294	...	35	...	...	3	45	23	...	...	45	...	45	...	...	6	80	...	80	...	...
For Europeans and other foreign races	...	...	...	...	...	...	...	...	...	...	...	...	...	...	...	...	...	...	...	...	...	...	...	...	...	...	...	...	...	...	...	...	...	...	...	...
Total ...	5	515	374	381	81	134	6	405	104	...	280	9286	6462	583	634	8701	8	5628	3647	3	80	2309	1480	100	57	2199	...	1458	848	3	365	12,110	14	7491	4599	6

CHAPTER XVII.

ROADS AND COMMUNICATIONS.

SABHI KHAN (see p. 48) was probably the first road-maker in the district. His roads, or jangáls, as they are called, are to be found in the northern and north-western parts of the district, especially in thanas Gournadi and Kotwalipara (now transferred to Farídpúr). They were very broad and high, and though now broken and even obliterated in many places, they are still used by the country-people. A section of one of these may be seen near the Palardi police station, and it has been made part of the modern road from Barisál to Gournadi.

Sabhi Khan was in all probability a man of energy and public spirit, and I have no wish to depreciate unduly his merit, or that of the other Mahomedans of like stamp who made roads in Bengal in the old days of the Moghal empire. I am not sure, however, that the decay of his roads is not a proof of the comparative uselessness of merely individual effort, and of the evanescent character of improvement for which the time is not ripe. I suspect that Sabhi Khan's jangáls would never have fallen into decay if they had been really wanted. At least it is difficult to see how they could become covered with jungle if people were daily in the habit of traversing them. Probably many of the old Mahomedan roads were made for military purposes, and their usefulness ceased when these purposes had been accomplished.[1] It is but fair to notice that Sabhi Khan, on making his roads, appears to have made provision for the physical and spiritual wants of wayfarers, for he dug tanks by the roadside at Sabhi Khan's Pár and elsewhere, and he erected a handsome mosque at Ramsiddhi. Of course I cannot positively say that the tanks and mosque were made by him, for natives have a habit of ascribing every improvement to one distinguished man.

Major Rennel in his "Memoir on Roads in Bengal" has given a list of routes in Bákarganj, and his map (republished by Colonel Gastrell) shows a road passing from Bákarganj to Kótarhát, Sutaluri, Gournadi, and then across the swamps to Khulna and Maxadpúr. No doubt this route is in part composed of Sabhi Ḳhan's jangál, but I suspect that much of it was merely a track across country, and only open in the cold season, or rather just before the rains; for thanas Gournadi and Kotwalipara, and indeed Bákarganj generally, are most traversable in the months of April and May. Kótarhát is now a deserted place, but the name seems to imply that it was once a place of importance, and there are remains of an old road (now repaired) which led from it to Bákarganj in the days when the latter was the headquarters of the district. In old times there was a munsif's court at Kótarhát. Sutaluri, as the name implies, was an old seat, I believe, of the weaving or of the thread trade. It is situated on the road from Barisál to Jhalukátti, and is near Gurudham. It still contains some ornamented ruins, and there is a *mat* or funeral monument in it, which, though the top has

[1] One great cause of the destruction of the Mahomedan roads was the absence of sufficient water-way. Lime and skilled labour were scarce, and hence, though large bridges were put up here and there at important places, there were few or no culverts, and the height of the earth-way was the chief thing relied on for resistance to the floods.

fallen off, is still, I believe, the loftiest structure in the district.

The oldest roads made during the English administration were probably those leading from Bákarganj to Sibpúr, and to the Golabari and Kótarhát. The Sibpúr road is about five miles long, and still is in tolerable repair, and has several bridges. The headquarters of the district were removed to Barisál in 1801, and the oldest road in that neighbourhood, I believe, is one which led from Barisál to a market (now deserted) known as the Khazanchi's (treasurer) Hát. It is about four miles long, and has been repaired, and is now known as the Dapdapia road. It is part of the road to Bákarganj. The road from Barisál to Madhabpásha (about seven miles) is also an old one, and is due to the liberality of a Hindu lady (Parbati Chaudharine).

The following remarks on roads, &c., in Bákarganj appear in a volume entitled "East India Affairs," and printed by order of the House of Commons, 1819: "The nullahs and ditches which intersect the town of Barisál require deepening to admit the tide and carry off the stagnant water. The only road about the station has been lately repaired, and the prisoners are now engaged in making bricks to lay on it. A road is intended to be made near the station, by which much jungle will be cleared. A road from Barisál to Gournadi, which is on the route to Dacca, would be very advantageous, merchants being at present prevented from resorting to Barisál from apprehensions of the risk attendant on navigating the large rivers between it and Dacca."[1]

The road which Mr Sage desiderated so long ago has

[1] Mr Sage, in Appendix E to Superintendent of Police's Reports, 15th May 1816, p. 239.

only recently been made. It is very useful for foot-passengers, but is not adapted for carriages. None of the district roads, indeed, are readily traversable by carts, and it is not necessary that they should. The rivers will always furnish the readiest mode of transporting heavy goods. There are perhaps some forty or fifty carts in or about Barisál, and there are a considerable number in Dakhin Shahbázpúr (where the ryots use them to bring home their grain from the fields), but, speaking generally, there are no carts in Bákarganj. The numerous rivers and khâls in the district, and consequently the great number of ferries or expensive bridges required in order to make the roads suitable for carriage traffic, are a most insuperable obstacle to the making of carriage-roads.

The road to Gournadi goes *viâ* Lakutia, and consists so far of a very good road, made by Ram Chandra Rai, zamindar of Lakutia. This same gentleman also made a very good khál for boats alongside of the road. The other principal roads are Barisál to Jhalukátti, Barisál to Nalchiti, Barisál to Bákarganj, and Barisál to Táltolli.

Of subdivisions, Dakhin Shahbázpúr is the one which is best supplied with roads. There are a road and canal across the island from Bhola to Daulat Khan, and there are footpaths to Ghazipúr, Dhaniya Maniya police station. In Perozpúr subdivision there is a towing-path, and a road from Kumarkháli to Raierkátti. In Patuyakháli there are no roads, except a footpath for a few miles along the bank of the Patuyakháli dōn.

It has often been said that every man in Bákarganj has his boat, and that roads are not required. This, however, is a mistake. It is very far from being the case that every ryot has his boat, and even those who have, often find it much quicker and easier to walk than to row against the tide, &c. Women and children also often travel, and they neither have boats nor can they afford to hire them. The amount of walking which is done in the district is in fact very great, especially in the dry season. In some large tracts of the district—the island of Dakhin Shahbázpúr, for instance—there are no rivers, and consequently hardly any boats, and nearly everybody walks. Roads, then, are wanted in the district, but they should be merely raised footpaths, and, above all, the kháls which intersect them should be bridged. For this purpose wooden bridges, and even bamboo bridges, are quite sufficient. The number of bamboo bridges, or *chárs,* as they are called in the district, is very great. Every village has two or three, and in some parts every homestead has one.

Towing-paths also are much required, especially on the highway from Barisál to Calcutta, and I am glad to say that these have been in part supplied. There are no towing-paths in the Sundarbans, and navigation there is almost entirely dependent on the tides.

Not much has yet been done towards the canalisation of the district. However, channels have been made from Bhola to Daulat Khan, and from Barisál to Lakutia. The Jhalukátti khál has been deepened, &c.

Now that the road cess has been introduced in the district, we may expect that many canals and roads will be made.

The Government ferries are Rahamatpúr, Dwarika, and Shikarpúr, on the road to Gournadi ; Jagua, on the road to Nalchiti ; and Kalijiri, on the road to Jhalukátti. There are also ferries at Perozpúr station, and between Daulat Khan and Hattia, and Tamizudin and Manpúra. The Barisál town ferry belongs to the town committee. There are numerous private ferries.

CHAPTER XVIII.

BARISÁL.

BARISÁL, the largest town in the district, and the seat of the principal courts, is situated on the right or west bank of the Barisál river,[1] and is 183 miles nearly due east from Calcutta, and about 75 miles south of Dacca. It is, however, only accessible by water from either of these places, and the voyage from Barisál to Calcutta occupies from four to seven days, and from Barisál to Dacca about three days. Barisál did not become the seat of the courts till 1801, but Rennel's map shows that it was a place of some consequence many years before that time. I have also quoted in another chapter a remark of Mir Kassim, which shows that Barisál was an important salt *chauki*, or place where the salt tax was paid, in the middle of the last century. In Rennel's time the town seems to have been confined to the south side of the Jailkhana khál. The town is composed of the five villages of Barisál, Bogura, Amanatganj, Alikandi, and Kaunia. The village of Bárisál is a very small one, and lies in a pargana of its own called the Gird-i-Bandar, which appears to have been formed out of pargana Chandradwip as a site for the bazár. The English church and the principal public offices are situ-

[1] I believe the proper name of the river is the Kirttankhola, though I never heard it called so.

ated in Barisál proper. These offices consist of the civil and criminal courts, the Collectorate, the registration office, &c.

The present dimensions of the town are of recent origin, it having been enlarged with the view of making it a more suitable basis for the registration of vital statistics, and also in order to increase the collections from the taxes. Formerly only portions of some of the five villages I have named were included in the town, but now they have been entirely incorporated. This has given a survey boundary for an arbitrary one, and has enabled us to know the area of the town with some exactitude. From the survey papers it appears that the area is nearly six square miles (5 square miles, 588 acres). The population within these limits appears to be 13,332, including 1124 of a boat population. The population therefore is very sparse for a town, being only about 2000 to the square mile, or about four times the prevalent rate (482 to the square mile) in the district. The fact is that great part of the so-called town consists of scattered villages, interspersed with trees and gardens, and even rice-fields. In truth it may be said that, with the exception of the bazár, every house in Barisál is more or less a *rus in urbe.* I believe that the towns in other Bengal districts are similarly constituted. When, therefore, it is justly stated in the Bengal Administration Report for 1872-73 that "the absence of large towns is one of the most remarkable statistical features in Bengal," and reference is made to "Rangpúr, the capital of the great district of Rangpúr, containing only 6100 souls, and to Jessore 8152, each of these districts having a population of over two millions," these facts, extraordinary as they are, do not bring out the whole singularity of the case. For even these petty towns have their populations distributed over wide areas, and are "half town and half country."

More than half of the inhabitants of Barisál are Mahomedans, and the other half are Hindus, with the exception of about 150 Christians. The place has no manufactures and no trade, except that it is to some extent an entrepôt for cloth from Calcutta, which is distributed from Barisál over the district. There are one bazár and two markets, one for fish and one for general produce. The latter is held on Tuesdays and Saturdays. Barisál is a calling-place for steamers, and its river is navigable by them all the year round. It contains an English church (built in 1845), a Baptist chapel, a Brahma Samaj meeting-house, three *akras* — namely, two of Madan Mohan and one of Jagannath—five *kalibaris*, and five *manashas*, though only one of the latter is in a separate building. The Mahomedans have one mosque and three or four places of prayer. There are a charitable dispensary, established in 1847; a public library, founded by Mr Kemp (now a Judge of the High Court) in 1855; a large civil and criminal jail, &c. There are a very good English school,[1] a vernacular school, a normal school, a girls' school, and one or two *pátsálas.* There are two printing-presses—viz., the Purna Chandrodai and the Satya Prakásh. Four newspapers are published at it—viz., the "Barisál Bártabaha," the "Hitsadini," the "Bala Ranjika," and the "Satya Prakásh." There are a burial-ground for Christians, one for Mahomedans, and a burning ghât for Hindus.

The town is largely occupied by the professional classes, such as pleaders and attorneys, and their servants.

[1] The present schoolhouse is, I believe, an escheat to Government. It was formerly inhabited by Dr Spencer, who committed suicide in it on 20th July 1836.

They are only temporary residents, and hence at times, when the courts are closed—such, for example, as the Durga puja holidays—the town is almost deserted. As the pleaders and shopkeepers do not make the town their home, there are comparatively very few women in it, and even of these a large proportion are professional prostitutes. This puts the climax to the facts above mentioned about the paucity of towns in Bengal, and shows how the genius of the people is opposed to agglomeration in great centres; for not only are the towns few in number and small in point of population, and that too not closely packed together, but there is hardly any home-life in those parts of the towns, such as the bazár, &c., where houses are contiguous enough to form streets.

The affairs of the town are managed by a town committee appointed under Act 6 of 1868 (Bengal Code). There are 3042 holdings, and these, for taxation and other purposes, are arranged in ten wards. The income of the committee is about Rs.7000 a year, Rs.6000 of which are derived from the tax on houses (at the rate of three anas a month), Rs.600 from the town ferry, and the remainder from the cattle-pounds, proceeds of fishing licences in the tanks, &c. The committee also generally receive a grant from the road fund. In 1814, 522 houses were assessed to the chaukidari tax, the monthly collections were Rs.65, and there were 17 chaukidars. In 1819 there were only 378 houses assessed, and the monthly collections were only Rs.46 (M. 28, 5, 19). There were then 13 chaukidars at Rs.3 a month, and a dafadar at Rs.6. In 1820 there were 1316 houses in the town (M. 4, 7, 20). In 1826, 564 houses were assessed. The Magistrate's cutchery was not finished till 1830, and previous to that time the Magistrate held his court in his own house, and got an allowance of Rs.40 a month on this account (M. letter, 1826). In 1827, Rs.1500 were given by Government and Rs.925 subscribed for improvements in the town, and some tanks were dug in consequence, &c. I do not know when the present Barisál band was made, but it is mentioned incidentally by Mr Chapman, in a letter dated 22d May 1819, that he had left court at about 5 P.M., and that on returning from his ride he was walking on the bank of the river with three other gentlemen. The letter I have quoted describes a mutiny which had arisen among the sepoys of the Provincial Battalion owing to one of their number having been put in irons.

On 25th February 1833 the Magistrate refers to the bad repute of Barisál for unhealthiness, and says that a fire which occurred in the town showed by removing the houses the bad state of the sanatation. The town now has tolerably wide and straight streets, and clearly it owes them to English influences, for natives, when left to themselves, have no idea of keeping highways clear of houses.

Barisál has for a considerable time been diluviating, and it appears that within the last twenty years about a third of the bazár portion has been washed away. There is a report of 6th December 1854 on the subject, and there is a map, made in 1857, and now in the possession of the town committee, which shows, by comparison with the present state of the town, the amount of land which has been carried away.

CHAPTER XIX.

GENERAL REMARKS.

ON reviewing the history of Bákarganj for the last eighty years, it seems impossible to deny that some improvements have been effected. Gang-robbery has been in a great measure suppressed, and the cases which still occur seldom exhibit the circumstances of atrocious cruelty which used to characterise the crime. Widow-burnings have ceased, affrays have become less frequent and less bloody, and the wrongful confinement of the peasantry and other acts of high-handed oppression have become comparatively rare. The rights of landlords and tenants have been defined, extensive tracts of country have been brought into cultivation, and trade and population have largely increased. School education has been introduced, and has made some progress; and there has been, I think, some change even in the character of the people, who no longer deserve the sweeping terms of reprobation employed by Mr Wintle in 1802.

As regards the cause of these improvements, I think that every unprejudiced person must acknowledge that they are mainly due to the introduction of the English Government. That this has been the chief cause seems evident from the fact that it is the only important change which has taken place in the country during the last two hundred years. If, then, the English Government has not been the cause of the improvements which we see, why did they not occur at an earlier period? If other things were the same then, and the form of government was not worse, why was it that much of the country was a jungle, that the rivers and creeks were full of piratical boats, and that life and property were everywhere insecure?

It is natural that enthusiastic Bengalis should regret the days of their native kings, when Bákarganj was ruled by a Rajah of Chandradwip, and Jessore had a prince who was powerful or audacious enough to dispute the supremacy of the Emperor of Delhi. But, in sober truth, there seems little reason to regret the extinction of any of the Hindu dynasties. Taken at their best, they seem to have been chiefly beneficial to idle Bráhmans, and other unproductive classes. There is no evidence that any one of the Chandradwip Rajahs was a man of superior ability or virtue; and we know that one of them was insane, and that the last lineal representative of the family was an ignorant voluptuary. Pratápáditya, the King of Chandecan or Jessore, and the most famous and powerful of the so-called "twelve suns of Bengal," seems, from his biography, to have been a brutal tyrant who fell into his proper place when his conquerors shut him up in an iron cage.

We may also remind our Hindu friends that nine out of the twelve above-mentioned luminaries are described by the Jesuit priests as being Mahomedans. Until lately we had a good illustration of the working of a petty Hindu kingdom in the native state of Kuch Behar. The Rajah of this little country was not, it is true, independent after the treaty with the British Government in 1773, but he enjoyed considerable freedom of action, and we may judge from the way in which he used it how he would have acted if he had been totally uncontrolled. Now it was my fortune some years ago to be stationed at Kuch Behar for many months, so that I had an opportunity of studying its history in the old records, &c., and I can confidently state that the condition of the worst-administered district in Bengal is better than that of Kuch Behar under its native Rajahs. The most famous of the ancestors (Harendra Narain) of the present Rajah, and the one who, I am sorry to say, seemed to be most highly thought of by the native amlah, was a debauchee and a murderer, who only escaped punishment from the unwillingness of the Governor-General of the day to interfere in the internal affairs of the country. Not many years ago there was a native Rajah of Jyntia in Sylhet, and he lost his territories (in 1835) partly from long misgovernment, and partly because he was believed to have connived at the kidnapping of four British subjects for the purposes of a human sacrifice. Another Rajah with whom I was acquainted, and who, though not really independent, claimed certain privileges and the possession of a quasi-sovereignty over the neighbouring hill-tribes—I refer to the Rajah of Susang in Mymensing—made use of the latter in his quarrels with other zamindars, and tried to screen them when they had committed a diabolical outrage on a Bengali household, and had murdered a whole family—man, woman, and child—of fifteen or sixteen persons.

One of the best-known instances of a modern Hindu kingdom in Bengal is the territory which used to be known as Independent Tipperah, but which is now officially designated Hill Tipperah. There is now a political agent at Agartolla, the capital of the state, and things have perhaps improved, but some years ago Tipperah was the resort of all the fugitives from justice belonging to the neighbouring districts. I remember also that when, some fifteen or sixteen years ago, a boundary dispute was decided against the Rajah, and a tract of country which he claimed was declared to belong to the district of Sylhet, he revenged himself by burning the villages in question, and by carrying off the inhabitants into his own dominions. Another instance of a Hindu, or at least a semi-Hindu state, is to be found in the country of Manipúr, and I can testify from personal observation that things are not in a very flourishing or progressive state in that territory.

With more reason the Mahomedan part of the population, and even the inhabitants generally of Eastern Bengal, may regret the days of the Nawabs and their deputies, for there was a vigour and a power of organisation among the Mahomedan rulers which were wanting among the Hindu princelings. We see the difference between them in the way in which they treated the Arracanese invasion. The Hindus were unequal to the contest, and fled under the pretext of avoiding contamination; the Mohamedans, on the other hand, took the more manly course of grasping their nettle, established themselves at Dacca, where the danger was greatest, raised and maintained a fleet, and swept the rivers and their estuaries clear of the Arracanese and the Portuguese pirates. Bengalis, indeed, and especially those of Eastern Bengal, have much reason to be thankful to the Mahomedans, for it is to them that they owe in great measure their preservation from the Burmese. But for the conquest by the Mahomedans of Sandwip and Chittagong, it is probable that much of what is now known as Eastern Bengal would have been a portion, and a deserted and despised portion, of the kingdom of Arracan or Burmah.

It must be admitted, also, that Eastern Bengal (though not that part of it which forms the district of Bákarganj) has declined in importance, if not in prosperity, since the English conquest. Dacca is no longer the seat of a great trade, and presents the melancholy appearance of a decayed city. Various reasons may be assigned for this, but the principal one of course is the destruction of the weaving interests by the importation of Manchester goods. English power also was not always as beneficent as it now is, and there was a time when our English laws, and still more our English desire to make rapid fortunes, wrought sad havoc in Eastern Bengal. This was the time of the outrages and tyrannies at the Bákarganj bazár referred to in a former chapter, and which exhibited what Lord Macaulay has called "that most frightful of all spectacles, the strength of civilisation without its mercy." This probably was the most unhappy period in the modern history of Bengal. There were abuses under the Hindu rulers, and also under the Mahomedan governors, but we suspect that the thirty years before the Permanent Settlement were more acute in their misery than any which had gone before. It says much for the vigour of our Government that we have been able not only to heal the wounds inflicted in that terrible time, but also to raise the body politic to a higher stage of health and wellbeing.[1] Perhaps some

[1] "It must give pain to an Englishman to have reason to think that since the accession of the Company to the Dewanny, the condition of the people of this country has been worse than it was before; and yet I am afraid that the fact is undoubted, and I believe has proceeded from the following causes: The mode of providing the Company's investment; the exportation of specie, instead of importing a large sum annually; the strictness that has been observed in the collections; the endeavours of all concerned to gain credit by an increase of revenue during the time of their being in situations, without sufficiently attending to what future consequences might be expected from such a measure; the errors that subsist in the manner

will say that I am attributing too much importance to administrative action, and they may be disposed to remind me of the dictum of Mr Buckle, that governments can do but little towards the advancement of a country. But, in the first place, if the fact really be that Bengal owes much of its progress to the English administration, it cannot be set aside in favour of the notion of any individual writer, however eminent; and secondly, I think I can show that there is no contradiction in the matter. Mr Buckle, in saying that governments have not done much for civilisation, is not referring to governments composed of foreigners. He begins his arguments by the following remark: "In the first place, we have the obvious consideration, that the rulers of a country have, under ordinary circumstances, always been the inhabitants of that country, nurtured by its literature, bred to its traditions, and imbibing its prejudices. Such men are at best only the creatures of the age, never its creators. Their measures are the result of social progress, not the cause of it" (vol. i. p. 250).

It is plain, therefore, that his argument does not apply to the case of our Indian Government. He would not, I think, have denied that it might exercise great influence over the civilisation of Bengal, any more than he would have denied that the Roman or the Norman government of England had powerfully affected the condition of that country.

of making the collections, particularly by the employment of *amils*. These appear to me the principal causes why this fine country, which flourished under the most despotic and arbitrary government, is verging towards its ruin, while the English have really so large a share in the administration." (Extract of letter of Mr Becher to the President, dated 24th May 1769, quoted by Sir Philip Francis in a paper printed at p. 931 of the Ninth Report of the House of Commons. See note about famine of 1770 in Appendix for a notice of Mr Becher.)

Two circumstances in the progress which Bákarganj has made under English rule appear to me to be deserving of attention. The first is that the non-official Englishman, or interloper, as he used to be called, has had very little to do with it. I do not mean to say that the district has not been largely influenced by Calcutta merchants, nor that English literature has not produced a perceptible effect on its educated classes. I only wish to point out that hardly any non-official Englishmen have resided in the district as indigo-planters or traders, as has been the case in the neighbouring districts of Farídpúr and Jessore. Opinions will differ about the effect of the absence of these classes, and some will think it has been a great loss to the district. Still it cannot be denied that the peasantry of Bákarganj, or, in other words, four-fifths of the population, are at least as comfortable as those of Jessore or Nadiya, and that they have therefore done very well without indigo. For my own part, I consider that Bákarganj is to be congratulated on its escape from a class of residents who were not subject to the same laws as the rest of the community.[1] Almost the only non-official English residents whom the district has had have been the Baptist missionaries, and they did not enter it till 1830. Their influence has been almost entirely confined to its north-west corner, but there it has, I think, been very beneficial. At least I am sure that the presence in the district for many years of a man so simple and gentle-hearted as the late Mr Sale must have done good, and I know that he was esteemed by all the natives who knew

[1] At the time of the Indigo Commission (1860) Morrellganj was included in Bákarganj, and Mr Morrell's evidence (answer 2390, p. 234) gives a curious picture of the abhorrence which his ryots had for the cultivation of indigo. The same evidence gives some interesting details about the cultivation of the Sundarbans.

him. His predecessor, Mr Page, was a man of much vigour and energy, and exercised great influence over his flock.

The second circumstance is that few if any of the Bákarganj officials appear to have been men of great ability, and that none of them has left any deep impression of himself on the district. Mr Douglas, who made the Permanent Settlement, was a man of exceptional breadth of view and humanity, and Mr Massie seems to have been energetic and able; but they lived at Dacca, and were thus too far away to exercise much influence. None of the other early Magistrates or Collectors appears to have risen much above mediocrity, and there is at least no one who stands out in the manner in which Mr Westland has made Messrs Henckell and Rocke to stand out in the early history of Jessore; though, indeed, even with regard to Mr Henckell, one has a suspicion that he was more energetic than prudent, and that his schemes for the reformation of the salt administration, &c., ended in failure. Certainly his plan for cultivating the Sundarbans appears to have brought loss to Government, and to have embroiled him with the zamindars.

The names of the older officers have quite gone out of the memories of the Bákarganj people. The name of Mr Battye, who was Magistrate in 1811, survives officially from his having built a bridge, and from an outbreak in the jail having occurred in his time. It appears also from a letter of the Court of Directors that he was very successful in putting down dacoity. Mr Chapman, who was Magistrate in 1819, is remembered from his connection with the burial-ground, which appears to have been formed by him, and from his name having been given to a tank which is said to yield the best drinking-water in Barisál. Mr Garrett was an active and public-spirited officer, and is remembered for the improvements he made in the town, and for his having assisted in the formation of the first English school. The name of Mr Shawe, who was Magistrate in 1845, and who at a later period became Judge of Sylhet, is remembered on account of his activity in road-making, and of his having built the English church; while his contemporary, Mr Sturt, is remembered for the extravagance of his entertainments, the defalcations which occurred in his treasury, and above all, perhaps, for the great *éclat* with which on one occasion he had the Kali puja celebrated in the bazár as a means of averting the cholera.

Another officer (Mr Morris Beaufort) is remembered on account of his having sentenced a notoriously oppressive zamindar to a term of imprisonment, and then compelled him to work at the road leading from the Magistrate's house to the cutchery. The path is to this day known by the name of Nil Kanth Rai's road.

Perhaps the names which linger longest in the memories of the people are those of the Settlement officers, for they are intertwined with their dearest interests. I have referred in another chapter to the great fame in the eastern districts of Sir Henry Ricketts. Similarly Mr Dampier's name will long remain in the island of Sandwip on account of his settlement of it, while that of his assistant, Sir Frederick Halliday, is remembered in Noakháli for his settlement of the island of Hattia, &c.

In Bákarganj one of the most noted names among those of Settlement officers is that of Mr James Reilly, who settled the large Government estate of Tushkháli, and who was in fact Collector of the district during the incumbency of Mr Reid.

Of late years I do not know that any name has been more widely known among the people than that of one who was never anything higher than an uncovenanted Deputy-Collector and Deputy-Magistrate. I refer to the late Babu Dinu Bandhu Maulik, who held office in the district for several years, and acquired a great influence over the people. He left the impress of himself on nearly every department of the administration, but was especially famed as a good police-magistrate. So useful was he that he never could get leave of absence, and I think it is not too much to say that his premature death, when only about thirty-four years of age, was in a great measure owing to overwork. Curiously enough this man, who was so popular with the natives, and who also did so much good service, was far from being esteemed by some of the higher authorities, and more than once narrowly escaped dismissal.

In the above review I am, of course, only speaking of officials. If I were to mention non-officials, there are at least two who have exercised more influence than any judge or magistrate. I refer to the Mahomedan preachers named Keramat Ali and Dudhu Mia. The name of the latter is widely known, and he and his father, Shariyatoolah, may be called the founders of the sect of Ferazis. Dudhu Mia's character, however, was stained with vices, and I am not prepared to say that his influence has been beneficial. On the other hand, from all that I have heard, Keramat Ali, who was a native of Juanpúr, was a man of a very pure and disinterested character, and did much good by preaching sound morality. He has certainly exercised much more influence over the common people than Keshab Chandra Sein, and I should think that he was the truer and more modest man of the two.

RELIGION.—The mention of these two men brings me to the consideration of religion, and of the possibility of the country's ever becoming Christianised. At present, as we have seen, two-thirds of the population are Mahomedans, and I cannot say that there seems any likelihood of their soon throwing off the shackles of their faith. Some might even say that there is an appearance of their wishing to draw them tighter, for Feraziism is undoubtedly a puritanical movement, and an endeavour to return to the supposed greater strictness of the primitive Church. But such movements may indicate fear rather than strength, and may testify to a dying out of Mahomedan faith, just as the spread of Ultramontanism is significant of the vogue of infidelity. However, the great body of the peasantry seem to be still sincerely attached to their religion, which after all does not interfere much with their life, nor call upon them for any important sacrifices, except in the month of fasting. Singularly enough, the educated Mahomedans do not exhibit any signs of scepticism, and appear to reverence their Koran almost as much as their more ignorant brethren. If the fact be so, it is not a little strange, for the Koran is, at least in Sale's translation, such an unintelligible and wearisome book, that it is difficult to imagine how any intellectual person can believe it to contain a divine message. The number of educated Mahomedans, however, is very small, and I have had little opportunity of judging of their real sentiments. It may be, therefore, that free-thought has made more progress among them than I am aware of.

Among the Hindus the prevailing worships are those of Kali, or Durga, and Vishnu. The worship of Siva is comparatively rare. The common people are considerably addicted to idolatry, and are fond, especially the womankind of them, of worshipping sacred trees, &c. I have seen a tree near Sarupkátti almost covered with hair, which had been hung up by parents in fulfilment of vows that if their child recovered they would cut off his hair, and make a votive offering of it to the tree, or rather, I suppose, to the goddess who was believed to reside there. The educated Hindus have for the most part lost all faith in their religion, and are deists or atheists. Many of them reject the doctrine of a future life. The organisation of the Brahma Samaj, however, is not making much progress, and many Hindus seem inclined now to draw back and to return to the customs of their country, even where they are tinged with idolatrous associations. Christianity is not making any progress in the district, and I do not see the least likelihood of its ever becoming the prevalent religion. Although there is an English church at Barisál, there is no resident clergyman, and the spiritual wants of the members of the church are attended to by the Dacca chaplain, who visits the place once a quarter. It is to be hoped that in time the principle of disestablishment will be at least partially carried out in Bengal, and that people who are so very "churchy" that they cannot enter a Baptist chapel will not be indulged at the public expense in their exclusivism.

Considerable as has been the progress of the Bengal districts under English rule, it would doubtless have been much greater under more favourable circumstances. Probably the frequent changes of officers have been the greatest obstacle to improvement. A gentleman who has resided in Barisál for about five-and-twenty years tells me that during that time he successively served under twenty-four Collectors of the district and nine Commissioners of the division. Bákarganj has been worse off in this respect than other districts, for it has generally been disliked as a residence, and therefore most officers who have been appointed to it have tried to get away as soon as possible. Other districts, however, have not been much more fortunate. Dr Taylor, in his "Topography of Dacca," tells us that "from the year 1781 to 1839 fifty-nine civil servants have filled the office of magistrate, but of this number thirty have only been in temporary charge; the average duration, therefore, of each Magistrate's appointment has been two years, the longest period four years and twenty-seven days. The number of Collectors for the same time was thirty-seven; twenty of this number have been acting Collectors: the longest period for which a permanent Collector has held office is six years and forty-five days." Nor is it only the Collectors and Magistrates who have been frequently changed. Transfers have been quite as rife among the subdivisional officers, the deputy-magistrates and deputy-collectors, the police officers, &c. At one time the Board of Revenue went so far as to pass an order that no native ministerial officer should remain in the same district more than three years. The result of this notable order (which was passed with the idea of diminishing corruption) was that poorly-paid natives were driven from their homes, and subjected to much expense and inconvenience, and that hardly any one remained in a district office who had local experience, or who could help his newly-arrived Collector out of a difficulty. At length, after much heart-burning and distress had been occasioned, and after the efficiency of many offices had been crippled, the Board were pleased to place the order in abeyance, though I am not aware that it has been formally cancelled. Attempts have been made of late years to diminish the frequency of transfers, but they have not been very successful, and in fact the inherent difficulties of the matter are too great to admit of the hope that they will ever be overcome so long as the administration is in the hands of foreigners.

In the report on the administration of Bengal for 1872–73, Sir George Campbell writes as follows: "It must be admitted that in the inferior grades of the service, covenanted and uncovenanted, permanency has not yet been attained. The present leave and service rules are so favourable to change, the varieties of climate and of amenities or disamenities in Bengal stations afford such temptations to seek change, the habit of going frequently to Europe has so much grown among the European servants of Government, and so many of the native servants so persistently strive by every device to avoid and get rid of out-of-the-way and disagreeable stations, that it is very hard indeed for those who administer so great a government with such a mass of Government servants to hold its own against so many who, for one reason or other, seek change. So many interests are set in motion, that it is a matter of extreme difficulty to avoid the necessity of making several changes when a vacancy occurs before things settle down. It is, in fact, a sort of game of chess, as it were, in which the Government is very unequally pitted against a great many players, and it is hardly possible to give to each move the attention and the calculation of contingencies which is necessary to avoid being taken at a disadvantage by one or other of them. The Lieutenant-Governor has been, he may say, shocked to find how many changes have occurred during the year among the subdivisional and other subordinate officials of some districts, in spite of all his struggles to avoid change."

In the above extract the Lieutenant-Governor deals

only with changes among the subordinate officers. But the changes among the heads of great departments are nearly quite as frequent, and are more injurious to the public service. The Governors-General, the Lieutenant-Governors, the Judges of the High Court and of the District Courts, and the Commissioners follow one another in rapid succession, and hence there is great want of stability in our administration.

One effect of such frequent changes is to give an air of grandeur and solidity to everything in the country which is permanent. Victor Hugo somewhere remarks, that whatever was the real character of Louis XIV., he acquired a semblance of greatness from the mere length of his reign, and from his thus presenting an appearance of immobility amidst the revolutions and changes of the kingdoms around him. In like manner, amidst the incessant flux of our administration, the inert Bengali landowner, living from youth to age in his ancestral home, and distributing a rude and unequal justice among his tenantry, or the village watchman going the rounds of his native hamlet year after year, forms a not unimposing picture of steadiness and uniformity.

The moral which these facts teach seems to be, that we should endeavour to place the internal administration of the country as much as possible in the hands of natives. And in doing so, we should, I think, not only appoint Bengalis to appointments in Bengal, but should, other things being equal, give the preference to inhabitants of the district, and even of the subdivision, in which the vacancy occurs. Bengal cannot afford to be administered by foreigners, and the inhabitants of one part of India are often almost as much foreigners in another part of it as Europeans are. A Bengali of Nadiya or Hughli will not serve in Eastern Bengal for less than Rs.200 a month, but the same man would gladly take office near his home for one-half of this amount. Already we have made a commencement towards localising the administration by choosing our rural registrars from among the inhabitants of the registration circle, and it only remains to give them magisterial powers. Of course this can only be done gradually, and on proof of the fitness of each officer to discharge judicial duties. The system of appointing honorary magistrates, and of thus making zamindars and others discharge the duties of country justices of the peace, has been lately revived in Bengal, and has had some good effect. I think, however, that it will not become really successful until more confidence is placed in the gentlemen selected for the duties, and they be not absolutely debarred from trying cases occurring in their own estates. At present the more property a zamindar has, the less useful is he as an honorary magistrate, because the fewer are the cases in his neighbourhood which he is supposed competent to try.

Interesting attempts have of late been made to develop municipal institutions, and to form what have been called village communes. And there is no doubt that this is eventually the direction which reform in Bengal will assume. The days of individualism and personal government seem to be over in that country. We have got beyond the days of the strong man of Carlyle and the Panjáb, who is to put everything to rights by a glance of his eye. Personal government of this kind may do very well among the hill tribes and in some other parts of India, but it is quite out of date in

Bengal.[1] A late Lieutenant-Governor, who was endowed with rare energy and quickness, but who came to Bengal with notions derived from less-advanced parts of India, made a vigorous attempt to establish personal government; but though his intensity, and still more the strength of his position, enabled him to make himself felt in the remotest villages of his government, yet no permanent effect was produced. Many of his measures have been silently abandoned or changed by his successor; and it seems to me that, great as Sir George Campbell's abilities undoubtedly were, the chief good effected by his administration was the demonstration it afforded of the hopelessness of any merely individual attempt to counteract a national will.

No doubt it seems melancholy to some that the days of hero-worship are over. They have trusted that some great man would deliver them and their country from the evils under which they laboured, and have been disappointed that he has not come. Tennyson has expressed this sentiment of sadness at the growing greatness of the world in the passage where he speaks of the

[1] "While I admit that the abridgment of discretion by written laws is to some extent an evil—though, under the actual circumstances of India, an inevitable evil—I do not admit the proposition which is sometimes advanced, that the natives of India dislike the abridgment of official discretion. This assertion seems to me not only unsupported by any evidence, but to be contrary to all the probabilities. It may be allowed that in some cases discretionary government is absolutely necessary; but why should a people, which measures religious zeal and personal rank and respectability by rigid adherence to usage and custom, have a fancy for rapid changes in the actions of its governors, and prefer a regimen of discretion, sometimes close upon caprice, to a regimen of law? I do not profess to know the natives of this country as well as others, but if they are to be judged by their writings, they have no such preference. The educated youth of India certainly affect a dislike of many things which they do not care about, and pretend to many tastes which they do not really share; but the repugnance which they invariably profess for discretionary government has always seemed to me genuinely hearty and sincere."—*Maine's Village Communities*, Appendix I. p. 215.

individual withering and of the world becoming more and more.[1] But, in fact, the complaint is a somewhat idle and querulous one, and need not seriously disturb us. True it is, that as the world advances, its dependence upon any individual man becomes less and less; but when we consider the shortness and uncertainty of human life, this is a motive for rejoicing rather than for sorrow. It is better that nowadays, if a great man die, he leaves five hundred as good as he, than that, as when Charlemagne or Akbar died, there should be no one to fill the void. Nor need we fear that the individual must *wither*, for the world is made up of units; and no assemblage of withered individuals, however great, will ever make a prosperous world. If, then, the world is to wax greater and greater, as apparently it will, individuals must rise higher and higher, though at the same time the absolute importance of any one of them must diminish.

Although we feel assured that some reform in which the whole country takes a share must be the ultimate remedy for Bengal, and that comparatively little can be done by individuals, yet it is not easy to predict the form which the change will take. Some have thought of reviving the village system; but, in fact, this is a system which never had a vigorous existence in Lower Bengal, and is now altogether decayed. The village system, of which we hear so much, may work well in Madras and the North-Western Provinces, but in Bengal it seems to be an anachronism. Besides, it is a Hindu institution, and therefore we cannot expect it to flourish

[1] "Knowledge comes, but wisdom lingers, and I linger by the shore,
And the individual withers, and the world is more and more.
Knowledge comes, but wisdom lingers, and he bears a laden breast
Full of sad experience, moving toward the stillness of his rest."

The words are those of a man who has been soured by disappointment and treachery, and are quite appropriate in his mouth. We need not take them to be expressive of the poet's own sentiments.

in Mahomedan districts such as Bákarganj and the other districts of Eastern Bengal. Villages in Bákarganj are very different from villages in the North-West, or even in Western Bengal. The houses in them are not grouped together, and there is little feeling of companionship among the different householders. The old village boundaries have also been obliterated in many cases by the formation of chars or by diluviation. There is certainly nothing in them which corresponds to the organisation which we read of in Elphinstone. There is no village accountant or village barber, nor even was there originally any village watchman, for the last is the introduction of the English Government, and was unknown till the last fifty or sixty years. And the village watchman, or chaukidar, as he is called, bears traces of his being a new institution; for we often find that he does not even live in the village he is supposed to guard, and it is with great difficulty that he ever gets his pay from the villagers.

"In Backergunge the villages are more scattered and less defined than in Jessore and Farídpúr; indeed in many parts are not defined at all, each villager having ordinarily selected as the site for his house the spot which appeared to him to be most eligible in relation to his agricultural pursuits, and wholly without reference to any future village community. This want of definition became a source of great difficulty when compiling the map of the district in the Surveyor-General's office. It was often impossible to say whereabouts to fix the dot or other conventional mark to designate the village." —*Gastrell's Report.*

Nor is there any feeling of local patriotism or of fellowship among the inhabitants of the same village. The village is in most instances of too recent origin, the houses are too scattered, and ryots migrate too readily from one village to another to admit of the growth of such feelings. Bráhmans and other non-agricultural classes live for generations on the same homesteads; but, as a general rule, the tenancy of cultivators is of short duration, and I think that if the ryots of a village were interrogated, it would be found that most of them had been settled in it for less than twelve years. Some villages are chiefly inhabited by one caste or profession. Thus Kalasgram is full of Bráhmans, Banaripara is full of Kayasts, and Baukátti has for generations been celebrated for the number of its thieves. But, as a general rule, the inhabitants of a village are a heterogeneous assemblage, and have few ties with one another. At least one-half of them are generally Mahomedans, and the remainder is composed of Hindus, who again are subdivided into castes and *dals* which do not intermingle. The land of a village does not belong to the village community, nor are there any waste or pasturage lands in which all the villagers and *no others* can share. The occupancy right in each plot generally belongs to a ryot, but the rights of receiving rent, &c., are generally held by some taluqdar or zamindar who often lives a great way off.

These last rights are not always or even generally vested in one man, so that the inhabitants of a village have frequently different landlords and different rates of rent. In fact it may be said that they have often nothing in common except contiguity of residence, and even this does not always exist, for the houses in a village are often an hour's journey apart from one another.

Within certain limits the people of Bákarganj are great travellers, and at all events they cannot be described as never losing sight of their native village. The absence of railways or steamboats prevents them from undertaking distant journeys, but they frequently visit the headquarters of their district to look after their lawsuits, to consult their landlord's agent, &c.

Their relatives and friends are widely scattered, and the facilities for locomotion afforded by the numerous rivers and the general possession of boats are so great, especially during the rains, that they spend much time in paying visits either with or without their wives and families. Thus a man will have his home in one pargana, his father-in-law's in a second, his son-in-law's in a third, and almost innumerable uncles and cousins—*dharam-pitas* and *dharam-putras*—scattered over the country. Every now and then one of his friends or relatives gives a feast, and as the Bengali ryot is generally only accountable to himself for the employment of his time, and is not a labourer paid by the day, there is nothing to hinder him from accepting the invitation, or from spending two or three days in a jaunt with his wife and children. Owing to the scarcity of land in the more populous parts of the district, and to the possession of herds of buffaloes, &c., it is no uncommon thing for a ryot to have two homesteads. In one he lives with his wife and family, and the other, called his *do-alia bári*, he visits during the cultivating season, and often inhabits for two or three months at a time.

For all these reasons I think it will be impossible to make the village the unit of administration, and that it will be necessary to take something wider, such as the thana or the registration circle.

DESTRUCTION OF WILD ANIMALS.—There is one improvement which I think might be accomplished without great difficulty, and which would be of great benefit to the people. I refer to the destruction of tigers, leopards, crocodiles, and other wild animals. I have often wondered that the British India Association, or the People's Association, or some other of the societies which Young Bengal delights to form, has not taken in hand a work so simple and so clearly useful. A very moderate amount of organisation and of expense might suffice to stamp out the plague of noxious animals in most districts of Bengal. In Bákarganj the greatest number of deaths by carnivorous animals is caused by crocodiles, and yet, strange to say, no reward is ordinarily allowed by Government for their destruction. There is said to be a tribe of men in the Dacca Division whose peculiar business it is to harpoon crocodiles, and as Government has not thought fit to undertake the task of extirpation, I think that the wealthy zamindars of the division could not do better than employ this tribe to do so.[1] Tigers and leopards are numerous in Bákarganj, but it is somewhat surprising to find how few human beings are killed by them. They are principally destructive to cattle and goats. Yet it would be a great mistake to suppose that because tigers and leopards only kill a few men in the year, their ravages are not very injurious to the community. We cannot measure the harm they do by the number of human beings whom they kill or wound. The distress and panic which they cause, and the obstruction which they offer to the performance of

[1] The chief sufferers from alligators are women and children, who are struck down by them (the alligator is said to knock them down with his tail) when bathing or when fetching water, and who have not the strength or the presence of mind to recover themselves. It is very rarely that Europeans are carried off by them. Colonel Wilford, however, mentions ("Asiatic Researches," vol. xiv.) that Mr B. Plaisted, one of our early surveyors, was carried off in the Sundarbans by an alligator, which he mistook for the rotten trunk of a tree.

work, are evils of much more general consequence. Thus a tiger may perhaps kill only one man in a village, but the terror which he produces will spread over a whole pargana, and prevent people from travelling at night, delay postal communications, &c. So the fact of a crocodile's being seen in a reach of the river, or of his having carried off, or attempted to carry off, any one from a ghât, will produce uneasiness among thousands of bathers, and of women who have to come daily to the river to draw water. In matters of this kind it is the indirect effects which are most serious. The direct injury inflicted by a dacoity may not be very great, but the indirect effect may be to paralyse the trade of a large bazár.

We may apply this consideration when reflecting on the benefit which the British Government conferred on the country by the abolition of satí. When we look at the returns of widow-burnings from the various districts, the surprising thing, perhaps, is not that there were so many cases, but that there were so few. In Bákarganj, in the year of the cholera (1825), when upwards of 25,000 persons died in a few months, the total amount of satís was only sixty-three. It is evident, therefore, that the great majority of the Hindu widows abstained from the rite. But this must not make us conclude that its abolition was of small consequence. The real evil of it, perhaps, was the sickening dread which every Hindu wife, and all who loved her, must have felt whenever her husband was ill, or even when she was given in marriage. And, perhaps, worse than even this must have been the loss of self-respect felt by every Hindu widow who could not bring herself to submit to being burnt.

Wild pigs are extremely destructive to the crops, and

I am sorry to say that some Englishmen have been selfish enough to try to prevent the peasantry from killing them. Of late years the sport of pig-sticking has been revived in the district of Dacca, and I have been creditably informed that the Commissioner and the Magistrate deprived many of the native shikaris or sportsmen of their guns, on the pretext, indeed, that there was danger of their being used in affrays, but really lest the pigs should be killed, and the sport of the gentlemen thereby interfered with.[1]

Much loss of life is caused by snake-bite, and as no remedy against the poison has yet been discovered, it is probable that the only thing to be done is to endeavour to extirpate snakes. This, however, is obviously a more difficult and expensive work than the extirpation of tigers and crocodiles. Government already has moved in the matter, and a small reward is given in certain places for the killing of the cobra de capello.

Note to General Remarks.

As I have said that Bengal cannot afford to be administered by foreigners, it may perhaps be supposed that I am one of those who advocate the immediate abandonment of India by Great Britain. Such, however, is not the case. I have a great respect for Dr Congreve, and I

[1] A correspondent of the "Times" gravely objected a year or two ago to the destruction of tigers, on the ground that it interfered with sport! This reminds us of Gibbon's note about Commodus and the African lions: "The African lions, when pressed by hunger, infested the open villages and cultivated country; and they infested them with impunity. The royal beast was reserved for the pleasures of the emperor and the capital; and the unfortunate peasant who killed one of them, though in his own defence, incurred a very heavy penalty. This extraordinary *game law* was mitigated by Honorius, and finally repealed by Justinian." Bad as this was, it was less exclusive in its selfishness than the behaviour of some of our modern sportsmen, for the lion-fights gave pleasure to a whole capital.

presume every one must admire a man who has made such sacrifices as he for his convictions, but I think that the time has not yet come for the step he recommends. Granted that we wrongfully got possession of India, still to abandon her now would be to act like a man-stealer who should kidnap a child, and then in a fit of repentance abandon him in a tiger-jungle. I think that we should look forward to the time when India can be left to herself, and that we should hasten its coming by putting the internal administration more and more into the hands of natives. For example, probably nearly all the judicial offices in Bengal might be held by natives. They will work for less pay than Europeans, and their knowledge of the language and customs of the people, and their not requiring long furloughs to Europe in order to recruit their strength, give them an immense advantage over foreigners. I do not overlook the advantages possessed by Europeans, but I think that none of them counterbalances the superiority of the Bengalis in the above-mentioned points.[1]

I would suggest also that no more appointments should be made to the India Civil Service as at present constituted, or at least that the number should be greatly restricted. Those who are already in the service must be provided for in some way or other, but I think that the Government is only making additional embarrassments for itself by bringing more young men into the service. Already some of those admitted complain that they have been enticed by false pretences.

[1] Another advantage which is perhaps of even greater moment, is that by employing natives, Government can get the services of men of mature age. It does not seem fitting that extensive judicial powers should be exercised by persons under twenty-five or thirty years of age.

APPENDIX.

(A.)

I.—FOUR SETTLEMENT REPORTS FROM THE COLLECTOR OF THE DACCA DISTRICT, DATED 6TH APRIL, 5TH AND 26TH MAY 1790, AND 31ST JULY 1792.

To the Honourable CHARLES STUART, President,
and Members of the Board of Revenue,
Fort William.

GENTLEMEN,—I have the honour of your letter of the 18th ultimo, transmitting for my information and guidance a copy of the Resolution of his Lordship in Council respecting the future settlement for Bengal for the period of ten years, and directing that I proceed with all practicable despatch to make the settlement of the district under my charge in the manner and agreeable to the principles therein laid down.

You also enclose for my information extract from your letter to his Lordship in Council, alluded to in the 7th article of the Resolutions, and containing your opinion relative to the amount of the jamma realisable from my district, founded on the information with which you were supplied by my predecessor, Mr Day, in answer to your circular letter of the 10th August 1787, directing me to refer thereto in the formation of the ensuing settlement as far as the suggestion therein contained conform with the Resolution of his Lordship in Council now communicated to me.

You further enclose me copies of your Resolutions, and those of his Lordship in Council, to the Collectors of Bazhai regarding the ganjes, bazárs, and hauts held within them, to which you desire my particular attention, as well as my answer to the several queries therein stated.

You also desire I will notify to the landholders, by publishing the same at the several cutcherries of my district, that the ensuing settlement for ten years, if approved by the Court of Directors, will become permanent, and no alteration take place at the expiration of that period.

I shall, in obedience to your orders, commence on the Ten Years' Settlement with the least possible delay.

As Government's motives for concluding a Makarrar jumma dus salah is to secure to the Honourable Company a certain fixed revenue on fair and equitable rates, and to afford ease and give confidence to the landholders, their under-renters, and ryots, I think it a duty I owe my employers, myself, and the proprietors of the lands, and those under themselves, early to lay before the Board my sentiments on the orders transmitted me.

By the extract of your letter to his Lordship in Council, dated the 14th October 1788, to which the seven articles of his Lordship's Resolution alluded, it should seem that in forming the ensuing settlement I am to be guided in fixing the jumma of each mahal by Mr Day's plan of settlement of 1195, which accompanied his letter of the 17th January 1788.

However unwilling I am to animadvert on Mr Day's proposed plan of a Ten Years' Settlement, yet a regard for my own character, and from a perfect conviction that I cannot conclude the settlement with many of the mahals at the jumma recommended by him, impels me to deliver my sentiments freely on the subject, relying on the Board's candour for putting a favourable construction on the motives by which I am actuated.

It is necessary to observe that Mr Day did not send down his proposed plan of settlement for upwards of six months after this district had been visited by the most dreadful calamity ever remembered by the oldest inhabitant of the district, and which deprived it (by Mr Day's calculation) of upwards of 60,000 of its inhabitants, who either miserably perished, or were reduced to the painful necessity of forsaking their habitations in search of a precarious subsistence. Mr Day visited some of the pargannahs where the famine raged with the greatest violence, and had ocular proofs of the extreme misery to which the wretched inhabitants were reduced. He saw the pargannahs inundated, whole crops destroyed, and cultivation totally neglected. He had the mortification of beholding hundreds of the poor wretched inhabitants daily dying without the means of affording them the smallest relief. After a local investigation of the cruel effects of the inundation, after a full conviction of the very heavy loss many of the principal pargannahs sustained both in its inhabitants and crops, and the consequent decline of cultivation, it is a matter of great surprise that Mr Day should, in many of the pargannahs which had suffered so materially by the inundation and loss of tenants, recommend an increase to be taken in the ensuing year's settlement. That gentleman observes that his plan was founded on the idea of a Ten Years' Bandobast; admitting of this, can it be supposed that districts which had been deprived of one-half of their natural resources, could in the short period of one year so far recover as to yield the customary revenue, much less bear an increase, which would have added to the miseries they had already suffered, and in all probability have obliged the remaining ryots to desert their habitations and seek refuge in more favourable districts?

I shall now proceed to point out to the Board those pargannahs which I am well satisfied cannot bear the jumma of 1194, but where even an abatement on the present year's assessment will be absolutely necessary in some of them.

1194. *Pargannah Rajnagar.—Jumma, Rs.*97,194-15-17-3.

This pargannah Mr Day visited in person, and in his letter to your Board under date the 20th December 1787, reporting on the state of the district and the effects of the inundation, observes that this pargannah presented such a scene of distress as he never before beheld, the land being then totally inundated, the country not showing the least appearance of cultivation, and the inhabitants in general being on raised stages. He at the same time expresses his apprehension that Government was likely to experience a very heavy loss at the close of the year in consequence of the late calamity.

Notwithstanding the wretched state in which Mr Day found this pargannah, yet he recommends in his proposed plan that the settlement be concluded for 1195 on the jumma of 1194.

The Board acquiesce in Mr Day's proposal, and direct him to conclude the settlement accordingly.

The Collector in consequence called upon the proprietors to enter into engagements on the proposed terms, but they positively declined, saying, "to engage at the rate of 1194 for the pargannah of Rajnagar and Kartikpoor would be subjecting themselves to a very considerable loss, from the absolute inability of the lands after the calamity which attended them during the last year."

In consequence of the zemindars declining to lease their lands on the terms of 1194, the Board direct the pargannah to be advertised for farm, and the settlement of 1195 to be tendered to the proprietors at the amount of the highest offer.

The pargannah was accordingly advertised for farm, but no offers being tendered, the Collector on the 4th of September 1788 transmitted the proposals of the zemindars for leasing it on an abatement from the jumma of 1194 of Rs.36,404.

The Board observe in their reply, under date the 23d of September, that "the offer of the proprietors of this mahal being extremely disadvantageous—being a deduction from the jumma of last year of no less a sum than Rs.36,404—we cannot accede to it. We authorise you, however, to make an offer of it to the proprietors at the remission Rs.8934 from the jumma of 1194, that in the event of their not accepting of it, the mahal be held khass."

The proprietors having refused to enter into engagements on the proffered terms, the mahal was held khass; and to show that it was little capable of yielding the jumma of 1194, I must observe that Government sustained a loss of Rs.47,272. This balance even exceeded that incurred in 1194, which amounted to sicca Rs.45,179.

It will probably be remarked that the settlement has not been concluded this year on the jumma of 1194. This I acknowledge, but I must beg leave to observe that an abatement of Rs.8934 was allowed in Bozergomedpore, and a further sum of Rs.13,791 in Kartikpore, both mahals dependent on Rajnagar; but the latter sum cannot be considered as an abatement on the jumma of Rajnagar, for supposing Kartikpore to have been the property of another person, a similar deduction must have been granted in consideration of the dreadful calamity it experienced in 1194. So that, in fact, the abatement allowed last year on account of Rajnagar was the remission of the increase laid on Bozergomedpore in 1194, being, as before stated, Rs.8934; and the late Commissioner's report will show that this abatement was very inadequate to the heavy losses sustained in the pargannah in the two preceding years both in its crops and inhabitants, and nothing but the apprehension which four of the proprietors entertained lest the proposals made to your Board by Kebal Ram, the remaining proprietor, would have been accepted, could have induced them to have entered into engagements on such high terms. They were fearful, in the event of Kebal Ram getting possession of the land, that he would have continued in the entire management and control of the zemindari in the same manner as his brother Gopal Krishna had done, by which means they would have been totally excluded from all participation or concern in the lands.

I have every reason to apprehend that a balance will be incurred at the close of this year of at least Rs.25,000. That the zemindars have collected more than they have paid into the Government treasury is beyond all doubt, but the amount appropriated by them for their maintenance does not amount to 5 per cent. on the jumma of the zemindari. The profits of their private lands, from the best information I have received, do not exceed Rs.15,000, and this profit enjoyed by two of the proprietors only to whom they appertain.

By his Lordship's instructions the zemindars are to enjoy a profit of 10 per cent. from their lands. The proprietors of Rajnagar will cheerfully relinquish their lands on these terms rather than engage on the jumma of 1194. They are men of rank and family, and have long been in the habit of living splendidly; and should they engage on the jumma of last year, the whole of the profits arising from the niz taluks will not be sufficient to answer the dues of Government; and as the proprietors have no other resources than their lands, they must, if deprived of a moderate profit from such land, be reduced to extreme indigence, and would be under the disgraceful necessity of disposing of their lands for a subsistence. For these reasons, and in order to secure a certain revenue to Government, I would recommend that an abatement of Rs.20,000 be allowed in the jumma of Rajnagar for three years, and at the expiration of which the same be resumed on a rusud jumma of three years.

1194. *Pargannah Kartikpúr.—Jumma, Rs.*25,791.

This pargannah forms a part of the zemindari of Rajnagar. Mr Day, in his proposed plans of settlement, recommends that an increase of Rs.4000 be laid on this pargannah, observing that he had no doubt of the ability of the lands to this addition without subjecting the renters to any additional tax above what they have paid for some years back to the zemindars.

Had my predecessor adverted to his letter under date the 20th December 1787, written about a month prior to the transmission of his proposed plan of settlement for 1195, I humbly conceive he would not have recommended the above increase, for in describing the state of the pargannah he makes the following remarks : "This mahal, I am sorry to inform the Board, has suffered in an equal degree with that of Rajnagar, to which it is contiguous, and is under charge of the same sazawal. The balance due from it to the end of Kartik is Rs.11,200, in part of which I much fear very little will be realised, as the only sources left in the pargannah for the liquidation of this, as well as the remaining kists, are the boro crops and the produce of betel-nut, which, from the proportion I am informed they bear of the pargannah resources, will scarcely suffice to pay either one or the other, and a considerable balance is of course to be expected from this mahal at the end of the year."

What Mr Day foretold actually happened, for at the close of the year 1194 a balance of Rs.12,238 was incurred.

Again, Mr Day, in explanation of the balance exhibited in his touzi account for Aghan, transmitted a few days previous to his proposed plan, speaking of the arrears due from Kartikpúr and Rajnagar, expresses his apprehension of realising the same, owing to the unfavourable state of the lands; and that the general failure of the crops, together with the loss the proprietors have experienced by the death and desertion of many of their under-tenants, he much fears will put it totally out of their power to make good their engagements with Government for the current year, a circumstance which nothing but the late unfortunate calamity would have prevented.

Surely after the deplorable state to which this pargannah was reduced by a total loss of its crops, and the depreciation of many of its under-tenants by death and desertion, it could ill bear the increase recommended by Mr Day. A loss of the harvest may be only considered as a temporary evil, but that of the tillers of the ground must be ever looked on as a most serious loss, and nothing can recover a district labouring under such misfortunes but great indulgence and much time.

The Board, in their answer to Mr Day's recommendation, seem to think that the pargannah is not equal to the increase, for they say, "You will call upon the proprietors for the increase you have proposed, or for such as may appear reasonable and can be levied without distressing them, the ryots and under-renters, due consideration having also been had to the late calamities of the season."

The proprietors being called upon to enter into engagements in 1195, so far from consenting to give an increase, they demand a deduction on the jumma of 1194 of Rs.9791, alleging that it was altogether out of their power to subscribe to any other engagement without risking the loss of their lands, a failure on their part being inevitable from the positive want of resources.

Mr Day, in his letter of the 11th July 1788, appears to be convinced that this mahal was not equal to the increase proposed, for, remarking on the balance of 1194 due from Rajnagar and Kartikpúr, he expresses his opinion as follows: "I was an eyewitness of the death of many when in the lands in the month of November last; and further, that many of the poor distressed wretches now daily perishing in the streets of Dacca were in the beginning of the year inhabitants of those mahals, but from the failure of their crops, having no means of support in the country, came to the capital to seek sustenance. Such, therefore, being the state of these lands, nearly depopulated, and the cultivation decreased of course in proportion, I cannot but consider the present heavy balance due from them irrecoverable, but further apprehend a considerable deficiency in the ensuing year's revenue to be unavoidable if an abatement be not made on their respective jummas on renewing the settlement."

Mr Day with great propriety might have added, considering the wretched state of the pargannah and the miserable situation to which the few remaining ryots were reduced, that unless an abatement was allowed for a period of years he saw no prospect of this mahal's recovering the heavy losses it had sustained by the inundation.

Mr Day, on the 15th of the same month, transmits to the Board the proposals of the zemindars of Rajnagar, Kartikpúr, and Bozergomedpúr for farming their mahals in 1195. The former they offered to take on a deduction on the jumma of 1194 of 36,404. On Kartikpúr they demand a deduction of Rs.9991, and on the latter they agree to an increase of 8934. Mr Day, in his letter which accompanied these proposals, begs to call the Board's attention to them, and observes "that the immediate loss arising in the two former is heavy, but, from the present state of the pargannahs, does not think that more with certainty, or without endangering a greater loss hereafter to Government, can be obtained from them than what has been offered."

Time has shown that Government has experienced a greater balance than the abatement required by the zemindars.

The Board in their orders to the Collector, under date 12th September 1788, speaking of Kartikpúr, made the following remark: "Considering the opinion expressed by you in your report of the 17th January, of ability of the lands to bear an increase of Rs.4000 on the jumma of last year, and also your recommendation that this increase should be levied at the ensuing settlement, we are altogether at a loss to account for your having submitted to us without comment proposals from the proprietors at an abatement from the jumma of 1194 of no less a sum than Rs.9991, making in all a difference in the jumma originally recommended by you of 13,791. Whilst we regret so disadvantageous a proposal, we deem it highly necessary, on your part, that you should furnish us with the fullest explanation of a result so widely different from what might have been expected from your own opinion and recommendation."

Mr Day, in answer to the Board's letter, says, "My letter of the 17th July has already pointed out that these lands have suffered afresh in the loss of the boro crop, which misfortune having befallen them subsequent to my report of the 17th January, must have added to the distress of the pargannah and its inhabitants. This, together with the year being so far advanced, no doubt influenced the proprietors in making so low a tender from the original jumma."

I have taken the liberty of submitting the above extracts to the Board to show the impracticability of making the settlement of this mahal upon the terms proposed by Mr Day, and the Commissioner's report, under date 28th October last, will show that Government sustained a loss in 1194 of Rs.12,238, and in 1195 the enormous sum of 16,205-2-12-2.

The Board being satisfied of the inability of this mahal, sanctioned the conclusion of the settlement with the proprietors of the present year on an abatement of the jumma of 1194 of Rs.13,791, and even this exceeded the assets of the pargannah in 1195; and from what I have said I cannot but recommend that the present jumma of 1196 be continued for three years, so that the lands may recover themselves, and that after that period an increase of 5000 be put on this pargannah on a rusud jumma of three years.

1194. *Jalálpúr.—Jumma, Rs.*103,902-12-7-3.

On adverting to Mr Day's proposed plan of settlement for 1195, he recommends that the jumma of this pargannah for 1194 be continued for two years, and that the deduction granted in 1192, amounting to 16,358, be resumed the two following years, half in each, by which the mahals at the expiration of four years will stand rated and yield to Government the jumma of 1188. He further recommends that "the mode of talukdari settlement be continued, or that the mahal be let to farm." Mr Day seems to have forgotten the loss and sufferings this pargannah and its dependencies experienced, and the misery to which the under-tenants were reduced, by the dreadful calamity of 1194, or he would not, I humbly conceive, have recommended the above mode of assessment. His letter of the 20th December 1787 evinces that many of the principal pargannahs dependent on this zemindari were nearly ruined by the inundation. In speaking of the pargannah of Mohabutpúr, Naroollapúr, and two or three others, he observes, "This year the owsh crop in these pargannahs appears to have been nearly wholly destroyed, and that of the aman in a considerable degree prevented. The loss, therefore, which those lands have sustained by the late inundation may be estimated at nearly seven anas proportion of its grain revenue. Notwithstanding this heavy loss, the Arzamin has paid up his revenue in full to the end of Assin; but in doing this there is every reason to believe he is become much in advance for the renters to liquidate his advances, if any such are due, as well as the remainder of the revenue to the end of the year. There is now only left the boro crops and the produce of the betel-nut plantations. From the latter, for the reason assigned in my report for Rajnagar, I fear little is expected."

The Board, relying on the accuracy of Mr Day's statement, authorise the continuation of the assessment of 1194, and direct that the same mode of settlement be adopted. A sazawal was in consequence intrusted with the management for 1195; and the balance incurred that year being 25,999-14-17-3, will show how far Mr Day was warranted in recommending a continuation of the jumma of 1194. The causes of this arrear are fully stated in the late Commissioner's report, transmitted under date the 28th October, to which I must beg leave to refer the Board.

The settlement concluded this year with the proprietors is an abatement of 16,901-12-17-3 on the jumma of 1194, which has been sanctioned by his Lordship in Council. By Mr Day's proposed plan, this abatement must not only be resumed at the ensuing settlement, but an increase of 8175 be added to the jumma.

The settlement of 1197 must therefore stand at 112,081-12-7-3, being an increase upon this year's jumma of Rs.25,080-12-17-3.

To satisfy the Board of the total impracticability of this increase being levied, I must beg to make the following remarks in addition to what I have stated in my report of the balance of 1194 and the assets of 1195.

From 1191 to 1195 this pargannah was held khass, and suffered very considerably in its resources by the loss of the crops and in inhabitants in 1194. Notwithstanding every extortion and oppression of the sazawal, Government sees a balance at the close of the year of 22,638-12-17-3, although it appeared on examining the sazawal's account that this arrear had been realised by him, and which has since been recovered; yet my report will also show that this collection did not arise from the produce of the lands solely, but from a sale of the talukdar's houses, cattle, implements of husbandry, and their private lands. Notwithstanding these violent measures adopted by the sazawal realising the revenue, there still appeared a deficiency at the close of the year of Rs.9956-6-10.

The zemindars, in order to encourage cultivation, and to recover the lands which had become waste by the death and desertion of many of their under-tenants in 1194, were induced to let them out to other talukdars at a reduced rate. Yet notwithstanding the efforts of the zemindars, and the abatement allowed this year by Government, there is every reason to believe that the assets of this district are not equal to the present dues of Government. The Security is greatly in advance to the proprietors, and finding on a scrutiny of the Moffossil resources that they fall short of the saddar jumma, withholds any further assistance, and solicits an examination of the Moffossil receipts; but as he became responsible of his own accord for Government dues, I shall use every exertion to compel him to fulfil his engagements, though I apprehend there will be a balance at the close of the year of Rs.4000 or Rs.5000.

Sensible of the declining state of Jalálpúr proper, Bangrolah, and Mohabutpúr, and confident that this zemindari is not equal to the present jumma, I am induced to recommend that a deduction of Rs.7000 be granted on it at the concluding the settlement for the ensuing year. That this abatement be resumed at the expiration of three years, when the jumma of Rs.1200 will stand at the present year's rate of assessment. This indulgence will not only prove beneficial to Government in securing to them a certain and regular payment of their dues, but will give confidence and encouragement to the talukdars and ryots to exert themselves in the improvement and cultivation of their lands; but, on the other hand, should Government be disinclined to allow of the above abatement, I apprehend a further loss will be experienced, for the under-tenants finding that the demands of Government are heavier than the earnings of their labour will produce, will be compelled to forsake their habitation and retire to some district where they may peaceably enjoy the fruits of their industry.

1194. *Edeelpúr.—Jumma, S. Rs.*95,115.

In Mr Day's proposed plan of settlement for 1195 he observes "that no cause can be traced why the different deductions have been granted, and as Manek Bose has had it in farm and always paid his revenues punctually, I should suppose he would have no objection to enter into engagements as heretofore on an increased jumma. I would therefore recommend that at the ensuing settlement an increase of 4885 be laid on, fixing the jumma at one lac of rupees."

The Board approve of the above-proposed increase, and on account of the notorious bad characters of the zemindars, direct it to be continued in farm. I humbly conceive that the increase proposed by Mr Day was made without due consideration of the loss this pargannah sustained in its crops and inhabitants by the dreadful calamity of 1194. This conjecture is confirmed by Manek Bose's refusing to renew engagements in 1195, unless a considerable abatement was allowed him on the jumma of 1194. In consequence of this refusal the mahal was advertised for farm, but no one offering for the same, it was held khass.

The Board, in their letter of 23d of September 1788, make the following remark: "Your holding this mahal khass being in conformity to our orders, we necessarily approve of it, but cannot help remarking on it as a circumstance somewhat extraordinary, that no proposals should have been tendered for the farm of a pargannah at the jumma of 1194, which you, in your report of the 17th January, deemed capable of paying an increase on that jumma of Rs.4885."

At the close of the Bengal year 1194 a balance was incurred in this pargannah of 25,128-11-15. The farmer pleaded total inability to discharge this, alleging that he sustained a loss equal to that sum. However, on his houses and effects being attached, and himself put under restraint, he, to avoid the disgrace of having his property sold at public auction, discharged the balance by borrowing, and mortgaging his houses; and well knowing the loss the pargannah sustained in its resources in 1194, he prudently refused to renew engagements for 1195 on the terms of the preceding year. The late Commissioner's report on the assets of 1195 will show that the causes of his refusal were but too well founded. It will further show that Government sustained a loss that year of Rs.30,541-7-8.

The zemindars having for a period of years been deprived of the management of their lands, and anxious once more to get possession of them, entered into engagements this year at a jumma exceeding the resources of the Moffossil; security being taken from them for the regular discharge of their dues is the reason that the revenues have to this period been paid up with tolerable punctuality, though the Security has declared to me that he is in advance to the zemindars upwards of Rs.10,000. The proprietors being sensible of their inability to discharge the debt contracted with the Security, and with a view to encourage him to a continuance of his assistance, have given a writing purporting that, in the event of their not being able to liquidate the amount advanced by him on their account, they will sell a portion of their lands to pay the same.

By Mr Day's proposed plan of settlement the jumma of this pargannah must stand rated at the commencement of 1197 at sicca Rs.100,000, which is an increase of the present year's jumma of Rs.19,999, and an excess on the amount paid into Government treasury last year of Rs.35,426-7-4.

The late Commissioner's report will fully show that the pargannah now stands overrated, and consequently altogether unable to bear the excess recommended. Government wish to secure a fair and equitable jumma, and his Lordship in Council's instructions evince equal anxiety to afford the landholders a reasonable profit from the produce of their lands.

Although confident that the assets of the pargannah are not equal to its present jumma, yet from a conviction that the lands are capable of great improvement, I would recommend the present assessment to be continued for the space of three years.

With whom to conclude the settlement is a matter that merits the consideration of Government.

With the proprietors—I fear they will not engage on the jumma of last year; but, in the event of their agreeing, security must be taken from them, or the regular discharge of their dues will be precarious. They are many in number, and in needy circumstances. They are reputed men of very bad character, and have long been under the stigma of entertaining dacoits in their pay. One of them, Ram Kanth, was confined for near six years in the Phouzdari jail of Backergunge, Dacca, and Moorshedábád, for abetting and participating in the robbery and plunder of the Company's factory at Soonargunge.

Should it be farmed, no person, I apprehend, will agree to the terms of last year, and at the same time allow 10 per cent. for a provision to the zemindars.

The present Security, who is well acquainted with the pargannah, a man of responsibility and fair character, having for a series of years had the management of it, has offered to farm it for the term of ten years on the jumma of last year for the first three years, and then offers an increase of Rs.4000 for the remaining seven years, provided he be not obliged to pay the 10 per cent. to the proprietors; that on the event of his being necessitated to pay the 10 per cent., he requests an abatement on the jumma of the current year equal to the sum to be allowed the zemindars; that at the expiration of three years he will give an increase of 4000. Considering the very ruinous state of the pargannah, and the noted bad characters of the proprietors, I cannot but give the preference to farming the mahal; but should his Lordship in Council not approve of this mode, I beg to suggest the expediency of holding the pargannah khass, but in doing this Government must not expect to realise the jumma of the present year, as I have before remarked that the resources of the mahal are not equal to that assessment.

I have been told from respectable authority that the northern parts of the zemindari lost three-fourths of its inhabitants in the dreadful calamity of 1194. Much time, great attention and indulgence, and regular advances of takávi are absolute requisites to restore this pargannah to any degree of cultivation. The loss of inhabitants must almost be considered as irretrievable, and the only mode left of increasing cultivation is by granting pecuniary assistance and giving every encouragement to the remaining husbandmen.

I trust what I have said on the subject of the state and capacity of this mahal will enable your Board to determine on a mode for its future management.

1194. *Chandradeep.—Jumma, Rs.*85,725.

My predecessor, in his proposed plan of settlement for 1195, recommends an increase of sicca Rs.15,000 be laid on this mahal, on the plea that the zemindar enjoys a net profit equal to that sum from the hissajat lands, besides avowed advantages on the gross realisation from the lands on which the present jumma is assessed.

The Board, at the same time they approve of the increase, express their hope that it will not be productive of distress to the zemindar or his family, or to the under-renters or ryots, and in that confidence they direct the Collector to call upon the zemindar to enter to engagements accordingly.

Of the increase recommended, 3000 was secured in 1195, and the additional sum of Rs.1000 laid on at the concluding of the settlement for the current year.

The proprietor of this pargannah is a youth of seventeen years of age, but as no attention has been paid to his education, he remains in total ignorance of the minutiæ of the Moffossil collections. His time is wholly spent in the luxuries of a zenanah, and his mother, wishing to continue in the management of the pargannah, supplies him with the means of gratifying his pleasures. The mother entrusts the executive part of the business to her brother, who is in every respect unfit for and unworthy of the office.

With care and good management an increase might be obtained from this pargannah, and to effect this I would recommend that the present jumma be continued for one year, that the gomastas report its state to me, and that according to such information the settlement be concluded with the zemindar on a fair and equitable jumma for the remaining nine years.

1194. *Narullapúr.—Jumma, Rs.*126,569.

Mr Day in his plan, speaking of this mahal, says, "The opportunity I have lately had of ascertaining with some degree of accuracy the gross amount of the sum annually realised from a part of this pargannah (Hosseenpúr and Hosseenshy) leads me to conclude that the jumma of which the pargannah at large is now rated is by no means equal to its ability, and that the balance remaining of the deduction of 1187 should be resumed at the next settlement. This, however, must depend on the truth and falsity of the pleas urged by the zemindar's agents, who allege that the impoverished state of Pautpossar and other parts of his district renders the excess of jumma, which appears to have been and is now collected from the other two above mentioned, absolutely necessary to enable them to perform their engagements with Government. I would, therefore, recommend that this plea of the bad state of Pautpossar be inquired into previous to concluding any settlement with the zemindars, when, should it appear to be false, the increase before proposed should, in my opinion, be levied, and the pargannah will then stand rated at the jumma of 1179, being Rs.136,687-9-3."

To the above proposal the Board make the following reply: "We direct that you will call upon the zemindars to enter into engagements for Hosseenpúr and Hosseenshy, with the increase proposed by you, and which you inform us you have ascertained their ability to pay; and that you conclude the settlement of these pargannahs accordingly. In respect to the assessment of Pautpossar, we await your report on the result of the investigation now making into the alleged losses in that pargannah, and in other parts of Narullapúr, which we require you will transmit to us with the least possible delay."

The zemindar's naibs being called upon to renew engagements for the pargannahs Hosseenpúr, Hosseenshy, with the increase proposed, observe that they can have no objection to an increase on the above pargannahs; at the same time they hope that equal justice will be done them on the assessment of Pautpossar, &c. &c., in which case they are satisfied and ready to engage, under the consideration that Government shall not insist on the liquidation of the present balance, in which case a renewal of engagements on their part is altogether impossible without the consent of their principal, to whom they shall immediately communicate the orders now received.

The agents' answer being communicated to the Board, they approve of the settlement of Hosseenpúr and Hosseenshy at the increase agreed on, and direct that Pautpossar and the remaining lands be published for farm, and that should the zemindar decline to engage for the highest amount offered, the Collector conclude the settlement with the farmer offering the same, subject, however, in either case to the approbation of the Governor-General in Council, should any remission be necessary from the jumma of last year.

Pautpossar, &c., pargannahs were in consequence advertised for farm; that no tender being made, and the proprietors requiring the enormous abatement on the jumma of 1194 of Rs.41,393-14-15-1, the Board directed, under date the 23d September 1788, these mahals to be held khass.

The balance due to Government from the zemindari at the close of the year 1194 stood at Rs.28,020-10-12. Of this arrear the Board recommend to his Lordship in Council a remission of 20,000, from a conviction of the losses sustained in the pargannah. His Lordship consents to a remission of half the balance, provided the zemindar would agree to discharge the remainder in the course of 1195. This offer the proprietor declined. However, the amount has since been recovered from him, as the Board remark in their letter of the 15th May last that they shall stop the same from his mosharah.

In 1195 Pautpossar, &c., being held khass, Government sustained a balance of 35,782-15-7-2.

The late Commissioner's report will show that these pargannahs suffered very considerably in their funds during the dreadful calamity of 1194, and that the settlement concluded with the proprietor for the current year exceeded the resources of the pargannah in 1195. I cannot, therefore, but earnestly recommend that the present jumma, being 113,001, be continued, and the settlement be concluded with the proprietor for the term of three years, after the expiration of which an increase of Rs.5000 be paid on a rusud jumma of three years.

1194. *Russoolpúr.—Jumma, Rs.*26,749-6-5.

Mr Day, sensible of the inability of the mahal, recommended in his proposed plan of settlement for 1195 that the jumma be fixed at Rs.22,000; but the Board disapproving of the abatement proposed, and the zemindars refusing to renew engagements on the term of 1194, the Collector was directed to advertise the mahal to farm, but no tenders being made, the pargannah was held khass. The balance sustained in 1195 amounted to the enormous sum of 15,817-9-17-2, and in 1194 the proprietors fell in arrears 16,365-5-13-2, the particulars and causes of which are fully stated in the Commissioner's report.

The settlement for the current year was concluded with the proprietors at the jumma of Rs.18,766, and the sole management given to one of the partners with the sanction of the Board; and I have the pleasure to observe that, by the mode adopted, the revenues have been paid with great punctuality. And if I might presume to recommend, I should propose the management be continued with Zey Odeen; and I am urged to this recommendation from the incapacity of one of the partners, and from the known refractory conduct of the other, who is the proprietor of the five and three anas share of Edrokpúr. The Board will see by my touzi account for Phangoon the heavy balance due from these divisions, and the steps I was obliged to adopt in consequence of the contumacious conduct of the zemindar. Zey Odeen is a mild capable man, and I have no doubt if the sole management of this mahal be left with him for ten years, that cultivation will be considerably extended, and Government revenues increased in proportion. If the Board should approve of this mode, I beg to recommend the present assessment be continued for three years, at the expiration of which period an increase of 5000 be taken on a rusud of two years, by which means Government jumma will stand in 1201 at 23,766, which is an excess on Mr Day's assessment of Rs.1766. I think it my duty to observe that the other two proprietors will strenuously oppose Zey Odeen's being vested with the sole management, but whether their objections are to be admitted and Government dues thereby endangered, must be determined by the Board. I shall only add, that in the event of the sole management devolving on Zey Odeen, he should enter into an obligation to divide the profits equally between the other partners, or to allow them their share of the 10 per cent. adjudged to the zemindars as their proportion of the Moffossil funds.

I have now, gentlemen, as my duty required, laid before you the state and ability of the principal mahals under my superintendence. If for the reasons adduced you deem it necessary to conclude the settlements on the terms proposed by me, I request to be furnished with your speedy orders.

I shall do myself the honour of transmitting you my remarks in the course of a few days on such of the petty mahals which in my judgment are not capable of bearing the assessment recommended by Mr Day.

In respect to your queries regarding the hauts and gunges, I shall reply to them with the least possible delay.—I have, &c.,

(Signed) W. DOUGLAS, *Collector.*

DACCA, *6th April* 1790.

To the Honourable CHARLES STUART, President,
and Members of the Board of Revenue,
Fort William.

GENTLEMEN,—I am now to reply to that part of your letter of 18th February which respects the hauts, bazaar, and gunges, and their attachment and separation from the mahal revenue.

As the immediate attachment of the bazaars, &c., would have greatly interrupted the collections of the land revenue, which must have taken place by deputing persons into the Moffossil for that purpose, and from the confusion which such a step would have occasioned, I judged it a matter of expediency to postpone the attachment till the close of the collections, lest the Honourable Company should have sustained a loss in the collections thereby, more especially as the zemindars and renters of every denomination considered themselves as entitled to the profits arising from them, and a depreciation of them would have been held forth as a plea for withholding balances probably to a considerable amount.

I did not fail, however, to institute an inquiry into the several articles of sayer collection, as directed by your Board, and from inquiry I perceive that the sayer collections general are constituted in this district under the name of mahals; for instance, the tax collected from the washerman is called the Gazzer-mahal, that from dried fish the Mehai-mahal; and so of others, the mahal deriving its name generally from the country name of the profession or article each should happen to bear.

Here it is necessary to observe that most of the mahals comprising the sayer are either included in the Shire Chundanah or Shawbunder.

In respect to the advantages or disadvantages to be expected from the continuance or discontinuance of them, I can only give my opinion, and leave the result to you for determination.

As these taxes are all, exclusive of the bazaars, hauts, and gunges, wholly separated and unconnected with the land revenue, the continuance or abolition of them cannot affect any other persons than those immediately employed in their collection or from whom they are levied; and it will rest with Government to give up the profits derived from them by their discontinuance; but in order to form a judgment of the expediency of such measure, a particular account of the mode of collecting and the rate of taxation is necessary.

As far as I have been able to learn, they are in general of the same nature as taxes on the same articles in other countries, and I am inclined to think they are not considered as oppressive even by the natives themselves, excepting a few in this district, which I shall have the pleasure of recommending to the Board to be abolished in the course of making the present year's settlement.

I shall not therefore take on me to recommend their discontinuance, whereby the Honourable Company must sustain considerable loss; while at the same time the benefits arising to individuals would scarcely be a compensation for giving up so much revenue which is necessarily appropriated to the general defence of the State, and of the benefits of which every individual participates. I therefore see no reason why professional men, tradesmen, and artificers of every kind should not contribute their quota to such a useful and necessary purpose, as well as the ryot or husbandman, more specially in times of pressing exigencies.

The mode of collection and rate of taxation is, I perceive, not very well defined, and is in some measure even arbitrary. I should therefore recommend that a moderate and fixed rate of taxation be determined on by the Honourable Board, to become a general and permanent rate, to be adhered to strictly in all instances, and every deviation punished exemplarily; that this rate should be published throughout the pargannahs, and the Collector directed to see it properly executed, which, with a proper situation of the persons employed in the detailed parts, might have a very salutary effect, overrule every objection to the nature of the taxes, and secure ease to the subject, while at the same time it would afford a source of revenue to Government.

In respect to the bazaars, hauts, and gunges, I conceive them to be on a very different footing from the sayer; and here I beg leave to acknowledge the receipt of the Board's letters of the 19th and 26th ultimo. On this subject I have carried the Board's orders into execution in attaching all bazaars, gunges, and hauts, whether situated on rent-free lands of different descriptions or otherwise, and as soon as I receive the Moffossil accounts, I hope to be able to propose from these lights a plan for the future management of them; at present I cannot venture to hazard a conjecture. I beg leave to submit my answers to the several queries put to the Behar Collections:—

Question 1.—Whether in admitting the rights of the zemindars to a property in the soil, they do not consider the gunges and bazaars as much a part of that property as any part of the lands in their possession?

Answer 1.—Admitting the right of the zemindars to a property in the soil, I certainly consider the gunges and bazaars as much a part of that property as any part of the lands in their possession.

Q. 2.—If they do not, to point out the ground of the distinction.

A. 2.—The former being admitted, all argument respecting the second falls to the ground.

Q. 3.—To report whether the zemindars claim the gunges and bazaars as their property, and whether they make any, and what objection to the separation of them.

A. 3.—The zemindars certainly claim the gunges and bazaars as their property, unanimously object to the separation of them, and have delivered in a petition to that effect, which goes enclosed, No. 1, with a translation stating their objections.

Q. 4.—To report if there are not gunges, bazaars, hauts, and sayer in the lands held by the proprietors of altamghas and the tenants of jageers, and whether persons of this description would object to the separation of gunges, &c. &c., and the grounds of such objection.

A. 4.—No doubt but there are many gunges, bazaars, and hauts in the rent-free lands, and the proprietors have the same objection as the zemindars to their separation; they claim them as their right held under certain grants. To show how extremely averse the proprietors of charity lands are to the separation, I must beg to state the remonstrance of a respectable old man who holds Narraingunge.

"I hold Narraingunge in virtue of a sanad granted by the Company for the purpose of defraying the expenses of the takoor, for feeding the poor, and for my own support. To this day the gentlemen have not resumed Debouter, Bormouter, Lackarage, Aymah, Piraun, and Fakiraun lands of ancient establishment, and the proprietors have been suffered to enjoy them unmolested. I have been an old and faithful servant of the Company, and have held Narraingunge these thirty years; and now that I am worn down with years and infirmities, and have no other means of support, I learn that a darogah is appointed to Narraingunge to attach the same. This news have overwhelmed me with grief, and as I am too ill and too weak to wait on you, I have sent my son to you to represent my miserable situation. He will show you my sanad. Let me beseech you to give a favourable ear to his representation; but if you do not, it were better that you take away my life, or expel me from a district where I can no longer remain without incurring shame, trouble, and infinite distress. Hundreds of beggars who are daily fed by me are clamorous for food, and you have not only deprived me of the means of supplying their wants, but shut the door against my performing my religious rites by taking possession of the gunge."

If any partial deviation from a general rule could be departed from, it ought to be done in the instance of this man.

He served the Company from eleven years of age, and held the office of Dewan to the Dacca Commercial Resident for eleven years, the duties of which, I am told, he executed with zeal, integrity, and credit until age and infirmities compelled him to relinquish the station.

There are several petty bazaars in this district, the sole profits of which are employed in defraying the expenses of different musjeds and takoors, and for the performance of religious ceremonies. The proprietors of these have resorted to me in crowds, and are become very clamorous in consequence of the late orders, and declare that attaching their bazaars is not only an infringement of their established rights, but strikes at the fundamental principles of their religion, as they are now deprived of the sole resource by which they were enabled to defray the necessary establishment of officers kept up for the performance of their religious ceremonies; that their houses of worship must now be shut up, and their priests dismissed. They freely say that Government had better deprive them of their existence than prevent the performance of their religious rites.

Your Board must decide how far these representations can be [not legible], they are well founded. I am also satisfied that the revenues to be derived from them will be absorbed in defraying the establishment necessary to be entertained for collecting the same.

His Lordship must determine how far bazaars which come under the above description can in justice or policy be resumed. It is only for me humbly to observe, that by suffering them to continue in the hands of the present proprietors, Government will afford ease, comfort, and relief to many hundreds of the poor inhabitants who are daily supported from the produce of them.

Q. 5.—As far as right of property is concerned, to discriminate between the rights of zemindars and those of jageerdars and altamgadars, in case objections on this ground should arise to the separation of the gunges, &c., from the jurisdiction of the latter.

A. 5.—I conceive there is a wide distinction between the property of the zemindars and altamgadars.

The former is liable to be deprived of his lands in the event of his declining to renew engagements on the terms proposed by Government, and for each deprivation he receives a certain stipend. Whereas the altamgadars hold their lands rent-free, and in perpetuity. The jageerdars, again, hold theirs on a different tenure, for on the death of the proprietor the jageer escheats to Government. Zemindars can have no claim to it, he having received an abatement from his jumma at the time such jageer was granted.

Q. 6.—Whether the abuses now prevailing in the gunges are of such a nature as not to be corrected by rules and limitations without taking them under their own charge?

A. 6.—I apprehend the abuses are of such a nature as cannot be corrected but by taking them immediately in charge for Government. It may then be practicable, by proper rules and limitations, with diligent and active officers.

In recommending for adoption a new system, which is likely to affect every renter in the country, I am aware that much caution, diligent inquiry, and a thorough knowledge of existing evils are necessary, and that great changes should not be hastily adopted; yet, from the nature of the abuses committed, the almost impossibility of detection, particularly in the [not legible] of the country, and the difficulty of obtaining redress and retribution, and from a persuasion the intended change will be attended with very salutary effects, every exertion shall be used on my part to carry his Lordship's orders into immediate and effectual execution, and I shall endeavour to fulfil the wishes of Government with unremitted zeal, activity, and integrity.

I beg to be favoured with your early orders respecting abatement to be granted the zemindars in consideration of their being deprived of the gunge, haut, bazaar collections, as you will perceive by the petition No. 1 that they have refused to renew engagement unless some compensation be made them. I apprehend that any farther delay in concluding settlement will be attended with a serious loss in the present year's revenue, for although I have taken every precaution to prevent anticipation of the revenues, yet the zemindars will endeavour to exceed the same, and clandestinely collect.—I have, &c.

(Signed) W. DOUGLAS, *Collector.*

DACCA, *5th May* 1790.

To the Honourable CHARLES STUART, President,
and Members of the Board of Revenue,
Fort William.

GENTLEMEN,—I have the honour to acknowledge the receipt of your secretary's letter of the 14th instant, enclosing copy of the Resolutions of the Governor-General in Council in the Revenue Department, under date 12th May 1790, revoking the 16th article of the General Regulations for the Bengal Settlement passed in Council on the 10th February last, as far as it regards who are actual proprietors of the lands composing their talooks, with the exception of that part of it which prescribes rules for fixing the amount of the assessment to be imposed upon their talooks, and directing that all talookdars who are proprietors of the soil and who now pay their rents through the mediation of a zemindar be immediately separated from the jurisdiction and authority of such zemindar, and the rents of the latter be adjusted, exclusive of the talooks so separated, and ordering that the settlement be concluded with the talookdars themselves.

As the measure involves a question of considerable magnitude, as far as it applies to the district in my charge, and the persons who are the immediate objects of it, I conceive it becomes a point of duty in me to take this early opportunity of stating to your Board the advantages or disadvantages which are likely to arise from an adoption of it in this district, as far as my local knowledge and the inquiries I have hitherto been able to make extend; and in doing this I rely on the candour of the Board to exempt me from any intentional inclination of opposing measures which may be established for the general benefit of the country. I trust the unremitting zeal and attention I have shown in endeavouring to carry into execution the late orders of Government will secure me from any suspicion, while at the same time a simple statement of facts, though they may operate in some measure against the intended Regulation, becomes in me an indispensable piece of duty, as the ensuing year's revenue may be affected thereby.

The first question that occurs is, What is a talookdar, and what the essentials that constitute him an actual proprietor of the soil?

As I was not satisfactorily informed on this subject, I recurred to the most authentic evidence, written or verbal, within my reach, and I find they are in this district of four kinds, besides a similar description of renter called a howladar, as follows :—

1. *Jungleboory.*—Previous to the division of the country into pargannahs and tappahs, and fixed what is called the tuxeembandy, many persons undertook to cultivate jungle and waste lands, and when the tuxeembandy was made, these new-cultivated lands were constituted talooks, and included in the zummabandy of the nearest zemindar by the Government of that time; and if any increase or remission was granted the zemindar, a proportional part fell to the talookdar. If the zemindar withheld from the talookdar any part of this, he was at liberty to complain to the Government, who compelled the zemindar to allow the talookdar his proportion of the remission. If the talookdar died leaving heirs, they got possession of this land in the same manner as their predecessor, and the zemindar had nothing to do with them, but receive his malgujari agreeably to kistibandi; but if there happened to be no heirs, the zemindar was the manager for the behalf of Government.

2. *Zur Khorid.*—The talookdars under this denomination were at liberty to sell their talooks by bill of sale, with or without the permission of the zemindar; and on failure of heirs the zemindar could take possession, and sell the lands, or keep them, as he might be inclined. These talookdars were subject to increase or entitled to remissions proportionately with the zemindar, agreeably to their respective jumma.

3. *Pattah Talookdar.*—The zemindars and chowdries could grant hereditary talookdary pattahs to any person for lands belonging to themselves, called their neez, whether cultivated or uncultivated, in which pattah it was stipulated that the talookdar should have possession of the whole lands agreed upon, and that the management should descend to his heirs for ever; but this talookdar could neither sell nor make over by deed of gift the lands of his talook, neither could the zemindar dispose of it, but on failure of issue it reverted to the zemindar. Pattah talookdars were subject to increase and remission along with the zemindar.

4. *Ausat Talookdar*, or talookdar within talookdar, is the same in respect to a talookdar that a jer khareed talookdar is to a zemindar.

5. *Howladar.*—In the pargannah of Bickrampore a custom prevails that if any talookdar sell any part of talook to another person, upon receiving the purchase price he calls him a howladar of so much land, who pays his rents to the talookdar; but if any dispute arises between the talookdar and howladar, he can get his howallah separated from this talookdar and included in some other talookdary lands; is subject to increase and decrease of revenue along with the other renters, and the property is hereditary and transferable.

The above is as accurate a definition of the different talookdars of this district as I have been able to procure, and it remains with the Board to decide what description of them, or whether the whole are to be considered as having an actual property in the soil, and to be separated from the zemindars.

The number of talookdars in this district is computed to be upwards of 20,000. Many pargannahs have already a talookdary settlement, the zemindars standing between them and Government in the light of tahsildars.

I am authorised by the Resolutions of the Governor-General in Council to appoint tahsildars in those pargannahs where the talooks are too numerous to receive the revenues immediately from the talookdars. This mode I must consequently adopt in many pargannahs, but in doing this the zemindars will murmur, as long custom and possession have given them a sort of hereditary claim to the management, from which they derive pecuniary advantages, as well as influence and consequence. The new tahsildars, it is true, can for some time to come have no hereditary claim, though there is no doubt but possession may at some future period give them a handle to set up pleas of the same kind. Thus, then, a new set of men will be set up who may claim property to which they have no title, at the expense of those who are already admitted to possess or supposed to have a right in the soil.

In the mahal Katarabu the zemindars have not a foot of ground—all talookdary—yet they claim a right to the lands, and are allowed the usual *russoom.* May we not suppose them to have been originally only talookdars, and from long possession have set up hereditary claim? And may we not also from thence infer that our talookdars may have a sense of their own interests sufficient at least to attempt a similar claim?

I beg to subjoin a list of some of the principal zemindaries of this district, showing the talookdary jumma, the neez jumma of the zemindars, and the number of talookdars in each zemindary:—

	Crown Lands.	Talookdars' Jumma.	Total Jumma.	No. of Talookdars.
Pargannah Jalalpore .	11,000	76,001	87,001	2148
Pargannah Chandradeep	17,000	72,725	89,725	400
Pargannah Bickrampore	2,010	25,642	27,652	268
Pargannah Rajnagar, &c.	92,555	20,118	293,673	400
Tappeh Mysurdee . .	4,000	14,004	18,004	561
Pargannah Essakabad .	1,700	2,000	3,700	200
Tappeh Hydrabad . .	1,237	750	1,985	200

From the above comparative view of the property of the talookdars and zemindars, it appears that the latter possess but little real property of their own, and that a separation of the talookdars would reduce many of them from affluent circumstances to a state of indigence, and the titles of Rajah and Zemindars, which they are allowed to enjoy, will become a mere empty name.

To ascertain the rights and tenures of such a number of talookdars as 20,000 must take up a great deal of time, and cannot be accomplished in less than two or three years; and sensible that the revenues of the current year must sustain considerable loss by any further delay in concluding the settlement, and anxious to prevent anticipation of collections which unavoidably must happen by any longer procrastination, notwithstanding every precaution has been taken on my part to prevent it, I cannot but earnestly recommend that engagements be entered into immediately with the zemindars as heretofore, with a notification of their agreeing to the separation of the talookdars whenever Government shall think proper to do so, and that the separation from their authority be gradually effected.

There can be no inconvenience in adopting this mode, as the zemindars are obliged to state the sudder jumma levied from every talook, mouza, and village under their authority, and grant pattahs to the talookdars, by which means illegal exactions will be prevented, and the talookdar will have it in his option to continue under the authority of the zemindars, or pay his revenues directly to the Collector. It is a matter of doubt with me whether, by emancipating the talookdars from the present authority and jurisdiction of the zemindars, it will free them from the exactions they have hitherto been subjected to, as, considering the number of them, the agency of tahsildars will be necessary, it being impossible for a Collector to treat directly with 20,000 or 30,000 different renters, more especially when his time is fully occupied in new and other important regulations, and I am not sure the management of a tahsildar is preferable to that of a zemindar; for my own part I should give the latter the preference, because a zemindar may entertain hopes of the management being continued to him from good behaviour, but a tahsildar has no right to entertain any such idea, and he will, looking to the present moment only, endeavour to enrich himself at the expense of those who are placed under his authority, unless indeed Government choose to confirm him in his office, for a space of time. There is another inconvenience attending the collection of a tahsildar in this district, which I believe does not exist in any other to so great a degree—namely, the dispersed situation of the lands. The lands of a talook are not one continued spot of ground, but extend through many pargannahs and detached in small and separate parts, and nothing but an actual measurement of the whole district can ascertain to whom the property belongs.

The zemindars, feeling their interests affected by the new regulations, will endeavour to conceal, combine with, and connive at the concealment of others; hence a defalcation of revenues, endless disputes, and consequent investigations attended with expense, will be the consequence, and I am convinced nothing but an actual measurement of the whole district can render the regulation of Government so effective as they could wish. Experience proved the collections of a native collector to be defective, and this induced the sovereigns of this country in former times to grant lands upon lease to the inferior renters under the most respectable of that class of people now denominated zemindars, for management and collection, finding the inferior landholders too numerous and too distant for receiving their collections at the sudder, and the collections of a tahsildar too defective to adopt the system universally. The zemindars also had the privilege of administering justice in their respective jurisdictions, acting something like justices of the peace in our own country, settling trifling disputes, and rendering easy and speedy redress to the injured party, which would have been rendered very difficult indeed if a poor man has a travel to the Huzzoor and prefer his complaint through a regiment of corrupt mutsuddees, every one of whom must have been bribed before he could obtain what a respectable zemindar could have granted him on the spot in a day's attendance.

The powers with which the zemindar was invested, I believe to have given rise to the present claims of the zemindars to the right of having the talookdars under their authority, and they are certainly not entitled to complain, if upon proof of ill-treatment or exactions, they should be separated from them; but it is, I think, doubtful whether the appointment of tahsildars is calculated to remedy the evil, while at the same time it affords, as I mentioned before, a handle to the zemindars to combine with one another, and with talookdars, to conceal lands and defraud Government of its just dues.

I shall conclude with observing that the talookdars whose distance from the sudder cutchery is considerable, and whose revenues do not exceed two, four, or six rupees per annum (and there are many such in this district), will find much inconvenience and loss of time in travelling to Dacca with their monthly instalments of two, four, and six anas, and the possibility of entertaining vakeels is out of the question from the amount. The jurisdiction of a tahsildar must extend through several pargannahs, and include these distant petty talookdars, and his authority over them must be very inefficient from their separate and dispersed situation, and hence an opportunity will be afforded for collusion.

W. DOUGLAS.

DACCA, *the 26th May* 1790.

To WILLIAM COWPER, Esq., President, and
Members of the Board of Revenue,
Fort William.

GENTLEMEN,—I have now the honour to transmit to you the proposed Novennial Settlement of this district, commencing with the Bengali year 1198 and ending with 1206, for your information and orders.

As in my letter of the 8th August last I expressed my hopes that the increase to be obtained by separating the talukdars would equal the expense of the tahsildari establishment required for this district, but as my expectations have not been realised it becomes necessary to explain to you the causes which have occurred to frustrate my hopes at the time I addressed your Board, transmitting for approval my tahsildari establishment. I conceived that the talukdars of the following mahals would be entitled to separation—viz., Selímábád, Chandradeep, &c., Nazirpore, Sultanábád, and Aurangpore—but upon investigating into their right to that indulgence, I find but few who are entitled to separation, the major part of them holding their lands on similar tenures with the jungleboory talukdars of Bozergomedpúr, who are considered as leaseholders, and therefore continue subject to the authority of the zemindars. Had the talukdars of the pargannahs above mentioned been separated, I am confident that my expectations for increase would have been secured.

Your Board will perceive in my account settlement that the lands of sundry talukdars who have been separated from different pargannahs remain khas. This has arisen either from the non-attendance of some, the death of others, or because their jama has not been finally adjusted, owing to the difference between the jama stated in the accounts delivered in by the zemindars and the account declared by the talukdars to have been annually paid by them. However, in my detailed account settlement, which I shall hereafter have the honour of laying before you, I hope to show that all taluks now held khas are either intrusted with their respective proprietors or farmed out, and in settling their jama I trust to secure some additional increase to Government.

The zemindary mahals which still continue khas I shall have the honour to report upon in the course of a few days.

Your Board may probably observe that a small increase has been obtained from the lands of the zemindars. To this I reply, that could any excess have been obtained from them without endangering the future prosperity of the district it should have been effected; but many of the pargannahs have not yet recovered the losses they suffered in the direful era of 1194 by a deprivation of many thousands of ryots, who either died or emigrated in that year. The Rajnagar zemindary is a melancholy instance of the truth of this assertion. This mahal was under the immediate superintendence of Mr Thompson for two years, and notwithstanding every attention was bestowed, and every encouragement given, yet he found it impracticable to secure the former jama. In 1196 it was found necessary to allow a deduction of 22,725. In 1198 a further abatement of Rs.20,000 was granted, and in concluding the eight years' settlement the further sum of Rs.6447-7-2-2 has been allowed, notwithstanding the sum of Rs.15,860 was added to the zemindary by a resumption of the profits of Pitambar Sen's neez taluks. Consequently if that sum had not been annexed to the jama of the zemindary, a deduction equal to its amount must have been allowed. It should therefore appear that in the short space of four years this pargannah has declined in its assets in the enormous sum of Rs.65,032-7-2-2.

Great difficulty was experienced by the tahsildars in realising the revenues from the talukdars, owing to the scattered situation of the lands composing the pargannahs under my superintendence. To remove this inconvenience, and to afford ease and relief to the separated talukdars, I propose, with your sanction, to divide the district into eight compact zillahs, and to place the same under eight tahsildars. Should your Board approve of this measure, I will do myself the pleasure of submitting to you the establishment necessary for carrying this plan into execution, the adopting of which will be affording great relief to petty talukdars, many of whom have to travel two days' journey to pay monthly the trifling sum of Rs.2 or 3, and Government revenues will be realised with greater ease and punctuality.—I have, &c.

(Signed) W. DOUGLAS, *Collector.*

DACCA, *the* 31*st July* 1792.

II.—LETTER OF MR MASSIE TO THE BOARD OF REVENUE ABOUT THE PERMANENT SETTLEMENT, DATED 24TH MARCH 1801.

GENTLEMEN,—It appearing to me, that in consequence of the *Malguzari* lands having been declared by the existing regulations responsible for such arrears as might become due to Government therefrom, sufficient regard was not paid in this district at the conclusion of the Decennial Settlement to the ascertaining and recording the names of the actual proprietors of such lands for the time being; in consequence of which the Government not unfrequently suffers losses in its revenues in cases where the proceeds of sales of certain lands are not sufficient to answer the balances due from such lands, as it cannot be ascertained what other lands the defaulting proprietors are possessed of; and individuals are often unable to recover the amount of their just demands by a sale of lands after decisions have been passed in their favour by the courts of justice; and it also appearing to me that if some easy and effectual mode of ascertaining and recording the names of the actual proprietors of lands could be adopted, it would be attended with the most beneficial effects as well to Government as to individuals, I therefore beg leave to trouble your Board with a few remarks on this subject for your consideration.

2d. Your Board will be pleased to observe that a practice has prevailed in this district from time immemorial, and still prevails, of conducting all the affairs of an estate from generation to generation in the name of the original proprietor of such estate or some fictitious name formed by him, under which cloak the actual proprietors for the time being are kept concealed, and what the consequences of such concealment are I have stated above. But before I proceed further, I deem it necessary to lay before your Board the following extract from the proceedings held in this office at the time of the conclusion of the Novennial Settlement, my remarks on which will, I trust, satisfy your Board that what I have already advanced is not incorrect, nor the evil complained of imaginary.

Dacca Jalálpúr, Revenue Cutchery, *the 20th May* 1791.

This being the day fixed on for commencing the settlement for nine years, in obedience to the orders of the Board under date the 29th of December 1790, and several taluqdars and zamindars being in attendance in consequence of the advertisement published in The Collector commences the settlement accordingly.

*Taluq Hujuri, Mirza Jehan.—J. Rs.*630-8.

Ram Sankar, gomasta, being in attendance, gives in proposals for the ensuing settlement. He is informed that as the settlement is to be made for nine years, he must give an increase so as to make the jama equal to Rs.701. He acquiesces. Resolved the terms be accepted.

*Taluq Hujuri, Sib Ram Mullick.—J. Rs.*23.

Dip Chand, proprietor, enters into engagements for this mahal upon an increase of Rs.2, making the aggregate Rs.25. Accepted.

*Taluq Hujuri, Sib Ram Kalsi.—J. Rs.*6.

The proprietor delivers in proposals with an increase of Rs.1, making the jama 7. Accepted.

*Taluq do. (i.e., Hujuri), Ram Sankar Sein.—J. Rs.*98.

Kowala Kanth, gomasta, being in attendance, delivers in proposals with an increase of Rs.2, making the jama Rs.100. Accepted.

*Taluq Putchkowl.—J. Rs.*107-6.

Ram Nar Singh, gomasta, being in attendance. This man declines entering into engagements on the terms of last year. The Board to be addressed. Ordered the settlement be postponed for the present. The zamindar having acceded to the terms of last year, it becomes unnecessary to address the Board.

*Taluq Hujuri, Birju Sundar.—J. Rs.*294-9-4-3.

Ram Sankar, gomasta, being in attendance, gives in proposals with an increase of Rs.3-6-15-1, making the jama Rs.298. The vakil represents that his constituent holds a taluq under taluq Baidinath, which he requests may be separated and annexed to his own.

Accepted for this taluq, and that the Board be addressed on the subject of the latter requisition.

The proprietor of Baidinath being in attendance, is asked whether he has any valid objections to make to the separation thereof. He replies that he has none ; but he observes, that as some of the taluqs under him are ruined, that the profitable taluqs, among which is this one, belonging to the taluqdar who wishes to be separated, used formerly to make good the loss he sustained upon the others, consequently if he is separated, an adequate abatement must be allowed him.

*Taluq Hujuri, Abul Moolah.—J. Rs.*125.

Kishen Mohan, gomasta, declines entering into engagements on the terms of last year, though a deduction has been allowed them last year, alleging that his taluq is overrun with jungle and the lands unfit for cultivation.

Ordered. The Board be advised. Unnecessary, the zamindar having agreed to the terms of last year.

*Taluq Sha Khalil.—J. Rs.*178.

This taluq stands rated in 1194 at Rs.138. An increase was obtained in 1195 of Rs.40. On a reference to Mr Day's plan, the jama of 1169 is recommended as the standard for the conclusion of the settlement, which the Board approve of. It appears, therefore, that the present jama is deficient in Rs.102-1-17-2. The vakil therefore is desired to enter into engagements with that increase. He declines, there not being assets. (The zamindar's terms were afterwards acceded to.)

*Taluq Chand Ram Pabaz.—J. Rs.*45-7-10.

Byjunnath, gomasta, delivers in proposals, with an increase of Rs.4-8-10, making the jama Rs.50. Accepted.

3d. The foregoing extract, your Board will be pleased to observe, contains one day's proceedings, in which only the name of one proprietor is mentioned as being in attendance, and even he in the previous counterpart proceedings is stated to be a gomasta.

Mr Massie then gives specimens of some of the *tahuts*, thus: "Mirza Jehan, signed by Mirza Jan, by the pen of Ramraman Naib, gomasta. Taluq Ram Sankar Sein, by the pen of Kamla Kanth Sarma," &c. &c., and adds, "From these signatures, any person unacquainted with the practice that has hitherto prevailed in this district, would of course suppose that all the persons named as the proprietors thereby, were in existence at the time of the conclusion of the Novennial Settlement, and that the several gomastas named were appointed by them to enter into engagements on their parts, but I must observe that it would appear there were then no such persons as Mirza Jan, Ram Sankar Sein, Abul Moolah, Sha Khalil."

He adds, "With regard to the settlement of the separated taluqs, from the immensity of their number, the proceedings appear to have been still more summary, and the difficulty of finding out the proprietors consequently increased, as your Board will perceive from the following extract."

He then gives an extract in which fifteen taluqs are put down without any proprietor being named, the note appended being merely that Ram Kanth, gomasta, enters into engagement on the Mofussil jama.

III.—BÁKARGANJ IN 1801, BEING A LETTER FROM MR WINTLE, DATED 7TH JANUARY 1802.

In obedience to the orders of Government of the 29th October last, I have now the honour to forward my reply to the interrogatories therewith transmitted. I fear it may not be thought so full and particular in some points as perhaps is expected, and I am sensible that it does not contain all that might be said on several questions; but as an apology for its defects, I take the liberty to state that I have had but little time since I was nominated to this district to turn my mind to the framing of Regulations, as my attention has been fully occupied by official (and in some measure extra) business ever since my first arrival in the zillah. When I took charge of the office, I found an immense accumulation of *fouzdarry* business, occasioned by my predecessor's sending out a *girdwar* who apprehended upwards of 350 persons, whose examinations occupied both the acting register's and my own time most fully for several months. Before this was finished, an order was passed for the removal of the sudder station to Burrishol, the carrying which into effect, by clearing away jungles, erecting jails, buildings, &c., and laying out a new town, has taken up all the time and attention I could spare from official avocations to this moment, so that though I have had every inclination to take minutes and propose amendments where I found the Regulations deficient, I really have been unable to find time. . . . I however hope that the reply, though deficient in some points from being written amongst sundry busy employments of surveyor, architect, &c., in addition to my judicial avocations, may not be deemed totally useless; and that your Lordship will believe my greatest wish is to give satisfaction to, and obtain the approbation of Government, by a faithful and diligent discharge of my public duty.

(Signed) J. WINTLE, *Judge and Magistrate.*

ZILLAH BACKERGUNGE, *7th January* 1802.

Question 1.

The number of causes depending on the 31st December 1801 was as follows, viz. :—

Before the Judge	117
Before the Register	315
Before the Native Commissioners	1274
Total	1706

Question 2.

The Civil Courts of this zillah were not established until April 1797. The number of causes depending at the end of each year is inserted underneath, which will show the proportion those now depending bear to former years, viz. :—

	1797. On the 31st December.	1798. On the 31st December.	1799. On the 31st December.	1800. On the 31st December.	1801. On the 31st December.
Before the Judge . .	276	269	220	384	117
Before the Register . .	260	290	121	40	315
Before the Native Commissioners . .	133	160	759	2461	1274
Total of each year . .	669	719	1100	2885	1706

Question 3.

The number of causes decided in the past year (1801) is inserted below, but they fall short of what may be decided when the Judge holds regular courts. The Judge's Court was not opened till my arrival on the 25th February, as I was not allowed to leave my former station for some months after my appointment to this zillah. From May to September inclusive four court days also in each month were lost by my being obliged to come once a week to Burrishol to look after the works carrying on at the new station. The Judge's Court was, besides, shut during the months of November and December, on account of the removal of the station, to enable the omlahs, vakeels, and pleaders to erect habitations at the new Residence, and to give time for removing the prisoners, cutcheries, &c. The number of causes decided was as follows ; in which statement I have thought it proper, for the information of Government, to insert causes disposed of by nonsuit, &c., and other business that is not brought on the regular file, viz. :—

Tried by the Judge.

In appeals from the decision of the Register .	49	
In appeals from the decision of the Native Commissioners	3	
	—	52
Decreed on trial	46	
Dismissed on nonsuit	80	
Adjusted by Razeenomah . . .	10	
	—	136
Total		188

By the Register.

Decreed on trial	187	
Dismissed on nonsuit	146	
Adjusted by Razeenomah . . .	38	
Total		371

By the Native Commissioners.

Decreed on trial	63
Dismissed on nonsuit	2467
Adjusted by Razeenomah . . .	1204
Total . . .	3734

Remarks.—Besides the above, 338 summary causes, according to the 7th Regulation of 1799, 49th Regulation of 1795, and 6th Regulation of 1800, were decided by the Judge. *N.B.*—The number of Commissioners were not complete previous to my taking charge.

Question 4.

The number of causes that must necessarily be depending cannot be stated with any certainty, because, though a pretty exact calculation may be made of the number that ought to be decided, the question must in a great measure rest on the number of suits instituted annually, which may vary exceedingly. This court having been established but a few years, the number of causes filed has annually increased, particularly in the past year, and may still increase. But as it is necessary to have some criterion to form an opinion upon, I think the past year's file (or 1801) the properest to go by. Agreeable to that, I conceive that, supposing the three tribunals to be regular and attentive in the discharge of their duty, there must yet necessarily be about the under-mentioned number of causes always in arrear, or nearly six months' business—that is to say, that a suitor may obtain a decision in six months from the period of instituting his suit, viz. :—

Before the Judge	60
Before the Register	310
Before the Native Commissioners . . .	900

The various official business the Judge has to perform prevents his giving his attention solely to the decision of regular suits. The reason of the number of causes now depending not being reduced so low as they might have been is principally to be ascribed to the causes mentioned in the answer to the 3d question, which, however, were temporary, and not likely to operate hereafter.

Question 7.

Litigation has certainly been checked by the establishment of the fees and stamp duties mentioned in this question, as far as respects frivolous and unfounded suits, but not in regard to real causes of action, which are as much sued for as ever. I do not think the several charges attending the institution of lawsuits too considerable, as far as relates to suits for large demands; but they appear in many instances to be too heavy on suits for small demands, as will appear by the following statement on a demand for two rupees, which would be much more were the suit for landed property. This the plaintiff has to pay to Government alone, exclusive of the expense of serving the processes before his cause comes to be tried, though, it is true, that eventually the defendant will have to pay it in addition to his own expenses, viz. :—

Stamp paper for plaint	0	4
Fees for filing ditto	0	2
Stamp paper for security for vakeel's fees .	0	4
Fees for filing ditto	0	8
Stamp paper for security to make good expenses of suit	0	4
Fees for filing ditto	0	8
Fees for issuing a summons'	0	8
Stamp paper for a copy of defendant's answers .	0	4
Stamp paper for a copy of rejoinder . .	0	4
Stamp paper for vakalant namah . .	0	4
Fees for filing ditto	0	8
Stamp paper for petition for issuing subpœnas .	0	4
Fees for filing ditto	0	8
Fees for three witnesses	1	8
Issuing subpœna	0	8
Two vouchers (only)	1	0
Total . . . Sicca Rs.	7	6

To suggest the means by which the expense might be lessened to the individual, without subjecting Government to much loss of revenue, requires some consideration and more time to arrange than the various duties I have at present on my hands will allow. Hereafter, when I have more leisure, I shall offer such suggestions on this point to Government as may appear to me deserving of its notice.

Question 10.

The vakeels in general, I believe, discharge their duty to their clients with as much honour and fidelity as a native usually possesses. I have never met with a native, high or low, who possessed much of the first quality, and their portion of the latter is but small, as far as seventeen years' intercourse with them enables me to judge.

Question 14.

There are several private schools in this zillah, where the Hindu law is taught, but no Mahomedan. The Brahmins, who are at the head of them, either have rent-free lands, or subsist by the bounty of their students. Some of them also receive presents for performing marriage and religious ceremonies.

Question 15.

The general moral character of the inhabitants of this district (if I may be allowed to use the expression) is at the lowest pitch of infamy; and very few exceptions, indeed, to this character are to be found. There is no species of fraud or villany the higher classes will not be guilty of, and to these crimes in the lower classes may be added murder, robbery, theft, wounding, &c., on the slightest occasion. In fact it is hardly going too far in asserting that the whole of the inhabitants of this district are dacoits ; for the lower classes in general must in a great measure support themselves in that manner, as few of them really work at trades, or cultivate sufficient lands for their maintenance; and the zemindars and talookdars, with very few exceptions, undoubtedly entertain and protect dacoits secretly, who are the principal actors in all affrays between the former respecting disputed lands, boundaries, &c. I fear the system of law established by the British Government has not had much effect in improving their moral character. Fear is the only passion that can operate to any purpose with the natives of this part of the country; they may be restrained from committing crimes from the dread of punishment, but I apprehend that no precept or example will ever induce them to be in love with virtue or honesty, from their purity only. Strict justice and rigorous laws can alone keep them in order.

Question 16.

The inhabitants undoubtedly consider their private rights and property to be far better secured by the present constitution of the country than ever they were under the Mogul Government, and that they are not liable to infringement by the executive authority itself, by the executive officers of Government, or by individuals.

Question 17.

The cultivation and population of this district are in a state of improvement; but from all I can learn from the natives, commerce has declined, the principal articles of which formerly consisted of salt and cloth; but since the Honourable Company has monopolised the first, and made advances for the second, many individuals have given over their dealings. Religious buildings are less frequently erected; and for domestic purposes, little or no improvement seems to have been made in those constructions. The natives are enemies to innovation, even in the form of their houses, and are too indolent to imitate neatness or taste. The grand cause of the decline of commerce and religious buildings seems, however, to arise from what in other countries forms not only the strength, but tends to the riches and prosperity of the State—increase of population. In this, it only operates to its impoverishment, if the opinions of the natives themselves have any force; for they say that when the population was less, their ancestors were rich, and had a capital which could be spared for the purposes of commerce and the erection of religious edifices; but as their descendants have multiplied so much of late years, such sums, divided and subdivided amongst them, gives to each but a small pittance, and has destroyed all the great fortunes. From my own observation and intercourse with the natives, I believe there is some truth in this reasoning; and unless a spirit of enterprise and honest activity can be infused into the natives at large, I see no means of their becoming either richer or happier. The lower classes of natives in this district are too indolent to try to better their situations by labour and exertion, though there is no doubt that the lot of the ryot, labourer, and mechanic has considerably improved under the English Government. My opinion respecting the population and cultivation of the district is founded upon inquiries from the natives and my own observation.

Question 18.

I believe the inhabitants of this district are perfectly satisfied with the British Government, and that they are fully aware of the great freedom they enjoy under it, beyond what they could ever taste under either the Mogul or Hindu administrations.

Question 19.

The present system of police is in general well calculated to ensure the apprehension of offenders, and only requires some additional rules, which are proposed in the answer to question 33.

Question 20.

The police establishments of this district are not adequate to the duties required of them, there not being a sufficient number of thannahs at present to admit of their being placed at ten *coss* from each other, agreeable to the 4th section, 2d Regulation of 1793, some of them being a much greater distance asunder. They appear also to have been in the first instance injudiciously placed, and not so disposed as to afford security to the district, equal to what the actual number of stations should do. Three or four more thannahs will be necessary, which I shall propose to Government as soon as I have leisure to prepare a new arrangement of the stations.

Question 21.

I am of opinion that the number of crimes committed annually has diminished in the past year, in comparison to what I understand were formerly committed; but as there does not appear to have been any regular account kept previous to my appointment to this zillah of the crimes committed within the jurisdiction of each darogah, it is not an easy matter to assert positively whether they have annually diminished since the year 1793 or not, the Adawlut Calendar not being a sufficient criterion to judge by (particularly the past years, which includes many crimes committed in former years), for many crimes were formerly, and are still sometimes committed, where the perpetrators escape being apprehended or discovered. I however keep a regular account of all crimes that come to my knowledge of the darogah's, whether the parties are taken or not. An account of the number of trials in each year since 1797, agreeable to the Calendar, is inserted below. No calendars prior to that year are to be found in the office. The second sessions of the last year not being concluded, the first sessions only is inserted, viz. :—

Crimes.	1797.	1798.	1799.	1800.	1801. 1st Sessions.
Murder	2	19	22	22	21
Dacoity	11	15	17	19	39
Dacoity and murder	1	7	9	8	5
Theft	2	13	8	5	4
Receiving stolen goods	...	1	1	1	...
Bribery	1	1	...	1	3
Perjury	2	1	8	...	12
Forgery	...	1	...	...	1
Wounding	1	1	2	1	6
Resistance to Court's authority .	...	...	...	...	4
Total	20	59	67	57	95

Question 22.

The crimes of enormity most prevalent in this district are murder; dacoity, with murder; dacoity, with wounding with spears, &c.; dacoity simple; dacoity, and burning with lighted *masáls;* dacoity, with putting bamboos to the back and chest of a person, and drawing them close with twisted strings, in the manner of a vice, until he is breathless, and sometimes the breastbone or ribs are broken; dacoity, with putting chilli powder (cayenne pepper) into the eyes, mouth, nose, and ears,—all these for the purpose of extorting confessions where the sufferers' effects are kept or hid, and which are usually inflicted by dacoits at the time of committing robberies; violent wounding with *daos*, &c.; affrays and assaults.

The cause of the prevalence of the first is that the inhabitants of this zillah in general are of the lowest class, and both the men and women are extremely passionate in their dispositions, and loose and profligate in their manners. Infidelity on the part of the women, and jealousy on the side of the men, most frequently are the occasion of murders, but sometimes a dispute about a kid or a *hooka* is sufficient for that purpose. Passion also often leads to the commission of self-murder, which is more frequent in this zillah than in any part of the country I have resided.

Dacoity (which often includes many crimes) arises from two causes—viz., 1st, That dacoits consider themselves as much a distinct caste or profession as any other caste; and it is very common for several generations to be dacoits. I have heard of an instance of a dacoit recommending to his son at the foot of the gallows to continue the profession, notwithstanding his own ill-fate. 2d, That the idle and ill-disposed begin first with pilfering, &c., and gradually advance from one enormity to another.

Question 23.

The generality of the inhabitants of this district do not keep arms in their houses. Such respectable persons as keep arms have these for defence against dacoits. The latter have the largest quantity of arms. They consist of *talwars*, spears, bows and arrows, *raibánses* (a long iron, somewhat like a spit, fixed at the end of a bamboo), *khangauns* (a long talwar), bludgeons.

Question 24.

There are the ruins of three old mud forts—two at Sujábád, pargana Chandradwip, and one at Sangrám, pargana Uttar Shahbázpúr—which were formerly built as a defence against the incursions of the Mugs. Some old cannon, it is said, are there remaining, but I have not had time to visit these places.

[Question 25 was about the population. Mr Wintle was not able to answer it, but thought that the proportion of the Hindus to the Mahomedans was 10 to 6.]

Question 26.

There is no person of rank except Rajah Jai Narain, *alias* Durga Koer Narain Rai, late zamindar of Chandradwip. The names of the most respectable persons are inserted underneath, but none of these have more than twenty-five or thirty followers. They never appear to go abroad with more than three or four barkandazes, armed with talwars and shields, and four or five peons.

1. Mir Hoosein Uddin Chaudhari, zamindar of tappa Nazirpúr.
2. Sib Narain Rai Chaudhari, zamindar of Selímábád.
3. Mir Asad Ali Chaudhari, zamindar of Shaistábád.

Ram Dulab Chakrabarti,
Bhowani Prasad Chakrabarti, } taluqdars, Chandradwip.

Kirti Chandra Rai, taluqdar, Ratandi Kalikapúr.

Sib Chandra Rai and Kirti Chandra Rai, taluqdars, pargana Arangpúr.

Khaja Mahomed Dyom and Khaja Chand, taluqdars, taluq Salkneenah.

Bhowani Prasad Rai, merchant at Sutaluri.

Question 29.

There are few or no roads besides those I am now making at Barisál, except an indifferent one at Bákarganj, about four miles long.

Question 30.

The convicts are employed from sunrise to sunset (two hours at noon for eating excepted) in making roads, clearing jungle, digging tanks, and raising the ground about the new station.

[In reply to question 32, Mr Wintle says that he does not think commissions should be issued to zamindars and others to act as justices of the peace, &c.; and in reply to question 33 he makes many suggestions about the appointment, &c., of village chaukidars.]

Question 34.

The tax on spirituous liquors has certainly rendered drunkenness less prevalent. [Still Mr Wintle thinks drinking has become more general within the last few years.]

Question 38.

[Mr Wintle thinks that dacoits and thieves have increased since the abolition of the Mahomedan punishment of amputation.[1]]

[1] This report is in a printed volume in the India Office Library. Mr Wintle was probably a better magistrate than he was a writer. His report is full of tautology; but if he had anything to do with the choosing of Barisál as a site, and if, as appears, he laid out the town, he must have been a shrewd executive officer.

The same volume contains reports from the Collectors, but Mr Massie's does not contain anything of special interest. He states that in 1792 Mr Douglas made an estimate of the population of the Dacca District (which then included Bákarganj and Faridpúr), and that it came to 938,712.

Mr Wintle does not state the population, but it appears from Mr Adam's Report on Education in Bengal that it was afterwards furnished, for he states the population of Bákarganj in 1801 to have been 926,723, and that Hindus were to Mahomedans in the proportion of 5 to 3.

The fort of Sangrám referred to in answer 24 has now disappeared, but the name is still known in the Mendiganj thana (see note, p. 43). From answer No. 2 it appears that Mr Wintle did not know of the Civil Court's having existed in 1782 (see p. 311).

(B.)

ÁKTRACT FROM MR PELLEW'S ARTICLE ON THE PHYSICAL CHARACTERISTICS OF BÁKARGANJ.

THE district of Backergunge is situated wholly within the lower Delta of the Ganges—that is to say, in that part of the Delta where the beds of the watercourses are all below the level of the sea at high tide. All of these are in consequence subject to tidal influence, and although during the height of the rains the water does not turn in the principal channels, but flows constantly towards the sea, it rises and falls as considerably as in the dry season. Owing to the incessant motion of the water at a considerable velocity, all the channels (which are innumerable) are kept open and navigable for boats proportioned to their size, and there is probably no part of India where such perfect access by water to every part of the district can be obtained. The district is, in fact, covered with a network of khâls most intricate in their windings and intercommunications, and apparently without any order or regularity. But although in a district so essentially flat, an organised system of natural drainage would scarcely be looked for, we find that in fact the whole district, except where the great Megna and Aryal Khan river have obliterated the old features of the country by recent deposits over its northern and eastern portions, may be divided into distinct drainage districts, each of them containing corresponding features.

In undulating tracts of country the drainage ordinarily radiates from elevated centres towards the circumjacent coast-line. In alluvial formations, on the contrary, owing to the excess of deposit on the edges, the water flows inwards from an elevated surrounding and enclosing ridge to a central basin, from whence it is conducted to the exterior along watercourses, piercing through this surrounding ridge. And this order is followed not merely in tidal districts like Backergunge, but in all alluvial formations, however elevated—as, for example, in Sylhet [or in Behar.]

Each of the drainage circles or districts of Backergunge, then, possesses its central basin or reservoir of swamp towards which the surface slopes in every direction from the exterior. On the exterior edge of the area, where it abuts on the large tidal rivers (which everywhere divide one drainage circle from another), the land is well raised and covered with villages. The intermediate space is covered with rice cultivation, and the centre is a lake or *beel*, varying in size and depth with the season of the year.

From points not very far from the centre of this beel, and quite submerged in the rains, numerous little watercourses proceed in every direction towards the edge. These can only be recognised by the fact that a current flows along them, and by the narrow submerged rims of deposited earth which enclose them on either side and partially separate them from the beel proper. Beginning almost in nothing, many combine to form others, which, though still within the beel and with banks submerged by its waters, present more defined features. At last, by the coalescence of many, a waterc urse is formed, with banks which, though but a few feet wide and sl ping rapidly towards the beel-water, are yet in the dry season above the water. After further convergence of such channels, we find ourselves (supposing we are attempting to find our way out of the beel by water) in a khál of moderate dimensions, with banks which are not submerged except in the height of the rains; we are still probably many stages from the great rivers, whose banks are permanently above the water, and which are some hundreds of yards in width. But it is useless to particularise further. The numerous khâls which originate in the depths of the central reservoir terminate in some two or three considerable channels which open into the circumposed main watercourse. Between this latter and the beel there is no water communication except through these two or three channels and their ramifications. Even if a short cut were artificially made direct into the beel, it would in a few rainy seasons, by sucking in at the ebb tide the water from all directions, create for itself a branched system of terminations under water, which in the dry weather would be exposed to view.

The whole system depends on the principle that inundating waters, if in a condition to lay down deposit, do so chiefly upon their actual banks, and thus tend to shut themselves off from the tract of submergeable country beyond. As the banks rise, the rush of water over them at ebb and flood is intensified, and at length bursts open channels of communication. These throw up enclosing banks in their turn, which process gives birth to new connecting channels piercing these new banks, and the process is repeated till the communicating channels become so small as scarcely to be noticed.

It is obvious that in this manner the drainage of flat surfaces is performed in the most effectual manner. In undulating or mountainous countries the drainage derives sufficient force from gravity to maintain the channels open, but in alluvial flats the slow passage of the water would scarcely suffice. If in a tidal district the drainage channels merely flowed from the interior of each patch of land towards the circumference, they would soon fill with sediment brought in by the tide, which would ebb and flow in them with but slight velocity; but where these channels are the only means of communication between two considerable bodies of water constantly differing from each other in level, a high rate of speed is easily maintained.

In the rainy season the drainage reservoirs are connected much more directly with the exterior than during the remainder of the year. The water, from various causes, stands at an average at least six feet higher than in the dry season, and completely submerges all the interior articulations of the system of relieving channels. Only the larger and more external have their banks above the water;

the smaller feeders are supplied both from their extremities and over their own banks. The greater volume of water which then requires passage is thus amply provided for; whilst in the dry weather, when the drainage volume is weak, the water is unable on account of the fall in its level to leave the reservoir except through the extreme ends of very small channels. The banks of the different classes or grades of channels, each in turn, begin to fulfil their proper functions, as the level decreases, and in this manner the waterway is always exactly proportioned to the volume to which it is required to give passage.

In districts of alluvium raised above tidal influence the rise and fall of the rivers during the rainy season produce similar effects. The water on the swamps being only connected with these by narrow channels piercing the banks of the rivers, is always, unless the river remains very long at exactly the same level, either above or below that level, and the channels are incessantly occupied in restoring the balance.

The swamps or drainage reservoirs are themselves an interesting feature in the physical geography of Backergunge. They vary greatly in size, in accordance with the area of the tract they drain, and the amount of *filling up* which they have undergone. In the eastern portion of the district, the alluvium from the Megna has completely obliterated the whole drainage organisation, which has become enveloped in one uniform mound sloping towards the west, and forming the right bank of this immense watercourse. In the western portion of the district where the system of drainage prevails which we have endeavoured to describe, the swamps during the rainy season fill up the whole of each drainage tract, except its extreme margin and the banks of the primary channels which penetrate that margin. In the dry weather they become reduced to the extent of the nucleus or central portion from which the relieving channels take their rise. This nucleus is often of considerable depth, and is generally covered by a floating surface of matted grass and earth on which Nul, Hoogla, and Koonda reed sometimes grow; at other places it is covered with a short, coarse, but very green grass, abounding in snipe. In parts where the covering is thick enough to support the cultivators, rice is sown in the dry season. It is dangerous to tread on this shaking surface except where the straw *hiras*, or small retaining embankments which mark the fields, show that people have been before. Even through the midst of this quaking bog the small ramifying watercourses are to be found, and on their margins, though two or three feet deep under water, a firm footing is generally obtainable. Their beds also are ordinarily composed of a hard mixture of sand and clay, and it is only in the interspaces that the floating surface exists. The smaller beels are very useful as village boundaries. The inhabitants on either side cultivate as far as they prudently can, and abandon the centre to jungle and water-fowl.

From the beel on every side the country rises with considerable slope, the first footing being generally found in the watercourses. The drainage towards the beel is along successive terraces of rice-fields, each a few inches lower than the next above it. The water is retained in the higher ground for cultivation by means of the little hiras or banks (here constructed of straw as well as earth) common throughout Bengal. It may be repeated here that all the surface drainage of the tract surrounding each beel flows towards it, and never into the penetrating channels, whose banks are always higher than the ground outside, and always slope away from the channel.

The level of the sea at the head of the Bay of Bengal, and on the tidal watercourses of the Delta, is subject to a considerable annual alteration. It is a doubtful point whether this alteration is to be attributed to the influx of fresh water in such immense quantities, or to the banking up of the sea by the south-west monsoon. As the increased elevation occurs during the rainy season, when both these influences are at work, it is extremely difficult to decide the question, and both are probably concerned in the result. The change of level is not confined to the head of the bay, but is found some distance down the east coast of India. In Backergunge the difference in mean level must be at least four feet. This is an important point, for, as the whole district of Backergunge is nearly horizontal, the water at high tide in the rainy season floods nearly the whole of it, and the inhabitants are obliged to raise their houses on mounds. It is owing to this alteration in the level of the tides, rather than to the mere local rainfall, that the change in the level of the beels takes place.

(C.)

I.—PRICES.

THE following interesting facts regarding prices are extracted from a manuscript volume in the India Office :—

"Rice, which forty years ago was two and a half maunds per arcot[1] rupee, is now [November 1800] one and a half maunds per arcot rupee. Salt, which at the same period was one arcot rupee per maund, is now four sicca rupees per maund. Oil, which was

[1] The arcot rupee seems to have been worth about one per cent. more than the Government rupee. As regards the price of salt in old times, see Sir Philip Francis' letter of 22d January 1776, where he says that the Company had declared in their letter of 20th November 1767 that they had rather that even the duties should be reduced than that the price of salt to the consumer should ever exceed Rs.140 sicca per 100 maunds.

two and a half arcot rupees per maund, is now four arcot rupees per maund. Other articles were also enhanced in price. *Cappas* [cotton], which used to be at the rate of from four to five puns per sír, was last year at six, and is this year at nine puns. Thread of all kinds, excepting the finest, is much dearer now than formerly. In 1787 and 1788 a great number of spinners died of famine; this and the increased price of necessaries of life are considered as the principal cause of the present dearness of thread. Labour is likewise raised; the pay of a weaver forty years ago was from one to one and a half arcot rupee, and of a journeyman from eight anas to twelve anas per month. The pay of the former is now from two and a half arcot rupees to three and a half arcot rupees, and of the latter from one arcot rupee to two arcot rupees. Rent also is said to be raised, and what formerly was eight anas per *pakhi* [a little less than a bigha] is now twelve anas."

In the same letter reference is made to "the great diminution in the demand for the fabrics of this province, which has prevailed since the commencement of the present war in Europe" (Letter of Mr John Taylor, Commercial Resident at Dacca, dated 30th November 1800, and forwarded to the Court of Directors by Commercial Letter from Bengal dated 1st December 1801). Mr Taylor gives interesting particulars of the cultivation of cotton and of the weaving processes. In a postscript, dated November 1801, he states that the population of the city of Dacca had been estimated by the Magistrate to be 200,000.

Some interesting statistics about prices will be found in appendix to a report of Board of Customs, Salt and Opium, 26th January 1832 (Calcutta, 1833). See especially p. 120.

II.—India Office Records.

The India Office in Westminster contains Revenue Consultations of the Dacca Factory from 1736. Many papers appear to be wanting, and those which remain do not possess much interest, as they are chiefly taken up with details of the weaving business and of the Company's investment. Those were days when, as Lord Macaulay has remarked, "the ablest servants of the Company were busied only about invoices and bills of lading." How unprepared we were for a larger conception of our duties is shown by the following extract from a Dacca minute of 20th July 1763, which was written by Messrs Leycester and Senior on their return to Dacca after they had quitted it on the outbreak of the war with Mir Kassim: "Having recovered our factory, &c., with the assistance of the Meckly detachment, and also taken possession of the city, the collections and the revenue of so large a district is an important business which we are not much acquainted with, and having no man belonging to the factory equal to so great a charge, it is agreed to call on the officers of the Government to resume the management of their several offices in the name of our honourable masters till we are informed from the President and Council through what channel these matters are in future to pass."

The records extend from 1736 to 1763, then there appears to be a blank up to 1772, when we have the report of the Committee of Circuit. Then come the reports of the proceedings of the Provincial Council, which commence in 1774 and go down to 1779. The following notes are arranged chronologically, and contain such passages as appeared to me of interest, especially with reference to Bákarganj:—

August 1737.—Aga Bákar, foujdar, is said to have taken Rs.3000 as hush-money from the chaudhari of a pargana in connection with a theft of cloth from the Jagdea Factory.

October 1737.—On the 30th ult. and 1st inst. there happened a storm here and in the adjacent countries, the most violent that has been known in the memory of man. It began at eleven o'clock of the night, and blew very violent from north-east till seven in the morning, when it returned from the south-west with double violence. This storm destroyed almost every boat and vessel that was on the river, and ashore blew down vast numbers of buildings, and among the rest the honourable Company's bungalows that were for the use of the washermen and their workmen at Tezgong and on the wharf. A consultation of the 17th idem refers to information having been received from the President of the loss of several of the Company's ships in the hurricane.

N.B.—This is the storm which did so much damage in Calcutta and the Sundarbans, and which is referred to in the "Gentleman's Magazine" for 1738–39. See "Calcutta Review" for March 1859, article "Gangetic Delta."

24th November 1737.—Letter from Mr Pomfret of Jagdea, dated 18th idem, stating that they have advice that the Mugs are come out in great numbers, and the country around them being full of dacoits, who have already done considerable mischief, &c.

Another storm took place on 31st May 1739, and the three following days.

December 1744.—Sergeant Cooper being sent with 30,000 arcot rupees to Jagdea, reports that there were a great many Mugs in the way. Resolved to send him all the European soldiers in the factory.

4th June 1745.—A sloop returning from Dacca to Calcutta had been attacked by dacoits near Serampore, who had plundered the crew of what they had and murdered five of them, after having cut the rigging, sails, cables, &c. Having information also of several sloops and boats being on the way from Calcutta to Dacca, and that as the ways between this and Bawkergange (*sic*) are greatly infested with dacoits, it was agreed that a party of ten men, with a sergeant, corporal, and ten Baxeries, (?) be sent down as far as Bawkergange, and convey hither all vessels belonging to the English.

30th December 1745.—Apprehensions about the Mahrattas.

January 1746.—Resolve to put a parapet wall round the factory as a protection against the Mahrattas.

1749.—Mr Nicholas Clerembault became chief. He had joined on 9th March 1744, when he took his seat as the youngest of Council.

30th December 1754.—Raj Ballab Duan intimates that on the change of the head Nabobship of Dacca, which is now in the name of Muradda Doulla, he expects a large present, and even hinted the sum of Rs.10,000. Resolved to give him Rs.3000, if the payment is absolutely necessary.

15th November 1755.—Nicholas Clerembault, Esq., chief of this factory, departed this life of a violent fever. Doubtless this is the Columbo Saheb whose tomb Bishop Heber mentions.

23d October 1757.—Nabob communicated his apprehensions of his safety.

July 1763.—Council had fled from Dacca, and taken up their quarters at Luckypúr.

22d July 1763.—Mir Jaffar Ali Khan proclaimed Souba.

We now come to the report of the Dacca Committee of Circuit, 1772, which is in a separate volume. It does not, however, contain much which is interesting. There is a long report in it, dated 25th September 1772, from William Makepeace Thackeray, about the lime quarries in Sylhet. He was appointed Collector of that district on 10th October 1772. The volume also contains long reports of the disputes between Gokal Ghosal and the zamindars of Sandwip, and would doubtless be very interesting to any one writing the history of Chittagong or Noakháli. The following is the advertisement, dated 3d October 1772, which the Committee of Circuit published when they proceeded to settle the land revenue :—

"Notice is hereby given that the lands of the Dacca District, as also those of Sylhet, will be let in farm for the term of five years, agreeable to the conditions that have been already advertised ; all persons therefore who are willing to farm, and can produce respectable securities, are directed to deliver in sealed proposals specifying the amount rent they offer to give for each pargana separately." It will be seen from this that the claims of zamindars and taluqdars, or the rights of the tenantry, were not much considered in those days.

17th February 1774.—Regulations about the post office.

5th April 1774.—Petition from Mani Ram Dabee, son of Dyal Chaudhari, claiming Buzurgumedpúr. States that his father reclaimed it from jungle, and that during the administration of Murshid Kuli Khan, Aga Bákar infamously sent people to seize on the daughter of Dyal Chaudhari, whereon he, being driven to the greatest pitch of desperation, relinquished his estate and effects, and destroyed all the female portion of his family. Petitioner afterwards tried to recover the property, but was thwarted by the intrigues of Raj Ballab's sons. The latter replied, saying that they bought the property in 1167 from Mirza Mendi, the brother, and Mahomed Salé, the son of Mahomed Sadok, who was son of Aga Bákar. They added that in 1737 the property belonged to Udai Rajah and Mahomed Reza, after which Aga Bákar got it, and recorded the estate in his son Sadok's name. (This is the name in the old Collectorate papers.)

3d May 1774.—The Calcutta Council rejected the claim on the ground, first, that Dyal Chaudhari had been regularly dispossessed by the government of the Nazim for rebellion; and secondly, because Aga Bákar was regularly appointed to the zamindari by the same reigning government about thirty-three years ago, in the light of a reward for his services in reducing the rebellious Dyal Chaudhari. There is also a petition, dated 6th May 1774, from Mirza Mendi and Katissa Khanam, setting forth that on Aga Bákar's death in 1160, Mahomed Sadok absconded, upon which Raj Ballab confiscated his effects. In 1164 Mahomed Sadok returned, and obtained the wadadari of the pargana for his son, Mahomed Salé, under the seal of Nawab Jaffar Ali Khan, and was himself reinstated in his zamindari. In 1166 Mahomed Sadok died, and in 1167 Raj Ballab dispossessed petitioners. Apparently this petition was dismissed.

20th June 1774.—Much correspondence about char Bhuta, and reference to a trial about it in Luckypúr Civil Court 10th June 1773.

Idem.—Reference to Calcutta about an order, dated 17th May 1774, directing that from 1st July 1774 no person shall be allowed to buy or sell a slave who is not such already by former legal purchase, and any kazi who shall grant any kawala after that date for the sale of any slave whatever shall be dismissed.

The Dacca Council writes, "As it is an established custom throughout the Dacca districts to keep in bondage the offspring of slaves who have once become so, agreed that we address the honourable President and Council of Revenue, requesting to be informed whether the benefit of the Regulation is to be extended to the future offspring of such persons who may at present be in slavery." The Calcutta Council replied on 12th July as follows: "In those districts where slavery is a general usage, or in any way connected with, or is likely to have an influence on the revenue, which we are informed is the case in Sylhet, and may be so in the other, especially the frontier parts of your division, we must desire you particularly to advise us what is the usage, and every circumstance connected with it, and we shall then give you such direction as we may judge necessary; but considering your question in the meantime in the light of a general proposition, we are of opinion that the right of masters to the children of the slaves already their property cannot legally be taken from them in the first generation, but we think that this right cannot and ought not to extend farther, and direct that you do make publication accordingly."

5th July 1774.—Severe orders from Calcutta against the impressment of ryots as coolies by travellers.

11th July 1774.—Appointment of foujdars. Boundaries of Bákarganj thana—south, Aurungábád pargana; north, Sundarkul; east, Jalálpúr; west, Syedpúr in Dacca.

30th July 1774.—French letter from M. des Granges, reporting that the French have abandoned their Dacca factory.

13th August 1774.—The President and Council of Calcutta send a price-current of grain, which has been made the standard for collecting the Government duties upon throughout the provinces, from which, the Collectors have been informed, they are not on any account to deviate. The standard is fixed so very low that it must remove every just ground of complaint from the rice merchants.

The Government duty of 2½ per cent. was to be levied according to this standard, which was to be current over Bengal, Behar, and Orissa. I give the more important items:—

	Mans.	Sírs.		Mans.	Sírs.
Horse grain, per rupee	1	26	Rice, 1st sort, per rupee	1	10
Green grain (*sona möog*), per rupee . .	1	10	Rice, 2d sort, „ „	1	20
			Rice, 3d sort „ „	1	30
Barley, per rupee .	2	30	Paddy . „ „	2	20
Ashar „ „ .	1	20	Mustard „ „	1	0
Wheat „ „ .	1	10	Tíl . „ „	0	30

21st August 1775.—Petition from Gopal Kissen, zamindar of Buzurgumedpúr, asking for remission of the *phanri malwa* (called here *phannaly malwa*, and also *panny malwa*), on the ground that it had been abolished when taxes on grain were removed. In these proceedings we at last meet with an explanation of the term, a witness stating that the tax was a duty levied on grain, timber, and all kinds of goods under transportation. The Calcutta Council relieved Gopal Kissen from the obligation of paying it (see p. 100).

1775.—Frequent notices of a Mr Wood, who was salt agent at Jainagar—*i.e.*, Jhalukátti.

18th January 1776.—Report on French factories states that the French carry on a trade in rice and cotton thread at Bákarganj, where a gomasta resides continually, with two or three sepoys.

29th July 1777.—Extract from Court of Directors' letter stating that they had revoked their orders to let the lands to the highest bidders, and signifying their pleasure to have them occupied by hereditary zamindars. Strict orders are given for insisting on every zamindar and farmer giving leases to their tenants.

21st July 1777.—Report on the arcot rupee, which has been "the only specie of general currency in this country time out of mind, and yet they never were coined at the Dacca mint." Also send proposals for the settlement of the Dacca Province.

11th July 1778.—Notice of declaration of war between France and England. Flight of M. Chevalier. List of all the Europeans in the Dacca Province. The total is about fifty.

8th September 1778.—Mr Hatch claims to be put in charge of Sylhet. Mr Holland dissents, and supports Lindsay.

Complaint of Chandradwip zamindar against Baksh Ali, foujdar of thana Barisál (10 September 1779).

19th November 1778, *Arangpúr.*—Case between taluqdars and zamindars. Vakil of zamindars states a division took place in 1158, after death of Janaki Ballab, into four equal shares, and again in 1172. This was found correct, and Board ordered taluqdars to pay the shareholders.

2d September 1779.—Remarks of Calcutta Council on settlement of Dacca districts for 1186—*i.e.*, 1779: "We particularly enjoin you never, in any instance whatever, to propose any abatement of any nature whatever unless you can at the same time clearly point out how such deficiency may be supplied. In short, it is our determination that the Dacca Division shall yield to the Government an annual revenue of Rs.2,985,549."

There is also a separate volume giving in detail the settlement for 1184—*i.e.*, 1777.

N.B.—The Dacca papers contain many interesting reports about the Jyntia Rajah, Sylhet, Sandwip, &c. There is much correspondence about Sandwip in a volume for 1774, but by far the fullest report on Sandwip is to be found in the Bengal Revenue Council Reports for 1780, vol. vi. This voluminous report extends over 491 paragraphs, exclusive of appendices, and contains a genealogical table of the Sandwip zamindars, and a statement of its revenue from as far back as 1069 A.H.—*i.e.*, 1662—when the Moghals first got possession of it. The report is written by Mr Jonathan Duncan (I presume the famous Jonathan Duncan of Benares and Bombay). He was sent to Sandwip to report on the murder of one Mahomed Kain, and lived on the island for a considerable time.

III.—Famines of 1770 and 1787.

Dr Hunter observes, in his "Annals of Rural Bengal" (p. 28), that the only non-official description of the famine of 1770 by an eye-witness is a metrical one; but, in fact, there is a tolerably full description of it in a letter in the "Gentleman's Magazine" for September 1771, vol. xli. p. 402. The letter was forwarded to the editor by one J. C., who describes himself as having just received it from a very worthy friend of his in the Company's service in Calcutta.[1] The same letter appears in the "Scots Magazine" for September 1771, vol. xxxiii. p. 454; and there are also references to the subject at pages 160 and 216 of the same volume. See also the "Gentleman's Magazine" for February 1772, p. 69. It is probably to the above letter that Warren Hastings refers to when he speaks of the effects of the famine having been made known "to the public by laboured descriptions, in which every circumstance of fact and every art of languages have been accumulated to raise compassion, and to excite

[1] Though the letter is from a Company's servant, it is non-official in the sense in which Dr Hunter uses the word, or otherwise Lord Teignmouth's verses could not be called non-official.

indignation against your [the Company's] servants" (Warren Hastings' letter, Appendix G of Dr Hunter's Annals, p. 380). It would appear, however, from Charles Grant's "Observations on the State of Society in Asia" (General Appendix, No. I., to House of Commons Report of 1833), that the French of Chandarnagore were the first to accuse the English of being the authors of the famine, and probably therefore detailed descriptions of it are to be found in the French papers of that period. Mr Grant himself gives some particulars of the famine. His paper was written in 1792, and he tells us that he derived his information partly from his own observations and partly from a manuscript account by Mr Becher. Mr Becher was then resident at the Durbar (Murshídábád), and was, I presume, the person quoted by Sir Philip Francis (*vide* note, p. 376). Mr Grant says Mr Becher saved the country in 1770 by laying in 60,000 mans of rice for the use of the army, and that he was a man noted for his honesty and humanity. "His anxiety and exertions for alleviating the miseries of that whole period ended in an illness which almost cost him his life. Yet on his return to England he found himself traduced as the author of the famine." Unfortunately the charge of turning the public distress into a source of private profit was true as regards some servants of the Company, and Mr Becher had only himself to thank for the odium he incurred, inasmuch as he neglected to restrain or even give up the names of those who had through their native servants not only "monopolised the grain, but compelled the poor ryots to sell the seed requisite for the next harvest." (See Court of Directors' letter, Appendix B, p. 420, Hunter's Annals.)

Notices of the 1787 famine will be found in "Calcutta Gazettes" of 20th September 1787 and 27th March 1788. The last shows that Bákarganj rice was sent to Dacca.

IV.—Establishment of Civil Courts at Bákarganj.

At p. 889 of the Sixth Report of the House of Commons there is printed a Revenue Department Consultation, dated 6th April 1781, which gives us the details of the first establishment of a court of civil justice at Bákarganj. The following is an extract from the preamble: "The Board, taking into consideration the present state of the administration of civil and criminal justice throughout the provinces, pass the following resolution: That to remedy the inconveniences occasioned by the too extensive jurisdiction of the Mofussil Dewanny Adâlats established by the Resolutions of 28th March 1780, and thereby promote the more rapid and effectual administration of justice, the following Courts of Civil Justice, including those now existing, be established throughout the provinces." Then follow the names of eighteen courts, among which Jessore appears under the name of Moorly. The boundaries given of Bákarganj are as follows: "The jurisdiction of Buckergunge (*sic*), consisting of that portion of the Dacca Province lying on the south-west of the Ganges or Padma and the Cally Ganges, and to the west of the Meghna from Chandpúr to the sea; having as its western limits the eastern frontier of Boosna and Jessore, down to the mouth of the river of Raj Mongal, including also all the islands belonging to and situated on the coast of the Dacca Province, except the pargana of Sandwip and its dependencies."

The Resolution farther directs that the Civil Judges shall have the power of apprehending dacoits, &c., though not of trying them, and that the Nawab be requested to withdraw all his phousdars except the phousdar of Hughli.

The above orders are also published in Colebrooke's Digest, vol. iii.

V.—Character of the People.

The following interesting remarks on the character of the Bákarganj population, &c., are taken from a letter by Mr Meredith (?) Parker, printed in the appendix to Mr Plowden's salt report. Mr Parker's letter is dated 15th September 1832, and the object of it is to rebut the assertion that the molunghies or salt-makers were not free agents:—

"I believe I am well warranted in asserting that no portion of Lower Bengal, with the exception perhaps of the Nuddea district, has ever been considered so difficult to manage. I speak with reference to matters of police, as the Twenty-four Parganas, the Jessore and Bákarganj zillahs, the chars and islands at the mouth of the Meghna and Chittagong, but more especially the belt of cultivated land which accompanies or invades the line of the Sundarbans in the three first-mentioned districts. It need scarcely be observed that everywhere people dwelling on the frontiers of great forests, the pioneers before whose hatchets these forests recede, people who dwell in islands surrounded by broad and dangerous rivers, or on the sea-shore, are noted, as compared with their fellow-countrymen in other parts of the same land, for hardihood and roughness of character, nor am I inclined to believe that Bengal offers any exception to this nearly general rule. Now, four-fifths of the molunghies belong to the above class, and certainly no more unfavourable selection could be made for trying the experiment of coerced labour if all Bengal had been searched for the purpose. Attempts at coercion which might bewilder and intimidate the quiet weavers of Dacca or Murshidábád, would, I apprehend, meet with a very different reception from the borderers in the Sundarbans; the woodcutters and fishermen of the Twenty-four Parganas, Jessore, and Bákarganj; the ryots of Bhulloah

[Noakháli], ever braining each other in boundary disputes; and the litigious, unmanageable people of Chittagong. For my own part, had I a public measure of an unpopular nature, or which would be considered oppressive by the ryots, to carry into effect, I confess I should prefer being appointed to make the experiment in any portion of Bengal rather than in the districts I have adverted to, and I believe the Magistrates and other public officers who have had experience of them would agree with me in this preference."

In the same letter Mr Parker asserts that cultivation is essential to the salt manufacture, as the rice straw is used for boiling the water. This seems too strongly put, but still it is satisfactory to know that there is not necessarily any opposition between cultivation and salt-making. We may therefore hope that the reclamation of the Sundarbans and the chars will not prevent the revival of the salt trade.

VI.—Dacoits.

There is a curious passage in Mill's "Logic," where he speaks of the English bringing with them into Bengal the phrase "landed proprietor," and of the confusion which it led them into. "They gave an absolute right to one who had only a limited right, from another, because he had not an absolute right, they took away all right, drove whole classes of men to ruin and despair, *filled the country with banditti*, created a feeling that nothing was secure, and produced, with the best intentions, a disorganisation of society which had not been produced in the country by the most ruthless of its barbarous invaders" (book iv. chap. v. Natural History of the Variations in the Meaning of Terms).

This passage apparently refers to the formation of the Permanent Settlement, and makes it answerable for the filling of the country with banditti. But as regards the eastern districts, at all events, the quotations given in my book show that dacoity flourished there long before 1790. I suspect that Mill borrowed the illustration from his father, who was prejudiced against the Permanent Settlement.

VII.—Early Travellers in Bengal.

An interesting article might be written on this subject, but as I am only dealing with the history of one district, it would be out of place for me to go into much detail. With the help of my friend Dr Wise I have searched a great many books in the hope of finding some particulars about early Bákarganj, but the result has been disappointing. In conducting an inquiry of this kind, one is, I think, most struck with the tremendous amount of waste with which the carrying on of the world's work is accompanied. The same facts are repeated in scores of books in the same or in different languages, so that about nine-tenths of them are superfluous; and hardly any book can be found which goes farther than its neighbours, or gives any information which is novel and valuable. The earliest European traveller in Bengal appears to have been Varthema (Vertomannus) of Bologna, who was in Bengal about 1507. His travels have been translated for the Hakluyt Society (1863), and the editor discusses in the introduction the question of the site of the town of Bengala or Banghella, which Varthema describes himself as having visited. The editor supposes that it was situated between Hattia and Sandwip, and it has occurred to me that perhaps it is after all identical with Fitch's Bacola. Le Blanc of Marseilles, who was in Bengal some ten years before Fitch, speaks of Bengala as being the principal town of Bengal, but adds the important observation that the native name of it was Batacouta. Faria y Sousa, and perhaps some other writers, seem to call Bacola sometimes Baticala,[1] which is very near to Le Blanc's word, especially when we consider how easily *t* may be mistaken for an *l* in printing from a manuscript.

Le Blanc must have been in Bengal shortly after Cæsar Frederick, and, curiously enough, he too was forced by stress of weather to land at Sandwip. Unfortunately Le Blanc's travels were not published till after his death, and perhaps they were not written down till long after his return. At all events, they contain allusions to things—*e.g.*, the reception of the Jesuit priests by the King of Chandécan, which did not take place till some twenty years after his return home.

Another early traveller in Bengal is Sebastian Manrique (referred to in a paper by Dr Wise). He was in India and Arracan from 1628 to 1641, in the capacity of an Augustinian missionary. He describes Shahbázpúr, and also an island which he calls Sagaldiva—*i.e.*, he says, all-rich. He says that these islands had become depopulated on account of the continual wars between the Portuguese, the Arracanese, and the Moghals. He also describes Sandwip, and gives some particulars about Gonzales, whom he calls the Portuguese "King of Sundiva." He describes the Sundarbans and his shipwreck in the neighbourhood, but unfortunately I am not sufficiently acquainted with Spanish fully to understand him.

I may here note that the most complete list of early works on India appears to be that given in Don Antonio de Leon Pinelo's work entitled "Epitome de la Bibliotheca Oriental," &c., Madrid, 1737.

The earliest map of Bengal appears to be Gastaldi's (1561). A facsimile of it is given in the Hakluyt Society's translation of Varthema's Travels (Dr Badger's introduction).

[1] There was also a Baticala in Canara and another in Ceylon.

VIII.—FRANCIS FERNANDEZ.

Francis Fernandez and his companion Dominic da Sosa were the first Jesuits who visited Bengal, and they probably deserve the honour of being reckoned the first missionaries to the Bengalis. They were not, however, the first priests in the country, for they found a curate in Gullo on their arrival in May 1598. This Gullo appears to me to be identical with Bandel, which last was a name given to all Portuguese stations in Bengal. Fernandez describes it as being 210 miles from the mouth of the Ganges, and says that it took them eight days to ascend the river to it. Gullo was evidently one of the earliest, if not the very earliest station of the Portuguese in Bengal, and so we know was Bandel, the church bell of which bears the date 1599. When the Jesuits speak of their church at Chandecan as being the first erected by their order, they do not thereby deny the priority of that of Bandel. Fernandez and his companion stayed at Gullo till October, and they employed themselves there in the laudable work of establishing a hospital, which I suppose must have been the first in Bengal. From Gullo they went to Chandecan, and stayed there till December, when they went on to Sripúr. Fernandez describes Chandecan as lying half way between Porto Grande (Chittagong) and Porto Piccolo (Gullo?), and says that the king's dominions were so extensive that it would take fifteen or twenty days to traverse them. He adds, that it has a great trade in bees'-wax, which is produced in the jungles, so that there were Sundarbans then also. There were dacoits also, and Fernandez says they encountered great dangers from them and from tigers on the way from Gullo to Chandecan.

Fernandez' first letter was written from Sripúr, and was dated either 14th or 19th January 1599 (both dates are given). It will be found at length in the edition of Pimenta's letter published at Venice in 1602, but the note of Aquaviva prefixed to this edition states that the letter was originally printed in Latin. It would seem, therefore, that the statement in my text (p. 29) is a mistake, and that the missionaries originally wrote in Latin. The edition states on the titlepage that Pimenta's letter was written from Goa on 25th December 1598, but the date given at the conclusion of the book shows that 98 is a mistake for 99. A Portuguese edition of the letter was published at Lisbon in 1602. There is a short biography of Fernandez in Bartholomé Alcazar's "Chronicle of the Jesuit Worthies of the Province of Toledo," Madrid, 1710. From it we learn that Fernandez was born at a place called La Villa de Huerta, near Toledo, and that he entered the University of Alcala in 1570, when he was twenty years old. He arrived in Goa in 1575, and died in 1602, when he was only about fifty-two, though Du Jarric and Alcazar speak of him as being weighed down by years.

(D.)

Two Bákarganj Cases.

1. *Story of Karimuddin.*

I only mention this story to show to what desperate lengths Bengalis will occasionally go in the prosecution of their revenge. Karimuddin was an idle, dissolute fellow, and a thief. One night he was seen by some of his fellow-villagers stealing fish from their nets, and they gave him chase but could not catch him, and so had to content themselves with giving him a volley of abuse. Karimuddin resolved to be revenged, and the method he took was this. He had an old father who had been bedridden for two or three years, and whom he felt to be a burden to him, so he actually took up a bludgeon and fractured his father's skull, and then hurried in with the body to the police station and laid a charge of murder against the people who had abused him. The case was investigated, and I am glad to say that the truth came out, and that Karimuddin was transported for life.

2. *Story of Jabar Ula.*

Some three years ago there was a Mahomedan peasant, named Jabar Ula, who lived with his wife and family on the banks of the river Meghna. The homestead was a joint one—that is to say, he and his family lived in one part of it, and another family, distantly related to his, occupied the remainder. The lands attached to the homestead were cultivated in common by the two families, an arrangement which led to occasional disputes about the produce. One day Jabar Ula had a quarrel with a woman of the neighbouring family about the division of a quantity of sesame or oil seeds which had been spread out to dry in the courtyard. Jabar Ula wanted to carry off his share, and the woman said he was taking more than he was entitled to. I suppose she used her tongue pretty freely, for at last Jabar Ula got so angry that he tried to strike her, and in doing so he happened to twitch off her upper garment. She rushed off to her brothers, who had just come in from the field, and complained of the affront. Her two brothers at once came into the courtyard, seized Jabar Ula, and gave him such a beating that he at last fell down insensible. Terrified at this, the two lifted him up, gave him water, and finally carried him into his house and laid him down on his bed. Some days after this Jabar Ula's wife sent word by the village watchman to the police station that her husband had died of his beating, and that the murderers had broken into her house and carried off the dead body. The police went out to the village, which was a good way off, and commenced an investigation. No trace of Jabar Ula's body could be found, and his widow gave a circumstantial account to the police of how her husband had lain insensible for two or three days after his beating, how he had got worse and worse, and how she and his mother had watched by his side night after night until he died. When they saw that all was over, and that they were widowed and childless, the two women gave way to their grief, and broke out into the lamentable cries which Bengali women use on such occasions. The accused heard them, and knowing what the cries meant, and that there was no safety for them if Jabar Ula's body remained where it was, and if the marks of violence on it were seen by the authorities, they broke into the room, which had only mat walls, and carried off the corpse. The widow could tell no more, but the accused were now arrested, and they told the rest of the story. They acknowledged to the police that all that the widow had said was true, and added that they had put the body on board of a small boat, rowed out to the middle of the stream, which was there two or three miles wide, and then flung the body into the river. On this they were sent into Barisál to appear before the Magistrate, and I well recollect that their confessions were recorded in my presence, that they were full and particular, and that each prisoner told the same story. The case was made over to another Magistrate, who examined the witnesses and then committed the accused to the Court of Session on charges of murder, &c. Before the trial came on the prisoners said to their attorney that they were innocent of the murder, and that Jabar Ula was not really dead. They, however, admitted that they had beaten him, and that they could not produce him. On this their attorney advised them to plead guilty, and to throw themselves on the mercy of the Court. "It is of no use," he said, "for you to deny the crime; you can't produce Jabar Ula, and you have no witnesses who can say where he is. On the other hand, his widow and his mother are prepared to swear that they saw him die, and that they saw you carry off his dead body. Your best plan is to plead guilty, and to plead the provocation Jabar Ula had given by insulting your sister." They took his advice, and acknowledged the genuineness of their confessions before the Magistrate. The witnesses for the prosecution were examined, and repeated the evidence they had given before the Magistrate, and the Judge convicted the prisoners, but passed a comparatively light sentence. As the body had not been found he acquitted them of the charge of murder, and sentenced them to six months' imprisonment for causing grievous hurt, and six months for concealment of evidence, in that they had thrown the body into the river. Altogether they got a year apiece. The prisoners went to jail, and made no appeal; but some seven or eight months afterwards, and while the prisoners were serving out their time in Barisál jail, we were all startled by a rumour that Jabar Ula had turned up, alive and in good health. It was true. A man had come to a country market to make some purchases, and a fellow-villager had recognised him as Jabar Ula. He had changed his name, and did not want to come forward, but the village watchman insisted on taking him to the police station. There he acknowledged that he was indeed Jabar Ula, and told a marvellous story to account for his reappearance. He had become insensible after he was beaten, he said, and remembered nothing farther until he felt a gnawing sensation in his back, as if some animal were biting him. This awoke him, and he found that he was lying in shallow water on the edge of a sandbank, and that a jackal had been biting him. The animal had come down to drink, and had seen Jabar Ula and thought he was dead. After this Jabar Ula saw a boat passing and hailed it, and was taken by it into the district of Noakháli. After that he lived in various places, but always in hiding, lest he should be discovered by his assailants and murdered by them. We tested his story by sending an officer with him to make inquiries in the various places he had visited. The result did not corroborate his story, and he now began to shuffle about the names of the places he had visited, and to tell conflicting stories. Among other things he dropped the story of the jackal, and said he had been saved by clutching at a plantain-tree which was floating down the river. He also gave up the story of his having been taken to Noakháli. And now, when the evidence of the witnesses in the Court of Session was more closely examined, it was found that the women of Jabar Ula's family had materially altered the statements they made to the Magistrate. Before the Magistrate they had sworn that they had seen the prisoners carry off the dead body of Jabar Ula. Before the Judge they said that they had fallen asleep, worn out with watching and fatigue, and that when they awoke again they found that the body was gone. Moreover, it was clear that the confessions of the prisoners must have been false, at least in part, for they had said that they had flung the body of Jabar Ula into the middle of the Meghna, and it is utterly impossible that he could ever have been saved if he had been flung in there, especially when reduced by illness. By this time the prisoners had heard of the reappearance of Jabar Ula, and had forwarded petitions declaratory of their innocence, and accusing Jabar Ula and his family of getting up a false case against them, and the police of having tortured them into confessing. The prisoners were now sent for, and they made similar statements in person, and no doubt these were the real circumstances. Of course the police denied that they had used any violence to the prisoners, and it was impossible to get proof of this so long after the occurrence; but at the same time they could not get out of the difficulty that Jabar Ula was alive, and that if the confessions were true he must have been dead. The affair was never wholly cleared up, but no doubt remained in the minds of the great body of the public that the case was altogether false except as regards the beating, and that Jabar Ula had, in revenge for his thrashing, slipped away in the night-time and hidden himself for months, having previously arranged with his wife and friends that they should say he was dead, and accuse the prisoners of having murdered him.

The case thus remains as a memorable instance of the lengths to which a man will go in order to satisfy his revenge, and of the danger of relying too much on confessions of guilt.

Note.—It seems proper to add that I was so convinced of the innocence of the prisoners in this case that I took upon myself to release them in anticipation of the orders of Government. For this irregularity I was deservedly censured, and three Judges of the High Court afterwards decided that there was no ground to interfere with the original conviction. However, the prisoners were not re-presented before the High Court, and there is no doubt that the general opinion in the district is that Jabar Ula never was flung into the river.

(E.)

THE LANGUAGE OF THE DISTRICT.

BENGALI is the vernacular of Bákarganj, and there are few provincial peculiarities except in pronunciation. I doubt if there be a single word whose use is exclusively confined to Bákarganj; and when we reflect how modern the district is, and what violent changes of boundaries it has undergone during its short life, we can hardly expect to find many peculiarities of language in it. In all the districts of Eastern Bengal we find a good many Arabic and Persian words, due no doubt to the influence of the Mahomedans. These words chiefly relate to administration and jurisdiction, but some of them relate to the arts and sciences, and to domestic life; and it is a shrewd remark of Ram Kamal Sen, in the valuable preface to his English Bengali Dictionary, that the words for *pen* and *paper* are of Arabic or Persian origin, showing that the Sanskrit-speaking people did not know how to make paper.

I once made out a list of such words and phrases as appeàred to me to be peculiar to Bákarganj, and sent it to the Commissioner of Dacca, but I am not aware that any use was ever made of it.

Mr Sutherland has given an interesting list at p. 192 of his report on Bákarganj (Principal Heads of the History and Statistics of the Dacca Division, Calcutta, 1868), and to this I beg to refer the reader. The following words and expressions are all I can give at present:—

Nisbat or *nisbati*, a brother-in-law (Arabic).

Kura, a bigha.

Mora, a basket of paddy.

Amiani, without settlement.

Badla, to work for another. This refers to an interesting usage of villagers mutually assisting one another by giving a day's ploughing or weeding. (See Mr J. Cockburn's evidence, ans. 458, p. 34 of evidence taken before Indigo Commission, and also paragraph 69 of the report, 1860.)

Bagchar, berm of road.

Khola (not *kola*, as in Sutherland), an open field.

Chár, a bamboo or supari bridge.

Át, the raised edge of a moat.

When a boat has sunk, boatmen employ the euphemism of *bhala haiache*, literally, it is good.

When the peasantry take to firing homesteads, as they sometimes do in a dispute about rent with their landlord, they are graphically described as setting the red horse a-running (*lál ghora dauran*).

There is a curious expression for a mother-in-law in Bákarganj. She is called *diwanji—i.e., diwan* or manager. Probably this is in allusion to the fact that she is generally the real mistress of the house, the daughter-in-law being too often a mere child.

(F.)

Note to Page 75.

I have not printed the song about Kamala on account of the difficulty in procuring Bengali types.

Note to Page 142.

I believe that the Mr Thackeray here referred to was not the father of the novelist. The father of the latter appears to have been a Mr Richmond Thackeray, who died in 1815.

INDEX.